MW00337057

Additional Praise for
Doug Kass on the Market
A Life on TheStreet™

"Doug Kass was my favorite bear, long before Warren Buffett discovered him. He is a reality check on the mindless cheerleading that takes place on Wall Street."

—Barry L. Ritholtz
Chief Investment Officer, Ritholtz Wealth Management
Columnist, *Washington Post* and *Bloomberg View*
Host, *Masters in Business* on Bloomberg Radio

"*Kass on the Market: A Life on the Street* is essential reading for anyone wishing to understand and contextualize the investment landscape during these last turbulent years. Doug's writings are often quite prescient and always interesting."

—Dan Greenhaus
Chief Global Strategist, BTIG

"Everyone is a genius in a bull market, but it's the ability to successfully maneuver thru all types of markets that separates the men from the boys. Doug Kass has done that in his long career, and this book provides amazing insight and invaluable stories that reflect his great ability to think outside the box in a business where many feel comfortable just following the herd. As Dougie would say, run, don't walk, to read this book."

—Peter Boockvar
Chief Market Analyst with The Lindsey Group

DOUG KASS

ON THE MARKET

DOUG KASS

ON THE MARKET

A LIFE ON
TheStreet™

DOUG KASS

EDITED BY DANIEL ROBINSON

WILEY

Cover Design: C. Wallace

Cover Photograph: © Jeffery Salter/Jeffery Salter Photography

Published by John Wiley & Sons, Inc., Hoboken, New Jersey.
Published simultaneously in Canada.

For general information on our other products and services or for technical support, please contact our Customer Care Department within the United States at (800) 762-2974, outside the United States at (317) 572-3993, or fax (317) 572-4002.

Wiley publishes in a variety of print and electronic formats and by print-on-demand. Some material included with standard print versions of this book may not be included in e-books or in print-on-demand. If this book refers to media such as a CD or DVD that is not included in the version you purchased, you may download this material at http://booksupport.wiley.com. For more information about Wiley products, visit www.wiley.com.

Library of Congress Cataloging-in-Publication Data:

Kass, Douglas A.
Doug Kass on the market: a life on TheStreet/Douglas A. Kass.
    pages cm
ISBN 978-1-118-89298-5 (cloth); ISBN 9781-118-89299-2 (ebk);
ISBN 978-1-118-89301-2 (ebk)

1. Investments. 2. Finance. I. Title.
HG4521.K278 2015
332.6—dc23

                              2014027687

Printed in the United States of America.

10 9 8 7 6 5 4 3 2 1

*This book is dedicated to
Chuck "Brown Bear" Zion—a wise, kind,
and cherished friend who died in the
World Trade Center tragedy in 2001.*

Contents

Foreword

S it down and strap yourself in. You are about to embark on a journey back in time that will teach you more about making money in the future than just about any source anywhere in the firmament. You are about to see what the market really looks like through the eyes of one of the greatest financial whizzes and wits of our generation, the one and only Doug Kass.

I have had the privilege of working side by cyber-side with Doug in our writing cave, TheStreet.com, for almost 20 years. In that time, I have come to respect and covet his views and his insights as I know you will as you read his real-time journal detailing the ecstasy, agony, and just plain madness of the world we call Wall Street. That's why I feel so honored to pen this foreword for a book that will stand the test of time for all sorts of markets—bull, bear, sideways, upside down, and the one we are in at the moment you read this, whatever it may be.

Doug's fond of lists, and you'll read many prescient ones in the pages ahead. They are filled with observations that only someone with as keen an eye toward making money as Doug could ever give you. Therefore, I think it is only fitting that I offer my top 10 reasons why you will love, laugh, and, of course, profit from my colleague's unique and remarkable insights.

Reason number one: Essentiality. If someone asks me what's the most essential voice I need to hear on Wall Street, I'd say one name without hesitation: Doug Kass. You need to know where he stands because so often he represents the view opposite you, the variant view, the one you most need to worry about before you place your bets on these pieces of paper we call stocks. How can you not want to know why you may be wrong? That's the essentiality of this man's unique commentary.

Reason number two: Fearlessness. So many people are cowed on Wall Street. They fear the powerful, they fear the retribution, they worry about what happens if they tell the truth. Doug Kass is the antidote to that fear. Whether it be a gentle yet still withering riposte against Warren Buffett—face to face, mind you, all detailed here—or the outright castigation of the rapacious bankers and pseudo regulators who are supposed to protect us from their machinations, Kass goes where pretty much everyone else fears to tread.

Reason number three: Self-effacement. Sure, Doug's gathered many of the best of his more than 50,000 entries since he started writing for TheStreet back in 1997, but some of my favorites here are the ones filled with humility, as the market, bull or bear, is a most humbling of animals. Doug doesn't have to be always right to learn from; sometimes it's the dissection of his own mistakes that makes for the most profitable of insights.

Reason number four: Insider's insider. If you are reading this book, chances are you have heard of a lot of big-name investors and always wanted to know what they are really like. By virtue of his successes and his knowledge, Doug knows the best and brightest personally and extols them in ways that give you the context that's invariably absent when we hear their utterances. Doug, as they say, is "in the room"—a room that you may never get to be in but will certainly come to feel comfortable with because of his candid observations about those with whom he surrounds himself.

Reason number five: He's not afraid to stick his neck out. At the beginning of each year, Doug lays out some predictions that may seem outlandish—that is, until they come true. It's uncanny that so many pan out, and the pan can be filled with gold. Oh, and no one is more brutal about the prognostications that didn't work out than Doug himself. No free passes for anyone, including himself.

Reason number six: You never know where he's going to come out. Some think Doug's a perma-bear. I say wait until you get to the entry entitled "Bottoms Up, Mr. Market," where Doug began an astounding series of articles that nailed the exact bottom of the worst stock market decline in our lifetime. Oh, and because each piece here is dated in real time, including those fabled March 2009 time-to-buy postings, there's no denying Kass his due. When a man who has been correctly bearish for thousands of points on the Dow suddenly and convincingly goes bullish, you want that judgment. Doug's generational bottom call will always stand the test of time. Thank heavens I listened to him in those darkest-before-dawn days and my viewers and readers rode his coattails to tremendous profits.

Reason number seven: Expertise. Doug's an old housing analyst by nature, and that expertise helped nail the subprime issue, the proximate cause of the great recession, well ahead of when the downturn snow-balled. His subprime articles written on the cusp of the Great Recession are warily prescient; if only the Fed had subscribed! His expertise goes well beyond housing, of course, but Doug's musings about all of the accoutrements of the industry—consumer sentiment, retail, interest rates, the Fed's role—make for some indispensable reading.

Reason number eight: Education into short-selling. Most people, including many hedge fund managers, think they know how to profit from the downside. They actually don't have a clue. I don't think anyone knows the tactic and strategies of successful short-selling better than Doug. It's a wonder, and a life-saver, or at least a portfolio saver, that he's willing to give them to you. And he does so in a clear, no-nonsense way.

Reason number nine: Impact. When Doug takes a variant view on a stock, particularly a loved stock, look out: there are going to be fireworks. Doug's insights, as you will see here, quickly turn into actionable ideas that can make for a very profitable trade or investment. Put simply, Doug can and does move markets. You need to know which way he is moving them.

Finally, and perhaps most important for these columns' longevity, Doug's a brilliant wordsmith. His writing is suffused with irony, mirth, outrageous story-telling, including the always hilarious insights from

Grandma Koufax—yep, that Koufax—and genuine warmth. Even if you aren't a stock junkie like I am, you'll most certainly get a kick out of the trenchant way he makes his points. He tells a terrific yarn.

For all of these reasons and many more, you will come to share the joy I have of cracking open the browser each morning to my favorite columnist to learn what I didn't think would happen before it actually occurs.

James J. Cramer, markets columnist, TheStreet.com,
co-anchor of CNBC's *Squawk on the Street,*
and host of CNBC's *Mad Money* with Jim Cramer

Preface

For over 15 years I have been a contributor to *TheStreet* and its subscriber-based products (currently *Real Money Pro*).

TheStreet, Inc. was founded as TheStreet.com by Jim Cramer and Martin Peretz in 1996 and went public in 1999. Since then, *TheStreet* has become one of the most popular and informative fountains of investment information of its kind.

I have always enjoyed writing, and Jim and his team have provided me with a platform in which I combine humor, pop culture metaphors, and even clever quips from my Grandma Koufax in an attempt to differentiate my words from the dry Wall Street research that permeates the investment narrative.

If I have been successful, it is probably because I write for myself. I ask myself in every column—and I typically write at least 15 columns a day—if I have learned something new and if the process of reading my diary has been an engaging and enjoyable experience.

This is easier said than done. After all, since 1998, I have likely written over 30 million words contained in more than 50,000 columns.

Ask yourself whether you discuss 15 new subjects in your own life with your friends and family each and every day.

With so much to express in my daily columns, I start my day early at around 5:00 A.M., and I end the day, subject to after-hours news, after 6:00 P.M.

That's a long day. But it has been rewarding, and I like to think that I still have something to say or observe.

My writings and investment/research process have been influenced by numerous legends as well as many regular folks and friends.

My journey was made possible by the tens of thousands of subscribers to *TheStreet, Real Money,* and *Real Money Pro.* We have shared experiences, corresponded frequently, and some of us have grown to be true friends.

The cornerstone and epicenter of my journalistic travels on *TheStreet* starts with Jim Cramer. Jim has been my collaborator, my defender and advocate, and he has provided me with the guidance of a shining star in the night. He has been generous with his time and kind in his criticism. All this has made the journey smooth, and the 15-plus years have flown by. Stephanie Link, also at TheStreet, has been helpful and has also been an important adviser to me over the past several years. Finally, TheStreet CEO Elisabeth DeMarse is a wonderful leader who has steadily guided the company through an ever-changing and increasingly difficult-to-navigate media terrain.

Perhaps my most significant personal influence is my Grandma Koufax. She was a successful businesswoman, investor, and feminist, who taught me about the stock market when I was in my mid-teens.

Other influential iconic figures for whom I have worked include Jerry "The Chief" Jordan, the best trader I have ever met; Larry Lasser, who taught me how to deliver a sound analytical argument; and Martin Hale at Putnam Management, who gave me a historical perspective. Omega Advisors' Lee Cooperman, the hardest-working hedge-hogger extant, and Steve Einhorn showed me the positive consequences of going belly to belly with a company's management and enlightened me about the advantages of looking more frequently on the optimistic side.

Our late national journalistic treasure Alan Abelson, of *Barron's,* as well as my first boss, Ralph Nader, taught me the benefits of being a skeptic, thinking outside of the box, and the value of investigative research, which is essential in developing differentiated and hard-hitting analysis.

Warren Buffett's invitation to grill him at his 2013 Berkshire Hathaway annual shareholders meeting provided me with a unique opportunity and contributed to one of the most enjoyable weekends of my life (which I shared with my son, Noah). By now, my copies of his letters to shareholders are all dog-eared. The Oracle of Omaha is simply the best professor any investor can be schooled by.

Others from whom I have learned include Yale's Bob Shiller, George Soros, Stanley Druckenmiller, "Uncle" Bob Farrell (the greatest technical analyst of all time), Leon Levy, *Grant's Interest Rate Observer's* Jim Grant, *Bloomberg's* Tom Keene, BTIG's Dan Greenhaus, The Lindsey Group's Peter Boockvar, *TheStreet's* Herb Greenberg, Richard Bernstein (who has helped me navigate the noise), Raymond James's Jeff Saut, the indomitable Dennis Gartman, the lynx-eyed Barry "Tell It Like It Is" Ritholtz, the research-intensive Jeff Berkowitz (Jim Cramer's former hedge fund partner), Bob "Scarsdale Fats" Brimberg, and Howard Marks (who teaches us all that there is more than one important thing to investing).

A special thanks to all of my friends at CNBC: Mark Haines (R.I.P.), Sir Larry Kudlow (my favorite host), the *New York Times's* Andrew Ross Sorkin, Becky Quick, "Judge" Scott Wapner, David Faber, and many others who have provided me with a forum for my investment ideas and views since 2003.

I owe a lot of gratitude to my Seabreeze associates Chris "The Fisherman" Brandon and Scott Budner, who put up with my idiosyncrasies and long hours.

Finally, I want to give a special shout out to my best pal, Barry Wish. Barry is a thoughtful and compassionate friend who has been my rabbi, especially over the past 15 years. His wise counsel has been a beacon of light.

I could not have produced the stream of columns without the steady hand of Daniel Robinson. Danny has been my editor for much of the past decade and has done the heavy lifting to bring this book to fruition. Despite his adoration of the Boston Red Sox, his friendship and creative pen have been invaluable.

What a long strange trip it has been and will, hopefully, continue to be for many years ahead!

Where It Began

Introduction

Back in early 1997 I received a call from Dave Kansas, the managing editor of *TheStreet.com*. I had known Dave from his early days at the *Wall Street Journal*, where he had frequently interviewed me. At the time, *TheStreet.com* was in its formative stage, and Dave asked me to write a column. I admired Dave professionally, and I agreed to author an irregular column called "The Contrarian."

Writing has always come easy for me, and I started my gig on *TheStreet.com* as a lark. I never thought that 17 years and tens of millions of words later I would still be writing.

This chapter starts with my first column written on *TheStreet.com* and later on depicts my journey on TheStreet and in life!

The Contrarian

May 1997

Today's stock market is bifurcated—it is a market of haves and have-nots. Increasingly, price action is influenced by the dominant investor of the 1990s, the mutual fund manager. With stocks in so relatively few hands, equities often move based on the strategies employed by these funds. This makes for the kind of inefficiencies and opportunities that we are seeking in this column. As Warren Buffett once put it, "Our job is to be fearful when others are greedy and greedy when others are fearful."

I have learned over the years that in the equity market, there are few truisms. Today's established doctrine often becomes tomorrow's false beliefs, as conventional wisdom does not always represent common sense.

It is important to recognize that a contrarian approach can be just as foolish as a follow-the-crowd strategy. What is required is thinking rather than polling. Bertrand Russell's following observation about life in general applies with unusual force to the financial world: "Most men would rather die than think. Many do."

The purpose of this column is to make investors think.

In future columns, we'll do this by taking a hard-hitting, iconoclastic look at individual securities and sectors of the market.

Our first column, however, will deal with a person, not a stock. It holds several important messages that apply, in this writer's opinion, to the current state of the stock market—a market that may have lost its moorings.

Four years ago this month, a dear friend of mine passed away. As the major markets register all-time highs and we move into the summer months, it seems appropriate to reflect upon my friend and to recall some of the lessons he taught me.

My friend's name was Robert Brimberg.

Bob headed Brimberg & Co., a small securities business by Wall Street standards. But by any measure, Bob was a "big man," who hailed from Scarsdale, a tony suburb north of New York. He was nicknamed Scarsdale Fats by author "Adam Smith" (George Goodman's nom de plume), who immortalized Bob in his 1967 best seller, *The Money Game*.

In the 1960s, as in the 1990s, money managers with billions under management were welcomed anywhere. But mostly they gathered at Bob's spartan room on Broad Street, where corned beef sandwiches were the plat du jour. No house silver, no perfectly groomed waiters, just metal folding chairs, paper napkins, and a big bowl of pickles and sour tomatoes were the standard offering.

Why were Bob's lunches the meal to be invited to? As Erich Heinemann recalled, "The price of admission was that you had to have something to say. Bob ran the only true salon for the investment community."

Bob put it this way:

> I had to compete. What have I got? Nothing. Those hot young research analysts at Donaldson Lufkin can write hundred-page reports, Bache can field a thousand salesmen. The white-shoe firms can fly the Old St. Wasp flags. So I thought: Who has the money? The funds. Be nice. Ask them to lunch.

And that is how Bob Brimberg became the Perle Mesta of Wall Street.

Ultimately, Bob moved uptown to a corner table at Harmonie Club. It was in that setting 20 years ago that I met Scarsdale Fats when he invited me to my first lunch. I was a wet-behind-the-ears 27-year-old portfolio manager, and Bob exposed me to the best and the brightest on Wall Street.

Scarsdale Fats's pointed questions and sometimes brusque manner cut through the pretense, and the poker-game aspect stimulated even the most knowledgeable of us to prepare for the lunch. And everybody came to be with the Yalie who was as comfortable talking about Kierkegaard as Keynes.

The Dow Jones Industrial stood at about 750 back in 1977, and we have been in a bull market ever since.

I (and many other people) owe a lot to Bob. Since his death and during my visits back to Harmonie Club for lunch (now as a member), I find myself gazing back to Scarsdale's corner table. I still vividly remember those spirited lunches and how much we profited from the conversation.

You see, Bob brought the sensibilities of a world-class bridge player (which he was) to our understanding of the markets. Above all, he taught us investment humility—that if you do not know who you are, Wall Street is an expensive place to find out.

Which gets me to the subject at hand. The market. For, as Bob put it to me one day in 1987, "Dougie, genius is a rising market."

And the market today, again, gets back to "Adam Smith's" *The Money Game*, in which the author recalls a character named Billy the Kid:

> [W]ho was in Leasco Data Processing, Financial General, and Randolph Computer, and a couple of others I can't remember, except that they all had data processing and computers in the title. When asked why the computer leasing stocks were so good, he responded, "Leasing has proved the only way to sell them and computer companies themselves don't have the capital. Therefore, earnings will be a hundred percent this year, and will double next year and will double again the year after. The surface has barely been scratched. The risk has barely begun."

As this piece is written, technology is on a tear. I am awash in nostalgia: Today's investors are similarly obsessed with the future of technology, the Internet and, for that matter, the top tier of industrial equities such as General Electric.

"Adam Smith's" fictional character, the Great Winfield, continues:

> The strength of my kids is that they are too young to remember anything bad, and they are making so much money they feel invincible. Now you know and I know that one day the orchestra will stop playing and the wind will rattle through the broken window panes and the anticipation of this will freeze us. All of these kids but one will be broke, and that one will be Arthur Rock of the new generation.

Bob, some things never change—this is still a kid's market. Being over 40 years old has been a liability in the bull markets of the 1990s. But don't forget, it took over 17 years (1982) to eclipse the high in the averages established in the mid-1960s!

And despite the market's monumental rise, remember that prices have no memory, and yesterday has nothing to do with tomorrow. Every day starts out 50-50 (to paraphrase Professor Eugene Fama).

Sic transit gloria.

A Longtime Bear Turns Bull

3/26/2001

Roy Neuberger, a great trader and the patriarch of Neuberger Berman, once told me to buy cyclical stocks when the factory doors of industrials are padlocked. The economy and the stock market's doors are now padlocked.

After weeks and weeks of pounding, it has become almost unthinkable that the market might rally. For new equity and low-grade debt financings, the capital markets are closed. Investment bankers are being fired by the large underwriters.

A year ago, it was almost unimaginable that the equity market would fall. A year ago, initial public offerings (IPOs) routinely rose by 100% on their first day of trading. Mutual funds were created just to buy new issues and to participate in the aftermarket trading of those new issues. The great bull market of the 1990s did its best to obviate the need for an historical perspective. In essence, experience and knowledge of the past was a liability.

No longer—the tide has changed. Growth-oriented mutual funds have faltered badly, and investors are withdrawing their investments. Value-oriented mutual funds are performing better and are becoming more popular with individual investors.

I have been bearish throughout the past two years, but over the course of the past two months, I've grown progressively less cautious. And now, I'm of the view that the equity market is putting in an important bottom.

Investors have finally recognized that they made a mistake in thinking that the technology capital spending boom of 1998–2000 was a secular phenomenon. And that recognition is at last being reflected in today's low stock prices.

The technology spending spree was not enduring—it was nothing more than a temporary ramp-up. It was abetted by a halcyon IPO market that provided issuers with zero-cost capital and by the compliant manufacturers of tech products that offered customers financing that, based on poor business models, was undeserved. In turn, this produced an unsustainable level of demand for technology products.

The resulting demand became so heavy that it fooled even the tech companies (and investors in tech stocks, who bid the sector to ludicrous price levels) into believing in a secular expansion in demand for optical fiber, routers, servers and other tech products. In response, the largest companies dramatically expanded the capacity of what their plants could produce.

Along the way, alas, the fuel for the euphoria in the form of plentiful debt and equity financing to lower-tier participants, combined with aggressive vendor funding to unworthy creditors—all the things that encouraged the hysteria—began to disappear. That was 12 months ago, to be precise.

In addition, it began to be acknowledged throughout the past year that certain areas of technology, such as personal computers and wireless phones, had reached a level of maturity that was suggestive of cyclical, slower growth.

A year ago, with Qualcomm, Dell, Micron Technology, and Nokia at the top of the investment world, this was unthinkable.

And earnings growth hit a wall. One by one, technology companies issued profit warnings. Then, all of a sudden, valuations began to matter, and the bifurcated market of the past decade reversed, big time.

Investors, analysts, and market strategists were in denial during most of the market reversal. And why not? It had paid to buy every previous decline.

Of course, the greatest myth—that commerce had entered a Web-centric world—was squelched. The suggestion that, in order to compete, a rapid deployment of an Internet strategy was the key to future profits, was replaced with the more traditional and prosaic notion that capital spending programs needed to be justified by quick paybacks.

Unfortunately, similar to the roads to riches of prior investment bubbles (e.g., railroads, radio, and automobiles), investors learned for the umpteenth time that the laws of valuation and of gravity have not changed. Even that forward-thinking (just kidding!) newspaper, the *New York Post*, has a new column entitled "The Dot-Com Dead of the Day," which appears in its business section every day!

That said, the speculative excesses of yesteryear have, in my estimation, been eradicated. Besides the changing investment landscape, in both sentiment and price (described above), I want to share additional reasons for my more constructive view:

1. Fear is palpable. The business media have begun to take an adversarial approach to their money manager and analyst interviewees who have performed poorly. Lame-O Awards are handed out to analysts who have recommended stocks that are down 75% or more, and Penguin Awards are given to brokerages that downgrade stocks after the companies have issued earnings warnings or traded down to less than $2 a share. While these awards might be justified, I find the manner in which they are given offensive, and it provides me with yet another contrarian indicator, as they were shameless cheerleaders just one year ago.

2. For some time, I have been of the view that layoffs at the two major television networks dedicated to market coverage (CNNfn and CNBC), as well as layoffs at the major brokerages, would presage a market bottom and indicate that the worst might be over. After all, it has been a great indicator in the past. And those layoffs are occurring now.

3. Since March 12, the broader S&P 500 and the Dow Jones Industrial Average (DJIA) have underperformed the tech-laden Nasdaq, as investors sell anything that is liquid or not down that much. This is a big and positive tell to me.

4. The redemption issue, or what I fondly call the nightmare scenario, appears to be an overblown concern. Dominant mutual fund family Janus has relatively large cash positions (in certain funds as much as 20%)—a rather large buffer in anticipation of withdrawals in relation to the concerns du jour. The tax issue, being that realized investment gains in early 2000 must result in the sales of stocks in order to meet April 15 tax payments, also seems to be an overblown concern. The market decline, beginning last spring through the year's end, in

large measure erased a lot of the gains. Regardless, tax selling will be over in a matter of weeks.

5. The dividend discount models—you remember those!—I use suggest that technology, currently making up about 17% of the S&P 500 (and down from more than 30% a year ago), represents real value. First time since 1997!

6. All now agree that the Goldilocks economy is dead. As a consequence of the broad acceptance of the new economy, all valuation benchmarks were broken by huge margins. But, similar to the children's story, the concept of an economy not too hot and not too cold was nothing but fiction. And price-to-earnings ratios fell back to Earth.

7. Most of the juicy short themes I have employed over the past two years (i.e., Internet, optical fiber, wireless phones, personal computers, semiconductors, handheld devices, etc.) are now incorporated in lower stock prices.

8. There are few signs of a turn upward in inflation. The specter of higher oil prices is no longer a threat. And no cost-push or demand-pull inflation is in sight.

9. A tax cut is on the way. With elections out of the way, we might even see the parties agree on additional ways to extricate the economy from the downturn.

10. Institutional cash positions have risen from a low of 4% a year ago to 6% today. This rise might sound trivial, but it is not. On the $4.3 trillion of fund assets, that is a rise of $86 billion in cash reserves. As well, money market funds are at an all-time record, ready to be committed to stocks once an uptrend is established.

11. A year ago, day-trading manuals populated the *New York Times* bestseller list. Today, some day traders are on the feds' most wanted list because of murderous sprees after losing all their money!

12. Two years ago, new language appeared, as *Wired* magazine introduced the phrase B2C (business to consumer) to our language. Now B2C is euphemistically referred to as "back to college."

13. I am being inundated by interest in my partnership, as investors want short representation. But where were they when the short pickings were abundant, as when Priceline.com traded at $100 or when

Yahoo! traded at $125 twelve months ago? Probably invested in the Janus funds!

14. Finally, I am getting a strong positive read from my point guard, partner, and trader—the Trading God. He has been bearish all the way down, and at 3:27 P.M. on March 22, he turned major-league bullish.

A decade ago, Warren Buffett advised investors to "be fearful when others are greedy and greedy when others are fearful." It may now be time to be greedy.

Until the distribution of those e-mails reverses, I suspect that the only question is, How high is up?

What a Long, Strange Trip It's Been

12/22/2004

Holidays are for fun, family, and reflection, especially as we near the year's end. I will concentrate on the reflection part today and hopefully give a sense of the factors that have molded my investment persona.

Fifty-some-odd years ago, I embarked on a rich personal and professional life full of successes and failures. Never dull, I have tried to embrace life and the markets with gusto and anticipation.

Soon after my birth, the DJIA embarked on a new bull market rally from about 160 to over 300 by the beginning of the 1950s. In 1950, the largest monthly change in the DJIA for the full year was only 14 points!

My grandmother, Grandma Koufax, was a great stock trader and investor. She owned her own business well before it was fashionable for women to be entrepreneurs. She was well ahead of her time. By the time I was 16 years old, she had taught me to chart stocks in a small notebook that I kept with me at all times. I charted my imaginary holdings daily and spent my Christmas and Easter holidays in a Long Island brokerage office watching the tape all day—at that time, the market was only open for a few hours each day—as if I were watching a movie. My preoccupation with the markets, especially during those holidays, led some of my friends to think that I was weird. In retrospect, they were insightful!

I made my first real trade while getting my MBA at Wharton. After weeks of analysis, I bought a couple of shares of Teledyne—and I really mean just a couple. Run by Dr. Henry Singleton, it was the Google of its time, a stock of the decade that went up nearly tenfold. With the proceeds of that first big trade, I purchased my first automobile, a Triumph sports car. By then, I was immersed in the stock market— you could say I was almost addicted—even before I had my first job on the Street.

At Wharton, I learned the theories behind portfolio management and securities analysis on the way to getting my MBA. While at the University of Pennsylvania, I met Ralph Nader and I coauthored *Citibank: The Ralph Nader Report* with Ralph and the Center for the Study of Responsive Law. My contribution to that book also became my master's thesis.

My first job was as a housing analyst at the venerable brokerage firm Kidder Peabody. I learned how to prepare company spreadsheets and about the integrity of independent analysis under Director of Research Johann Gouws, who had successfully led one of the first research boutiques (H. C. Wainwright) into prominence earlier. Interestingly, my office was next to Julian Robertson, soon to be of Tiger Management, who at the time was a retail broker!

After a few years, I ended up at Putnam Management, considered one of the premier money managers extant, in Boston. I worked under two individuals, Larry Lasser and Jerry Jordan (The Chief), who profoundly influenced my career by teaching me how to logically process data and to succinctly develop that data into a well-reasoned and profitable analytical conclusion. Jerry, in particular, taught me how and when to press an investment decision, a technique that is quite important in the hedge fund business today.

Glickenhaus & Co. was my next stop, where I honed my money management skills under the talented and legendary Seth Glickenhaus. It is through his influence that I became a contrarian and began to regularly take variant views against the market's prevailing bias. I had my own money management firm during most of the 1980s, and, while experiencing some periods of success, I learned the importance of a team.

In the late 1980s, I acquired a large 13-D position in a New York Stock Exchange (NYSE)-listed company, thinking that I was going to become the next takeover king. I quickly learned to stick to my knitting, analyzing and investing, not taking over companies.

But I should digress. During the mid-1980s I took up driving harness horses as a hobby. I broke a world record, and one of my horses, Kassa Branca (a play on words from the movie *Casablanca* and named for me and Brooklyn Dodger pitching great Ralph Branca), won a million-dollar race! Unfortunately in 1990, I was almost killed in a harness racing accident while driving in a race in Pennsylvania. I was in a body cast and wheelchair for nearly two years, and I still feel the physical pain daily.

The supine position gives one a lot of time to contemplate one's future.

By 1992, I was able to work again (though I still could not walk unaided) and while running the research and institutional department at First Albany, I met Alan Abelson of *Barron's*. That relationship led to a cover story that I wrote for *Barron's* on Marvel Entertainment (a negative assessment of Marvel's prospects, and the company ultimately filed bankruptcy). That start was followed by approximately 30 interviews and articles over the years in Abelson's column or in other areas of *Barron's*.

I believe my relationships with Ralph Nader and Alan Abelson as well as my period of time reflecting on life after my accident importantly framed the manner in which I have viewed markets and companies—a glass half-empty, if you will.

A stint with the remarkable Leon Cooperman at Omega Advisors taught me the tough hedge fund game and independence of analysis, after which I started my own partnerships, which I have had for nearly seven years.

I sit here grateful and satisfied, though looking forward to the continued challenges presented by the markets with enthusiasm and excitement.

It seems as if I have never had a dull moment in the investment business over the past three decades. What moves me is that it seems that there are new and different variables to consider every day, and with over 6,000 publicly traded securities, projects are rarely duplicated.

What a long, strange trip it has been.

Short-Selling

Introduction

Over the nearly four decades of my investment career, I have been identified as a short-seller.

Being a skeptic and going against the bullish grain started early for me in my career. Indeed, upon graduating with an MBA from Wharton, my very first research report (as a housing analyst at Kidder Peabody) was a decidedly negative review of the mobile home and recreational vehicle industry, a leading market sector at the time. The group imploded in the months following my sell-side research report, and, from that point on, a cynical view has been a prevailing thread and dominant theme of mine.

I am uncertain why I have been attracted to the "dark side." Perhaps I view the investment glass as half-empty as a result of two important professional influences: Alan Abelson of *Barron's* and my first boss, Ralph Nader. Alan and Ralph have both been, in their own right, true skeptics.

As a result, throughout my hedge fund career, I have approached the traditional long/short hedge fund business with a short bias, as contrasted to 99% of the long/short hedge-hoggers, who are almost universally long biased.

That said, I have always emphasized that, given the asymmetric reward versus risk on a short side trade—you can only make 100%, but you can lose, in theory, an infinite amount—risk control is integral in delivering superior investment returns from the short side. No concept or valuation shorts for me. Also, no heavily shorted stocks. Life is too short to be subject to painful short squeezes. As a student of history, I will never forget the lesson that I and others learned from Bob Wilson's infamous short of Resorts International that nearly bankrupted him.

This chapter contains some lessons I have learned as a short-seller and attempts to demonstrate some basic tenets in the short-selling process.

The Case for Short-Selling

5/15/2006

Many investors have a general misapprehension about short-selling.

They shouldn't.

When done conservatively and with risk controls in place, it is a fertile strategy for successful hedging and for the generation of absolute returns in most market settings.

In fact, short-selling and hedging are growing necessities in an uncertain world, especially during the more lumpy and uneven period of economic growth that is likely to follow the stock market bubble's piercing after four years of unprecedented fiscal and monetary stimulation.

Still, there are the skeptics.

Many consider short-selling a mug's game for a couple of reasons:

1. The gravitational pull (higher) of equities over extended periods of time (about an 8% annual rate of return); and
2. The asymmetric risk/reward of a short—one can make "only" a maximum return of 100% (in a bankruptcy), but an infinite risk is apparent on the upside.

In addition, many short-sellers have been decimated in rising markets because they have concentrated on heavily shorted (and speculative) equities and demonstrated little discipline in limiting losses. Moreover, some of those short-sellers have shorted on the basis of conceptual or valuation issues, the timing of which is inherently uncertain, and the market outcome has been consistently poor.

To put short-selling into perspective, of all the hedge fund asset classes, short-selling is the least populated and most underserved. By definition, this provides a unique opportunity to generate excess returns. The entire dedicated short pool in the United States is estimated at less than $5 billion, or about only 6% of the size of the Fidelity Magellan Fund.

Despite the influence of New York Attorney General Eliot Spitzer's attempts to regulate Wall Street research, the analytical output of Wall Street is still dominated by purchase recommendations. Wall Street exists for a purpose: not to produce disinterested research but to raise capital for a growing America by selling stocks and bonds. (The higher the market rises, the easier it has been to sell, but the more disingenuous the sales pitch becomes!)

Market participants want to look on the bright side. Individual and institutional investors and the management of the corporations are invariably biased and bullish. How else to explain that nearly every money manager interviewed in the media is constructive? Consider whether you have ever witnessed an interview with a corporate executive who was bearish on the future of his company.

In my numerous appearances on CNBC's *Squawk Box* and in other venues, I have never encountered such an animal. (This is one of the reasons I rarely visit corporate managers in assessing a company's outlook.)

All too often, short-sellers make tactical errors in establishing a short book. Among those common mistakes are the lack of diversification (along companies and industries), being fully invested (through thick and thin), the utilization of too much leverage, shorting hard-to-borrow stocks, shorting on the basis of valuation (or a concept or prices), and creating a short portfolio almost entirely based on the search for frauds (a needle-in-a-haystack approach).

For example, it would be a mistake to short a concept stock such as Google, or a "new paradigm" stock such as Phelps Dodge. (Although

Phelps Dodge is far from a concept stock, the shares have doubled during the past year and are emblematic of a new paradigm in industrial commodities. I may short this type of stock periodically but only with proper risk controls.) You need to keep your eyes on the road, your seat belt fastened, and one foot on the brake at all times.

1. Through independent analysis, develop a variant (and negative) view of a company or industry's prospects, its business model, or a company's quality of earnings. Logic of argument, power of dissection, and the rejection of convention and orthodoxy in seeking a variant view against the market's prevailing view should form the basis for initiating short ideas.

2. While discovering frauds seems like a sexy practice, it is impractical to structure an entire or a large portion of a short portfolio on the basis of frauds. (Even if one is successful in creating a short book consisting only of frauds, the timing and market acknowledgment of fraud might be unsuitable for a portfolio that is designed to prosper in market downdrafts.)

3. Never employ leverage. In fact, when conditions dictate inaction on the short side, raise the portfolio's cash positions, as it is better to be conservative than sorry.

4. Create a diversified short book. No individual equity position should exceed 2% of your portfolio's assets.

5. When a market is dramatically overvalued, I would strongly suggest the use of out-of-the-money calls (against your shorts) as a means of buying time for a short catalyst to develop (because market moves to the upside, as well as those to the downside, usually last longer than most investors anticipate). This also helps define individual equity and portfolio financial risk/exposure and allows you to sleep at night (and be of sound mind during the day).

6. Take losses quickly, and let your profits run. Remember that the basic rule to investing, in both buying long or selling short, is not to lose. (The second rule is not to forget the first rule.) The desire to stand out at any cost, or an unrelenting negativism, is faux pessimism.

Although the true contrarian resists too-popular trends with sometimes grim resolve, he must realize that being plain stubborn is not necessarily being smart. Crowds are not always nuts as a society, and the market's wisdom always deserves some respect. But I have learned that the greatest danger to prices and valuation is a slavish subjection to tides and trends, and that as distinct as each market/sector bubble might be, the psychology that drives investors is always the same.

In stocks, whenever you are certain that there is no way to go but up, look down. When everybody's blazing away, hold your fire. (And when everyone agrees the future is hopeless, invest or cover.)

7. Don't look for management to help you in your analysis. Indeed, don't bother visiting management except to develop an understanding of a company's business. Warren Buffett, in the late 1980s, wrote to the shareholders of Berkshire Hathaway that "managers lie like ministers of finance on the eve of devaluation."

8. Given the asymmetry of risk and reward, the construction of shorts is almost as important as the short itself. As mentioned previously, this can be accomplished by buying puts, or through the protection of out-of-the-money calls during halcyon times.

9. Avoid illiquid and heavily shorted stocks. If you don't, eventually a short squeeze will be the outcome, and there will be heavy losses with it.

10. Trade around your short positions, and ladder your shorts with the timing of expected catalysts (in terms of the calendar) to ensure superior performance and participation in market downdrafts.

Poor management, frauds, and eroding company or industry trends always will be in fashion, regardless of market conditions. That said, several new secular developments seem to be setting the stage for a rocky and below-trendline outlook for equity returns over the balance of this decade.

- *Uneven economic growth in 2006–2010.* After a period of speculation (similar to the late 1990s) followed by unprecedented fiscal and monetary stimulation, the 2006–2010 economy is likely be a much more difficult period for corporate managers and investment managers to navigate. A period of lumpy and uneven economic and profit growth (and a continued debasing in the U.S. dollar) seems likely, which is a rich environment for short-selling.

- *Growing geopolitical danger.* The geopolitical landscape has changed for the worse, and unfortunately, it is not likely to improve for years. This risk will almost certainly be accompanied by the headwinds of higher commodity and energy prices.
- *A secular rise in the rate of inflation.* The benign inflationary backdrop of the past two decades seems to be in the process of being reversed.
- *A widening schism between haves and have-nots.* The social and economic risks associated with the increasingly disenfranchised lower- and middle-income classes (and their deteriorating real incomes and lack of participation in the economic recovery/boom) pose an intermediate-term threat to the domestic economy.
- *A brave new world reliant on asset appreciation is filled with risk.* An economy based on continued asset appreciation (equities and homes), as compared with the more traditional role of wages and salaries as locomotives for growth, holds new risks. This will serve as a slippery and uncertain slope for policymakers and investors.

Short-Sellers under Fire

9/29/2006

After years of the sell side bearing the brunt of litigation by individual and institutional investors, short-sellers have recently been the target of a number of lawsuits by public companies including Overstock, Biovail, and Fairfax Financial.

I have no idea as to the validity of the claims behind these three suits, but I do have a general view that the role of short-sellers on markets is a constructive one. As well, I have an interesting anecdote about when I was a target of a suit in the early 1990s, which makes me somewhat more sympathetic to the defendants and which could be instructive about the current ill feelings toward the short-selling community.

But some background first. I am a professional short-seller, and I have generally found those in the short-selling community to be more inventive, more detailed, and more informed in their analysis of companies.

Importantly, I have found that serious fundamental short-sellers, as contrasted with the momentum-based short-sellers who dominate the short-selling landscape, are very good stock analysts. Indeed, the two leading practitioners, David Rocker of Rocker Partners and Jim Chanos of Kynikos, are the best securities analysts I have ever met. Their understanding of balance sheets and power of analytical dissection is far superior to any other analysts I have met in my 30 years on Wall Street. Why is this so?

I don't know exactly why, but it could be in part that most analysts tend to be cheerleaders because it's in their best interest for stocks to go higher; short-sellers have to look at both sides (particularly the risk factors), so they tend to be more well-rounded in their approach to stock analysis.

Though at times vociferous, short-sellers are dramatically outnumbered by long buyers, so in the aggregate, they are far less vocal compared to the legions of generally bullish talking heads in the media—particularly among Wall Street sell-side analysts, who remain more cheerleaders than anything else.

As such, I believe this is one of the reasons that short-sellers are more likely to be the targets of lawsuits alleging nefarious conduct.

My own experience as the target of a suit by a company for my negative analysis came when I started to do some research on Marvel Entertainment.

In 1991–1992, Marvel was the Internet stock of its time, with comic book collecting all the rage. Marvel Entertainment (then controlled by conglomerator Ron Perelman) was a hugely successful 1991 IPO. Coupled with Perelman's string of profitable takeover transactions, Marvel became the darling of the momentum crowd and enjoyed a several-billion-dollar enterprise value (market cap minus debt plus cash) despite its leveraged balance sheet, one-product profile and modest earnings.

During 1991, I began to canvass comic book stores to determine the value of Marvel's franchise position and growth prospects. At the time, comics were 100% of Marvel's product offerings, and as my research expanded, it increasingly became clear to me that the popularity of comic book collecting was ebbing—traffic was falling at comic-book stores and some were even closing.

I could also tell Marvel had begun to lose its creativity, stuck in a creative rut of muscular male superheroes and buxom and sexy female superheroes.

Leading independent comic book publishers began taking market share from Marvel, and younger, hipper readers were increasingly turned off by Marvel's product line. I talked to comic book buyers, and they were telling me that they were more interested in the independent, edgier comic book offerings. Stated simply, Marvel was headed for a fall.

After completing my analysis of Marvel Entertainment's declining fortunes, I thought about sharing it with several of my friends in the media.

Then I got a different idea.

For 20 years I had admired *Barron's*' Alan Abelson. I had considered him a journalistic treasure, someone who was iconoclastic and willing to consistently write (in vivid prose) about contrary views against the market's prevailing (and bullish) bias.

So one day I headed down to Dow Jones headquarters and up the elevator to Mr. Abelson's office on the 16th floor.

There was one problem. I had never spoken to Abelson and didn't have an appointment. The receptionist said Abelson does not meet with walk-ins. At that very second, Abelson appeared.

Seeing me in a wheelchair and obviously feeling bad for me, he led me to his office saying he had about a minute for me. I asked him about Marvel Entertainment, and he explained that he been doing some preliminary work on the company. I told him that I had spent weeks doing research on Marvel, and that I had written up a synopsis of my findings.

He then asked me to give him a copy of my findings and that he might get back to me at some time. That sometime was later that night, when he told me that, with the assistance of his editor, it would make a great cover story for *Barron's*.

And that Saturday morning in February 1992, only three days after my initial meeting, my story on Marvel Entertainment ("Pow! Smash! Ker-plash! High-Flying Marvel Comics May Be Headed for a Fall!") appeared in *Barron's*.

When markets reopened on Tuesday, Marvel's shares fell by almost 20%. This occurred despite First Boston (Marvel's investment banker on its IPO) reiterating a buy on the stock and raising estimates.

Not surprisingly, Marvel's management ridiculed my article, citing the company's strengths. Weeks later, Perelman's Marvel Entertainment filed suit against me and my employer, charging that our clients (at the time I had just started to run First Albany's institutional division) front-ran the article by shorting the shares (they did not, as no one knew about it) and that my analysis was ill-founded and inflammatory. On the contrary, it was well-researched with copious notes and documentation.

Marvel Entertainment lost the suit.

Two years later, Marvel Entertainment filed bankruptcy—and two years after that, they filed bankruptcy again!

And I became known as a short-seller.

So what's to be learned here? It's lonely to hold a contrarian view against a company that's held in very high esteem, and it can be a lonely fight to hold to one's conviction when you don't follow the herd.

But it's that very herd mentality—which often overvalues companies—that can make short-selling such a lucrative line of work.

How to Short

3/30/2007

As a dedicated short-seller, I incorporate some basic tenets and disciplines in my portfolio management.

One of those principles is to avoid hard-to-borrow and heavily shorted stocks.

Yesterday, Dendreon announced that the Food and Drug Administration said its Provenge drug (the first active cellular immunotherapy and the first biologic approved to treat prostate cancer) was safe and that there was "substantial evidence of efficacy."

Dendreon has a float of 80 million shares; its average trading volume is about 3 million shares a day. Short interest, however, totals 20.3 million shares (up nearly 4 million shares from the prior month), or about 25% of the float!

I avoid heavily shorted stocks in which short interest is a large percentage of the float or shares outstanding, such as at Dendreon. To me, high short interest is a nonstarter.

Dendreon closed at $5.12 a share on Wednesday—it didn't trade on Thursday—and is currently trading up by over 230%, to $17, in the premarket!

Dendreon is a classic example of why a short-seller should avoid heavily shorted stocks.

Month-to-date, the S&P 500 is up by over 1% in March. It is safe to say (barring an extreme event) that March will likely end up positively, which would put 13 out of the last 15 months in positive territory.

Despite this extraordinary (and historically abnormal) run, at the slightest downtick, I sense a lot of angst in the market by hedge fund operators. From my perch, this means that investors (especially the hedge fund and fund of fund kind) are far longer (or levered) than most surveys reveal.

As I have mentioned previously, I don't put much credence into the various sentiment studies, most of which can be subject to, well, very subjective interpretation.

It is my view that, within the context of the investment process, sentiment studies are often simplistic, linear crutches, especially when used in a vacuum.

For example, a lot of the short-interest figures are influenced by structural market changes and the introduction of new securities that require hedges on the other side or investors on the other side.

Surveys can also be undependable because they often rely on relatively small samples.

I am aware of instances in which the respondents simply didn't tell the truth or the surveys relied on the bias of advisers or letter writers who teach but don't invest.

Finally, many massage the output to produce a desired outcome (e.g., if you don't like the fact that last week the *AAII* bearish percentages have moved close to a one-year low, change your calculation to a 12-month moving average that doesn't exhibit as much of an extreme reading). You get the picture.

In conclusion, technical analysis plays an important role in the investment mosaic, but making investment conclusions solely by observing squishy sentiment measures can be dangerous to your financial health.

I believe there is far too much emphasis on unreliable sentiment voodoo that can be interpreted any which way and often too little emphasis on economic and company fundamentals (which, by the way, are also open to massaged metrics).

And those fundamentals are fading faster than you can say Sanjaya Malakar.

Lehman Can't Blame Shorts

4/2/2008

Yesterday, in an interview on CNBC with Maria Bartiromo, Lehman Brothers' chief financial officer (CFO), Erin Callan, called on the Securities and Exchange Commission (SEC) to investigate potentially abusive tactics of short-sellers, who she claimed were responsible for the continued pressure on her company's shares. (It is important to note that I currently have no stake, long or short, in Lehman's shares.)

Callan's claim was shared by many Lehman shareholders, members of the media, and others, including our own Jim Cramer.

Implicitly, Lehman's CFO seemed to place a primary role on short-sellers as the proximate cause for Lehman's share weakness. And, by inference, Ms. Callan dismissed the role that the following items may have had in the slide of the company's shares:

- Lehman's disappointing earnings and revenue results, down 30%;
- A levered balance sheet in which Lehman's liquidity is, to some degree, dependent upon "the kindness of strangers";
- Its broad mortgage and fixed-income exposure; and
- An uncertain profits future, though she alluded to the likelihood of continued challenges "for several quarters to come" late in the interview.

Lehman's CFO contended that "perception trumps reality" and that the $4 billion convertible raise this week "endorsed the value of the franchise"—even though, days before, Callan dismissed the need for capital.

When push came to shove, however, she claimed an escalation of the rumors and observable trading volume in Lehman's shares necessitated the capital-raising mode, which caused about a 6% dilution in the company. Her contention was that recently the normal daily trading volume had risen by nearly tenfold, suggesting that short-selling (which purportedly continued to pressure Lehman's shares) was dramatically on the rise.

Let's examine her claims that short-sellers have had an untoward role and have pressured Lehman's share price.

- At yesterday's close, Lehman's equity capitalization stood at $24.45 billion.
- Lehman has 551 million shares outstanding, and its float is approximately 528 million shares.
- As of March 11, 2008, only 46.5 million shares were short, representing only 8.4% of the outstanding shares and only 8.8% of the float.
- Over the past three months, Lehman's average trading volume was about 29 million shares a day, and over the past 10 days, the average trading volume was nearly 45 million shares. Therefore, days to cover are only 1.6 and 1.0 days, respectively, very low ratios.
- The short interest has risen by only 3.3 million shares since last month.

Now, let's do a quick compare and contrast with Merrill Lynch:

- The short position in Merrill is about 37 million shares, or 4% of the outstanding shares and of the float.
- The short position has risen by 5.5 million shares in the last 30 days and represents 1.2 days to cover on the three-month average daily volume and slightly less than 1.0 days based on the last 10 days' average trading volume, not materially different than Lehman.

Next, let's move on to an analysis of the put trading in Lehman in order to see if this issue pressured the company's shares. Similar to the other brokers, the outstanding interest in the out-of-the-money puts has increased, but the amount of skin in the game is insignificant (as the put values are in pennies). The purchase of out-of-the-money put options does not impact a company's share price, though it does increase the stock's volatility. For example, there are 25,000 April $10 and April $15 puts open; they trade at only $0.04 and $0.08, respectively.

In summary, I believe that the placement of Lehman's $4 billion convertible was a wise capital move for the company, and an even wiser move was made in placing the security with a small group of current stakeholders, which precluded more short-selling through the convertible arbitrage. That being said, the allegation that short-sellers unduly influenced the price of Lehman's shares seems to have little basis in fact.

It is my continued view that short-sellers—and I am clearly talking my book—play a far less important role in influencing share prices generally. The dedicated short community is well under $10 billion, less than one-fifth the size of Fidelity's Magellan Fund. There is no empirical evidence that the short-selling asset class, the elimination of the uptick rule or that the role of short-sellers (as part of the long/short hedge fund class) are in any way responsible for the bear market of 2007–2008.

There are ample fundamental reasons (especially of a credit kind) for the market's weakness, but the short-selling blame game is quite simply a figment of the bullish cabal's imagination and an easy excuse for their mistakes.

Stop Pointing Fingers at Short-Sellers

4/25/2008

Not surprisingly, certain corporate managements and several members of the media have sought out scapegoats to rationalize their own fundamental mistakes. Rather than looking in the mirror and 'fessing up to their own managerial errors (i.e., their lax due diligence, increased corporate misdealings and operational shortcomings), short-sellers have recently been the repeated targets of many.

"We have met the enemy and he is us."

—Walt Kelly, Pogo

Bear Stearns' senior management, days before it almost failed, was quick to accuse short-sellers as conspiring to accelerate the company's downfall. During that period, Lehman Brothers CFO Erin Callan chimed in as well and called on the SEC to investigate the abusive tactics of short-sellers, who she claims were responsible for the continued pressure on Lehman's share price. And in early March, Ambac's Michael Callen ridiculed the short-sellers and continued the refrain of accusing short-sellers for the fall in his company's share price, which was down by nearly 50% this week.

In the media, Ben Stein and CNBC's Dennis Kneale, seemingly acting as shills for the bullish cabal, have been at the epicenter of the blame game against short-sellers.

I have long felt that finger-pointing is a giant waste of time, and, quite honestly, the only thing that might be more of a waste of time is commenting on it.

Yesterday, CNBC's Dennis Kneale, who I happen to generally respect and like, suggested that the SEC should have imposed a larger financial punishment against a trader, Paul Berliner (who was employed by the Schottenfeld Group), for spreading a false rumor that the Alliance Data Systems/Blackstone Group takeover was in jeopardy.

I agree with Kneale that it was a good thing that the SEC nailed Berliner, but I strenuously disagree with the finger-pointing against short-sellers for the following three reasons:

1. As I have often written, investors and policymakers should have taken a cue from the early read by short-sellers in their analysis of the housing, subprime, rating agencies, and credit issues, which substantially presaged the problems before they surfaced. A lot of money would have been saved. As has been documented in numerous academic studies, stocks with high short interest ratios typically underperform the market dramatically, as it is often a sign of systemic problems. Consider Overstock, Ambac, MBIA, MGIC Investment, Biovail, and many others.

2. For every stock that is rumored to go down, there are a hundred that are rumored to go up. When will the SEC go after the latter?

3. And what about corporate executives (especially of a tech kind) who routinely cheerlead and then dump shares? Shouldn't the SEC address this as well?

Blame Game Is Dishonest

8/25/2008

I am struck by the fact that such a large number of respected money managers have purchased huge positions in many of the financial stocks that have dropped so dramatically over the past two years.

I am also struck by the fact that so many of these money managers blame their ailing positions and poor overall investment performance on short-sellers rather than on the inadequacy of their own research and analysis.

David Dreman (Dreman Value Management), Richard Pzena (Pzena Investment Management), Bill Miller (Legg Mason) and Marty Whitman (Third Avenue Management) have doubled and tripled down their ownership of Fannie Mae, Freddie Mac, Ambac, and MBIA—among other impaired financial intermediaries.

"The most nefarious aspect of the short-sellers revolves around their concerted efforts to destroy, or at least diminish, the companies' existence as going concerns."

—Marty Whitman, Third Avenue Funds' third-quarter 2008 letter

The confidence expressed by the above-mentioned managers in their ownership of shares of companies such as Freddie Mac is especially stunning—or frightening, depending on one's book. For example, Bill Miller reported holding about 50 million shares of Freddie Mac at the end of first quarter 2008—worth about $1.3 billion, or slightly more than $25 per share, at that time but purchased at a much higher prices. Last week, Miller announced that he raised his holdings in Freddie Mac during the second quarter by over 60% by adding 30 million more shares, bringing his total holdings to 80 million shares. Freddie Mac closed trading on Friday at $2.81 per share.

Under the circumstances, blaming the poor share price performance for a stock such as Freddie Mac on the purported iniquitous scheming and market influence of short-sellers seems outside the realm of reality.

Perhaps, it is as one of the hedge fund industry's icons told me years ago, "The value of a large investment organization is greatly over-exaggerated." It might also be that the above examples of dip-buying

"There is a certain measure of the moralist in short-sellers. As detectives on Wall Street, they enjoy revealing the emperor without his clothes."

—Kathryn F. Staley, *The Art of Short Selling*

"This vast right-wing conspiracy has been conspiring against my husband since the day he announced for president."

—Hillary Clinton

represented an error in judgment and/or intransigence on the part of these great investors, or perhaps their outsized losses (both in dollars and on a percentage basis) were simply a function of poor analysis and then denial.

Whatever the reason, I can only talk from my own experience. Above all, when I invest, I try to be honest with myself, I critically test others' views (and the market's prevailing bias), I weigh changing fundamentals, and I attempt to employ a rigorous loss discipline.

As I wrote earlier, there are several common threads in the commentary of the chastened investors in Fannie Mae, Freddie Mac, Ambac, and MBIA—and that list can be extended to Citigroup, Wachovia, Radian Group, PMI Group, MGIC Investment, and other financial stocks held in the portfolios of the Dremans, Pzenas, Millers, and Whitmans out there—as a large amount of money has been lost in these stocks, and the short-selling community has become their scapegoat.

From my perch, considering the depths of the current economic problems, to blame the substantial share price declines in financial stocks on a short-selling conspiracy is as silly as the above quote from Senator Clinton.

I run a hedge fund dedicated to short-selling. My goal is to deliver absolute returns in any market or economic cycle. Sometimes I achieve success; sometimes I meet with failure. I and other dedicated short-sellers represent a small minority (estimated at less than $5 billion) within a hedge fund universe that approaches $3 trillion in assets under management and a mutual fund industry that exceeds $10 trillion in size.

I attempt to create a short book by identifying companies whose business models are exposed to changes in the competitive landscape—often through new challenges such as technology and the Internet. There are no short-sellers I know of any consequence—and I know most of them—that rely on spreading rumors in order to move their targeted shorts lower in price. The short-sellers I know rely on hard-hitting analysis. We have to because, over the long run, stocks rise in price.

Call me old school in my view, but investors ought to be accountable to their investment managers and corporations accountable to their shareholders.

Yale University Professor Owen Lamont once said, "When security prices are wrong, resources are wasted, and investors are hurt." Wall Street does not produce (and never has) disinterested and objective research. They are in the business of selling products (stocks, bonds, and, ugh, in recent years, derivatives). And Wall Street compensation has, for decades, been a "heads they win, tails they win" proposition.

> Short-sellers are our first line of defense against securities manip-
> ulators who would pump and dump worthless securities. It is
> important that the stock lending market work efficiently in order
> for the short-sellers to be able to do their job. By preventing
> fraudulent manipulators from hyping overpriced stocks to the
> stratosphere, they can prevent investors from buying overpriced
> stocks.
>
> —*Professor James J. Angel, Georgetown University*

In summary, short-selling is vital to the balance and functioning of the equity markets.

Investors (individual and institutional) must look into the mirror of honesty regarding their mishaps as playing the blame game card is unprofessional, dishonest and, quite frankly, is getting long in the tooth.

It's time to pay more attention to short-sellers when their analytical arguments are well reasoned and documented.

So listen up.

11 Ways to Fix the Short Ban

9/23/2008

Last week's hastily crafted regulatory response to ban short-selling must be immediately corrected or terminated.

While it is probably true that the recent fiscal effort has its own set of problems but is probably a necessary jolt to a deeply challenged financial system, the series of poorly constructed and reactive regulations in the SEC's selected ban (and enforced disclosure) of short-selling will likely have unintended negative consequences.

My prediction is that the only naked short-sellers that are caught and prosecuted in the SEC's hunt will be day traders who have bypassed the current shorting regulations as they trade on their REDIs and other trading platforms—that is, the same day traders who took stocks up to ludicrous levels nine brief years ago in the Internet bubble and set the stage for the Nasdaq collapse.

There are many risks associated with the SEC's plan. The principal risks include a liquidity drain that could cause capital to exit the markets and undermine the financial system as well as a loss in confidence that market participants are on an even playing field.

That being said, here are some of my suggestions for changing and enforcing last week's rules:

1. First and foremost, reinstate the uptick rule. This is so fundamental and so obvious that it is almost beyond my comprehension why a revision of this rule was not considered first and before the other recommendations were instituted.

2. A timeout on short-selling of financial stocks and a brief cooling-off period are reasonable, but it should have been focused only on our major financial institutions as contrasted to a broad sweeping policy and commentary that has essentially vilified short-selling. When a General Motors is added to the SEC ban on short-selling because it has a bank stuffed in it, the ban is preposterous. No doubt, if markets continue their descent, companies with captive financing arms—that is, nearly every manufacturer and retailer—will request to be exempt from short-selling.

3. Remove short-selling disclosure rules. The unintended consequences are broadly negative and counter to the basic goal for all participants in our equity markets to play on a level field.

4. Make a strong comment that short-selling is a necessary practice and contributes to the efficiency and liquidity to our markets.

5. Focus on comprehensive disclosure and filing requirement rules for all activities in the credit default swap market not just in equities.

6. Turn the SEC into a committee instead of a political appointee; include people that actually understand how short-selling, the stock market, and economy function as well as equal representation from those at short-only, quantitative, and long/short hedge funds so that people who short stocks have representation. Remember, the SEC also instituted this policy previously, probably because cronies asked for it, which is central to the problem.

7. Actively prosecute and severely penalize those convicted of wrong-doing (spreading rumors, naked short-selling, touting stocks, etc.), and that includes the majority of the inappropriate activity taken by the long-biased world (arguably, at the root of many of our current problems).

8. Include the activities of proprietary brokerage trading desks and other business units of the brokerages themselves in any investigative activity about inappropriate trading in shorting of financial stocks or overall credit default trading. Request the tape of all trades and commit human resources to a thorough investigation of the role of these brokers shorting products of other brokers.

9. For those that package and sell long-dated risk, tie compensation to the long-dated risk turning out money good as opposed to the risk being sold—and the same goes for the buyers.

10. Remove the rule that allows public companies to buy back their own stock in last 30 minutes of trading. To me, this was the most mystifying of all of last week's SEC initiatives and indicates that those making the rules must not have a clear understanding of the game. What's the point? Do the regulators want financials to mark up their own stocks into the close? (Encouraging banks to ply their needed capital to mark up their stocks is distasteful and poorly reasoned.) What kind of rule is put in place to deliberately encourage companies to manipulate their own stock prices? Even worse, the ones that do so will be the ones that have little to do with the larger problem in the financial system; they are likely smaller companies with less liquid stocks and typically promotional-style managements that could use shareholder dollars to mark up their own stocks into

the close at the same time as insiders sell them. Besides having nothing to do with the primary problem, this rule will ultimately further burn individual investors and erode the confidence of institutional investors in fair markets.

11. Companies begging to be added to the "do not short" list should be ashamed of themselves, especially great companies such as General Electric. Indeed, I would like GE's chairman to publicly say that the decision to put his company on the list is dumb. Exploiting and executing well in fair markets is what has made General Electric one of the best and most respected companies in the world. GE should act like it and be proactive.

Leave the Short-Sellers Alone

8/12/2011

Four European countries are banning the short-selling of stocks in their markets to try to halt the precipitous plunge in value of troubled European banks, a step that some experts say could intensify fears and ratchet up risks of another financial crisis.

Belgium, France, Italy, and Spain have decided to impose a temporary ban on short-selling, beginning on Friday, according to a statement from the European Securities and Markets Authority released Thursday evening, after markets had closed. . . .

The ban on short-selling carries echoes of the 2008 financial crisis, when the Securities and Exchange Commission temporarily banned short sales in the U.S., a move that resulted in a brief rally but ultimately did little to arrest the market's free fall. . . .

In France and Spain, the ban on short sales will last for 15 days, and will only apply to stocks in the financial sector, according to the *Globe and Mail*. Belgium will ban short sales on four financial stocks for an unknown period of time. It was unclear which stocks the Italian ban would affect, or for how long it would be in place.

A spokesman for the U.K. Financial Services Authority told *Bloomberg* that Britain has no plans to ban short sales.

> —*Alexander Eichler, "Italy, France, Spain, Belgium Ban Short-Selling in Order to Protect Markets,"* Huffington Post, *August 11, 2011*

Yesterday the U.S. stock market rallied, in part, on the announcement that several countries in Europe were imposing a ban on selected short-selling. (This morning, there are rumors of an even broader short-selling ban in Europe.)

A September 2008 short-selling ban in the U.S. failed miserably (as the market's drop actually accelerated after it was instituted) and will likely fail in Europe now.

Such short-selling bans smack of desperation; they are artificial, interfere with natural market forces and are anti-free market (though typically instituted by free-market policymakers). Bans are ineffective Band-Aids that often raise red flags, may result in investors selling their longs (as bans make them nervous) and reduce the cushion of potentially latent buying from short positions put on.

As I have written recently, what should be clear in looking at the dismal U.S. and eurozone economic numbers in the first half of 2011 and in the falloff in confidence is that there is a pressing need for outside-the-box, creative, hard-hitting, thoughtful, and pro-growth fiscal strategies. Our country needs (among other things) a series of Marshall Plans aimed at reviving the housing market (and denting the shadow inventory of unsold homes) and an aggressive fiscal strategy that will generate jobs growth. But, given the partisanship observed in the debt-ceiling and budget circus, how can investors be confident that these needs can be met, especially as we are closing in on the November 2012 elections?

Instead of hard-hitting solutions, we get short-selling bans.

It is almost laughable, but the poor state of our world's economic affairs makes it sad.

Back in the fall of 2008, I wrote the following op-ed in *Financial Times* about short-sellers and the blame game:

This Blame Game Is Short on Logic

After acquiring General Re in 1998, Warren Buffett, the veteran investor, learnt the hard way that "derivatives are like hell, easy to enter but almost impossible to exit."

Four years later, Mr. Buffett, chairman of Berkshire Hathaway, argued that highly complex financial instruments and derivatives were time bombs and that these "financial weapons of mass destruction" might harm the economic system. His caution was prescient—like that of many others who have identified company frauds or diagnosed previous credit cycles gone wild. Yet most of these gloomy messengers have been ignored. Since Mr. Buffett's warning, financial markets have imploded and policymakers have failed to address the abuses that created the crisis, from the excess leverage of banks to ratings agency failures.

Instead, public policy has become focused on a blame game aimed at restricting the short-selling of securities—especially of a financial kind. In July, Christopher Cox, chairman of the U.S. Securities and Exchange Commission, announced a plan to curb improper (naked) short-selling. In doing so he has (de facto) attempted to limit the activity of short-sellers. Mr. Cox seems to be implicitly blaming the shorts for the unprecedented fall of bank, government-sponsored agency and brokerage stocks over the past year—even though short-sellers were the very group that warned of the dangerous credit cycle and its consequences.

Short-selling runs deep in financial history. Perhaps the first case dates to 1609 when the Dutch trader, Isaac Le Maire, targeted the shares of the shipping company, Vereenigde Oostindische Compagnie (the Dutch East India Company). VOC was the first multinational corporation in history and had broad powers. Nonetheless, Le Maire, concerned about threats of attack by English ships, sold VOC's shares short. After learning about Le Maire's tactics, the stock exchange governing VOC's trading banned short-selling (although the ban was later revoked).

In the early 1630s, the Dutch economy fell into a depression following a speculative peak in the trading of tulips. Again, short-selling raised the ire of regulators, many of whom saw it as magnifying the effect on the Dutch economic downturn. As a result, England banned short-selling outright.

Almost 420 years later—in the late 1920s—short-sellers warned of the consequences of speculation. But in the aftermath of the Wall Street crash of 1929, many blamed them and the uptick rule—which banned short-selling on downticks—was instituted (and stayed in effect until 2007). More regulation governing short-selling came into force in 1940, with a ban on mutual funds from short-selling (though that law was lifted in 1997). In early 2005, the SEC again sought to restrict the practice.

Yet short-sellers have served as financial watchdogs, as many of their warnings have been spot on. The delusional dotcom boom in the late 1990s brought Cassandra-like utterings from the short-selling cabal that proved insightful but were largely ignored. After the subsequent 75 percent collapse of the Nasdaq, a bull market in corporate fraud emerged and short-sellers such as David Rocker, founder of Rocker Partners, highlighted accounting problems at companies such as Sunbeam, Tyco and Lernout & Hauspie. Kynikos' Jim Chanos played a role in uncovering the largest fraud in history when his contrary-minded analysis warned of Enron's accounting shenanigans—which were emulated (but ignored by investors) in the banks' recent dalliance with structured investment vehicles.

By the middle of the decade the property cycle was in full bloom and David Tice of the Prudent Bear Fund warned of the dire ramifications of a downward spiral in home prices on the levered balanced sheets of Fannie Mae and Freddie Mac. Soon thereafter, Nouriel Roubini, the economist, voiced particularly pessimistic forecasts about the housing market's impact on credit.

Drawing a line between economic and market progress as against fantasy is a role taken by the few. Short-sellers provide an anchor of objectivity in an investment world populated by those more interested in rewards than in uncovering systemic risks. This week, Mr. Cox said the SEC would announce new

regulations to restrict short-selling. Instead of more regulation, the chairman and investors should begin listening to what short-sellers have to say about our economy and credit markets.
—*Doug Kass,* Financial Times *(August 21, 2008)*

Weeks later, a short-selling ban on financial stocks was instituted in the United States, and I wrote the following in mid-September:

> *"We believe that to err is human. To blame it on someone else is politics."*
> —Hubert Humphrey

Several weeks ago, I wrote an op-ed column in the *Financial Times* that spelled out my view that short-sellers shouldn't be restricted in their activity and shouldn't be blamed for the abuses in lending, credit formation and in the growth of the unregulated derivative markets that got us into the mess that we are in today.

Indeed, history has shown—Enron, Tyco, Sunbeam and so on—that market participants should be attentive in listening to the analytical warnings of the short-selling community.

A few seem to be coming to their senses—in certain cases from surprising corners. For example, here is an email exchange I had with Ben Stein (for whom I now have newfound respect) last night:

> Ben Stein: I am bound to say after all this time that you understood this so much better than I did, especially the mentality on Wall Street that would lead to this that it is profoundly humbling.
>
> Doug Kass: Thank you, Ben. My Grandma Koufax would call you a "mensch." My constant proddings were not meant to be ad hominem attacks against you but rather to deliver my analysis and underscore my sense of foreboding that was based on my analysis of the abuses and egregious risk taken in the credit, housing and derivatives markets.

Some observers such as *Bloomberg*'s Michael Lewis get it.

Others recognize that the blame lies squarely on the shoulders of regulators, borrowers (and lenders), banks (did the shorts tell Citigroup's Chuck Prince to "keep on dancing"?), broker-ages (did the short-sellers OK obscene compensation packages in the "heads I win, tails I win" culture on Wall Street in which those monies earned were withdrawn out of the firms while levering their capital to 32-1?) and the Three Stooges of 21st Century Finance (who reside in the administration, Treasury and Fed and proved, once again, to be reactive not proactive). All of these players gleefully drank from the spiked punchbowl of credit excess over the past decade, believing in another new paradigm (and uninterrupted growth) for the housing and credit markets, but failed to have a vision of the dangers associated with their careless risk-taking and lack of due diligence.

> *"If they can get you asking the wrong questions, they don't have to worry about answers."*
> —Thomas Pynchon, *Gravity's Rainbow*

From my perch, it seems far-fetched to blame short-sellers for the general lack of regulatory scrutiny and enforcement, the absence of risk controls and a continuum of reckless management decisions at the world's leading financial institutions (banks, brokers, hedge funds, private equity, etc.), all of which have combined to create a black swan event that has resulted in a credit market gone amok and a shadow banking system often under the radar of regulators.

Increasingly this week, however, all too many seem to be suggesting that the short-sellers are the root of all evil and are to blame for a plunge in share prices (especially of a financial kind). Indeed, SEC Chairman Cox instituted new short-selling rules last night, which included a requirement to disclose daily short positions, and some institutional investors, such as CalSTRS' CIO Christopher Ailman, are not permitting their investment holdings to be loaned out to short-sellers, citing clear evidence that short-selling is the root cause of the decline in the shares of leading investment banks.

Here are some of my reasons why the current popular game of blaming short-sellers is misplaced:

- I simply can't accept the basic assertion that there is currently a great deal of naked short-selling going on. Yesterday, I undertook an experiment and tried to borrow 250,000 shares of Morgan Stanley from my prime broker (one of the very institutions that is complaining about short-sellers!); it took less than three seconds. Every other financial on the SEC's list is readily available to borrow, so why the heck would anyone illegally short without a borrow?
- Short interest in the publicly traded investment banks has dropped in the last month. (For example, Morgan Stanley's short interest has dropped by 3 million shares in the last month, to 45 million shares, and stands at a low 2.8 short interest ratio, and at only 4% of Morgan Stanley's float.) According to Short Alert, from early July to late August (the most recent data available), the short interest in the 34 companies classified as Investment Banking Brokerage by S&P dropped from 9.42% of all shares outstanding to only 7.55%, for a 20% decline. So not only are critics of short-selling wrong that shorting has increased but it appears that covering by the short community served to provide stability to the markets.
- Fails-to-deliver from naked short-selling account for a small percentage of market capitalization, according to the Depository Trust and Clearing Corporation. Currently, fails are about 31,000 positions daily (including both new and aged fails) out of an average of 54 million new transactions processed every day by the National Securities Clearing Corporation. In dollars, fails-to-deliver-and-receive amount to only about 1.4% of the daily volume.
- Short-selling (or buying of protection) is now rampant in the credit default swaps area, an unregulated market that the very investment banks who are complaining about short-sellers pushing their shares down have argued to keep unregulated!
- As to the rumor-mongering, one should not look at the short-sellers, we (or more precisely the SEC) should look at

the very investment banks that are complaining the most loudly about short-sellers. Chinese Walls in brokerages have long fallen, as it is widely recognized that investment firms' proprietary desks are shorting each other's stocks (and pulling capital from each other), likely with information from their own investment banking arms. What if it turns out that Goldman Sachs was shorting Morgan Stanley and Morgan Stanley was shorting Goldman Sachs—and that they both were shorting Fannie Mae, Freddie Mac and American International Group.

- Finally, where are the hedge funds making all this money shorting stocks (illegally)? The dedicated pool of short-sellers (which stands at about $5.5 billion, or about 9% the size of Fidelity's Magellan Fund) is simply too small to have a meaningful impact on the markets. Based on ISI data, most hedge funds tied to a long/short strategy are relatively inactive, and many are liquidating out of fear of ever-greater losses and redemptions, which leaves us with the dominant quant funds that use algorithms, not fundamental security analysis or rumors, as their operating methodology. No doubt, some of these are shorting the weakness in financials based on their modeling.

In summary, the blame game is counterintuitive to the facts (above) and seems motivated by investors' and financial managements' rationalizing their poor investment and business decisions, many of which have caused unnecessary pain for a lot of Wall Streeters who have become victims of their senior managers' misdeeds.

In Defense of Short-Selling

10/8/2012

With what seems to be under the guise of sound twenty-first century central banking, the Fed's policy of providing ever more easing through the manipulation of interest rates and even possibly aiming at raising asset prices (such as equities), I continue to hear the following objections from many investors and traders:

- Why bother selling short?
- Isn't short-selling a mug's game?

Over the years, in search of a variant view, my analysis has often led me to reject general expectations and orthodoxy. At times, this has put me at odds with consensus, as I am sometimes bullish when others are bearish and bearish when others are bullish.

Sometimes I get it right—sometimes I get it wrong.

Markets are invariably moved by the unexpected or what the crowd is not anticipating, particularly at inflection points. Part of my job (as I see it) is to game whether the crowd is correct of view or wrong (and should be faded). Legendary hedge fund manager Michael Steinhardt once said that developing a variant view is what puts distance between ordinary and superior investment performance.

As we all know, the objective of establishing a profitable, non-consensus view is easy to talk about but hard to isolate in analysis and put into practice. Since the crowd is more typically optimistic, over the course of time, this pursuit has led me to specialize in selling short—and, at times, I have maintained sizeable short positions (even as stock markets advanced).

It appears the basic objections to short-selling are that:

- When economies stumble, public policy (fiscal and monetary) comes to the fore and defends against an acceleration of economic and corporate profit weakness and often inhibits natural price discovery;
- Risk and reward are asymmetric in short-selling;
- The historic average annual positive return for equities is an insur-mountable headwind; and
- The exercise of selling short is analytically time-consuming—long ideas are dished out on a silver platter by Wall Street's research departments and are usually confirmed by management, which is not true of shorts.

I couldn't disagree more. Financial concepts have their seasons, and the market's numerous dives over the past decade combined with the uniqueness of today's structural worldwide economic challenges and the increased frequency of black swan events suggest that, when timed properly, a great deal of money can be made on the short side.

Sometimes a market gets terribly overvalued—as it did in the late 1990s, when investors adopted the notion that the DJIA was destined to reach 36,000 (i.e., that there shouldn't be a risk premium on stocks) or embraced the notion of a new paradigm (i.e., an uninterrupted economic boom), which created unique opportunities on the short side.

Other times (more often than the above condition), individual securities or sectors are embraced by market participants and levitated to unimaginable valuations, which also creates an opportunity on the short side.

Mainly, it seems to me that opportunities to challenge biases are much more pronounced and more easily identifiable on the short side, no matter what the market conditions are, mainly because those searching for such weaknesses are substantially in the minority. And few are comfortable with the short side, which makes for an inefficient market.

More than any time in history, it can be argued that the secular headwinds (e.g., fiscal imbalances, structural unemployment, debt-laden private and public sector balance sheets, etc.) to worldwide economic growth represent powerful gusts that challenge a smooth and self-sustaining trajectory of global economic growth.

These factors (and others) are likely to lead to a more tentative and inconsistent growth backdrop in which corporate managers will likely find it more difficult (than in the past) to navigate the currents.

In summary, short-selling and hedging seem to me to be a necessity in an increasingly uncertain world. After all, farmers do it, oil exploration companies do it, miners do it, even property owners do it by selling forward with long-term leases.

Moreover, short-selling creates portfolio stability and a hedge against the inherently positive bias of analysts, managements and even human nature. Rather than being a mug's game, I have concluded that short-selling is a useful tool that can provide profits in almost any market setting.

One should never be obsessed with short-selling or any specific investment strategy, but given that there is little permanent truth in the markets and given the aforementioned factors that will likely weigh on global economic growth, I have concluded that short-selling is a neces-sary part of an investor's repertoire—or at least mine.

Lessons Learned

Introduction

What we learn from history is that we do not learn from history.
—Benjamin Disraeli

I have accumulated four decades of investing lessons—most of them are serious but some are less so. Many are presented here.

In this chapter, I explain how playing poker might help us as investors, the significance of the bond market's message, how to right your investing wrongs, the importance of time frames/exposures and risk profiles, how to identify market bubbles, and why price is what you pay but value is what you get.

I even garner some advice from legendary North Carolina State basketball coach Jim Valvano.

Sniffing Out Bad Stocks

4/2/2001

During the bull market of the 1990s, research on Wall Street lost much of its integrity and, increasingly, most of its value in helping individual and institutional investors make sensible investment decisions.

Consider that fewer than 1% of all Wall Street research reports are outright Sell recommendations. This is a particularly astonishing figure given that nearly 85% of the stocks listed on the New York Stock Exchange are down year-to-date. It says to me that analysts are simply not doing a good job or are not acting independently.

Indeed, Wall Street research has deteriorated to the point at which its analytical output has been rendered almost useless.

To be sure, there are excellent analysts at many brokerage firms, but unfortunately, they are few and far between. Independent analysis has become nearly nonexistent, replaced instead by hidden agendas (analysts indentured to investment banking clients) and research that is neither thorough nor detailed. Instead of acting as analysts, analysts have been reduced to stenographers and cheerleaders.

Even with stocks so depressed, it is ever important to pay attention to possible indicators of trouble. So, how can the individual investor be on the watch for troubled companies that are candidates for sale or shorting?

Following is a list of 11 early warning signs that often serve as indicators of trouble:

1. Management that complains about short-sellers and appears to be more interested in stock price than the company's fundamental business.
2. Competitors that are having problems or are exiting the business.
3. High turnover of key managers.
4. Increasing days of inventory on hand and increasing days of receivables.
5. A company that is having a light quarter but is blaming it on the weather ("orders are slipping into the next quarter").
6. Companies that are late in reporting and that withhold vital information.

7. Companies that do not return analysts' phone calls, especially when they were previously outgoing.
8. A company that has missed its estimates or where the bull story is not playing out, yet Wall Street hasn't given up on the stock—instead, the bullish analysts make excuses.
9. A company that has previously been a growth story, but sales have flattened.
10. On a different note, watch out if the company is controlled by Ron Perelman.
11. If senior management wears more jewelry than your mother, wife, or girlfriend.

For those investors with larger portfolios who have the resources but not the time to do their own analysis, there are a number of valuable services that provide independent research away from Wall Street. These services specialize in finding companies/industries to avoid or to sell short. The services can be relatively expensive—but you get what you pay for.

Laugh at Your Own Expense

4/23/2001

- *Portfolio manager:* The person to whom the host of a TV game show says, "You *are* the weakest link."
- *Institutional investor:* Past year's investor who is now locked up in an insane asylum.
- *Stock analyst:* The idiot who just downgraded your favorite stock.
- *Broker:* What your account representative made you during the year.
- *Momentum investing:* The art of buying high and selling low.
- *Value investing:* The art of buying low and selling lower.
- *P/E ratio:* The percentage of investors wetting their pants as the market crashed during the year.
- *Standard & Poor's:* Your life in a nutshell.
- *Bull market:* A random market movement causing an investor to mistake himself for a financial genius.

- *Stock split:* When your ex-wife and her lawyer split all your equities equally between themselves.
- *Market correction:* What happens the day after you buy a stock.
- *Cash flow:* The movement your money makes as it disappears down the toilet.
- *Call option:* Something people used to do with a telephone in ancient times before e-mail.
- *Yahoo!:* What you yelled after selling it to some poor sucker for $500 a share.
- *Windows 2000:* What you jump out of when you are the sucker that purchased Yahoo! for $500 a share.
- *Bill Gates:* God's banker.
- *Alan Greenspan:* God.

When the Bond Market Talks, Listen

11/18/2004

While I recognize that capturing a turn in the economy is never an easy task, I once again have to go against the consensus—and this one might be more important than my usual contrarian forays.

From my perch, economic and corporate profit projections are simply too high. And future expectations for the course of intermediate-to-longer-term interest rates (which are generally expected to rise) might also be misplaced.

I had thought that despite a contrarian and negative view of the economy as we move into 2005, a collapse in the price of crude oil (which has occurred) would have been viewed in the very short term as economically stimulative and would hit fixed-income prices and raise yields. So, I shorted the iShares Lehman 20+ Year Treasury Bond Fund (TLT).

I was wrong (despite the renewed and added evidence of inflationary pressures), and I have materially reduced my TLT short as my expectation has been unfulfilled.

This morning I would like to discuss the implications of the current term structure of interest, also known as the yield curve, and why it is signaling slower economic growth.

While the stock market has had a rather mediocre forecasting record, the yield curve is the closest thing to a crystal ball that economic prognosticators have.

One common misperception about monetary policy is that the Fed controls all interest rates. The Fed controls only short-term interest rates, via the federal funds rate; market participants influence all other interest rates.

The shape of the yield curve has served to effectively forecast turning points in both the economy and the capital markets for decades. With the exception of 1966, an inverted yield curve has correctly predicted every economic downturn in the past 45 years.

There are four types of yield curves: normal (example: December 1984), steep (example: April 1992), inverted (example: August 1981), and flat or humped (example: April 1989). Each shape tells us something about prospective economic growth and future stock market performance.

- A positively sloping or steepening yield curve typically is consistent with accommodative Fed policy and economic prosperity, and it usually produces an equity market that evokes positive investment returns over time.
- A flattening or negatively sloping yield curve typically is consistent with restrictive Fed policy and slowing economic growth, and it usually produces a headwind to equity market returns.

The yield curve (3-month bill up to the 10-year note) has consistently flattened in the last half of this year, and that flattening process is now accelerating.

This is contrary to the expectations of economic bulls and, to this observer, solidifies the argument that economic forecasts (and corporate profits) for next year are pie in the sky.

While I would note that the yield curve is not yet inverted—just flattening—an inversion has presaged a recession and poor stock market outlook in almost every cycle in modern economic history.

When the bond market talks, we should carefully listen.

Today, the general level of interest rates and the flattening of the yield curve are giving unambiguous signs that the economy is slowing.

Poker Is Flush with Insight for Traders

1/24/2005

This weekend I participated in several events at Jack Binion's Gold Strike Casino in Tunica, Mississippi, leading up to the estimated $5 million World Series of Poker, which started Monday.

I did well and managed to pay for my trip, winning a small tournament. But in the end, I decided that my day job should trump playing in the finals (along with about 700 other participants and a first-place prize of about $2 million dollars!), which would have taken most of this week to determine its outcome.

Moreover, after observing Gus Hansen, Phil Ivey, Johnny Chan, Chip Reese, Men "the Master" Nguyen, Sam Farha, and Barry "Robin Hood" Greenstein play on table No. 29 for nearly 40 hours straight (and with average pots in the neighborhood of $300,000), I concluded that I had little chance to survive into the final table this Thursday.

It would be like trying to out-trade Stevie Cohen, Stanley Druckenmiller, George Soros, and Leon Cooperman!

It was an extraordinary weekend on many different levels, but as always, I want to relate my experiences to the stock market.

Poker and trading/investing hold many similarities, and after spending a brief period of time with the greatest poker player of all time, Doyle "Texas Dolly" Brunson, here are some of the parallels between both activities.

Poker, like trading/investing, is a game of people. In both activities, one needs to get inside the head of one's opponent or the collective head of the masses to be able to consistently win. Importantly, in both venues, one has to know what makes your opponent or the market tick. And one has to know the mood of one's opponent or the psychological condition of investors who set share prices.

Neither poker nor the market can be played purely mathematically or statistically. Many computer programmers have tried to game poker and the stock market, but they have failed. A program is unable to understand the perception of the moment, as judgment requires a human mind.

So, after spending 18 hours a day for four days playing poker, here are some of the specific parallels I have observed.

Pay attention, and it will pay you. Concentrate on everything when you are playing/trading. Watch and listen; remember to do both and relate the two.

Understand when to play aggressively. It's the winning way. Don't be a tight or loose player/trader; be a solid one and recognize when it is time to press your bets/positions. To attain superior returns in poker and investing over the long run, grind it out (in stocks until you are up 30% to 40%, and then if you have convictions, go for a 100% year). If you can avoid losing and put together a few 100% years, you can achieve outstanding long-term investment performance.

Tells: Look for them, and you will find them. Poker players and stock markets have tells—giveaway moves that are very revealing. Learn to recognize them. History is your textbook. (For example, improving corporate financials usually presage a rally; conversely, deteriorating financials usually augur poor market performance.)

ESP: It's a jellyroll. In those rare instances when all your card knowledge and market judgment/knowledge leave you in doubt, go with your strong feelings and not against them.

Honor: A gambler/trader's ace in the hole. A good reputation and respect from others will put you in good stead.

Be as competitive as you can be. Go into a poker game and into a trade with the idea of completely destroying your opponent or scoring a major investment coup. If you win a pot or make a successful trade, nearly always play the next pot or make the next trade shortly thereafter—within reason. Although the cards and trades might break even in the long run, rushes do happen, and momentum often feeds upon itself. When you earn the right to be aggressive, you should be aggressive. When you have a tremendous conviction in a poker hand or trade, you have to go for the jugular.

Art and science: It takes both. Both activities are more art than science—that's why they are so difficult to master. Knowing what to do is about 10% of the game. Knowing how to do it is the other 90%.

Money management. The same sound principles of money control apply to the business of tournament/professional poker and to successful investing. The way to build long-term returns or poker winnings is through preservation of capital and home runs.

The important twins of poker/investing—patience and staying power. Come to the poker table or to the markets with enough time to stay and play for a while.

Alertness is key. You must stay alert at all times.

So is discipline.

Never let your mind dwell on personal problems. Never play/trade when you are upset. Make a conscious and constant effort to discover any leaks in your play, and then eliminate them.

Control your emotions. Allowing your confidence to be shaken can turn a simple losing streak into a terrible case of going bad. Keep your emotions in check. When you lose a pot or make a poor investment decision, get up, walk around the chair, or take some deep breaths. Don't lose your poise. If a trade or a poker hand does not work out, walk away from the position/hand. Be confident enough about your ability to win afterwards.

Schedule vacations. It is important to give both your mind and your body a rest.

My Tenets of Investing

4/10/2006

"You've got to be very careful if you don't know where you are going because you might not get there."

—Yogi Berra

Arguably, the investment and asset-allocation processes can hold more weight and are more complex than nearly any other business decision. A host of variables, known and unknown, contribute to the investment alchemy. As well, subtle and unconscious influences and personal biases affect the process, as we all seek the market's metaphorical green jacket.

What follows are some basic tenets that form my investment consciousness, which are admittedly simple to write about but more difficult to execute.

Know Thyself, Work Hard and Don't Get Emotional

- If you don't know yourself, Wall Street is a poor place to find yourself. There is a reason why there was a church on one side of the old New York Stock Exchange building and a cemetery on the other.

- If you enter the hedge fund biz, remember Darwin. It is survival of the fittest, the smartest, and the most practical. The hedge fund industry is populated by some of the most obsessive and idiosyncratic practitioners extant, most of whom are highly educated and possessive of a greater-than-normal cerebellum. Differentiate yourself by your process and by routinely working harder than anyone else—for example, my day routinely starts at 5:00 A.M.—for as John Maxwell wrote, "Successful and unsuccessful people do not vary greatly in their abilities. They vary in their desires to reach their potential."
- Do not get emotional in making investments, and however eloquent the strategy is, it is the results that count. The ecstasy of getting investment performance right is always eclipsed by the agony of getting it wrong. If you are uncertain or temporarily lack confidence, raise your cash positions.

The Investment Process Is Methodical

- If you are a fundamentalist, write a brief synopsis of each investment analysis/conclusion. It will serve to crystallize your investment analysis and is an excellent personal and investment discipline. Moreover, an ex-post facto reflection on why one achieved past success or failure is usually illuminating, instructive and often leads to fewer mistakes. After all, as Benjamin Disraeli wrote, "What we have learned from history is that we haven't learned from history."
- If you are a technician, keep all your charts, just as the fundamentalist should write up a summary of each investment. Reflecting on past mistakes and successes is as important to a technician as it is to a fundamentalist.
- A combination of fundamental and technical input is usually a recipe for investment success.
- Regardless of one's modus operandi (fundamental, technical, or a combination of both), logic of argument and power of dissection are the two most important ingredients in delivering superior investment returns. Common sense, which is not so common, runs a close third.

Stay Objective and Independent

- Neither be a Cassandra nor a Sunshine Boy! It is much easier to be critical than to be correct, as financial disasters are always impending, according to the ursine crowd. Conversely, the outlook is never as perfect or clear as it is seen by the bullish cabal.
- Within limits, stay independent in view. Above all, remember that equilibrium is rarely observed in the stock market. To quote George Soros, "Participants' perceptions are inherently flawed" (at least to varying degrees).

Investment Discipline Is Key

- Let your profits run, and press your winners, as knowing when to seize opportunity is one of the basic principles of investing. But stop your losses, as discipline always should trump conviction. Edwin Lefèvre wrote in *Reminiscences of a Stock Operator*, "I did precisely the wrong thing. The cotton showed me a loss and I kept it. The wheat showed me a profit and I sold it out. Of all the speculative blunders there are few greater than trying to average a losing game. Always sell what shows you a loss and keep what shows you a profit." Woody Allen put it even better: "I don't want to achieve immortality through my work. I want to achieve it through not dying."

The Past Is Not Necessarily Prologue to the Future

- History should be a guide, but not a jailer. There is little permanent truth in the financial markets, as change is inevitable and constant. Do not extrapolate the trend in fundamentals in your company analysis nor the trend in stock prices. Be independent of analytical and investment conclusions, greedy when others are fearful and fearful when others are greedy, but always remember that holding on to a variant view has outsized risk as well as outsized reward.

Risk and Reward Should Be Assessed Properly

- In buying a stock, remember that risk/reward is asymmetric. A long can climb to indefinite heights and one can only lose 100% of the value of each investment. (Buy value, but only with a catalyst.) When longs have high short-interest ratios, investigate the bear case completely.

- In shorting a stock, remember that risk/reward is asymmetric. A short can only return 100% (a bankruptcy) but can rise to indefinite heights. (Never make conceptual shorts without a catalyst.) Avoid shorts when the outstanding short interest exceeds five days of average trading volume.
- Use leverage wisely but rarely, as financial markets are inherently unstable. While the use of leverage can deliver superior investment returns when the wind is at the back of your investments, it can also wipe you out when events fail to conform to your expectations. Only the best of the best consistently time the proper use of leverage.

Knowledge of Accounting Is a Must, but Meetings with Management Have Little Value

- There is no substitute for a thorough knowledge of financial accounting. Accounting can be misleading, opaque, and unaccountable, but free cash flow rarely lies.
- If you must meet with management, do so to understand a company's core business, but remember that managements infrequently, if ever, view their secular prospects with suspicion. In the late 1980s, Warren Buffett wrote in a letter to Berkshire Hathaway's shareholders that "corporate managers lie like ministers of finance on the eve of devaluation."

Be Open to Others' Ideas, but Rely on Your Own Analysis

- Always be self-critical, and once your view is formulated, be open to criticism from others that you respect. Take their criticism and test your thesis (constantly). Avoid what G. K. Chesterton once mused: "I owe my success to having listened respectfully to the very best advice, and then going away and doing the exact opposite." Bullheadedness will get you in trouble in the investment world.

Only Invest/Trade When Distractions Are Limited

- Invest/trade/speculate only if you are not dependent upon the investment profits to maintain your standard of living.
- A stable personal and financial life, outside of investing, is typically a necessary ingredient to investment success.

- Take vacations and smell the roses. When you return you will be rejuvenated and a better investor/trader.
- Be well rested and in good shape physically. "Investing is 90% mental. The other half is physical" (another Yogi-ism!).
- Keep your investment expectations reasonable, and expect to make mistakes, as perfection is not attainable. Nevertheless, by all means try to chase perfection, as the by-product will be investment excellence.

Read and Learn from the Best

- Learn from those investors who have excelled by reading and rereading the classic books on investing.

12 Investment Principles for the Abyss

1/17/2008

I have been concentrating on what an investor should do when he/she is staring into the abyss, and I have deduced that, regardless of market conditions, investors should adhere to the following sound investing practices:

1. Err on the side of conservatism.
2. Learn from the best, in classic investing books or through conversations with trustworthy individuals.
3. Avoid advice from those who lack flexibility and are dogmatic.
4. Be more concerned with return of capital than return on capital.
5. Trade/invest with below-average positions in order to take advantage of the market's volatility and opportunity.
6. Take a base on balls, hit a single, but don't go for the fences.
7. Buy straw hats in the winter.
8. Buy only the best-of-breed in periods of economic/market uncertainty.
9. Always leg into a position.
10. Be patient.
11. Buy when your hands are shaking; sell when you become over-confident and complacent.
12. Always remember investing is about common sense.

My Recession Checklist

1/22/2008

Notwithstanding the attempts by many to marginalize the role of the U.S. economy on worldwide economic growth, most of the world's economies will soon feel our pain.

That bullish cabal will recognize the existence of the downturn only after the fall in equity values (and after digesting the conclusive economic evidence that is forthcoming)—in other words, after it is too late to prepare investors.

The short-term economic outlook is now practically cast in stone, and the sharp downturn in equities will only serve to exacerbate the growing economic weakness and loss of confidence on the part of consumers and businesses.

Expect market assumptions for retail sales, business spending, and, most importantly, corporate profits to be ratcheted down in the weeks ahead.

In order to properly navigate the investment terrain, investors must answer the following five critical questions:

1. How long will the recession last?
2. How deep will the recession be?
3. How will corporate profits be affected?
4. What will the response be in the capital markets?
5. What wild cards could change the economic and capital market backdrop?

What follows is a summary of my conclusions, and these conclusions will serve as a blueprint for my overall market views and attendant investment strategies.

How Long?   Most recessions are relatively brief—under a year in duration. The evolving supercycle of credit availability (mainly through securitizations) over the past decade, coupled with its unique profile/character of egregious risk-taking as seen from the eyes of both creditors and borrowers, is unlike any cycle in modern financial history. Problems in the residential real estate category have spread like a wildfire throughout the broader economy, putting a pinch on the banking system and, in a marked reversal, serving to restrict credit to many borrowers.

Corporations of all kinds now face a closed window of credit securitizations, so American industry's ability to grow lies squarely on direct bank lending. Unfortunately, with money market rates at 2.75%, the 10-year Treasury note at 3.55% and the federal funds and discount rates at 4.25% and 4.75%, respectively, banks have little incentive to lend, especially in a questionable economic setting.

The securitization market is broken and will take years to repair. Accordingly (and subject to the magnitude of the negative wealth effect of the eventual stock market hit), the 2008–2009 recession will likely be deeper and lengthier than those of the past. Even more important, the aftermath of the recession will linger, producing a period of inconsistent and uneven growth that will be difficult for corporate managers and investment managers to navigate.

How Deep?   Despite the current appearance of a tardy and timid Fed and a generally unresponsive and unimaginative administration, fiscal and monetary stimulation will be swift in its implementation and will, in the fullness of time, buffer somewhat the magnitude of the falloff in gross domestic product (GDP). More aggressive policy moves could be hastened by the proximity of the presidential election in November 2008.

Impact on Corporate Profits?   A profit drop of about 10%, skewed (and deepening) toward the second and third quarters, is about what we should expect in 2008. Mitigating against some of the profit pressure will likely be a reasonably swift decline in commodity prices (especially of an energy kind) and still historically low interest rates. Nevertheless, corporate pricing power will not likely stabilize until well into 2009 (at the earliest), so corporate profits in 2009 will likely be flat to up 5%, well below market expectations.

Response from Capital Markets?   As we have seen in January, markets see through and quickly reject incessant cheerleading (especially in the media). Most of the fall in the stock market and the rise in the fixed-income market have probably already occurred in an environment that, more than ever, adjusts so rapidly to changing economic conditions.

A possible explanation for this phenomenon is that the dominant investors today (i.e., the world's hedge funds) move more swiftly than the dominant investors of the past (i.e., bank trust departments in the 1970s and mutual funds in the 1980s and 1990s)—and so do individual day traders. Another possible explanation is that the Internet platform and other communication devices provide an almost instantaneous information flow.

As mentioned earlier, the economic choppiness will produce abrupt market moves to the downside and the upside, which will be difficult to navigate but ideal for the opportunistic investor. Perma-bulls, perma-bears, and trend followers will be frustrated, but those who remain market-agnostic and sell the rips and buy the dips could be rewarded.

Possible Wild Cards?   On the negative side, more worldwide stock market weakness (reinforcing the existing economic vulnerability), tardy and indecisive policy decisions (both monetary and fiscal), another leg down in the housing market, any event that further seizes up the credit markets, and a sharp rise in energy product prices could all prove to have a disruptive effect on the economy and markets.

On the positive side, a decisive move to insure and underwrite counterparty risk by the administration would serve to stabilize the mortgage, bond, and other credit markets and could produce an immediate and immensely positive impact on stocks around the world. As well, a more aggressive easing than is generally anticipated by the Fed could have a salutary impact on equities and business conditions.

Kill the Quants, Punish the ProBears

2/27/2009

> The mission of the U.S. Securities and Exchange Commission is to protect investors, maintain fair, orderly, and efficient markets, and facilitate capital formation.
>
> As more and more first-time investors turn to the markets to help secure their futures, pay for homes, and send children to college, our investor protection mission is more compelling than ever.

As our nation's securities exchanges mature into global for-profit competitors, there is even greater need for sound market regulation.

And the common interest of all Americans in a growing economy that produces jobs, improves our standard of living, and protects the value of our savings means that all of the SEC's actions must be taken with an eye toward promoting the capital formation that is necessary to sustain economic growth.

The world of investing is fascinating and complex, and it can be very fruitful. But unlike the banking world, where deposits are guaranteed by the federal government, stocks, bonds and other securities can lose value. There are no guarantees. That's why investing is not a spectator sport. By far the best way for investors to protect the money they put into the securities markets is to do research and ask questions. . . .

It is the responsibility of the Commission to:

- interpret federal securities laws;
- issue new rules and amend existing rules;
- oversee the inspection of securities firms, brokers, investment advisers, and ratings agencies;
- oversee private regulatory organizations in the securities, accounting, and auditing fields; and
- coordinate U.S. securities regulation with federal, state, and foreign authorities.

The Commission convenes regularly at meetings that are open to the public and the news media unless the discussion pertains to confidential subjects, such as whether to begin an enforcement investigation. . . .

The Division of Trading and Markets assists the Commission in executing its responsibility for maintaining fair, orderly, and efficient markets. The staff of the Division provide day-to-day oversight of the major securities market participants: the securities exchanges; securities firms; self-regulatory organizations (SROs) including the Financial Industry Regulatory Authority (FInRA), the Municipal Securities Rulemaking Board (MSRB), clearing agencies that help facilitate trade settlement; transfer agents (parties that maintain records of securities owners); securities information processors; and credit rating agencies. . . .

Common violations that may lead to SEC investigations include:

- misrepresentation or omission of important information about securities;
- manipulating the market prices of securities;
- stealing customers' funds or securities;
- violating broker-dealers' responsibility to treat customers fairly;
- insider trading (violating a trust relationship by trading on material, non-public information about a security); and
- selling unregistered securities.

—SEC mission statement, "The Investor's Advocate: How the SEC Protects Investors, Maintains Market Integrity, and Facilitates Capital Formation" (taken from the SEC website)

Most investors (who are long-biased), and indeed the U.S. stock market as a whole, are disadvantaged in a market dominated by momentum-based quant funds and by ultra-bear ETFs, both of which prey on a weakening hedge fund industry riddled by redemptions and by a community of individual investors whose confidence is badly broken.

These quant funds and ultra-bear ETFs, which bypass Federal Reserve Regulation T margin rules governing the extension of credit by securities dealers and brokers in the United States, wreak havoc in a market that needs all the regulatory support it can get.

Today's investors no longer walk tall, as they have seen their portfolios shrivel up. For several years, institutional and individual investors have been competing on an uneven playing field dominated by the powerful quant funds and ultra-bear ETFs that not only have a disproportionate role in total New York Stock Exchange trading but, more importantly, have had an undue influence on pushing stocks lower during the course of the bear market.

Investors are not only facing an unprecedented economic, credit and financial outlook coupled with the uncertainty of public policy but they are also competing against quant funds and ultra-bear exchange-traded funds (ETFs).

As referred to earlier, in the SEC mission statement, our capital markets exist for the benefit of society, and a market dominated by quant funds and ultra-bear ETFs does little to help society.

There has never been a period of time during which the markets had so much money around that could profit from declining prices and invoke economic pain on society. That is what makes the current bear market so much more difficult to navigate than 1930, 1938, 1970 or 1974. Quant funds and ultra-bear ETFs have muddled the ability of the markets to shift assets from weak hands to strong hands.

How do you get people out, if they never run out of firepower (i.e., can short, cover, short, cover all day)?

Under Christopher Cox, the SEC has dropped the ball on a number of key issues over the past several years. The agency's policy (and indifference) almost certainly contributed to our current economic and stock market woes.

It is important that the SEC addresses the dominance and unwieldy influence of quant funds (through the reinstatement of the uptick rule) as well as the circumvention of margin rules by the ultra-bear ETFs in order to "maintain fair, orderly, and efficient markets." It is also important that the SEC considers regulation of the credit default swap market, a market that the Committee neglected and incorrectly left as materially deregulated in recent years.

Our stock market's playing field is no longer level, and, almost without question, the two players above have contributed to an acceleration of the market's downtrend in 2008 and 2009.

I am hopeful that the SEC will not wait in addressing the role of quant funds and ultra-bear ETFs until it is too late to rescue our stock market. Remember this is the same organization that crippled the markets with Sarbanes-Oxley, though, so I am not going to hold my breath.

Chase Value, Not Price

5/14/2009

In my professional investment career, since graduating the Wharton School in 1972, I have seen multiple bull- and bear-market cycles. And, almost without fail, I have observed that far too many investors worship, trade, and invest at the altar of price momentum, though their investment strategy is framed (publicly and sometimes disingenuously) on fundamental grounds.

While momentum trading has its benefits and can produce superior investment returns, it is not for me.

I am by no means an investment purist, but buying high and selling higher is not in my investment bag. Unlike Jim Cramer, I am no good at it.

Rather, I prefer to stick to the discipline of interpreting fundamentals, valuation, and sentiment through a logically reasoned, objective, and analytical process. This means that I maintain the self-control of sitting on my hands, selling and/or shorting when values are rich and buying (even recklessly sometimes) when values emerge as they did two months ago.

This is, however, easier said (or written) than done. It requires patience and, at times, a variant or contrarian view and strength of analytical conviction. It often also requires one to ignore the business media's staccato repeated sound bites of bullish breathlessness. Their intentions might be honorable, but quite frankly, the media, with few exceptions, have no or little skin in the game. Market participants are often required to ignore the delivery of the media's talking heads, who are too frequently theatrical and shallow in their advice rather than substantive in their analysis.

One day a hare saw a tortoise walking slowly along and began to laugh and mock him. The hare challenged the tortoise to a race, and the tortoise accepted. They agreed on a route and started off the race. The hare shot ahead and ran briskly for some time. Then seeing that he was far ahead of the tortoise, he thought he'd sit under a tree for some time and relax before continuing the race. He sat under the tree and soon fell asleep. The tortoise, plodding on, overtook him and finished the race. The hare woke up and realized that he had lost the race. The moral, stated at the end of the fable, is, "Slow and steady wins the race."

—Aesop, "The Tortoise and the Hare" (Wikipedia summation)

Today's investment mosaic remains unusually complex, and arguably, it's growing ever more complex, given the proliferation of hedge funds, the instantaneousness of news and the unique economic circumstances (i.e., the great buildup and the consequential unwind of credit)—among other unprecedented conditions.

Regardless of one's style, the preceding factors will contribute to a secular increase in market volatility, and accordingly, that expected heightened market turbulence should lead traders/investors to maintain smaller-than-typical positions and attempt to supplement a buy-and-hold strategy with an opportunistic trading strategy.

For both for individual and institutional investors, erring on the side of conservatism should continue to be the dominant investment mantra.

My Grandma Koufax's words still resonate (as she paraphrased a New York City off-track betting slogan back several decades ago): "Dougie, invest with your *kepela* (head), not over it."

Chase value, not price. Be the tortoise and not the hare, given the unusual economic times we face.

Six Ways to Right Your Wrongs

9/21/2009

Being convicted in a view or in a series of views is important and a key to superior investment performance, but controlling risk at times of strategic misdirection can be equally important. Almost as critical a determinant of portfolio management as making money when your expectations are accurate and your portfolio is properly structured is dealing with how you handle yourself as an investment manager when you are wrong.

While you wouldn't necessarily know it by watching the business media, in which it appears that nearly every talking head missed the 2008 stock equity market collapse and bought the March 2009 generational bottom, over the course of one's investing/trading career, we all get out of sorts. And in a market that for 2008 and 2009 seems to have been a one-way street (down in 2008 and up over the last six months), money management and discipline is critical to surviving the extreme moves in momentum.

Here are six of my strategies to avoid large losses when your tactical view is wrong:

1. Always stay on top of individual stock fundamentals by talking to management, the competition, and company analysts and industry specialists.
2. Use out-of-the-money puts/calls as protection, especially with high-beta stocks.
3. Do not press losing positions.
4. Accelerate the review of every portfolio holding by rechecking the fundamentals at a 5% to 7% loss, and regardless of those fundamentals, automatically reduce positions as they approach a 10% loss.
5. Maintain a diversified portfolio. (I limit my shorts to 2% positions and my longs to 3% positions.)
6. Never employ leverage.

In conclusion, always remember that, by definition, the crowd usually outsmarts the remnants, and staying in the game when you are incorrectly positioned is almost as important as enjoying a period of investment prosperity.

Remember, it's really awful to lose opportunity, but what is even worse is to lose capital.

Four Stages of Market Turning Points

10/12/2009

It can be argued that there are four classical stages in a move from market bottom to market top and then back again.

- *Stage One:* It is important to recognize that market bottoms are made when investors lose all sign of hope, and fear is the dominating emotion. At bottoms, bears are deified and bulls are rebuked. Seven months ago, prices were beaten down, and the news flow was consistently reinforcing in its negativity. Economic expectations were uniformly bearish, as the credit and financial system seemed broken. Investors no longer believed. The fear of being in the markets overwhelmed market participants—so much so that on the day of the yearly low, a poll indicated that more than half of Americans believed we were entering the Great Depression II. Importantly, decades of buy-and-hold investing seemed to vanish and gave way to a preferred strategy of opportunistic trading.

- *Stage Two:* As stocks began their ascent from the March lows, signs indicated that things were getting less worse as the second derivative recovery commenced. The liquidity put into the system in late 2008 and early 2009 began to flow into the capital markets. Credit spreads improved as the curse of cash began to manifest. In time, fiscal and monetary stimulation began to assert a hold, and improving economic conditions followed.

- *Stage Three:* In time (and with the impetus of higher stock prices and recognition that there were signs of economic improvement), the fear of being in began to be replaced by the fear of being left out. As deflated company forecasts turned out to be too pessimistic, the news (importantly influenced by aggressive cost-cutting) improved, and share prices moved comfortably above the March lows.

- *Stage Four:* Tops are born out of a rally in optimism and when bullish commentary multiplies. At tops, bears are chastised, and bulls regain their popularity. And at tops, investors want to believe.

My position has been that I believe that it is different this time.

From my perch, the prospects for a self-sustaining economic recovery are in doubt in the face of numerous headwinds that are not only consequential in scope but some of which didn't even exist in the last few recoveries out of recessions. Despite the certainty in a smooth and reinforcing recovery that seems to be at the foundation of the bullish cabal, the magnitude of policy (both monetary and fiscal) decisions speaks volumes about how fundamentally different conditions are in October 2009 vis-à-vis past cycles. Moreover, the due bills from those remedies and the timing and response to the withdrawal of the outsized stimulation in 2008–2009 add further to the uncertainty of the slope of future economic growth and poses risks anew.

Whether the stock market is topping out and the economy's 2010 trajectory will disappoint is subject to debate, but what probably can't be debated (and something that truly astonishes me) is the brief period of time in which we have moved from fear to greed.

Moving On

3/22/2010

I have consistently attempted to analyze and strategize about the economy, the capital markets, leading industries, and individual equities.

I try to do this through logic of argument and hard-hitting and independent analysis. Often (maybe sometimes too often), my views are contrarian, as they were when I called for a generational low in March 2009 and again when I pulled in my bullish horns five to six months later, and I will sometimes stay outside of the consensus, even though I recognize that the crowd usually outsmarts the remnants.

One thing I am proud of is that I admit to my mistakes. Frankly, few admit being wrong; after all, it is more natural for all of us to accentuate the positives and our triumphs. No place is this more true than in the business media. If you believe the talking heads' commentary, everyone sold the 2008 high, bought the March 2009 low, and has stayed fully invested since!

I am fully aware that my mistakes over the past few months have been numerous and far-reaching. Above all, I have been steadfastly skeptical regarding the sustainability of the domestic economic recovery and convicted in the view that the foundation for a sustained move in the U.S. stock market was on shakier ground than the consensus believed.

I have been particularly concerned about the still-hobbled American consumer, the tentative recovery in residential real estate and the weight of the phantom housing inventory, the uncertain effect of the withdrawal of government stimulus, the long tail of the last credit cycle and the amount of time it will take the deep scars of the debt overload to heal, a tax-and-spend policy that is aggravating the country's already weak fiscal problems, our reliance on "the kindness of strangers" to fund domestic growth, and the likely onset of numerous nontraditional headwinds (such as rising corporate, individual, and capital gains tax rates as well as the financial disarray at the level of our state and local governments) that are growth- and valuation-deflating. Also, I have often noted the growing schism between the haves (cash-rich, highly profitable large corporations) and the have-nots (small businesses and consumers who face the burden of higher costs emanating from populist tax and regulatory policy), the outgrowth of which has produced an unprecedented disdain against the wealthy that has led to a series of administration-led populist and anticapitalist initiatives. Finally, the necessary austerity measures and consequent need to increase savings and deleverage at so many levels of the private and public sectors in the United States and around the world potentially pose risks to even the conservative forecasters of shallow yet sustainable economic growth.

While there might not be a causality, the consensus seems to have grown emboldened (or at the least very complacent), as share prices around the world have risen over the past 12 months. By contrast, I have opined that the risk/reward of U.S. stocks has turned negative, as it is my view that some of the recent signs of economic growth in many industries represented little more than a statistical expansion from historically depressed levels. To this observer, those signposts of growth are now too readily extrapolated by the bullish cabal. They may be signaling a false sense of prosperity.

All this said, I have been wrong—at least, Mr. Market has been saying so!

I may still prove to be correct in my economic and investment conclusions; as Warren Buffett has written (in paraphrasing Ben Graham), the market is a voting machine over the short run, but it is a weighing machine over the long run. Regardless of the eventual outcome, however, perhaps the single most important ingredient to being a successful money manager or individual investor is to control risk and avoid large losses when one's baseline expectations go awry. An example of when the majority of investors lost their discipline and failed to react in a timely fashion to changing financial and credit conditions that served to sink the equity markets would be 2008. Those who stood pat and didn't sell have only recently, as Jim Cramer writes, "gotten even."

Ideally, we want to be correct tactically and in composing our portfolios. This means being heavily invested in leading market sectors and in the leading stocks within those sectors during bull phases and being light, or even short, when headwinds arise.

Being wrong tactically and not getting obliterated remain essential ingredients toward delivering superior investment returns over the course of several cycles.

The discipline of recognizing the errors in the timing of one's analysis and, even more important, respecting Mr. Market's price action are integral parts of the investment equation—whether or not the price action is later confirmed or unconfirmed by the fundamentals.

There are many ways to control risk—buying out-of-the-money calls and/or puts is one way—but sucking it up and stopping out losses before they get too unwieldy are the best ways and most straightforward strategies to control risk.

Taking small losses is part of the game; taking large losses can take you out of the game.

Adapting to Mr. Market

6/22/2010

The disproportionate influence of high-frequency trading strategies has resulted in an increasingly volatile, trendless, and often random market over the past several months that is difficult for most investors (especially a buy-and-hold kind) to navigate.

> *"Everyone thinks of changing the world, but no one thinks of changing himself."*
>
> —Leo Tolstoy

Grandma Koufax used to say, "Dougie, take and adapt to what Mr. Market offers you."

I always listened to Grandma when she was alive, and I remember her investment tenets (and life lessons) since she has passed 15 years ago.

Here are eight ways that I have responded and adapted to the market's changing character:

1. While my portfolio management is almost entirely based on fundamental analysis, I have increased my "normal" cash positions in order to trade around my investment positions.
2. I am now a more active trader, trying to take advantage of broad and swift intraday moves.
3. When programs clobber markets, I have the cash reserves to add to positions I am convicted in analytically.
4. When programs ramp up markets, I automatically pare back positions, regardless of my fundamental conviction.

5. I am less concentrated and more diversified. No individual long equity position accounts for more than 3% of my partnership's assets, and no individual short equity position accounts for more than 2% of my partnership's assets.

6. I am also diversified across industry lines. No industry accounts for more than 12% of my partnership's assets.

7. I maintain solid risk control. If investment positions (long or short) drop by 7% or 8% from my cost basis, I automatically reduce the position's size (even if that reduction is modest), and I revisit my analysis, making sure that I still know more than Mr. Market does.

8. My partnership is never leveraged.

In summary, in these volatile times, be opportunistic (trade more frequently), stay unlevered, be diversified and err on the side of conservatism.

In Bernanke We Trust?

12/6/2010

Below are misguided comments made by the Fed Chairman over the past five years on derivatives, the financial crisis, housing and the economy.

> *"It is better to keep your mouth closed and let people think you are a fool than to open it and remove all doubt."*
>
> —Mark Twain

On the Economy

- In February 2006, Ben Bernanke, as President Bush's Chairman of the Council of Economic Advisers, was responsible for drafting the Economic Report of the President, which claimed the following: "The economy has shifted from recovery to sustained expansion. . . . The U.S. economy continues to be well positioned for long-term growth." In this report, Bernanke projected the unemployment rate to be 5% from 2008 through 2011.

- On July 20, 2006, Fed Chairman Bernanke referred to the economy as "robust" and "strong."

- On February 15, 2007, Fed Chairman Bernanke said, "Overall economic prospects for households remain good. The labor market is expected to stay healthy. And real incomes should continue to rise. The business sector remains in excellent financial condition."
- On July 18, 2007, Fed Chairman Bernanke said, "Employment should continue to expand. . . . The global economy continues to be strong . . . financial markets have remained supportive of economic growth."
- On February 27, 2008, Fed Chairman Bernanke said, "The nonfinancial business sector remains in good financial condition with strong profits, liquid balance sheets and corporate leverage near historic lows. . . . Projections for the unemployment rate in the fourth quarter of 2008 have a central tendency of 5.2% to 5.3%, up from the level of about 4.75% projected last July for the same period. By 2010, our most recent projections show output growth picking up to rates close to or a little above its longer-term trend, and the unemployment rate edging lower. The improvement reflects . . . an anticipated moderation of the contraction in housing and the strains in financial and credit markets."
- On June 9, 2008, Fed Chairman Bernanke said, "The risk that the economy has entered a substantial downturn appears to have diminished over the past month or so."
- On May 5, 2009, in front of the Joint Economic Committee, Fed Chairman Bernanke said, "Currently, we don't think [the unemployment rate] will get to 10%." In November the unemployment rate hit 10.2%.

On the Housing Market

- July 1, 2005: Bernanke, then President Bush's Chairman of the Council of Economic Advisers had the following exchange with CNBC:
  CNBC interviewer: Ben, there's been a lot of talk about a housing bubble, particularly, you know, from all sorts of places. Can you give us your view as to whether or not there is a housing bubble out there?
  Bernanke: Well, unquestionably, housing prices are up quite a bit; I think it's important to note that fundamentals are also very strong. We've got a growing economy, jobs, incomes. We've got very low mortgage rates. We've got demographics supporting housing growth. We've got restricted supply in some places. So, it's certainly

understandable that prices would go up some. I don't know whether prices are exactly where they should be, but I think it's fair to say that much of what's happened is supported by the strength of the economy.

Interviewer: Tell me, what is the worst-case scenario? We have so many economists coming on our air saying, "Oh, this is a bubble, and it's going to burst. And this is going to be a real issue for the economy." Some say it could even cause a recession at some point. What is the worst-case scenario if in fact we were to see prices come down substantially across the country?

Bernanke: Well, I guess I don't buy your premise. It's a pretty unlikely possibility. We've never had a decline in house prices on a nationwide basis. So, what I think what is more likely is that house prices will slow, maybe stabilize, might slow consumption spending a bit. I don't think it's gonna drive the economy too far from its full employment path, though.

- On February 15, 2006, Fed Chairman Bernanke said, "The housing market has been very strong for the past few years. . . . It seems to be the case, there are some straws in the wind, that housing markets are cooling a bit. Our expectation is that the decline in activity or the slowing in activity will be moderate, that house prices will probably continue to rise but not at the pace that they had been rising. So we expect the housing market to cool but not to change very sharply."

- On February 15, 2007, Fed Chairman Bernanke said, "The weakness in housing market activity and the slower appreciation of house prices do not seem to have spilled over to any significant extent to other sectors of the economy."

- On March 28, 2007, Fed Chairman Bernanke said, "The impact on the broader economy and financial markets of the problems in the subprime markets seems likely to be contained."

- On May 17, 2007, Fed Chairman Bernanke said, "We do not expect significant spillovers from the subprime market to the rest of the economy or to the financial system."

- On February 27, 2008, Fed Chairman Bernanke said, "By later this year, housing will stop being such a big drag directly on GDP. . . . I am satisfied with the general approach that we're currently taking."

On the Financial Crisis

- On February 15, 2007, Fed Chairman Bernanke said, "The Federal Reserve takes financial crisis management extremely seriously, and we have made a number of efforts to improve our monitoring of the financial markets to study and assess vulnerabilities, and to strengthen our own crisis management procedures and our business continuity plans."
- On February 28, 2008, Fed Chairman Bernanke said, "Among the largest banks, the capital ratios remain good, and I don't expect any serious problems . . . among the large, internationally active banks that make up a very substantial part of our banking system."
- On July 16, 2008, Fed Chairman Bernanke said that Fannie Mae and Freddie Mac are "adequately capitalized" and "in no danger of failing." Since then, Fannie Mae and Freddie Mac have received a $200 billion bailout and have been taken over by the federal government.

On Derivatives

While Warren Buffett warned that derivatives were "financial weapons of mass destruction" that pose a "mega-catastrophic risk" to the economy in 2003, Bernanke supported the deregulation of these risky schemes.

- In November of 2005, Mr. Bernanke was questioned by then-Senate Banking Committee Chairman Paul Sarbanes:
- **Sarbanes:** Warren Buffett has warned us that derivatives are time bombs, both for the parties that deal in them and the economic system. The *Financial Times* has said so far, there has been no explosion, but the risks of this fast-growing market remain real. How do you respond to these concerns?
- **Bernanke:** I am more sanguine about derivatives than the position you have just suggested. I think, generally speaking, they are very valuable. They provide methods by which risks can be shared, sliced, and diced, and given to those most willing to bear them. They add, I believe, to the flexibility of the financial system in many different ways. With respect to their safety, derivatives, for the most part, are traded among very sophisticated financial institutions and individuals

who have considerable incentive to understand them and to use them properly. The Federal Reserve's responsibility is to make sure that the institutions it regulates have good systems and good procedures for ensuring that their derivatives portfolios are well managed and do not create excessive risk in their institutions.

- On February 27, 2008, Fed Chairman Bernanke said, "If you have two investment banks doing an over-the-counter derivatives transaction, presumably they both are well informed and they can inform that transaction without necessarily any government intervention."
- On July 10, 2008, Fed Chairman Bernanke said, "Since September 2005, the Federal Reserve Bank of New York has been leading a major joint initiative by both the public and private sectors to improve arrangements for clearing and settling credit default swaps and other OTC derivatives. . . . I don't think the system is broken, but it does need some improvement in execution."

> *Take me out to the*
> *ball game*
> *Take me out with*
> *the crowd*
> *Buy me some peanuts and*
> *Cracker Jack*
> *I don't care if I never*
> *get back*
> *Let me root, root, root for*
> *the home team*
> *If they don't win it's*
> *a shame*
> *For it's one, two, three*
> *strikes, you're out*
> *At the old ball game*
>
> —Jack Norworth,
> "Take Me Out to the
> Ball Game"

America's Pastime Applies to Markets

3/6/2012

I have learned over my career that history is instructive—it rarely repeats itself, but it often rhymes.

That said, we must all recognize that the past is not immutable.

As a cousin to Sandy Koufax, I grew up immersed in the game of baseball. I watched numerous games with my grandfather, Harry Koufax (Grandma Koufax's husband!) at his home in Mount Vernon, New York. I used to watch the peaceful look in Grandpa Koufax's eyes when he sat watching the games in his big cushy chair, cigar in mouth. I have never forgotten that look: He was in baseball heaven. I think I have that same look today when I watch ball games. It's a look of contentment.

It wasn't only the Koufax connection that drew me to baseball; it was the purity of the game. Baseball is an untimed contest. The home run records, perfect games, the tar on the bats, the spit in the mitts all combined to create an almost genteel tradition among today's sports.

And that song. "Take Me Out to the Ball Game" is played during the seventh-inning stretch of every Major League Baseball game, with Harry Caray getting the credit for singing it first at a ball game in 1971. Call me sentimental or old-fashioned, but to this day, every time I am at a baseball game and I hear "Take Me Out to the Ball Game," I well up in tears.

When I think of baseball, the first thing that comes to my mind is a sense of historical perspective—a respect for Roger Maris's record 61 home runs in one season (1961), Hank Aaron's 755 career home runs, Pete Rose's 4,256 hits, Joe DiMaggio's 56 consecutive games with a hit, and Nolan Ryan's six no-hitters and 5,714 strikeouts.

Back in 2007, I got teary-eyed at the tribute to Willie Mays, the "Say Hey Kid," at that year's All-Star Game. Perhaps it was that respect for baseball's traditions. Or perhaps it was a sense of a historical perspective, like when Sandy Koufax refused to pitch Game 1 of the 1965 World Series because the game fell on Yom Kippur, the Jewish Day of Atonement.

It is the same perspective and respect and sense of history that seems to be missing in the analysis of today's stock market by many of its participants—most of whom, in the mounting competitive landscape of hedge funds, invest/trade at the altar of momentum.

To some degree, fear and doubt have been driven from Wall Street today. There

> *Where have you gone, Joe DiMaggio?*
>
> *A nation turns its lonely eyes to you.*
>
> —Simon and Garfunkel, "Mrs. Robinson"

> *Yer blind, ump,*
>
> *Yer blind, ump,*
>
> *You must be out of yer mind, ump.*
>
> —Damn Yankees, "Six Months Out of Every Year"

is no negativity bubble, but rather a bubble in complacency and in economic and stock market extrapolation.

One would have thought that lessons would have been learned by the unthinking speculation of day traders in the U.S. equity market in the late 1990s, which resulted in a 70%-plus schmeissing of the Nasdaq or in the horrendous stock market during the 2007–2009 period. But nothing has been learned. The same mistakes are being made over and over. Other errata—such as marking to market (collateralized debt obligations), trusting credit agencies (remember Enron, Tyco, etc.?), the use of margin debt, or even the buying of the crap that Wall Street packaged (again, collateralized debt obligations)—will be buried and lost to history, and I guarantee that these mistakes will be repeated in the future.

The availability and price of credit in 2005–2007 facilitated the housing bubble, which in turn followed the technology and Internet bubble of 13 years ago. It was a bubble that fed the private-equity boom and that, for a period of time, created a put under the market that served to reduce fear and produced the aforementioned bubble in optimism (and the concomitant use of leverage, such as the carry trade, by hedge funds and the aggressive use of debt worldwide).

I began writing and warning about the tip of the iceberg of credit on this site—namely, subprime lending—back in 2006, when the ABX BBB was trading at par; it ultimately fell close to zero. Back then, as the deterioration in subprime began to spread, talking heads in the media grew bored of the subject and swept it under the lending rug, dismissing its possible impact on our markets and the domestic economy.

For a while, credit spreads were contained and locked in a narrow range—surprising, considering how levered segments of our economy were, particularly at the consumer level—but the spreads eventually bottomed and, in the fullness of time, widened to levels never thought possible. In turn, the housing market experienced its roughest patch in history, and the residential market's credit contagion grew and was not contained to subprime; it infected all the debt markets. In time, the drop in housing activity accelerated, and there was a pernicious impact on operating results on the entire spectrum of America's companies (especially of a banking kind).

And the Great Recession of 2008–2009 came to pass.

In time, the loose lending of 2000–2006 moved well beyond the subprime mess and into motorcycle, automobile, and credit card securitizations by 2007. And it spread further to every town in the United States (and many abroad) populated by merchants that had encouraged the consumption binge (buy now and pay later).

The crack in the foundation of credit began to gain speed as the lending community grew more circumspect, and, in time, credit grew ever sparser.

The credit crisis was born, and the Great Recession moved speedily toward its height.

For a while in 2007–2008, with the pressure on, the quality of corporate profits and elevated profit margins were dismissed as companies influenced by activist shareholders would mask the evolving headwinds with share buybacks, which, in the fullness of time, served to leverage the one relatively remaining healthy sector: American business's balance sheet. (Look back at the prices that General Electric and Hewlett-Packard paid for their shares in buyback programs back then. It will make you sick! GE and Hewlett-Packard shareholders suffered the hangover effect of the poorly timed buybacks!)

As legendary hedge fund manager Michael Steinhardt said in a 2007 interview with *HedgeFolios*, "As expected, once companies are faced with having to discuss their quarterly performance, we get a new round of share repurchase announcements." He pointed to Sears Holdings, which lost more than 7% after it came out with a warning that "almost halves the analyst estimate for earnings and magically a $1 billion increase in its buyback is announced. . . . Clearly, not every buyback is being used to cover for operational deficiencies, but when a company is struggling to sell products at good margins, that should be more important than a decline in share counts."

Another legend—this one of a baseball kind—pitcher Satchel Paige once said, "Age is a case of mind over matter. If you don't mind, it don't matter." For a while, the metamorphosis of the credit cycle was ignored: Investors didn't mind; market participants, however, ultimately got a lesson in history.

Joltin' Joe has left and gone away?

Hey hey hey, hey hey hey.

—Simon and Garfunkel, "Mrs. Robinson"

My advice? Similar to Major League Baseball records, be mindful and respectful of the history of credit and stock market cycles.

This certainly does not mean that anything close to an economic Armageddon or stock market crash lies ahead (similar to what occurred in 2008–2009); it does mean that the economic ride will be increasingly lumpy and that the stock market ride will become increasingly bumpy.

The era of free and easy money is coming to a close at the same time as our recovery is growing increasingly fragile, but it's different this time, with secular challenges that present unique headwinds to a self-sustaining domestic economic recovery.

Consider that today's challenges (fiscal imbalances, structural unemployment, etc.) are more problematic than those that were encountered in the last cycle. Today's challenges suggest a lengthier period of rehabilitation. The solutions to these problems cannot quickly be dispatched, as they are our inheritance from the last cycle and, maybe even, a decade or two of risk and debt accumulation before that.

So, remember for the future, if you don't pay attention to Mr. Market's history, it could be, "one, two, three strikes, you're out, at the old ball game!"

Let the Trading Day Commence

6/7/2012

Over the course of the past week and through this upcoming weekend, college and university graduations abound around the country.

Six of my friends either gave commencement speeches last week or are going to give speeches in the next few days.

Several of them asked if I would publish the commencement speech I gave at Alfred University when I received an honorary PhD.

Here it goes. I hope you enjoy reading it. And a warm congratulations to all the 2012 graduates.

> Students, parents, grandparents, siblings, teachers, President Edmondson, members of the Administration and of the Board of Trustees, I am honored to be here today.
>
> I want to offer my sincere congratulations to this year's graduates on such an important day in your lives. I especially

want to congratulate the parents. And remember that they still need you, and maybe they will now listen to you. If you aren't sure who I am talking to, I am actually talking to both the parents and the students, so congratulations to everybody!

Today, I am going to briefly touch on my journey and then make some observations about what went wrong in our financial system and where we might be going economically in the years ahead.

The 1960s vs. the 2010s

We live in much different times than when I graduated four decades ago. After all, there was no texting or even cell phones back then. Instead, there was one public telephone on each floor of our dormitories. We ate blackberries; you text, phone, and e-mail with them. We got our news from newspapers; your generation gets the news from blogs and tweets. We wore watches. We took pictures with cameras. We navigated with maps. We listened to transistor radios. Again, you do it all with a cell phone.

We had VCRs that cost $750 each; you use YouTube at no cost, and you can upload 50 hours of YouTube videos in less than a minute. Laptops were nonexistent when I attended Alfred, and the term *laptop* had an entirely different connotation back then! We bought most of our books at the Alfred Bookstore, not on Amazon. We played pong in the Student Center; you play Wii in your dorm rooms. NASA used mainframe computers to go to the moon; you use an iPod, which is about 500× more powerful, to listen to Lady Gaga on the way to your next class.

We used the word *friend* as a noun; you use the word *friend* as a verb. Today, Facebook provides your forum for socializing; in 1970, our social life was centered on campus fraternities and at the only bar nearby, which we called "Down the Road" in Hornell, New York, which, of course, was literally down the road from school! Back then, our idea of search was not Google; it was, again, searching for members of the opposite sex at that bar, Down the Road, 40 years ago.

The fact is that the world we live in today is quite different than the world of 40 years ago.

You will soon search for work in an economy that is emerging from the worst recession since the Great Depression. You live in a world in which change occurs more frequently than at any time in history. You will raise your children with threats of terrorism and climate change—issues we were oblivious to four decades ago.

You will live in a world that is growing more connected. You will work with more people that don't look like you or don't come from where you came from. You will work in an economy that has shifted from manufacturing to information services.

These challenges, these changes might make you worry about the future.

But don't worry.

It is important to recognize that throughout all the challenges of the past two and a half centuries, America has a tradition of thriving through thick and thin. We have always moved toward "a more perfect union" and back toward stability and ultimately growth.

Sometimes, like now, we need the help of our government.

For example, when the markets crashed during the Depression, our government put in new rules and safeguards to ensure that it wouldn't happen again, just like we are doing today.

Two hundred years before I entered Alfred, President Lincoln said that the role for government is to do for people what they can't do better for themselves. His administration set up the first intercontinental railroad system and the first land grant colleges.

Franklin Roosevelt's administration instituted aggressive and unprecedented New Deal programs that left a lasting mark on the American landscape.

President Theodore Roosevelt said that the object of government is the welfare of the people; he broke up monopolies and established a national park system.

In the 1960s the Kennedy administration was responsible for founding the Peace Corps, signing the Nuclear Test Ban Treaty, and helping to end racial discrimination.

When I was at Alfred, the Johnson administration designed the "Great Society," created the "War on Poverty," and was instrumental in launching key legislation that protected our environment.

And in reaction to the unique economic times, today's administration is participating in equally profound change.

So while the challenges appear monumental, you will help and in the years ahead be a part of a community that overcomes those headwinds; you will adapt and contribute to these changing times.

The government won't guarantee your future, but the government will give you a good chance to succeed. But in order for our system to work, you must become part of the debate and contribute to the implementation of balanced and effective public policy.

When I was at Alfred, Dr. Timothy Leary developed the counterculture phrase: "Turn on, tune in, and drop out."

Don't follow his words. Don't be an island. Rather, become part of the process; help choose your leaders and criticize them if they let you down.

Joining in this debate is the responsibility of every graduate today.

I have stressed the dissimilarities of 2010 and 1970, but of course not everything is different today than in the early 1970s. For example, I have been reminded over the last two days that the setting at Alfred remains beautiful. Unfortunately, another similarity is that we are still at war today as we were in Vietnam back then.

Importantly, the University still provides a marvelous liberal arts education, and that education provides a potential springboard to a very successful professional career as it did back then.

My Journey

I have many recollections of Alfred University as an undergraduate—perhaps the most vivid of which was living in my car for a semester to save money. (Fortunately, my best pal, Sheldon, let me shower in his off-campus apartment a couple of times a week!)

The times were different than today, but, like all of you, my personality and character have been molded by many of my experiences at Alfred.

I would separate those experiences into two categories. First, I recall the close and nurturing relationships I had with some of the faculty at Alfred, with professors like Dr. Gary Horowitz and Dr. Myron Sibley, and the strong bond I had with the then-President of Alfred, Dr. Leland Miles. These relationships led me to the conclusion, popularized in the movie *Animal House*, that at Alfred, as at Faber College, "knowledge is good."

Seriously, though, I would strongly recommend that if in the future you are in a position to mentor someone, as the afore-mentioned Alfred teachers did for me, you will be, again, doing good.

The second category of experiences was a bit more personal and revolved around a remarkably bucolic setting, staged during a remarkable period of time 40 years ago in which I evolved and planned for the future.

- I remember a lot of emotion—the 1960s was a period of feelings.
- I remember my first love—I remember being shot down by my first love.
- I remember the experimentation.
- I remember the music, which seemed at the core of our being. I particularly remember attending the Woodstock Music Festival, and, as Sam Moore of the singing group Sam and Dave shouted out in his song, "Soul Man," you could say that I was also educated at Woodstock while a junior at Alfred.
- I remember traveling around the country to watch the Grateful Dead perform in 71 separate concerts.
- And I remember the killings at Kent State in Ohio, which made so many of us adopt a philosophy of nonviolence.

I strongly recommend that in the future you, too, hold on to your memories.

I graduated Alfred University in 1970, a bit earlier than most of my classmates, as I was anxious to move forward. My next destination, in keeping with the experience of the times and the turbulence of the 1960s, was a southerly one, to New Jersey, in the graduate program in philosophy at Princeton University.

After majoring in philosophy and religion at Alfred, as a good liberal and as an avid participant in the decade's "make love not war" peace movement, my first job was working with Ralph Nader in the early 1970s. At that time, the consumer movement was in full force, and being a "Nader Raider," as we were called, was viewed almost as prestigiously as being a partner at Goldman Sachs on Wall Street before the credit crisis hit in early 2008 and certainly before the news of recent weeks. With Nader, I wrote a book entitled *Citibank*, which presciently argued all the way back in the early 1970s that the banking industry had too much power.

The economy was in a recession in the early 1970s (as it was in 2008–2009), and as much as I enjoyed studying the writings of Søren Kierkegaard, Martin Buber, and Frederick Nietzsche at Princeton, I ultimately succumbed to economic reality: There simply was not a large need for philosophy PhDs at that time! So I continued my trip further south, with my next stop in Philadelphia and business school at the Wharton School at the University of Pennsylvania, where I got my MBA. Three days after graduating, I began my investment career in Lower Manhattan.

By taking that fork in the road to Wall Street, I suppose one may be reminded of something Mae West once said, perhaps relating to my journey, as I made the move from Nader to the business world, "I used to be Snow White, but I drifted."

What Went Wrong in the Economy?

So what went wrong with our economic and financial system in the past several years?

Wall Street was at the epicenter of all that went wrong in our economy over the past three years. A small cabal of bankers who created unwieldy, unregulated and unnecessary derivative products, or financial weapons of mass destruction, ended up producing an economic, financial, and credit disequilibrium that affected nearly everyone in the audience today. This was done under the not-so-watchful eyes of regulatory agencies and of our government.

Recklessness abounded. How else to explain investment banks that were leveraged to the tune of 35–1, which seems to be the equivalent of playing Russian roulette with five of the six chambers of the gun loaded. If one added up the off-balance-sheet liabilities to this leverage, you might as well have filled the sixth chamber with a bullet and pulled the trigger.

America rushed headlong into the twenty-first century without a proper understanding of what economic policies and financial tools were going to be required to prosper in a changing world. For more than two decades, the U.S. economy favored financial speculation over production.

The financial crisis impacted nearly everyone in our country, and, with those derivative products imported by the investment banks, AIG and several large money center banks to other financial institutions around the world, a massive credit crisis ensued, which nearly resulted in an unfathomable collapse in the world's banking system and securities markets.

Certainly, everyone in this audience has, to some degree, been impacted. Household net worths were decimated by the unprecedented stock and home price drops, and, to varying degrees, your parents' ability to help you pay for an Alfred education was hurt. The University itself lost money in its endowment and was forced to provide ever more financial assistance to its students. Teachers' head counts were reduced as were other important services curtailed.

We all won't forget the last few years, but I remain hopeful—and you should be, too—that the safeguards now being put in place will protect us in the future. But, again, to be totally effective, you must contribute to the debate that dictates policy.

Where Is Our Economy Headed?

In discussing this commencement speech with Dr. Edmondson several months ago, Charlie suggested that I offer my view as to where the economy and stock markets are headed. And that is how I would like to end this speech.

But first, I am reminded of a story of a professor at the University of Edinburgh Medical School who asks his class the question: "What part of the human body expands six times its normal size under stimulation?"

The professor points to a woman in the first row and asks, "Ms. Kennedy, can you answer the question?"

Turning beet red, Ms. Kennedy stands up and tells the professor that she can't possibly answer the question.

The professor then turns to a gentleman in the fifth row, Mr. O'Donnell, and asks him the same question. Mr. O'Donnell stands up erect and says, "The pupil of the human eye expands six times its normal size under the stimulation of light."

The professor congratulates Mr. O'Donnell on the correct answer and readdresses Ms. Kennedy by saying, "I have three responses to you Ms. Kennedy:

- Firstly, you haven't done your homework.
- Secondly, you have a dirty mind.
- Thirdly, you are destined to live a life of unfulfilled expectations!"

In a like manner, if you all think I am about to give you an accurate outlook for the economy and stock markets, you, too, will be living a life of unfulfilled expectations.

But, at least I work cheap, Charlie!

Here is what I see for the U.S. economy.

While it is my view that the U.S. economy faces a healthy near-term outlook, the secular problems put the recovery on a bit shakier ground than usual as a number of nontraditional headwinds and bills from the aggressive government fiscal stimulation are shortly coming due.

I remain particularly concerned about the still-hobbled American consumer, who is burdened by wage deflation and weak income growth, structurally high unemployment, lower housing wealth, elevated debt loads, and still-tight credit. The recovery in residential real estate seems tentative and will weigh on growth as will the uncertain effect of the withdrawal of government stimulus and the long tail of the last credit cycle and the amount of time it will take the deep scars of the debt overload to heal. Other concerns include our reliance on "the kindness of strangers" to fund domestic growth and the likely onset of numerous nontraditional headwinds (such as rising corporate, individual and capital gains tax rates as well as the financial disarray at the level of our state and local governments). Also, the growing schism between the "haves" (cash-rich, highly profitable large corporations) and the "have-nots" (small businesses and consumers who face the burden of higher costs emanating from populist tax and regulatory policy) must be carefully watched as it has produced an unprecedented disdain against the wealthy.

In the current cycle, credit, too, will be a lot less plentiful. Prospectively, China, another uncommon driver to world economic growth, holds some risks in the form of an overheated economy and in a credit and asset boom that includes hidden debt, unproductive real estate, and infrastructure projects.

Finally, the necessary austerity measures and consequent need to increase savings and deleverage at so many levels of the private and public sectors in the United States and around the world (like in Greece) potentially pose additional risks.

Former New York Yankees baseball player, Hall of Famer, and wordsmith, Yogi Berra, might say about the future that it's different this time, but it almost always is!

Conclusion

Let me conclude by mentioning something that Apple's Steve Jobs talked about in his Stanford University commencement speech five years ago, in which he highlighted a very idealistic magazine that many of us read at Alfred back in the late 1960s called *The Whole Earth Catalog*. In essence it was our Google in magazine form, but it was patched together not by sophisticated desktop publishing systems but by pictures taken from Polaroid cameras and words that poured out of typewriters.

By the time I graduated, *The Whole Earth Catalog* closed, and on the back cover of the final issue was a photograph of an early-morning country road—the kind you might find here in upstate New York.

Beneath it was a farewell message from the managing editor. The words were: "Stay hungry. Stay foolish."

I have always wished that for myself. And now, as you graduate to begin anew, I wish that for you.

Stay hungry. Stay foolish.

Good luck and thank you all for letting me be a part of your commencement.

A Delicate Balance

6/26/2012

Managing investment money (as distinguished from trading money) is not taking a black or white position; it is working off a complicated mosaic of fundamentals, sentiment/technicals, and valuation.

While it currently seems as though a risk-on/risk-off market requires one to be spot-on in our decision-making process over every day/week/month time frame, it is not the case. No one is that clairvoyant to accurately predict every wiggle. We can occasionally forecast and position a small portion of a portfolio for a short-term move in an attempt to produce a cash-register effect of locking in gains, but, in the main, we should recognize that the odds of succeeding may be remote.

We should aim for more balance and consistency in our portfolios. This means if, in a normal market environment a 60%/40% stock/bond fix is in line with your investment objectives and risk appetite, then a more uncertain investment backdrop (such as we face today) should have a stock/bond guideline of some lesser amount with a cushion of cash—perhaps 45% stocks, 30% bonds, and 25% cash.

Years ago, John Bogle brilliantly said, "We must base our asset allocation not on the probabilities of choosing the right allocation but on the consequences of choosing the wrong allocation." In other words, extreme positions of putting on or putting off risk (in cash or stock) are generally unsound and can produce negative consequences.

More balance, even in times of uncertainty, represents a more sound investment strategy.

Getting it right is not being all in or all out.

Thoughtful and hard-hitting analysis that generates exceptional information and knowledge of the historic interaction between companies, industries, and asset classes under similar circumstances are some of the basic ingredients for long-term and consistent investment success.

But, as Barton Biggs recently suggested, getting to know yourself will improve your investment behavior and returns:

> The investment process is only half the battle. The other weighty component [is] struggling with yourself and immunizing yourself from the psychological effects of the swings of markets, career risk, the pressure of benchmarks, competition and the loneliness of the long distance runner. . . .
>
> Understanding the effect of emotion on your actions has never been more important than it is now. In the midst of this great financial and economic crisis that grips the world, central banks are printing money in one form or another. This makes our investment world even more prone to bubbles and panics than it has been in the past. Either plague can kill you.

We have been in an environment of crisis since 2008.

It is an emotional setting filled with potential investment opportunity but also terror and potential investment losses.

An unemotional view and a balanced portfolio construction are apt to provide the road to investment success in the period ahead.

The Lion's Share

7/23/2012

A month ago, I was speaking to the legendary Ira Harris (one of the most influential Wall Streeters extant back in the day when he ran Salomon Brothers' Chicago office), who mentioned that he could not remember a time during his investment career when there was so much uncertainty as there is now.

In other words, there exists, as Sir John Mauldin points out in his commentary this week, more than the usual lurking "lions in the grass" (and in the open fields) these days.

In the economic sphere an act, a habit, an institution, a law produces not only one effect, but a series of effects. Of these effects, the first alone is immediate; it appears simultaneously with its cause; it is seen. The other effects emerge only subsequently; they are not seen; we are fortunate if we foresee them.

There is only one difference between a bad economist and a good one: the bad economist confines himself to the visible effect; the good economist takes into account both the effect that can be seen and those effects that must be foreseen.

Yet this difference is tremendous; for it almost always happens that when the immediate consequence is favorable, the later consequences are disastrous, and vice versa. Whence it follows that the bad economist pursues a small present good that will be followed by a great evil to come, while the good economist pursues a great good to come, at the risk of a small present evil.

—From "That Which Is Seen and That Which Is Unseen," an 1850 essay by Frédéric Bastiat (hat tip John Mauldin)

As John wrote over the weekend, most lions are readily seen—they are known, in front of us, and are usually anticipated. The lions in the grass and their distant cousins, the more random black swans, which have been spotted with a frightening frequency over the past decade, however, are not

"More than at any other time in history, mankind faces a crossroads. One path leads to despair and utter hopelessness. The other, to total extinction. Let us pray we have the wisdom to choose correctly. I speak, by the way, not with any sense of futility, but with a panicky conviction of the absolute meaninglessness of existence that could easily be misinterpreted as pessimism. It is not. It is merely a healthy concern for the predicament of modern man."

—Woody Allen

readily foreseen—those are the scariest and the most market upsetting. They spring upon us suddenly, unexpectedly (and some of them even inhabit my annual surprises lists), sometimes taking off an arm or a leg or causing our investment portfolio to plummet in value.

While those lions in the grass are grazing somewhere—one possible grass inhabitant might be the adverse implications of the current U.S. drought—let's review the visible lions that limit the upside and the downside to the U.S. stock market.

Core Market Challenges that Limit Upside

- *Fundamentals:* Top-line growth is moderating, and there is a limit to how long corporate profit growth (and margins) can be sustained. The U.S. bond market is delivering a more bearish economic vision than the U.S. stock market. While the U.S. economy stands tall relative to the other developed economies, any realtor will tell you not to buy the best house in a bad neighborhood.
- *Eurozone:* These ferocious lions are running amok in Europe. They represent the greatest threat to the well-being of the equity markets. Last week, in a vote of no confidence, the euro has hit a two-year low against the U.S. dollar.
- *Central banks:* With interest rates near zero, U.S. monetary policy is waning in its influence and could be pushing on a string.
- *Politics:* Governor Romney is considered by most market participants as pro-market and pro-business relative to the incumbent, but President Obama's lead in the polls continues. He remains the favorite—at this point in time, it's his election to lose.
- *Geopolitical:* The Middle East is heating up and so is the price of crude oil.

> *"Disaster has a way of not happening."*
>
> —Byron Wien, vice chairman Blackstone Advisory Partners

Core Market Positives that Limit Downside

- *Fundamentals:* Second-quarter 2012 results have failed to indicate that an imminent drop in corporate profits (or margins) will occur. Despite some falloff in the top line, corporations have controlled their fixed costs and continue to operate profitably even as the rate of global economic growth decelerates. Balance sheets are rock-solid, with reams of cash and liquidity. The CRB Index has fallen by nearly 15% from June, a tax cut to the consumer and a potential preserver of corporate margins. The residential real estate market has bottomed (in sales activity and price) and appears on the launch path of a durable, multiyear recovery. The U.S. stock market remains the best house in a questionable economic and investment neighborhood.

- *Eurozone:* Though not caged, these lions can still be domesticated by the region's central bankers and leaders through forceful policy. Most importantly, their whereabouts are well known by the markets.
- *Politics:* While the fiscal cliff is feared, there might be upside to expectations as even our dysfunctional leaders must recognize that a repeat of August 2011 will crush business and consumer confidence, our markets and our economy. History shows that our leadership rises in times of crisis. (Let us hope that Senator Schumer and others are listening.)
- *Central banks:* A broad-based (and market-friendly) global easing promises to be with us for some time to come.
- *Sentiment and expectations:* Investor sentiment remains subdued, mired in a lost decade for stocks, the Great Decession, and structural disequilibrium in the jobs market. Investor expectations have been dulled by the May 2010 flash crash, two large drawdowns (in 2000–2002 and 2008–2009), and numerous scandals (Madoff, Stanford, Peregrine, Liebor, etc.) and trading gaffes (at JPMorgan Chase and elsewhere). Retail investors and hedge-hoggers have derisked. Large pension plans are skewed toward low- or no-yielding fixed income and have not yet balanced back into equities. Frightened by the past, these (antispeculative) conditions suggest that, with so many turned off to equities (and turned on to fixed income), the pain trade is to the upside.
- *Valuations:* P/E ratios are undemanding relative to inflationary expectations, interest rates, earnings, and private market values. Most conspicuously, risk premiums are back to mid-1975 levels, a period that was followed by outsized gains in the senior averages.

How to Trade a Trading-Sardine Market Many of my most successful hedge fund friends have made their fortunes in buying and holding—namely, by discovering investment acorns that rise into mighty oaks. They contend that, regardless of the environment, there will always be those opportunities.

Many of these hedge-hoggers have prospered by bottoms-up stock picking and have often downplayed the macroeconomic backdrop.

They might be correct—and for many it has paid mighty dividends—but I contend, by contrast, that the unique conditions that exist today make the harvesting of those great investments ever more difficult. Indeed, there are numerous fundamental, valuation, sentiment and technical factors that support the notion that both the upside and downside might be limited.

In his seminal book, *Margin of Safety*, hedge fund manager Seth Klarman tells an old story about the market craze in sardine trading. One day, the sardines disappear from their traditional habitat off the Monterey, California, shores, so the commodity traders bid the price of sardines up, and prices soar. Then, along comes a buyer who decides that he wants to treat himself to an expensive meal and actually opens up a can and starts eating. He immediately gets ill and tells the seller that the sardines were no good. The seller quickly responds, "You don't understand. These are not eating sardines; they are trading sardines!"

The 11 factors discussed above that on one side limit the market's upside and on the other limit the market's downside seem to almost offset each other—ergo, we might be locked in a trading range. These conditions are likely set to deliver what I have termed in the past a trading-sardine market, not an eating-sardine market.

Investment Conclusion   In summary, the U.S. stock market is populated by an unusual amount of visible (fierce and not-so-fierce) lions in the open and likely several lions lurking in the grass.

For now, the pride of lions is holding the markets at bay, and reward vs. risk appears in balance.

As a result, there appears to be no real trend nor is there likely to be one over the short term and into the fall. Instead, as I recently mentioned, a range-bound market confined between 1,300 and 1,420 on the S&P 500 seems to be a reasonable expectation for the balance of the year. (Friday's close of 1,360 is a relatively balanced reward relative to risk.)

My strategy has been to be 20% to 30% (long or short) on either side of market-neutral, depending on my assessment of the near-term outlook.

In the trading-sardine market I envision, I plan to continue to trade the range and rent with a nimble, albeit conservative, short-term view over the next few months, rotating into sectors, as we recently did in the Market Vectors Oil Services ETF, and into individual securities as the opportunities develop.

More serious money is typically made by investing rather than via short-term trading. But, for now, as I look at the investment portion of my portfolio, I plan to be patient while waiting for the right pitch.

Even though there are, no doubt, conspicuous lions and less visible lions in the grass, as we move closer to the election, there will likely be more clarity and a meaningful trend will hopefully fall in place later in the year.

That trend might even produce an eating-sardine market and a good backdrop for investing.

Hopefully, at that point in time, we will have the courage to be the king of the investment jungle.

What to Do When You're Wrong

9/14/2012

Here is my checklist when things go differently than I expect in the markets.

- Most importantly, spend some time objectively reevaluating one's investment thesis.
- Be honest with yourself; challenge yourself.
- If conditions have changed, change your investment strategy.
- Seek counsel from smart investors you know and sit down and discuss your thesis and get his/her feedback.
- Take 10 deep breaths and do nothing for a while. Like *Being There*'s Chauncey Gardner, just be there and watch.

It's easy to grin
When your ship comes in
And you've got the stock
market beat.

But the man worthwhile
Is the man who can smile
When his shorts are too
tight in the seat.

—Judge Elihu Smails
(Ted Knight),
Caddyshack

- Try to stay balanced emotionally. (Physical exercise is usually a good idea. So is a good book.)
- Do not double down or average up until some time elapses and you have enough time to settle down, analyze your positions again, and get input from others.
- Finally, if you conclude your currently wrong-footed investment position will prove accurate, do not be dissuaded. Stand firm in view.

Beware the Stock Market Trading Jones

12/24/2012

Today, I see many traders and investors afflicted with what I call the stock market trading jones. Market participants feel compelled to overtrade. It comes in the form of a near-obsession in overtrading both on news-based dislocations (to the upside and downside) and on nondislocations in the normal course of business, typically through chart gazing. The need to play too many earnings reports and the desire to trade macroeconomic events reside among numerous other catalysts.

There are several obvious influences that contribute to the addiction of too-frequent trading:

- *Brokers*. Brokerage companies have made trading at home easy and inexpensive. Sophisticated Internet-based trading platforms allow individual investors to trade actively at markedly reduced commission rates relative to any other time in history.
- *Societal pressures that favor short term over long term*. As a society, we have grown increasingly impatient. The media (and for that matter our society) increasingly emphasizes short term over long term and instant gratification over building value through intermediate-/long-term value. Today, we even communicate more briefly than ever in staccato-like form via tweets of fewer than 140 characters on Twitter and the acronym soup of texting and instant messaging. How-to-profit books teaching us how to gain money and fame quickly outsell more thoughtful investing books such as Benjamin Graham's *The Intelligent Investor*. All of these pressures (in the pursuit of instant riches) contribute to excessive trading by individuals.

- *Quick solutions and foolish acceptance of a special sauce to investment success.* We too often seek quick solutions to complex problems/issues. Increasingly, traders seek a special sauce, an algorithm or stock chart that evokes the promise of immediate success, often shunning the heavy lifting and time-consuming analysis. In its simplicity, this also leads to excessive trading, as if the appearance of a chart is an almost mystical and certain way to produce the Benjamins. Technical analysis has a broad definition and when utilized intelligently can be a very helpful adjunct in making (and timing) trades and investments. But, too often, the decision to make so many of these trades is seen purely through the narrow interpretation of a stock chart, a view that historical price action will provide us with a guide into the future. I see this often in front of an earnings release. Does anyone really think that prior to, say, Nike reporting its most recent earnings, a trader can outsmart the legions of other traders by virtue of looking at a chart? Does that really make sense to any of you?

- *Shortening cycles.* In our fast-moving world, economic, corporate, and investment cycles are ever more truncated. Performance definitions grow ever briefer, whether it is the duration of a CEO's career, measuring a company's profit performance, investors' patience with their investments (manifested in heavy turnover and reduced holding periods compared to any time in history) or with defining investment performance.

All of the above factors contribute to the impatience and heavy trading manifested in the stock market trading jones.

I have believed that by developing a variant view through hard-hitting and investigative research (e.g., contacting company managements, their competition, suppliers or through other means), you will have a much better chance of succeeding with an occasional trade. But, even that fundamental approach (which is time-consuming and doesn't fit in with some who believe that trading gains can be as easy as gazing at a chart) represents a difficult journey toward trading success, especially when it, too, is done with too much frequency.

Regardless of the rationale for action, however, a large portion of traders simply seem to have a trading jones—a need to play, a need for action.

In my investment experience, I have seen many more professional traders armed with every trading system that money can buy (who have been inflicted by the jones of constant trading) blow up rather than succeed over time. Then, why should you, as an individual investor, be more successful?

The answer is that, in all likelihood, you will not be.

Nonstop Trading Is a Mug's Game So let me be direct and straightforward on this subject—nonstop, excessive trading is a mug's game.

Any market mathematician will tell you that the more trades you make the less successful you will be.

I have written for years that waiting for the right pitch in trading and investing is the way to succeed over the long run in this game.

I believe this now as strongly as ever.

Oaktree as Our Template A superior investment will likely trump the jones of too-frequent stock market trading.

Let me demonstrate this observation by looking at the chart of Oaktree Capital Group, a stock I have consistently praised since it went public in spring 2012.

Oaktree is a nonvolatile, low-beta stock. It's an intelligently and conservatively managed company that does not present the thrills and agonies of volatility that are possessed by many favorites of traders such as Apple, Google, or Amazon. Over the past six or seven months, however, the shares have steadily advanced and have provided a great risk-adjusted return.

In theory, a buy-and-hold of Oaktree (just to use one example) will likely have trumped the numerous trades of someone possessed of the stock market trading jones.

Or go to the Securities and Exchange Commission filings of some of the great modern-day investors such as Lee Cooperman's Omega Advisors. What you will find is a remarkably stable and consistent list of the hedge fund's top stock holdings—it's the real pro's proven and time-tested antidote to delivering superior risk-adjusted returns.

The Media Sell Constant Trading The business media is well intentioned and inhabited by a lot of my friends. I am respectful of their contributions, but they too often encourage the stock market jones.

By and large, the media have an agenda that is different from yours. It doesn't make them bad guys—their objectives of a growing audience and higher ratings are inherently dissimilar to your objective of making money.

Moreover, as I have recently chronicled, the media's reaction to events of the day (e.g., the sovereign debt crisis, the presidential election, the fiscal cliff, etc.) is often hyperbolic and simply wrong-footed (from an investment standpoint).

Always remember that they are in the press box and you are on the playing field.

Not surprisingly and understandably (it's in their basic interest), the media too often advance the idea of constant trading and even, at times, (by inference) the dream of instant investor gratification. For every long-term investor queried, it seems as if there are at least 10 traders (maybe more) questioned in the business media.

Maybe it wouldn't sell as well, but I wish there were more forums and time spent on long-term investing in the media.

Unfortunately, many investors watching and listening can't help from being influenced by the media's barrage and sometimes short-term emphasis of time frame. By contrast, long-term price targets (defined in years) are deemphasized, as these are not subject matter seen as capturing ratings and audiences, and typically take a backseat in discussions.

We are often inundated with ways to make fast money. By inference, the pundits and talking heads tell us that this is best accomplished by trading almost every market or individual stock wiggle, often based on technical levels and/or in the knowledge of how to react to certain triggers or events.

In the ultimate level of the absurd, the media conduct contests to guess where the S&P 500 and Dow Jones Industrial Average will close at month's end, what will be the exact jobs number and so on, as if these guesses will provide some sort of magic market elixir to delivering outsized trading gains. The thrust of many of the conversations on CNBC and Bloomberg are too often based on mindless guessing of short-term forecasts, of which few really have any edge whatsoever.

How often does a business show start with the moderator's saying something like this: "The S&P is up by half a percent today, so where is it going to end the day?"

Or the dialogue goes something like this:

- "What is the next move in Apple?"
- "How do we play IBM's earnings report tonight?"
- "Whither Research In Motion?"
- "If Friday's jobs report is 150,000 or more, how will the market react?"
- "How will the fiscal cliff debate impact the market today?"
- "Sovereign debt yields are lower today—how will our markets react?"

You get my point by now—continually going one on one against the trading world by guessing on near-term market and individual stock moves is a difficult (if not impossible) pathway to investment success.

Trade in Moderation   Importantly, I want to emphasize that there is a place for trading, as I believe intelligent trading can be a profitable adjunct to investing.

I am very much an advocate of opportunistic trading, especially when one concludes that the market is range-bound without a clear bias in either direction or, for example, when one can get in front of an earnings report with an informed and variant view or by responding quickly to an earnings quality in an earnings report (among other means).

Done effectively, trading can result in a cash-register effect, contributing to the aggregate returns in your investment account.

But only in moderation and only when the right pitch (read: enhanced reward vs. risk) is offered up.

"Millions of people die every year of something they could cure themselves: lack of wisdom and lack of ability to control their impulses."

—Irving Kahn, chairman, Kahn Brothers Group

Summary   My definition of a good trading setup is far narrower and more selective than most.

My advice is to stop multiple and numerous trades that one justifies by reacting to the media, based on technical analysis or based on any number of other reasons—unless you are very lucky, it will not pay off in the long run.

More likely, you will trade (and churn) your way into investment oblivion.

Addressing the Fiscal Cliff

2/13/2013

It is my contention that dealing with our debt and deficits (i.e., the fiscal cliff) is probably easier to resolve than most believe. As a matter of necessity, it must be accomplished by:

- Cutting spending;
- Reforming Social Security, Medicare, and Medicaid;
- Accelerating the pace of domestic economic growth;
- Reducing government waste; and
- Raising taxes.

"If you know the position a person takes on taxes, you can tell their whole philosophy. The tax code embodies all the essence of life: greed, politics, power, goodness, charity."

—Former IRS commissioner Sheldon Cohen

As a starting point, there is the U.S. tax code.

There is so much waste and accumulated abuse of our tax code that savings are abundant if our politicians only looked under those rocks.

As Ralph Nader has written, the U.S. tax code (all 7,500 pages of it) "is the victim of severe tampering and perforating by corporate lobbyists and tax attorneys and unattended to by inadequate IRS enforcement."

One particular abuse that should have bipartisan approval and that seems impossible to defend lies inside an innocent-looking, green-trimmed, white, five-story building in the Cayman Islands: the Ugland House office on South Church Street.

The unassuming but appropriately named Ugland House is currently the home of over 18,500 corporate entities that reside there for the express purpose of avoiding (though some might say evading) U.S. taxes. It houses hedge funds and other partnerships as well as some of the largest U.S. corporations extant—all of which benefit appreciably from the avoidance of current federal income taxes by assuming a Grand Caymans address of incorporation.

Considering that the Cayman Islands have a tax rate of 0.0% and the fact that some of the largest U.S. corporations received billions of dollars from the bailout, one would assume the government would recoup some of this corporate welfare in the form of taxes. Instead, some of these corporations have not paid any federal income taxes for years.

In late 2011, Citizens for Tax Justice analyzed the tax payments of 280 of the Fortune 500's largest companies. Seventy-eight of the 280 companies paid zero or less in federal income taxes during at least one year from 2008 to 2010. Thirty corporations paid less than nothing in aggregate federal income taxes over the entire 2008–2010 period.

How are America's largest corporations avoiding so many taxes? A practice called transfer pricing. This accounting practice lets companies buy and sell products and services with their own offshore subsidiaries and set prices themselves, according to David Evans in the *Bloomberg* article "The $150 Billion Shell Game" from 2004.

This practice is just as relevant nine years later. Corporations abuse the accounting practice by shifting profits overseas to avoid U.S. taxes. Their prices are set artificially high for imports and low on exports. In the United States, the corporations are allowed to claim the high expenses on the imports and the smaller profits on the exports in their IRS filings.

Profits earned through a foreign subsidiary of a U.S. corporation are not taxed until the cash is repatriated in a dividend back to the U.S. parent company. As a result, while the statutory federal corporate income tax rate stands at 35%, it is estimated that the effective tax rate of the largest publicly traded companies in the United States is closer to 20%.

Regardless of one's party affiliation, the very existence of the Ugland House appears indefensible.

Back to Nader: "Any significant push toward fundamental tax reform has to start by chipping away at the corporatized, commercial Congress which uses tax breaks, deferrals, credits and exemptions as inventory to sell for campaign cash in increasingly costly campaigns."

If the basic purpose of taxation is to raise revenue needed for public services. Why should hardworking citizens underwrite corporations who skate the tax code? How does filling the coffers of profitable companies who avoid taxes through a labyrinth of skillful tax avoidance—including Bank of America, General Electric, Oracle, Cisco Systems, Microsoft, Apple, Verizon, and so many other companies—and their ridiculously high-paid executives benefit the lives of everyday citizens?

At most large multinational U.S. corporations the tax department is a well-oiled and systematic profit center. In 2010, GE earned $7 billion in the United States but paid no federal taxes to the U.S. government. Verizon and Bank of America didn't pay federal taxes either. Yet all three companies were provided with the resources, public services, and infrastructure to conduct their business.

By most estimates, over $1 trillion of profit earned by U.S. companies sits in offshore cash and short-term investments in offshore holding companies and has never been taxed by the United States. Two conspicuous examples include Microsoft and Apple, which hold $50 billion and $100 billion in cash, respectively, in offshore accounts.

The ever-growing pile of offshore cash has introduced new potential risks to the balance sheets of these corporations at home. Companies are avoiding paying the taxes on the repatriation of their overseas profits but still have to fulfill the obligations to shareholders in the form of dividends, share repurchases, debt repayments, and pension contributions. Given the easy borrowing terms of low interest rates here in the United States, companies are taking on more debt instead of paying Uncle Sam in taxes.

While corporations continue to hoard cash offshore, they are simultaneously improving margins by shipping American jobs and factories abroad. Corporate profits improve but tax revenue is hardly impacted by the process. This has contributed to the loss of more than 5 million U.S. manufacturing jobs and the closure of more than 56,000 factories since 2000, according to Senator Bernie Sanders (I-Vt.).

Sen. Sanders has introduced new legislation with Rep. Jan Schakowsky (D-Ill.) with the Corporate Tax Dodging Prevention Act (S.250) in an effort to stop American banks and corporations from sheltering profits in places such as Ugland House and other tax havens to avoid paying U.S. taxes. The act will also cease rewarding companies that ship jobs overseas with tax breaks. The Joint Committee on Taxation has estimated in the past that the provisions in the bill will raise more than $590 billion in revenue over the next decade.

The legislation will certainly raise some arguments on Capitol Hill. The situation remains that the United States is the only major country that has substantial taxes on the repatriation of profits earned overseas. The GOP argues that the United States needs to move toward a territorial system for international taxation. Under this system, foreign-source income would be taxed only in the country where it was earned and not be taxed at all in the United States. This approach would reduce the tax burden on U.S. companies and eliminate the disincentive for corporations to repatriate their foreign profits, according to the Brookings Institute 2012 article, "A Sensible Plan to Bring U.S. Corporate Profits Home."

The major point of contention with this system is that certain profits would not be taxed at all in the United States.

The alternative proposition from President Obama is the international minimum tax. Under this proposal, all income of U.S. corporations must be immediately taxed, either by the United States or some foreign country, at a rate greater than or equal to this as yet unspecified international minimum tax rate. If a corporation reported profits in a country that collects no corporate tax, the U.S. would immediately tax those profits at the international minimum tax rate. This would help reduce the appeal of the tax haven, according to Brookings.

Very few people actively support the current system of taxing the foreign profits of U.S. corporations. A combination of the two systems would provide the best compromise: a territorial tax system for the valid tax-collecting nations and the international minimum tax rate for those that collect little or no corporate tax (e.g., the Cayman Islands). At this point in time, however, compromise is a four-letter word in Washington, D.C. Sen. Sanders's new legislation proposition is a good start toward addressing the tax dodging of U.S. companies.

What is the logic of this tax dodge by some of country's largest companies?

Seagate's Brian Ziel's explanation in 2004, which is commonly stated by other corporations as a rationale for overseas subsidiaries that do not pay U.S. federal taxes: "The competitive benefits relate both to taxes saved on certain income earned outside of the United States and the ability to efficiently deploy assets around the globe to remain competitive" (*Bloomberg*).

Corporations have prospered and have increased their share of GDP at the expense of the middle class, which has seen its wages and salaries stagnate while the cost of the necessities of life has steadily increased. Those large U.S. corporations that have opportunistically reduced their tax bills through Cayman Islands subsidiaries and other schemes are the same companies that have sliced fixed costs (and have recently achieved 57-year highs in profit margins) by paring down payrolls and utilizing temporary employees in place of permanent ones.

Perhaps before considering raising taxes on either the middle or even the upper class of U.S. wage earners, an explosive device should be detonated in order to destroy the rules that form the foundation of the ignominious Ugland House.

Tax what the large corporations burn, not what they earn, by getting rid of the shell game operated in the Ugland House in the Cayman Islands and elsewhere.

Citizens for Tax Justice estimates that tax havens in the Cayman Islands and elsewhere outside of the United States cost our government about $100 billion per year in tax receipts. Many of my hedge fund friends will no doubt push back from the notion of abolishing overseas tax havens, but we are entering a period of shared sacrifice in the four years ahead. Our legislators have hard decisions to make in reducing the country's budget deficit, but this seems one of the easier decisions.

There is an additional concern that is being addressed in Washington, D.C.: the notion of carried interest.

Carried interest is generally treated (preferentially) as capital gains in hedge fund and private-equity partnerships. The taxation of carried interest has been an issue for several years as the compensation earned by investors increased with the size of private-equity funds and hedge funds. Since private-equity firms tend to hold investments long term, the gains qualify as long-term capital gains, which have favorable tax treatment. Managers taking advantage of the maximum 15% tax rate on long-term capital gains have raised concerns. The view that managers are taking advantage of tax loopholes to receive what is comparably a salary without paying the ordinary 35% marginal tax rate is not sitting well with members of Congress nor their constituents. Taxing the gains at the marginal tax rate has drawn ire of several managers on Wall Street, but the move is necessary if Congress is going to close the tax loophole to address our country's budget issues.

After dealing with numerous other tax loopholes, our leaders in Washington, D.C., can begin to seriously address the enormous systemic waste that has been built up over the years in the bulging bureaucracy of our government.

Now there is some serious and heavy lifting.

One Shining Moment

4/8/2013

> *"If you laugh, you think and you cry, that's a full day. That's a heck of a day. You do that seven days a week, you're going to have something special."*
>
> — Jim Valvano, coach of the 1983 North Carolina State basketball team

> *"We were such underdogs that even my mother took the Houston Cougars and gave the points."*
>
> —Jim Valvano

Tonight the Michigan Wolverines face the Louisville Cardinals in the NCAA men's basketball tournament final in Atlanta.

March Madness is my favorite sporting event of the year. I have the most precious memories traveling with my youngest son to semifinal weekends and to Monday's finals. Our trips to the NCAA tournament have, in part, defined my relationship with him.

But this morning, my thoughts are on another game and that speech. Both can provide us with important life and investing lessons.

That game took place 34 years ago tomorrow in 1983. In that game (the NCAA finals), a seemingly outmanned North Carolina State Wolfpack faced the Houston Cougars who were led by two future NBA Hall of Famers in Hakeem "the Dream" Olajuwon and Clyde "the Glide" Drexler. Houston finished the regular season as the top team in the country and were collectively known as "Phi Slama Jama," so named for the fast-paced showmanship of their game. Going into the championship game, Olajuwon boldly predicted "the team with the most dunks will win."

Though only a No. 6 seed in their regional bracket, the North Carolina State Wolfpack was hardly a team of nobodies at No. 16 in the nation. It took an impressive late-season streak just to get them to that ranking, however, and nobody thought they had a chance against Houston (which had won 26 games going into the game against N. C. State). So it was quite a shock to see Lorenzo Charles dunk the winning two points in the last second of the game, and I will never forget Wolfpack coach Jim Valvano running around like a chicken with its head cut off.

And, oh, that 1993 ESPY Award speech that Jim Valvano gave just eight weeks before he died of cancer—I still cry every time it is repeated on ESPN.

James Thomas Anthony Valvano was the mischievous middle son born to Rocco and Angela. When he was 17 years old he wrote down on an index card his professional aspirations. He would play basketball in high school (he did at Seaford High School in Long Island) and college (he did at Rutgers), become an assistant basketball coach (he did at Connecticut), then a head coach (his first head coach position was at Johns Hopkins, then at Bucknell and Iona), achieve victory in Madison Square Garden (he did while at Rutgers), and finally cut down the nets after winning a National Championship (he did with N.C. State).

Some elements of Valvano's life lessons can be adopted into our investing strategy.

The investment mosaic is a complicated one, and no one rule always works. How-to books may sell copies and make money for the authors, but they don't

"No matter what business you're in, you can't run in place, or someone will pass you by. It doesn't matter how many games you've won. . . . How do you go from where you are to where you want to be? I think you have to have an enthusiasm for life. You have to have a dream, a goal, and you have to be willing to work for it."

—Jim Valvano

"Be a dreamer. If you don't know how to dream, you're dead."

—Jim Valvano

usually make the readers much money. There is no substitute for hard work in delivering superior investment returns. There are 86,400 seconds in a day; it's up to you to decide what to do with them. There is no secret sauce, magical elixir, or special stock chart that provides clarity to our investment decisions—rather, it is a by-product of hard-hitting research.

A variant view and second-level thinking are necessary reagents to good investment returns. In *The Most Important Thing: Uncommon Sense for the Thoughtful Investor* (Columbia Business School Publishing, 2013), author Howard Marks addresses these two subjects.

> *"I asked a ref if he could give me a technical foul for thinking bad things about him. He said, 'Of course not.' I said, 'Well, I think you stink.' And he gave me a technical. You can't trust 'em."*
>
> —Jim Valvano

In investing you must find an edge by often thinking of factors/ideas that others haven't thought. Importantly, you must also avoid being too early—especially if your investor base has a different time frame than yours.

Second-level thinking trumps first-level thinking in delivering returns. As Howard puts it, First-level thinking says, "It's a good company: let's buy the stock." Second-level thinking says, "It's a good company, but everyone thinks it's a great company and it's not. So the stock's over-rated and overpriced: let's sell." First-level thinking says, "The outlook calls for low growth and rising inflation. Let's dump our stocks." Second-level thinking says, "The outlook stinks, but everyone else is selling in panic. Buy!"

I am often asked why I don't usually listen to company executives or the guidance of their investor relations departments. To me, it is preferable to speak to people in the supply chain or to company competitors, for (to paraphrase Warren Buffett) managements often lie like ministers of finance on the eve of devaluation.

> *"My father gave me the greatest gift anyone could give another person: he believed in me."*
>
> —Jim Valvano

You gotta believe in yourself. Lehigh's basketball team believed it could beat Duke last year, and, in this year's tournament, No. 14 seeded Harvard upset No. 3 seeded New Mexico.

You gotta know yourself, too. Wall Street is not a great place to "find yourself." Psychology can be important; it often trumps cause-and-effect relationships that have been in place historically. Above all, have confidence in your own analysis (as long as it is thorough), even if your view is at variance with the consensus.

And, of course, Coach Valvano's most recognized quote: "Don't give up, don't ever give up."

Learn to survive under adverse market conditions by avoiding large losses, and learn how to prosper during good times. Generally speaking, by maintaining discipline and stopping out your losses, you can live another day in your investing life. It is not batting averages or on-base percentages that count in this game; it is how you control the risk in your portfolio. As an example, short positions can be hedged by owning cheap out-of-the-money calls, and long positions can be hedged by owning cheap out-of-the-money puts—especially in a low-volatility setting.

Laugh, think, and cry—I always do this time of the year, as I will tonight watching the NCAA tournament finals. (I like Michigan in the upset; they are 4-point underdogs.) But it's especially true this year after overcoming my own confrontation with cancer—it's been a shining moment for me.

You, too, can have many shining investment moments by applying some of Coach Valvano's life principles to your investing.

Time Frames and Exposures

4/22/2013

Late last week, I mentioned that we are likely to face a lot of volatility in 2013:

Volatility and disorder are likely a more constant state in a global economy that is experiencing a new normal that remains on tenterhooks, still experiencing the deleveraging and tail issues stemming from the last down cycle and, as a result, only experiencing a fragile trajectory of growth.

"We are not permitted to choose the frame of our destiny. But what we put into it is ours."

—Dag Hammarskjöld

To me, it's not good volatility; it's the outgrowth of uncertainty regarding economic growth and an unhealthy dependency on the policy of our monetary (Fed) and fiscal (our leaders in Washington, D.C.) authorities.

Regardless of whether volatility is heightened or reduced (or good or bad), among the three most important elements of one's trading and investing should be your time frame, appropriate exposures and risk tolerance/profile.

We all have different quotients of the above factors.

I will deal with two of the three factors: time frames and exposures.

To begin with, I view the market as a continuum in which one's time frame is an essential part of trading and investing.

As a matter of principle, I rarely have a gross exposure (adding my long and short gross exposures together) that exceeds 100%. On average, when I am bullish, I am typically as much as 65% net long (deducting my shorts from my longs as a percentage of the portfolio), and when I am bearish, I am typically as much as 45% net short (deducting my longs from my shorts).

In hedge fund circles, these exposure ratios place me in a conservative minority.

Depending on where we are in the market continuum determines the percentage of my portfolio that is committed to longer-term investments (both long and short) vs. shorter-term trading rentals (again, both long and short).

Under a normally trending (and upwardly sloping) market (and dependent upon my degree of confidence), I would have as much as 67% (when fully invested) of my portfolio in investment holdings (with a majority of longs), and I would have as much as 33% of my portfolio in trading rentals (again, a majority of longs).

But let's add two more market scenarios and characters—namely, a range-bound market and a downwardly sloped market—to the normally trending and upwardly sloping market getting us to three market scenarios.

Again, I change my exposures (investing vs. trading) dependent on the outlook:

1. *Range-bound market.* If I conclude that we are likely to be in a range-bound market, I would be more inclined to trade stocks, increasing the percentage of my portfolio committed to trading and reducing

my exposure to longer-term commitments. In this case, I might only be as much as 40% committed to investments and perhaps as much as 60% in opportunistic rentals, with a mix of both longs and shorts.

2. *Upwardly sloped market (normally trending).* If I conclude that we are in an upwardly sloping market, I would be more inclined to be a long-term investor in stocks. In this case, my portfolio might be as much as 60% to 70% (dominated by longs) in investment positions and 30% to 40% in trading-oriented positions (again, dominated by longs).

3. *Downwardly sloped market.* If I conclude that we are in a downwardly sloping market, I would be more inclined to be as much as 60% to 70% in investment positions and 30% to 40% trading-oriented positions. In theory, my portfolio, reflecting a downwardly sloped market, would be dominated by shorts, but, in reality, it's not practical, as the asymmetric risk/reward of short sales would reduce the overall commitment to shorts even in a correcting market phase. While I would likely be net short in both investment and trading positions, my degree of confidence in the market outlook would dictate that net exposure.

Let's now dig deeper into time frames.

To simplify, here are my definitions of time frames (note: yours may be different):

- A short-term trading position (rental) can be as little as a few hours or as much as several weeks.
- An intermediate-term trading or investing position is typically a month to 12 months in duration.
- A long-term investment position is typically greater than 12 months in duration.

It is important to recognize that sometimes very short-term positioning seems to contradict a market thesis, but adopting a near-term positioning that is at odds with an intermediate-term view may not be that illogical.

Let me explain.

I may do this in response to a number of different stimuli. Maybe the market has temporarily overshot to the downside and has become oversold. Perhaps the reason for the market's slide is not justified or an external shock contributed to the drop, and I expect the conditions to be remedied/addressed.

Or it might simply be my lame attempt to game or react to Mr. Market's volatility.

As I see it, my job is to be transparent in analysis (of markets, sectors, and individual stocks) and also to be transparent in my entry/exit points. Along the way, I try to provide other lessons—for instance, in risk control, as your investment/trading batting average does not necessarily link to superior returns.

But what must be recognized is your risk profile and time frames are likely different than mine (or anyone else's), so when I chronicle my investments and trading rentals, it is important to have the proper perspective so that you can better understand my tactics and strategy (which may or may not be appropriate to you).

Always consider your own time frames and risk profile/tolerance in determining the suitability of exposure and how you weigh your involvement in trading vs. investing.

Such a Long Time to Be Gone and a Short Time to Be Here

9/11/2013

September 11, 2001, still seems like yesterday to me. It is a day that I will forever remember vividly with clarity and disbelief.

To many of us, 2001 will forever be *annus horribilis*—the year of horror.

On this day, as has been the case for the past 12 years, my eyes remain full of tears as I write this column in memory of all of those I knew (and those I didn't know) who were lost in the World Trade Center, in Pennsylvania, and in Washington, D.C. It is said that death leaves a heartache that no one can heal but that love leaves a memory no one can steal.

And so it is today Tuesday, September 11, 2013, we observe the twelfth anniversary of the September 11 attacks.

As I have for each of those years, today I want to pass along my thoughts by writing this opening missive as a dedication to some of those who were lost—especially to my best pal, Chuck Zion (a.k.a., Brown Bear).

Chuck worked at Cantor Fitzgerald, the brokerage firm that lost nearly 700 employees 12 years ago. It was the hardest-hit company in the World Trade Center tragedy, accounting for nearly one-quarter of the building's deaths that day. I lost many friends at Cantor on September 11: Eric, Pat, Timmy—too many to count. So did many others. And of course, we all lost one of *TheStreet*'s own, Bill "Budman" Meehan.

In Cantor Fitzgerald's equity division, none had more of a presence (literally and figuratively) than Chuck Zion. He was known to his friends and clients as the Brown Bear, a sensitive, giving, and caring friend; father to Zachary; son to Martin and Jane; and husband to the amazing Carole ("Cheezy"). His love was pure, and there was never any pretense—not wordy, he was on point.

The largest producer over the past decade at Cantor Fitzgerald, Chuck was master of his universe. He was straightforward and clear-cut, a no-nonsense and respected partner who was remarkably generous but never, ever wanted others to know it. He gave often and substantially but always anonymously, without strings attached. Chuck, who also worked at Salomon Brothers and Sanford C. Bernstein, put on some of the largest trades in the history of the equities market. He was the player the "big boys" went to when they wanted anonymity. And I am talking multi-million-share trades, the really big prints. And it was Chuck who introduced me to Bill Meehan—he even had me fill in for Budman on a few occasions in the *Cantor Daily News*.

I cherished and loved Chuck Zion—he was my confidant and a brother that I never had. When I moved to Florida in the late 1990s Chuck introduced me to his father and mother, asking me to take them out once or twice a year, to look after them a bit. In time, Rabbi Zion and Jane became more than casual dinner mates; they became my mother and father, so Chuck and I really were like brothers (though absent the same blood).

I spoke to Chuck every morning at around 6:15 A.M. If I didn't call him on my direct line to Cantor's trading desk by 6:20, he'd get angry and yell at me in no uncertain terms. Invariably, legendary money managers Neil Weissman, Stanley Shopkorn, Dan Tisch, or Phil Marber (Cantor's former CEO) would interrupt our daily calls. He would take their calls, and then shortly, Chuck would call me back. We rarely talked about the stock market, preferring to talk sports and food (his favorite activity). Sometimes Chuck would tell me to check out Maureen Dowd's editorial piece in the *New York Times* ("Dougie, she is mandatory reading"), or who was on Imus that morning. I got him to buy a couple of harness horses with me for fun and he got a kick out of them as we followed their losing races. "We'll get him next time," he would say (his credo)— though we never did.

We played golf together (Chuck wrote the word *lost* on each of his golf balls because he lost so many of them that he wanted the other players to know they were his), usually with Phil Marber or Andy Smoller. We talked NCAA football and basketball, especially about Syracuse University's teams (his alma mater). But mostly we talked about our children.

The Friday before September 11 was my last day in the office, as I was leaving for Europe for 10 days. That day we spent a lot of time talking about his son Zack, reminiscing about the trip Zack and I had recently taken to New Haven to Yale University, where he watched me lecture at Dr. Robert Shiller's class on short-selling. Chuck was so proud of the way Zack had become a man. And he was nervously awaiting Greenwich High's football season with such anticipation. (They had won the state title the previous year, with Zack playing the offensive line.) Every time he talked about the upcoming season, his voice would rise several decibels. He was the proudest father on the face of the earth.

That Friday morning, the last day I spoke to Chuck, I was playing a Grateful Dead song in the background and I had Chuck on the speaker. Chuck was never what I would call into music. He was certainly not a fan of the Grateful Dead—maybe Motown but not the Grateful Dead. Surprisingly, in our early-morning talk, Chuck remarked how beautiful the song was. The song was "Box of Rain"—and the lyrics captured the concept of how short life can be only days before the disaster.

Chuck's *New York Times* obituary is still taped to my stock monitor in my office as an ever reminder of his loss. The paper is now aged, yellowed, and torn, but the scars still seem fresh.

Today, after writing this missive, I will again share Chuck's memories with his parents (Rabbi and Jane), his many friends (like Phil

Marber), and with numerous longtime subscribers (like Don Gher), who were business associates, recipients of his wise advice or friends with Brown Bear and who, as they have every year, will pass on their day's thoughts to me in e-mails or phone calls, which I eagerly anticipate and will always cherish.

Last night, subscriber Don Gher mailed me a classic story about Brown Bear. Don was thinking about Chuck and relayed that one of his pals, ex-Cantor (Los Angeles) and Dallas trader Eddie Weber, told him that one day he was at Cantor's NYC office, and he and Brown Bear walked out of the World Trade Center to grab lunch. There was a hot dog vendor there, and Chuck asked how many he had left. The guy said 12, and Chuck said, "Sold!" And then they proceeded to eat all of them. That was my brother, Chuck—an original. Don lit a candle for him at Mass on Sunday as he has done in each of the last 11 years. (Thanks, Don.)

I will never forget Mark Haines's report on CNBC of the first, second, third, and fourth incidents that day, as I watched the horror on a television on a cruise ship in the Mediterranean.

TheStreet's headquarters were physically very close to Ground Zero.

And I will never forget the real-time reporting (the confusion and emotion) on TheStreet on that fateful day, the revelation of the extent of the tragedy and the follow-up tributes by our contributors.

Ironically or sadly, Rosh Hashanah (the Jewish New Year) and Yom Kippur (the Day of Atonement) quickly followed on the heels of September 11, 2001. The most poignant recollection on TheStreet was the following post by Jim Cramer, who recalled an incident at his temple—to this day, it brings me to tears:

> At our synagogue last night on the eve of the Jewish New Year, our rabbi asked us to shout out the names of friends and family that we'd lost that day. There were so many names, it was frightening and I was glad we had left the kids at home. I felt honored to yell out Bill's name. And I feel honored to have gotten to meet and work with him in his short time on Earth. Oops, wanted to cry as I wrote that. Could feel it coming on. Nope, no can do. Not with that picture of him in my mind wearing that funny floral shirt. He wouldn't want us to remember him in any other way

than with laughter. God bless your soul, Bill. God bless the Meehan family.

—*Jim Cramer, "Remembering Bill Meehan"*

> *"All that's necessary for the forces of evil to win in the world is for enough good men to do nothing."*
>
> —Edmund Burke

> *"Revenge is an act of passion; vengeance of justice. Injuries are revenged; crimes are avenged."*
>
> —Samuel Johnson

Today, I will also share my fond memories of *TheStreet*'s and Cantor Fitzgerald's Bill "Budman" Meehan with his good pals Jim Cramer, Tony Dwyer, Herb Greenberg, and others, and we will all toast him as so many subscribers did in the fall of 2001.

Fortunately, on May 2, 2011, some very good and courageous men gained revenge for Osama bin Laden's deeds 12 years ago.

I hope that Osama bin Laden rots in hell.

But revenge doesn't reverse the loss of so many.

I suppose that living and remembering is the best form of revenge.

Thanks for reading this, and thanks for letting me wear my feelings on my sleeve.

Before the market opens and as you watch the annual tribute in downtown New York City, think about our lost loved ones and how lucky we all are.

We all miss you, Chuck.

> *"Stock market bubbles don't grow out of thin air. They have a solid basis in reality, but reality as distorted by a misconception."*
>
> —George Soros

10 Laws of Stock Market Bubbles

11/11/2013

The problem with bubbles is that if you sell stocks before the bubble bursts, you look foolish, but you also look foolish if you sell stocks after the bubble bursts.

Yale professor Robert Shiller outlined how to identify bubbles in his seminal book, *Irrational Exuberance* (Princeton University Press, 2000)—as you will read, there is some overlap in our identification process of bubble finding:

- The sharp increase in the price of an asset or share class;
- Great public excitement about these price increases;
- An accompanying media frenzy;
- Growing interest in the class among the general public;
- New-era theories justifying the high price; and
- A decline in lending standards.

Similar to Dr. Shiller, I have long felt that every bubble has distinguishable conditions leading up to them.

For me, bubbles typically emerge when the following five conditions are all met:

1. Debt is cheap.
2. Debt is plentiful.
3. There is the egregious use of debt.
4. A new marginal (and sizeable) buyer of an asset class appears.
5. After a sustained advance in an asset class's price, the prior four factors lead to new-era thinking that cycles have been eradicated/eliminated and that a long boom in values lies ahead.

Consider that all these conditions existed during the dot-com stock bubble (1997 to early 2000):

- Margin debt was inexpensive and readily available.
- Day trading shops and individual retail traders entered the market anew as the marginable buyer, lifting up share prices. The former (and some of the latter) was able to use 5× to 15× leverage.
- Traditional ways of measuring value in technology, in general, and the Internet, in particular, were abandoned in favor of "pay-per-views," "eyeballs," and the like.
- In turn, there developed the notion that technological innovation had likely repealed the economic/business cycles.

These conditions also existed during the housing bubble (2000–2006):

- The Fed lowered interest rates to generational lows. Correspondingly, mortgage loan rates plummeted to unheard levels.
- Banks and shadow banking entities lent freely with interest-only and adjustable-rate mortgages commonplace. No-documented or low-documented loans became readily available. Loans in excess of 100% of home value proliferated based on the notion that home prices would never decline.
- Individuals began to speculate in homes by virtually day trading homes, as the new marginable buyer (speculators) lifted home prices to unprecedented yearly price gains.
- The belief that home prices would never fall became the institutionalized and consensus view.

To my 5 conditions mentioned earlier, I add 5 more (several of these quantify the "degree of bubbliness") to complete my 10 laws of bubbles:

1. Debt is cheap.
2. Debt is plentiful.
3. There is the egregious use of debt.
4. A new marginal (and sizeable) buyer of an asset class appears.
5. After a sustained advance in an asset class's price, the prior four factors lead to new-era thinking that cycles have been eradicated/eliminated and that a long boom in value lies ahead.
6. The distance of valuations from earnings is directly proportional to the degree of bubbliness.
7. The newer the valuation methodology in vogue the greater the degree of bubbliness.
8. Bad valuation methodologies drive out good valuation methodologies.
9. When everyone thinks central bankers, money managers, corporate managers, politicians, or any other group are the smartest guys in the room, you are in a bubble.
10. Rapid growth of a new financial product that is not understood (e.g., derivatives, what Warren Buffett termed "financial weapons of mass destruction").

While some of the above conditions/laws have been met today, many have not.

While debt is cheap and plentiful to some, it is not universally so, as lending standards (especially mortgages and small-business loans) are relatively tight.

While investor sentiment is optimistic (and at multiyear highs), retail investors remain relatively noncommittal to stocks, and there is no new marginal buyer of equities (as was the case in the late 1990s). Nevertheless, the *Investors Intelligence* gauge of adviser sentiment (at a 55.2% bullish reading and only 15.6% bearish) is not only at the highest difference between the two in 2013 but at the most extreme reading since mid-April, a point in time when stocks experienced the largest correction of the current bull market that began in March 2009.

With over $50 billion of new-issue offerings thus far in 2013 (compared to $63.5 billion in the same period in 2000, the year the dot-com bubble burst) and follow-on offerings at a record $155 billion (year-to-date), conditions on this front are getting bubbly.

While some investors might be thinking that a new era lies ahead, they are in the minority.

In terms of valuations, they are somewhat higher than the average P/E multiple experienced over the last five decades, but they are not excessive.

On the other hand, the S&P multiple has expanded by nearly 20% this year, compared to only a 2.5% average yearly rise in valuation since 1900—that's a bit bubbly.

As to the consensus belief that the Fed can (without the benefit of intelligent fiscal policy) engineer self-sustaining growth, that is arguably a bubble-like notion/condition.

While quantitative easing today might be driving asset prices to potentially unsustainable levels, without stimulating much additional activity, those levels are not that out of the ordinary.

Finally, unlike the exporting of derivatives by our major money center banks that nearly bankrupted the world's financial system in 2007–2009, there is none of that today.

Bottom line: While equity markets might be richly priced relative to fair market value, I would conclude that we are not currently in a stock market bubble.

Yet.

My Stock Market Super Bowl Indicator

2/1/2014

On Sunday, one of the grand sporting events of the year will take place: Super Bowl XLVIII.

Back in January 2000, I created a brand-new stock market Super Bowl indicator as a contrary indicator, very similar to the cover of *Time*.

My indicator dictates that the more intense the Super Bowl television advertising by a group of companies, particularly in a specific industry, the more likely the stocks of those companies will perform poorly in the year ahead.

Barron's' Alan Abelson was kind enough to include and highlight my indicator in his "Up and Down Wall Street" during the weekend of the 2000 Super Bowl.

As the late Sir Alan wrote:

> As it happens, last week's tech wreck was accurately forecast by a remarkable new stock-market indicator, one we're proud to print for the first time anywhere, the Stock Market Super Bowl Indicator.
>
> Before you start yapping about it being old hat—or old helmet—we respectfully suggest you cool it. Pure and simple, our new indicator has nothing to do with the old Super Bowl indicator. Unlike the latter, its predictive power doesn't depend on the outcome of the Super Bowl or, more specifically, whether the winner represents the National Football League's American Conference or the National Conference.
>
> Our brand-new Stock Market Super Bowl Indicator is a contrary indicator, kind of like the cover of *Time*. Its critical components are the commercials carried on television coverage of the event and the identity of the companies doing the advertising. Its virtue is not as a forecaster for the market as a whole, but for individual sectors of the market.
>
> The indicator is the handiwork of Doug Kass, a kindly hedge-fund operator who, despite a propensity to short quantum leapers, wound up last year with an improbable performance matching Nasdaq's improbable performance.
>
> Simply put, the more intense the Super Bowl TV advertising by a group of companies, the more likely the stocks of those

companies—and others of a kindred ilk—will do poorly in the year ahead. For 2000, we're sorry to report, the indicator is flashing red for the Internet crew.

By Doug's count, roughly 12 of the 30 companies shelling out an average of $2 million for 30-second spots are dotcoms. That's four times the number of 'Net outfits that made their pitch on Super Bowl TV last year and compares with only one in each of the prior two years.

What's more, for the first time, an Internet company, E*Trade, is sponsoring the half-time show. That's known in locker-room lingo as piling on.

If nothing else, the greater the number of look-alike or sound-alike companies doing the shilling, the less the impact of the individual shills. And in fact, there seems to be more than a modicum of evidence that for the viewer, the link between the commercial and the sponsoring Web company barely registers.

Making the auguries all the darker for those dozen dotcoms is the sad history of the sole 'Net TV advertiser during Super Bowls XXXI and XXXII, autobytel.com. A '99 IPO, the stock peaked at $48 and, last we looked, was a hair under $17.

Without Wall Street, Silicon Valley would not have been able to remove the burden of salaries from its operating statements and substitute stock options for cash compensation. Without the lovely boost to earnings afforded by the incredible lightness of labor costs, earnings growth would be considerably less, and so the multiples awarded that growth would be merely ridiculous instead of absurd. There would be only a quarter as many West Coast billionaires and half as many millionaires.

In like manner, since the vast bulk of Internet companies are bereft of even a hint of cash flow, Wall Street has, via stock offerings, endowed them with the means of promoting their wares, not only on TV during the Super Bowl breaks but also in newspapers and magazines, on billboards and in subway cars and every other space known to advertising man.

If, indeed, we are rapidly reaching the point of cognitive congestion where the consumer is under such assault from so many dotcoms that they have begun to merge in his psyche into one big indivisible glob, that spells trouble in capital letters. And

not only for the 'Net companies, but also for the media on which
that vast flow of lucre has been lavished.
                                    —*Alan Abelson,* Barron's *(January 2000)*

Of course, the rest was history, as one of the largest stock market
declines (especially of a technology and Internet kind) occurred during
the following few years.

Last year, the food and beverage sectors were responsible for an outsized
41% of all Super Bowl advertisements—and, on cue, this defensive group
was an underperformer in 2013's sharp U.S. stock market advance.

$4 Million for 30 Seconds of Your Time   This year, Super Bowl ad
rates are through the roof and are expected to approach $4 million (up from
$3.5 million in 2013) for a 30-second commercial compared to about $2
million in 2000, $1.15 million in 1995, $700,000 in 1990, $222,000 in
1980, $78,000 in 1970 and only $42,000 in the first Super Bowl in 1967.

Rates approaching $10 million for a single commercial are going to
happen sooner than you might expect!

How Now, Super Bowl Advertisers?   Significant, again, this year is the
preponderance of consumer products companies that have anted up for 30-
and 60-second advertisements during the Super Bowl! Auto advertisers are
close behind. Combined, they represent the lion's share of Super Bowl ads.

Of the thirty 2014 Super Bowl advertisers, 12 are consumer-products-
related, accounting for 11.5 minutes of advertising (or 40% of the total
number of advertisers)—and that does not include PepsiCo, the beverage
and snack company that is sponsoring the halftime show. Eight advertisers
are automobile-related, accounting for 8.5 minutes of advertising (or 27%
of the total). Between consumer product and auto companies, the two
sectors account for 20 out of 30 advertisers, representing 20 minutes of all
Super Bowl commercials (or 67% of the total).

Summary   In summary, we might conclude from the historic causality
between my indicator and the industry composition of Super Bowl
advertisers that headwinds could be facing the shares of both the
consumer products (especially food and beverage) and auto manufacturing industries in 2014.

The Great Decession: Subprime and Credit/Debt Crisis

Introduction

In Bakersfield, California, a Mexican strawberry picker with an income of $14,000 and no English was lent every penny he needed to buy a house for $724,000.
—Michael Lewis, *The Big Short: Inside the Doomsday Machine*

During the 17 years that I have contributed to *TheStreet*, the most significant period (in terms of its near- and intermediate-term influence on the global markets and economies) was the Great Decession of 2007–2009.

Much of the blame for the recent downturn lies on the shoulders of the banking industry, whose appetite for leverage and financial steroids rivaled that of the New York Yankees' Alex Rodriguez.

The banking industry's exporting of financial weapons of mass destruction (based on the faulty assumption that home prices would never experience an annual decline) undermined and nearly bankrupted the world's financial system.

During the mid-2000s' run-up to the downturn, I strenuously warned of the consequences of this financial innovation, increased leverage, as well as the egregious lending (especially of a mortgage kind from a rapidly growing shadow banking industry).

In this chapter, I chronicle, at length, the ensuing market and economic devastation that followed in 2007–2009—and how, in the process, investors lost their innocence.

Trouble Looms for the Homebuilders

2/26/2004

Fed Chairman Alan Greenspan took center stage this week, and his comments have important implications for housing, the consumer and the economy.

Specifically, Greenspan suggested that the government-sponsored enterprises that finance and provide liquidity for the housing industry, Fannie Mae and Freddie Mac, have become too levered; if the companies miscalculate the risks inherent in their bloated balance sheets (like duration mismatches), there could be serious system-wide financial ramifications.

Importantly, the growth of government-sponsored enterprise (GSE) portfolios has a significant bearing on the future course of homebuilding, as changes in credit growth are almost always a sign of an industry slowdown. Already, the year-over-year change in Fannie Mae's purchases of securities is narrowing, while the year-over-year change in homebuilding share prices appears to be stalling.

Should Greenspan's words lead to pressures to slow down balance-sheet growth at the GSEs or to reduce their preferred lending status, homebuilding and homebuilding shares will suffer as credit extension to homebuilders will be reduced and the cost of home financings will almost certainly rise.

With the benefit of hindsight, the homebuilding industry has been the chief beneficiary of massive stimuli over the past three years, leading to artificial lows in mortgage rates (and a general improvement in consumers' ability to service an ever-expanding mortgage loan base), but a world without stimuli holds headwinds aplenty for the sector.

If I am accurate in my general assessment and absent the pricing umbrella of ever-rising home prices, the favorable operating history of rising margins for homebuilders will be threatened shortly on several fronts.

The sheer force of rising home prices over the past decade has provided the homebuilding sector with pricing power, allowing builders to raise their products' prices to levels barely foreseen even five years ago. Conditions are slowly changing as homebuyers are now threatened with their ability to afford ever-rising home prices, and the potential is for heightened consumer resistance to these price hikes.

The almost parabolic rise in home prices in certain markets has increasingly forced out buyers' (especially first-time buyers') ability to afford housing. We are already seeing moderating home-price increases on a national scale. Nationally, the rate of gain in home prices peaked a year ago at close to an 8% increase. Fourth-quarter 2003 prices rose by less than 5%.

The trend of decelerating home prices will likely be a feature of 2004–2005, and its ramifications for homebuilding growth are potentially profound. Of course, the aforementioned 5% rate of increase nationally is still historically high and points to its vulnerability, as it is nearly double the average home-price increase over the past 30 years.

Indeed, Hovnanian Enterprises has guided to a 3% reduction in its average realization in 2004. More builders will say the same in the months to come (serving to compress margins by 100 basis points this year after experiencing a 350-basis-point rise last year!).

Toll Brothers missed revenue guidance Thursday morning, citing bad weather's effect on closings. It also reduced the top end of 2004 estimated deliveries. Toll has an important presence in New Jersey and, as a high-end builder, seems vulnerable to Gov. McGreevey's recommendation to issue a $10,000 McMansion tax on homes in excess of $1 million in New Jersey, detailed in his budget for the upcoming fiscal year.

Rising home prices have been the underpinning of better margins as homebuilders' operating leverage is dependent on higher sale prices. On average, homebuilder margins have risen by a dramatic 275 basis points, to around 22%, since 1999, with Ryland Group and Hovnanian experiencing a nearly 500-basis-point improvement.

By my estimates, about 30% of the gross profit improvement in the past year for the homebuilders was a direct reflection of margin improvement, which came from an ability to raise home prices.

The rapid price rise in the homebuilders' cost of goods sold (principally land and building materials such as lumber) will further exacerbate margin pressure.

If home prices retreat, or even if the rate of increase in prices materially decelerates in the face of rising costs for land and building materials, homebuilder EPS growth in 2004–2005 will be increasingly dependent on unit growth.

But we already established the thesis that activity will be tempered by:

1. The likely easing in turnover (as interest rates rise); and
2. Pressures on consumer disposable income (rising taxes, health care, energy expenses) that will reduce the affordability of homes.

The likely diminution of pricing power could lead to rising incentives by homebuilders in the last half of 2004 or early 2005, further pressuring profitability. There are already some signs of a loss of pricing power by homebuilders as house-price appreciation is slowing. This is seen vividly in the greater-than-seasonal drop in gross margins at the leading homebuilders from the first quarter of 2003 to the fourth quarter of 2003.

From my perch, the cycle position of homebuilding is very much like that of technology in late 1999. Low-cost capital enabled technology to prosper, but it was ultimately the death knell for that sector, which experienced a crisis in profitability as pricing power completely eroded. In the same manner, housing's exposure to generational lows in mortgage rates has had the unintended consequence of moving home prices to levels where consumers will not only resist the prices, but increasingly can't afford to buy homes, especially if interest rates rise.

I have previously mentioned that cycle peaks are established when capital/debt is plentiful and cheap, whether it is technology or housing.

And similar to the 1999–2002 legendary implosion in technology, it will happen equally as fast and as unexpectedly in housing.

Because of the pressures on the GSEs, upgrades decelerating, evidence of moderating home prices, pressures on disposable incomes (which will negatively affect consumers' ability to afford a home), and the rising cost of materials and labor, the outsized improvement in gross margins will likely not be maintained, ultimately pressuring homebuilder profitability.

Stretched Consumer Nears Tipping Point

1/10/2005

At the risk of stating the obvious, the U.S. consumer has too much debt. I continue to believe that market participants have a flawed view of the sustainability of world economic growth. The root cause of my concern remains a levered consumer, and signs have emerged of the unwinding process. So for 2005 (as in 2004), I am taking smaller positions and fewer long-term positions. I think that an opportunistic trading approach makes sense until consumer debt unwinds.

Lest we forget the origins of the recent housing mania, I remind you that the recession of 2001–2002 was an unprecedented historic anomaly. It was a recession in which credit card and mortgage debt ramped ever upward, greased by an unprecedented series of interest rate reductions to practically zero. This translated into generational lows in mortgage rates, which had a twofold effect: Cash-out refinancings soared, and monthly payments fell (even as both housing prices and overall mortgage debt rose). In addition to mortgage debt, interest-free automobile financing has been rampant in recent years. The net result is total household debt of more than 80% of GDP, far greater than the 64% level at the beginning of the economic recovery in the early 1990s.

The Fed fueled a spending spree to offset the slow economy, so the real estate bubble served its purpose: it cushioned the U.S. economy from a collapse after the titanic tech bubble of the late 1990s.

Despite a wrenching recession and millions of layoffs, more Americans have big houses, big cars, and big-screen TVs than ever before. So there is no pent-up demand for large-ticket durables, which typically provide the catalyst for cyclical growth once a recession ends. This time around, however, there is little if any pent-up demand. Instead, most consumers have a mountain of debt. And much of the debt is backed by residential housing, where pricing defies logic and affordability. (When mean reversion does finally kick in, the result will be painful for both the consumer and the debt holder.)

In a nutshell, my thesis is that the consumer is spent-up, not pent-up, so a general rise in interest rates will have a speedier and more profound impact on the economy's growth path than investors anticipate. I say this because the equity market is priced close to perfection and certainly does not discount either slower growth or rising bankruptcies.

While these facts are blindingly obvious, most investors still underestimate the difficulty of unwinding all of this consumer leverage in the face of higher interest rates. I think that there is a fair chance that U.S. economic growth will be disrupted and maybe even derailed, as consumer spending stalls and bankruptcies soar. In fact, consumer bankruptcies have already begun to rise, though the impact on banks has been obscured by two factors: the securitization of consumer debt and a decline in corporate defaults. (Ironically, while consumers went on a debt-fueled spending spree, most companies slashed spending and have rebuilt their balance sheets.)

More recently, after the recovery in global equities in late 2004, I have warned and held steadfast in my belief that market participants have lost sight of or ignored building economic risks. And I continue to think that both the economy and corporate profits (especially margins) will disappoint in 2005. Despite my protestations, investors seemed to have feared nothing of late, and instead have adopted the mantra of *Mad Magazine*'s Alfred E. Neuman: "What, Me Worry?"

Evidence of complacency is widespread. Sentiment is at record bullish levels, with *Investors Intelligence* bull readings recently at the highest level since the October 1987 crash, and the CBOE Market Volatility Index (VIX) at decade-low levels. This complacency, combined with interest rates near record lows, has brought out the worst in herd behavior as desperate, momentum-based investment pros have grown immune to the risk side of the equation. Indeed, the move in the speculative darlings of the new millennium—for example, Travelzoo, Taser, Google, Sirius Satellite, and many others—has become reminiscent of the late 1990s bubble.

It's as if fear and doubt have been driven from the marketplace.

I highlight five warning signs from the fourth quarter that suggest that the U.S. consumer is now at the tipping point:

1. *Spending has been slipping:* Consumer spending has been slipping ever since the tax refund checks were mailed in the late spring and early summer. (Remember the Job and Growth Tax Relief Reconciliation Act of 2003?)

2. *Housing is getting speculative:* There have been signs that the speculative activity in the housing market is about to reverse. The hottest markets have shown the first signs of cracking, so the declines in Las Vegas and California could mark the inflection point in housing prices.

3. *Refinancings are down:* The consumer's refi needs are nearly sated, as shown by the 60% drop in refi activity since the spring. What's more, refinancing cash-outs—the opium of the consumer—have slowed to a crawl.

4. *ARMs are up:* Adjustable-rate mortgages and interest-only mortgages have more than doubled their share vs. fixed-rate mortgages as a percentage of new mortgages. Both of these developments are dangerous for consumers: ARMs shift the risk of higher interest rates from the bank to the consumer, and interest-only loans are the most leveraged way to participate in the real estate market. Why the risk? Because homebuyers are being priced out of the housing markets as the schism between affordability and home prices grows ever wider.

5. *Housing starts are plummeting:* November housing starts posted the biggest drop in over a decade, and investors ignored this. Instead, investors focused on old statistics such as existing-home sales. These data tell us more about the past than they do about the future. Remember, existing-home sales reflect conditions of two to three months ago (since a sale is booked at closing), while housing starts reflect activity at the signing.

The Fed revealed in the minutes of its most recent meeting that it is concerned about several forward-looking issues that I have repeatedly harped on. Stated simply, there might be unintended consequences from the protracted period of easy money.

- We have a real-estate-centric economy: For the reasons I cite above, we now have an economy that depends on a wealth-based, not income-based, cycle. This dependency is bordering on an addiction, and it must be recognized that the speculative rise in home prices over the last five years raises new economic risks that are far different from those in prior cycles.

- Low rates have induced complacency: Not only has an extended cycle of low interest rates increased the perils and risks of an asset-dependent consumer, it has also resulted in an acceptance of those low rates as the norm, which they are not. But it's not just consumers who forget that Fed will eventually take away the punchbowl. Investors have grown increasingly complacent, too, bringing risk-taking to a historically high level. Just look at the tightening of credit spreads and the boom in mergers and acquisitions.

- The Fed sees red: Certain members of the Fed virtually agreed with our assertion that the yield on the 10-year U.S. Treasury note connoted a less optimistic view of the economy than is reflected in equity prices. The Federal Open Market Committee (FOMC) meetings specifically highlighted the weakness in the November employment report and recent readings on initial claims for unemployment insurance. The Fed also expressed concern about the consumption binge in the United States and the low savings rate. While the Fed sees the risk in a deceleration in consumer spending, it does not see a slowdown as extreme as I do. I think the American consumer is an accident waiting to happen.

- Deficits can't last forever: The Fed also expressed concern about the twin deficits of mass destruction, the budget and current account deficits. I've noted in the past that the current account deficit has become a headwind at over 5% of GDP. This stands in marked contrast to a balanced current account in the early 1990s. Should an exchange crisis develop, foreign investors might demand a premium in the fixed-income market. (One analyst has already challenged the triple-A credit rating of U.S. government securities.) When the deficit headwind hits, the climb in interest rates is likely to be large and swift.

- The risk of inflation is rising: It's a fallacy to think that the consumer price index (CPI) accurately captures inflation. Housing, health care, tuition and local taxes are just a few of the areas that are not captured properly. (As for the "ex food and energy" CPI, that's great for people who don't eat or drive.) Cost pressure could hurt by raising interest rates and by reducing discretionary consumer income. But while the FOMC minutes focus on future inflation, I think it's already here. I think that we have already seen the pressure of inflation building (since the government reports on CPI are works of fiction!).

- Tech spending is slowing: The Fed cited recent indications of a softening in high-tech spending in the United States and abroad. Since tech accounts for the majority of corporate capital investments, a slowdown here would undermine one of the few remaining areas of potential growth.

All this said, the world is not coming to an end, nor does it preclude market rallies. But we should all recognize the consequences of policy decisions and remember the wisdom and lessons of history and adjust our risk profiles accordingly. For it seems as if in almost any cycle of speculative activity we forget Benjamin Disraeli's words: "What we have learned from history is that we have not learned from history."

Lest you think I have forgotten my humility as an investor, I'll repeat Warren Buffett's comment to shareholders of Berkshire Hathaway from 2004: "The cemetery for seers has a huge section set aside for macro forecasters."

When the Walls Come Tumbling Down

5/16/2005

History and Blood, Sweat & Tears teach us that "what goes up must come down."

Physics and Isaac Newton teach us that "for every action there is always an equal and opposite reaction."

While the hedge fund bubble and the convertible debt bubble have garnered most of the attention over the past two

"Nor is the people's judgment always true:
The most may err as grossly as the few."

—John Dryden

months, the markets have ignored—or put on the back burner—concerns regarding the real estate boom/bubble.

As seen by my analysis below, however, I remain a firm believer in mean reversion and that housing is heading for a hard landing as the issue of affordability will soon trump the historically low level of interest rates. Or, as Newton proclaimed, "A body in motion tends to remain in motion, or remain stopped unless acted on by a force."

From my perch, the ramifications of an unwinding in home prices could potentially prove as grave (in the 2006–2008 period) as the effect that the bursting of the stock market bubble had in 2000–2003.

And that is quite a bold statement.

How severe might the housing correction be?

In order to gauge the magnitude of the risk, it is interesting to look at the ratio of home prices as a multiple of average household incomes in England and in Boston, two geographic areas whose housing markets are exhibiting parabolic rises and appear eligible for the Bubble Hall of Fame.

In the United Kingdom, average housing prices divided by average earnings now stand at over three standard deviations above trend line (measured over the last 50 years); as recently as 1995, the ratio was one standard deviation below the average! Today, the variance in home prices to household earnings in England is even larger than the standard deviation imbalance of U.S. equities in March 2000, which represented the most conspicuous overvaluation in modern U.S. equity history. In order to move back to the historic trend line, home prices in England would have to fall by 38%.

In Boston—a good example of the red-hot coastal U.S. housing markets—median home prices stand at 2.5 standard deviations above the historical distribution. Twenty years ago, home prices were 1.5 standard deviations below the average experienced over the last half-decade.

In a recent CNBC special on housing, "The Real Estate Boom," I mentioned that the price-to-earnings (P/E) ratio of homes in the United States (average home prices divided by rental prices attainable) now approaches 34—eerily reminiscent of the bubble multiple on the S&P 500 in early 2000. If that ratio were to decline back to 20 (the average over the last 50 years), home prices would drop by 40%.

According to *The Economist* (March 3, 2005), based on the value of house rentals today, the housing market is roughly 30% overpriced in the United States.

Another way to look at house price vulnerability is to call upon the speculative rise in London home prices in the 1982–1988 period (when it peaked at two standard deviations above trend) and its subsequent deflation in the early 1990s. During that time frame, the ratio of home prices to average earnings fell from 5× to under 3×, signifying a meaningful drop in home prices.

It is important to note that although the break in the real estate markets was responsible for a considerable amount of damage in the world recession of the early 1990s, improving real wages buffeted its overall impact. In contrast, today's low inflation and lower income growth will likely be less of a cushion to a housing price decline than in the previous cycle.

Every single two-sigma event (a.k.a., bubble) in economic history has ultimately been broken, and with the piercing of an important asset class's bubble (such as real estate) invariably comes lower consumption and lower investing intentions, regardless of monetary or fiscal policy responses.

Remember above all else: When everybody else is doing it (as is the case in real estate!), don't. The more certain the crowd is, the surer it is to be wrong. If everyone were right, there would be no reward.

I have long felt that the consumer is spent-up not pent-up, and now, with the housing bubble near its final inning, I am positioning my portfolio in a number of shorts in companies that have relied on expanding turnover of the existing housing stock and rising home prices. What makes things even worse than many realize is that record refinancing cash-outs have levered the consumer ever more to the housing markets.

Furnishing companies, lenders, originators, remodeling companies and specialty retailing serving real estate will likely face a torrid headwind as we conclude this decade.

When the Walls Come Tumbling Down (Part Deux)

8/9/2006

At the core of my economic concerns for 2006–2008 is the swift and deep deterioration in the U.S. real estate market.

Housing has been—to paraphrase New York Yankee slugger Reggie Jackson's self-description—the straw that stirs the drink of the consumer and the economy.

The construction industry has been the most important catalyst for economic growth since 2001. The Fed took interest rates to unprecedented low levels, and mortgage lenders encouraged activity through creative mortgages that kept mortgage debt service even lower by requiring small monthly payments.

Indeed, economists at Merrill Lynch (and elsewhere) have pointed out that residential and nonresidential construction activity was responsible for nearly half of gross domestic product (GDP) and employment growth since 2001.

Equally important, the unprecedented rise in home prices (especially of a coastal nature) buoyed consumer confidence, allowed the consumption binge to be extended (through record refinancing cash-outs) and encouraged consumers to stop saving (comfortably relying instead on the appreciation of their homes).

I argued (prematurely) that the housing cycle was no different than past cyclical experiences, that the long boom forecast by industry participants (homebuilders and analysts) was fallacious and that, in the fullness of time, housing activity and prices were headed for a fall.

The major reasons for my forecast were twofold and differed from the declines of the past (which were influenced by job losses and other negative macroeconomic forces). Affordability (home prices divided by household incomes) had been stretched to levels never before seen, and a new class of buyers (speculators or day traders of homes) had artificially inspired rising home prices (very similar to day traders of stocks in the late 1990s).

Over the past nine months, the cyclical peak in housing activity has come and gone. Almost weekly, prior upward guidance by homebuilders has been replaced by the slashing of estimates, lower order rates and eroding backlogs. And the industry's inventory has mushroomed to multiyear highs.

The worst is yet to come for housing; it is moving toward a very hard landing. And with a further decline will be (important) attendant and adverse ramifications for consumer confidence and aggregate economic growth.

Housing led the economic recovery and will now lead the economy's contraction—a causal relationship far older than most hedge fund managers' (who have never seen a bear market) half-life of investing.

My home and my neighborhood illustrate how quickly real estate markets turn and how worrisome the downward trend in the housing market might become.

For five months of the year, I live in the tony town of East Hampton, New York. (I purchased the home three years ago.) I live in a nice 50-year-old home on a little more than an acre, which sits about five blocks from Georgica Beach.

When I left East Hampton for southern Florida (my winter residence) last October (which, coincidentally, was the statistical peak in housing), there were no homes for sale on my block (which consists of about 12 homes). However, upon returning to Long Island in late May 2006, four of the existing 12 houses had been demolished and replaced with new homes for sale. (I would estimate, on average, each home was about 7,000 square feet.)

All four homes have been for sale since May (by speculators/developers) with no bids. Moreover, three other existing homes on my block have been put on the market this summer. No bids there, either.

Real estate agents across the country routinely have Sunday open houses, and East Hampton is no exception. Those open houses on my street have come and gone; there has been no traffic.

East Hampton is symptomatic of many other coastal real estate markets. The hard landing in housing is upon us, and as usual, the cycle will be more extreme than expected—just as the climb was unexpectedly high.

During the halcyon times last spring, I participated in a CNBC town hall special titled "The Real Estate Boom," in which Dr. Robert Shiller of Yale University and I debated with optimistic industry participants and housing economists about the slope of the cycle. We were in the distinct minority. Many industry insiders still see a soft landing in housing. They are wrong.

As I mentioned previously, the statistical peak in housing (measured by new-home sales) was October 2005, only nine months ago (and with a unit drop in new-home sales since the peak of less than 20%). By contrast, the average postwar cyclical downturn for housing has been between 26 and 52 months, which has averaged a 51% drop in units.

As I wrote earlier, the worst is yet to come for housing, and with it, the multiplier effect on the domestic economy will be felt widely.

Housing Headed to the Woodshed

9/28/2006

"We do expect an adjustment in home prices to last several months, as we work through a buildup in the inventory of homes on the market. . . . This is the price correction we've been expecting—with sales stabilizing, we should go back to positive price growth early next year."

—David Lereah, economist, National Association of Realtors (*New York Times*, September 2006)

Wrong!

Lereah, whom I debated on CNBC's "The Real Estate Boom" in April 2005, is a very nice man and a capable economist. I recently had a most pleasant conversation with him at CNBC studios two months ago prior to a special on housing hosted by Bill Griffeth.

Lereah is also the author of the book *Are You Missing the Real Estate Boom? Why Home Values and Other Real Estate Investments Will Climb Through the End of the Decade—and How to Profit from Them* (Crown Business, 2005).

Not the most timely publication, Lereah's book was published within four months of the statistical peak in housing activity and prices in 2005. In fact, the paperback version came out in February 2006, when the down cycle was beginning to escalate.

I am in no way trying to embarrass Lereah. I am just stating the facts and my opinions. Don't think for a minute that the National Association of Realtors' Lereah was expecting a price correction last year, as stated in this month's *New York Times* interview above.

Back in April 2005 (on the CNBC special), Lereah and the managements of Hovnanian, Prudential Realty, and LendingTree were fully convinced (you might say glib) that the housing market was destined for a long boom. They saw a new paradigm of uninterrupted, noncyclical growth. One month later, Lereah was quoted as saying, "We simply don't have enough homes on the market to meet demand."

That was then, and it doesn't pay to dwell on the past. So let's look into the future. Unfortunately, many within the homebuilding business continue to talk their book despite clear trends that do not support their bullish view.

Forgive my preoccupation with the housing markets, but it has had a disproportionate role in economic growth since 2000 (and maybe before). This merits a continued discussion as to the possible slope of the decline and the nature of the inevitable recovery. The housing cycle, among other variables, is a key influence on aggregate economic activity.

I expect a hard landing, and I have roughly quantified my expectations as to when the housing market will bottom (2009). It is folly to think that an unprecedented rise in home prices (in real and nominal terms) will be over in relatively short order. Yet this has been suggested by Lereah and others.

Housing cycles are long, and they play out over many years. We have learned that the peaks are surprisingly high and the up cycles unexpectedly long. Unfortunately, so too are the depth and duration of the down cycles.

Days/months of inventory have only begun to rise as the glut of homes will be exacerbated by continued overbuilding, disposition of land, and the selloff of homes by flippers. And, as discussed previously, the consumer enters the current downturn in a weak position. Consumers are highly leveraged after the overconsumption binge of the last decade and after massive cash-outs of home equity.

Consider the dramatic sale of D. R. Horton homes in the Daytona Beach market in Florida. A message at the bottom of its advertisement reads: "Realtors Warmly Welcomed!" That's never a good sign.

These discounts include up to $90,000 a unit, or as much as 30% (plus a free washer/dryer and refrigerator). This is not unusual: Most homebuilders have offered large price discounts and/or large incentives (vacations, car leases, reduced mortgage rates, etc.) for several months.

For a moment, let's suppose that you were a flipper in the Daytona Beach D. R. Horton community who owned and speculated on a few homes without the intention of moving in. You just took a 30% haircut on your inventory, not to mention carrying costs of a mortgage, real estate taxes, and expenses to keep up the property (landscaping, utilities, etc.).

And when the unit is finally sold, you have to pay a real estate agent a 6% commission. That speculator likely put up less than 20% up front (probably far less), and is now out, by my calculation, about 50%. But making the situation worse is this: who wants to buy a used home when you can get a new one?

The ramifications of an extended housing downturn are broad—far broader than many realize. For example, the apartment real estate investment trusts (REITs), a sector I am short, argue that there has been no new construction, so supply/demand favors an escalation in rents. But just wait until speculators, unable to sell their condominiums and homes, resort to renting the units.

Or consider the implications for building materials companies like Eagle Materials, which warned on Tuesday. What about the sale of pickup trucks, which are often used on the construction trade? What does an extended downturn portend for carpet, gypsum, lumber and appliance manufacturers? Or for subprime and some prime lenders? And what do you suppose happens to the plethora of real estate agents and mortgage brokers? (Do they become day traders again?)

You get the point: The housing decline is just beginning to be felt. The fixed-income market recognizes this. But for now, equity market participants don't. Common sense has taken a sabbatical.

Don't believe the housing soft-landing advocates, and do recognize the broad economic impact that a protracted downturn will have on our economy.

The worst is yet to come.

Housing's Softness Has Long Reach

11/14/2006

The nearly uninterrupted and intoxicating rise in equities over the past four months has caused many normally sober market participants to underestimate the severity of housing's downturn and to ignore the likely broad multiplier effect of housing's hard landing on the economy.

The arm of the housing market is long, and the cycles (up and down) tend to be long, too. Importantly, the lag of housing's negative influence (from the statistical peak in housing) is typically long, too.

At first, furniture retailers are immediately affected by the slowdown in residential activity.

Then home remodeling retailers and appliance manufacturers falter.

Ultimately, the effect that a hard landing in housing has on economic activity—and the lower home prices that it portends—broadens and causes a deep retrenchment in consumption, and its scope and impact becomes all-inclusive.

By historical standards, the recent up cycle in housing was atypically strong (topping 6% of GDP for the first time since the post–World War II expansion). We are from a bottom in residential fixed investment and facing likely economic slowdown.

Earlier this month, Richard Fisher, the Dallas Federal Reserve's president, explained the factors that contributed to the unprecedented boom in housing over the past six years.

> In retrospect, the real fed funds rate turned out to be lower than what was deemed appropriate at the time and was held lower longer that it should have been. In this case, poor data led to a policy action that amplified speculative activity in the housing and other markets. Today, as anybody not from the former planet of Pluto knows, the housing market is undergoing a substantial correction and inflicting real costs to millions of homeowners across the country. It is complicating the task of achieving our monetary objective of creating the conditions for sustainable non-inflationary growth.

Stated simply, too-low interest rates fueled the speculative activity in housing and stretched affordability, which has resulted in an ever-expanding inventory of unsold homes. Today, a record level of builders' unsold inventory (including homes not started, homes started but not completed and completed home inventory) coupled with the residue of speculators' unsold homes speaks to a hard landing in housing, despite the protestations of many.

It is no wonder the Bureau of Labor Statistics reported a near 10% decline in home prices last month and that many homebuilders are reporting cancellation rates in excess of 40%.

Over the past 60 years, whenever residential fixed investment tops 5.5% of GDP and subsequently falls by at least 10%, a recession occurs. Already the ratio of residential fixed income to GDP (which peaked at 6.3% in late 2005) has now dropped by more than 10%. According to Guerite Advisors, the ratio has declined by another 17.4% in the fourth quarter of 2006.

Needless to say, there are other housing-related influences that will weigh negatively on forward consumption levels—adjustable option ARM interest rate resets; a clamping down on creative/ aggressive financing (as defaults/delinquencies grow); the absence of personal savings; still-stretched affordability ratios of home prices to household incomes, etc.—that suggest the housing landing will be hard, serving as a strong headwind to economic growth by weighing on the consumer and countering the relatively stronger position of the corporate sector.

Subpar Subprime a Growing Problem

2/8/2007

Last night, HSBC Holdings and New Century Financial—two of the three largest subprime mortgage lenders in the United States—reported disastrous credit losses stemming from their real estate origination businesses.

HSBC announced that its allowance for bad debts will rise to $10.6 billion (more than $1.75 billion above estimates) and New Century (whose stock fell nearly 20% on the news on Wednesday evening) projected a fourth-quarter loss and the need to restate its prior quarters because it materially understated subprime delinquencies and foreclosures.

Nationwide, the subprime default rate soared to 10.09% in November 2006—it stood at only 6.62% a year earlier. Despite a growing economy in early 2007, November's industry default rate exceeded the level of November 2001, which was recorded at the bottom of the last recession. The problem runs deeper than five and a half years ago, however, because nearly 15% of the mortgages made in 2006 were subprime. That is almost triple the penetration of subprime compared to 2000–2001.

Making matters worse:

- Subprime has never been more levered—just as the housing cycle has peaked. Loan-to-value ratios have risen from about 78% in 2000 to 86% today.
- Subprime has never been more dependent on the candor of borrowers. Low-documented loans have doubled to 42% of subprime loans over the past six years.
- Creative loans (non–interest paying, option ARMs, etc.) represented nearly half of all loans made over the past 12 months. At the turn of the decade these loans represented less than 2% of total mortgage loans.

Before the extraordinary start in home-price appreciation six years ago, bank charge-offs for home mortgages peaked at 45 basis points. If we simply move to that level again—and considering the preceding three factors, this seems reasonable—that would imply more than $40 billion in charge-offs.

Given the alarming swiftness in recent foreclosures and delinquencies, debt downgrades of subprime pools, and looser standards that accompany mortgage loan innovation, however, it is hard to believe that charge-offs won't exceed 2001 levels.

Many have dismissed the subprime risk, even though originators such as Sebring Capital and Ownit Mortgage Solutions were filing bankruptcy in late 2006 faster than you could say "five-year balloon mortgage."

For that matter, many other economic risks also have been dismissed, including the bubble in credit availability, a spent-up consumer, tightening labor markets and lower productivity, the rising CRB RIND Index and the attendant cost-push inflation.

Also dismissed are the bubble in emerging markets, the levered and vulnerable (long-biased) hedge fund and fund of funds (especially of a Swiss kind) industries, the broad and negative tax implications of the Democratic tsunami, and a more hawkish Fed than many expect.

After all, the current investor base sees no evil and hears no evil, as the market just chugs along ever higher.

That fungus of subprime credit is now clearly not only among us but is now upon us, and the implications for a tightening in mortgage credit will likely serve to contribute to the second leg down in housing over the balance of 2007.

The tidal wave of liquidity and cheap borrowing over the past seven years—which has permeated the mortgage, private-equity and stock markets—has created an attitude toward risk-taking unlike almost anything ever seen before.

Except for a brief period in late 1999–early 2000, the spread of risk-taking to risk-aversion has never been wider. Similar to eight years ago, this condition has produced a market that is currently priced for perfection and poorly positioned for any unpleasant surprises.

We entered 2006 with most investors holding the highest degree of confidence in rising prices for their homes. As it turns out, homeowners were materially disappointed last year.

We enter 2007 with investors having the highest degree of confidence in rising prices for their stock holdings. They, too, might be disappointed as the year progresses when the hidden fragility of an overpriced, overleveraged world will soon be revealed.

I have written that "in time we will undoubtedly see a mean reversion in home prices, interest rates, credit spreads (and losses), corporate profit margins . . . and in the world's equity prices."

Last night's subprime mortgage news that credit losses are skyrocketing is the first shot across the bow of the boat called market optimism.

Ratings Are Subprime's Dirty Secret

2/9/2007

The little-known secret in the subprime market is that the ratings agencies have been lax in their downgrades of subprime paper. The recalcitrant agencies (Moody's, Fitch, and Standard & Poor's) have quietly abetted the mushrooming of very aggressive subprime lending that has allowed the Wall Street firms selling these mortgage products to prosper.

According to Jim Grant, the number of downgrades at Moody's, for example, was even with upgrades in 2005. Last year, the downgrades/upgrades ratio rose slightly to 1.19:1. The problem is that the historical downgrade/upgrade ratio stands at 2.5:1.

Up to now, lenders (and borrowers) have greased the subprime market, making it the swiftest-growing portion of residential real estate lending from 2001 to 2007. Lenders relied on the candor of the borrowers, as nearly half of the subprime mortgages originated last year were no- or low-documented.

This week's *Grant's Interest Rate Observer* calls attention to a 13-month-old, $350 million asset-backed pool of mortgages, MABS 2006-FRE1. Foreclosures now stand at 9%, delinquencies at 10.5% and real-estate-owned at 3.5%. In other words, about 23% of the loans are problematic—and neither Fitch nor S&P has downgraded the issue. No doubt investors in MABS 2006-FRE1 (hedge funds, brokerages, institutions, etc.) mark the issuance to par (since it has not been downgraded).

But what will happen when the ratings agencies finally downgrade MABS 2006-FRE1? Answer: Investors will sell.

Anyone for a 60-bid?

The subprime fungus has only recently been uncovered, and the seriousness of the problem for the housing sector has only recently been uncovered in the "see no evil, hear no evil" capital markets of 2007.

What is astonishing is the almost universal view that the prime market is in good shape and that the weakness in subprime will be contained.

It will not be isolated, as nearly as half of all the mortgages made over the past 12 months—even those made to prime customers—are non-traditional, creative loans (interest-only, adjustable option ARMS, negative amortization, etc.). These, too, are vulnerable. At the very least, today's lemmings (a.k.a., mortgage lenders) will begin to restrict lending and will dramatically tighten standards. And Katy bar the door if this economy doesn't perform in a Goldilocks fashion.

Throughout the balance of 2007 and into 2008, mortgage defaults will accelerate into the prime market, as a result of a moderating economy, too-leveraged mortgage instruments, rising interest rates and ARM resets.

Credit is about to be less plentiful.

Subprime Fungus Will Spread

2/15/2007

Wednesday saw another large mortgage bank, Silver State Mortgage, cease originating subprime loans. Silver State Mortgage was, according to National Mortgage News, one of the fastest-growing wholesale lenders in the country.

The relatively healthy subprime originators, such as Washington Mutual's Long Beach Mortgage, are downsizing around the country faster than you can say BBB-minus.

In a related note, Standard & Poor's might have been reading my story from last week as it downgraded ratings on 18 securities from 11 mortgage-backed bond issues and put on review a number of other bonds sold by units of Goldman Sachs, Lehman Brothers, Barclays Capital, Countrywide Financial, and New Century Financial on Wednesday.

Many in the media have opined that the bears don't understand the conditions under which real estate markets collapse and that these conditions (suggestive of a broadening credit problem) are not present. And in a series of perfunctory conference calls over the past week, the leading brokerages have supported their case that there will not be a credit contagion emanating from subprime lending and that the brokerage exposure will be contained and limited, even though none of the banks disclosed their involvement in the subprime market (as agents and as principals).

It appears that the principal reason these observers are ignoring the subprime problem and its ramifications is that the equity markets are ignoring them. Ergo, it must not be a problem. This is the definition of a Goldilocks mind-set (see no evil, hear no evil) not a Goldilocks scenario.

The subprime carnage (such as HSBC's nearly $2 billion addition to subprime loan losses in the fourth quarter 2006) is ignored as is the commentary from merchant

> *"We began 2006 with a strong backlog that produced record deliveries. As the year progressed, however, market conditions worsened, cancellations increased, net orders declined and margins came under pressure. The result was a 2006 year-end backlog substantially below the year-earlier level. At a minimum this will likely result in a year-over-year decrease in our unit deliveries through the first half of 2007 and potentially longer."*
>
> —KB Home CEO
> Jeffrey Mezger
> (February 13, 2007)

builders such as KB Home and others (perhaps because their stock prices are also rising).

The credit containment argument ignores the parabolic growth and rising role of subprime lending (relative to total mortgage industry loans)—never before have lenders relied more on the candor and integrity of borrowers, and never before have underwriting terms been so lax. These are two toxic reagents, especially within the context of the biggest housing boom in history, in which real estate mortgage receivables have mushroomed to all-time records at the major (and minor) banks.

The "dot condo" *CondoFlip* website that encouraged investors/speculators to day trade condominiums (and proudly declared that "Bubbles Are for Bathtubs") has been dismantled and is no longer operational, replaced by a *Condo Super Center*. The site now admits, in a mea culpa, that "the condo boom was driven by overly ambitious speculators, many of whom had been successful in flipping condos in the past. As condo inventories grew and prices rose, many speculators realized that further purchasing was increasingly risky. So buyers just stopped buying."

There is an emerging credit crisis, and it will lead to rapidly rising charge-offs. Construction lending on land and condominium loans are the next area to implode. (Examples of exposed intermediaries are Fulton Financial, National City and Corus Bancshares.)

As night follows day, the enormous securitization markets will shortly begin to demonstrate the same sort of delinquencies we have witnessed in subprime mortgage lending. Then a continued acceleration of subprime loan problems will creep into the prime market (where equally creative mortgage loans have been made to prime borrowers).

Restrictive credit practices are just beginning to unfold as a consequence of the poor underwriting standards applied over the last decade. The more things change, the more they stay the same.

Subprime's Siren Call

3/12/2007

Maybe Jim Cramer is right when he writes "get over subprime's collapse" and in his view that the brokerage companies will be relatively immune from the subprime carnage.

But I doubt it.

It is far too easy and convenient to dismiss the subprime woes based on the notion that because it is on the cover of the *New York Times* or on the tongue of many market commentators, it is either discounted or not as bad as it seems. Rather than listen to the comments of others on the Street and in the media, I prefer to deal in facts as opposed to simple and glib sound bites.

Here is a tidbit from page 132—yes, I do read every page in these filings!—of Goldman Sachs's 10-K dated Nov. 24, 2006.

Securitization Activities

The firm securitizes commercial and residential mortgages, home equity and auto loans, government and corporate bonds and other types of financial assets. The firm acts as underwriter of the beneficial interests that are sold to investors. The firm derecognizes financial assets transferred in securitizations provided it has relinquished control over such assets. Transferred assets are accounted for at fair value prior to securitization. Net revenues related to these underwriting activities are recognized in connection with the sales of the underlying beneficial interests to investors.

The firm may retain interests in securitized financial assets, primarily in the form of senior or subordinated securities, including residual interests. Retained interests are accounted for at fair value and are included in "Total financial instruments owned, at fair value" in the consolidated statements of financial condition.

During the years ended November 2006 and November 2005, the firm securitized $103.92 billion and $92.00 billion, respectively, of financial assets, including $67.73 billion and $65.18 billion, respectively, of residential mortgage loans and securities. Cash flows received on retained interests were approximately $801 million and $908 million for the years ended November 2006 and November 2005, respectively. As of November 2006 and November 2005, the firm held $7.08 billion and $6.07 billion of retained interests, respectively, including $5.18 billion and $5.62 billion, respectively, held in QSPEs.

Note to Cramer: I am officially ordering a Code Red!

The fungus of subprime credits has grown in scope and in economic consequence over the past three months. We are now beginning to experience a full-blown bursting of the latest asset bubble, which could prove even more devastating than the piercing of the Nasdaq stock bubble in 2000. The impact of the subprime collapse on the availability of mortgage credit—and, in turn, consumer spending—is the primary reason why I believe the U.S. economy and corporate profits will materially disappoint and why the equity markets remain vulnerable.

"I guess we are a bit surprised at how fast this (subprime) has unraveled."

—Tom Zimmerman, head of asset-backed securities research at UBS, in a recent conference call for institutional investors

Many readily dismiss the potential spending consequences of substantially less capacity in the subprime mortgage-lending market and the emerging trend by mainstream originators and lenders to reduce lending in the primary mortgage market and for refinancing cash-outs.

Indeed, Jim takes the subprime issue one step further, noting that the mortgage house of pain will have a salutary market and economic result, as it will hasten the Fed's path toward monetary ease. Shockingly, many others can't comprehend the link between mortgage availability and consumer spending, claiming that the correlation between the two variables is unclear.

I have not touched on the outlook for considerably higher credit losses at the financial intermediaries that address the housing market, but I will underscore the perfunctory conference calls and the generally disingenuous role of Wall Street rating agencies that continue to hide the damage for owners of collateralized product paper as it relates to the collapse of the subprime market. It seems that at the end of every cycle's excesses, the investment community rationalizes the indefensible, owing to the enormous profitability of the products that are being peddled. The higher a market surges, the easier the product is to sell, but the less straightforward the pitch becomes.

Time and time again—whether it be junk bonds, tax shelters, technology stocks, high-priced initial public offerings (IPOs), glowing research reports—Wall Street (despite former New York Attorney General Spitzer's noble initiatives) continues to exist for the purpose of raising capital (i.e., selling stocks and bonds) and not for the purpose of producing objective research and making clients money.

The brokerages' ties (in packaging and trading mortgage products) and earnings exposure to the subprime collapse—they have 60% of the market share of the mortgage financing market—were covered in depth in yesterday's *New York Times* article by Gretchen Morgenson.

From my perch, the collapse of the subprime markets—delinquencies now stand at 12.6% for subprime and 4.7% for the overall mortgage market—within the context of the $6.5 trillion mortgage securities market will have a broad and negative multiplier effect on mortgage activity (housing turnover) and retail spending. It will also serve to further grease the current slide in new residential construction activity and hasten the drop in home prices.

It is important to understand housing's disproportionate role in terms of buoying employment and industrial production from 2000 to 2006 in order to appreciate how violent the reversal's effect might be on aggregate economic growth.

- The real estate industry has been responsible for 40% of the job growth since 2001.
- The rise in home prices has provided for 70% of the increase in household net worth since 2001.
- The increase in consumer spending and real estate construction spending has contributed to 90% of the growth in GDP since 2001.

Not only did new-home construction embark on an era of unprecedented growth, but the broad rise in national home prices gave way to the concept of the "home as an ATM"—a source of cash, a substitute for savings and an enabler of the consumption binge (which was above and beyond the income means of the average consumer).

During the 1990s, mortgage equity withdrawals averaged between $20 billion and $80 billion per year, or only about 0.50% of GDP. By contrast, average yearly mortgage equity withdrawals climbed to about $230 billion, or 2% of GDP, over the past five years and peaked at nearly 3% of GDP in the second quarter of 2006—or at an annualized yearly rate of almost $400 billion.

Several months ago, Freddie Mac forecast that mortgage equity withdrawals will drop by 20% this year and by another 30% in 2008. These projections were done before the subprime fungus spread, and I think its estimates are too high.

In 2006, subprime mortgage loans trebled (to 36%) as a percentage of all mortgages issued. "Liar loans," or non- and low-documented loans that relied on the candor of homebuyers (never an intelligent loan strategy) doubled (to 40%) over the same time frame. Creative loans (characterized by teaser rates, negative amortization, interest-only, etc.) became the new big thing in real estate and dominated the mortgages issued in 2006. Refinancing cash-outs proliferated, and, according to BankAmerica Securities, the average loan to a subprime borrower rose from 48% of the property's value in 2000 to 82% last year.

While the media have been focused on the D. R. Horton CEO's bleak forecast, every quarterly conference call with leading homebuilders last quarter confirmed the mounting restrictions of credit by mortgage lenders. Stated simply, it is growing harder and harder to get mortgages. In the interim interval, the subprime market's health has worsened and so has, on a daily basis, the availability of mortgage credit (the lifeblood of our economy's well-being).

In light of the recent adverse loan experience and bad publicity, most originators are avoiding these loans like the plague. Today, no mortgage lending officer at any bank or thrift will dare stretch lending standards to homebuyers, as the mandate of tightened loan-to-values and higher FICO scores are increasingly the directive from financial companies' management.

Moreover, the fixed-income market has a diminished appetite for packaged subprime loans and a diminished appetite for any collateralized product that includes subprime loans. It is unlikely that the institutional investors will hunger for this product for some time to come and originators will be faced with the hard reality that subprime loans will face more limited demand in the primary and secondary markets.

With financial intermediaries turning off the mortgage loan spigot, first-time homebuyers and trade-up buyers—who already are pressed by the lack of affordability (home prices divided by household incomes)—will have markedly reduced access to the residential real estate markets. As a result, the cyclical decline in housing will be forced into another down leg, just at a time when inventories of unsold homes remain elevated and the volume of ARM resets peaks (in third-quarter 2007). As a consequence, the gradual decline in home prices seen over the past 12 months runs the risk of becoming a full-fledged waterslide.

The mortgage market's new reality will serve to immediately (and adversely) affect housing turnover and reduce the demand for expenditures on many products. Exacerbating the decline in personal consumption expenditures will be the virtual disappearance of mortgage equity withdrawals.

Spending on everything from appliances, furniture, flooring, roofing, paint, televisions, telephones, and tools will suffer from the lower housing turnover and activity. The cessation of refinancing cash-outs could have an even broader effect, constraining discretionary spending on restaurants, apparel, vacations, remodeling projects, automobiles and other durables.

With the demand for a broad array of consumer goods and services moderating, corporate profits are at risk and will quickly disappoint relative to expectations. Up until now, the service sector has remained healthy (even while housing and autos weakened), but even the buoyancy in services will be pressured and put to the test in the months to come. In the fullness of time, the rate of job growth will decelerate even more markedly than we have seen over the past several months as construction unemployment accelerates and the contagion permeates the broader job market.

More tepid top-line sales growth will weigh on corporate profit margins (one of the cornerstones to my bearish case for equities and valuations) as operating leverage will be difficult to come by. Unfortunately, all this will occur at the same time cost pressures remain high.

The CRB RIND Index—an index of spot raw material prices—just made a multiyear high last week, while unit labor costs have upticked to levels not seen in years.

In summary, the credit contagion that started with the fungus of subprime lending will hit an already weakened housing market and could spread to other securitized markets. Its impact will be felt broadly and should have a pronounced negative effect on personal consumption, corporate profits, and stock prices. It will suck.

Four to Blame for the Subprime Mess

3/14/2007

There are four main culprits responsible for the expanding subprime debacle that threatens to upset the Goldilocks scenario that so many are trumpeting. I've listed them in descending order of importance:

Culprit No. 1: Former Fed Chairman Alan Greenspan did two big things wrong.

First, the former Fed chairman took interest rates far too low and maintained those levels for far too long a period in the early 2000s, well after the stock market's bubble was pierced. (Stated simply, he panicked.)

The Fed's very loose monetary policy served to encourage the new, marginal and nontraditional homebuyer—the speculator and the investor not the dweller—to embark on a speculative orgy in home purchases not seen in nearly a century.

Over time, home prices, especially on the coasts, were elevated to levels that stretched affordability well beyond the means of most buyers. Ultimately, despite relatively strong employment and low interest rates, the residential housing market crashed hard.

Second, Greenspan suggested—at just the wrong time and at the very bottom of the interest rate cycle—that homeowners retreat from traditional, fixed-rate mortgages and turn to more creative and floating rate mortgages (interest only, adjustable option ARMs, negative amortization, etc.).

He said this in February 2004 at a Credit Union National Association 2004 Governmental Affairs Conference:

American consumers might benefit if lenders provided greater mortgage product alternatives to the traditional fixed-rate mortgage. To the degree that households are driven by fears of payment shocks but are willing to manage their own interest-rate risks, the traditional fixed-rate mortgage may be an expensive method of financing a home.

One year later Greenspan continued the same mantra and cited the social benefits of the financial industry's innovation as reflected in the proliferation of the subprime mortgage market.

> A brief look back at the evolution of the consumer finance market reveals that the financial services industry has long been competitive, innovative and resilient. Innovation has brought about a multitude of new products, such as subprime loans and niche credit programs for immigrants. Such developments are representative of the market responses that have driven the financial services industry throughout the history of our country. With these advances in technology, lenders have taken advantage of credit-scoring models and other techniques for efficiently extending credit to a broader spectrum of consumers. The widespread adoption of these models has reduced the costs of evaluating the creditworthiness of borrowers, and in competitive markets, cost reductions tend to be passed through to borrowers. Where once more-marginal applicants would simply have been denied credit, lenders are now able to quite efficiently judge the risk posed by individual applicants and to price that risk appropriately. These improvements have led to rapid growth in subprime mortgage lending; indeed, today subprime mortgages account for roughly 10% of the number of all mortgages outstanding, up from just 1% or 2% in the early 1990s. . . . We must conclude that innovation and structural change in the financial services industry has been critical in providing expanded access to credit for the vast majority of consumers, including those of limited means. Without these forces, it would have been impossible for lower-income consumers to have the degree of access to credit markets that they now have. This fact underscores the importance of our roles as policy-makers, researchers, bankers and consumer advocates in fostering constructive innovation that is both responsive to market demand and beneficial to consumers.

But even as Greenspan was taking interest rates to levels that encouraged the egregious use of mortgage debt and exhorting the opportunities in creative and variable mortgage financing, there were some smart cookies out there who recognized the risks; here are quotes from two of the smartest who warned of the danger in the mortgage market.

> When I took economics in World War II, and we were studying the Great Depression, one of the reasons given was all the interest-only loans that came due. They were an indication of an economy getting into unsound lending. Ever since then it's been a rule that when you go into interest-only loans, you're very substantially increasing the risk of default.
> —*L. William Seidman, former chairman of the Federal Deposit Insurance Corporation and chairman of the Resolution Trust Corporation*

Our own Robert Marcin put it even more precisely (and vividly) in his prescient warning back in mid-2005.

> If Greenspan had a clue (remember, he didn't have one in the tech bubble, or maybe he did), he would jawbone the banking industry to tighten or even strangle lending standards for residential real estate. He should not kill the entire economy to slow the real estate markets. Now that bag people can buy condos in Phoenix with no down payments, maybe the Fed should get involved. You can't expect mortgage bankers to do anything; they get paid to lend money. But like Greenspan's unwillingness to raise margin rates in 1999, I expect him to do nothing until the market declines. Then, the taxpayers will be on the hook for the stupidities of the real estate speculators. Remember, I expect a sequel to the RTC in the future.
> —*Robert Marcin, "Making Money before Housing Crumbles"*

Greenspan will go untouched and will continue to give speeches at $200,000 a pop.

Culprit No. 2: Irrational monoline lenders such as Novastar, New Century, Fremont General, Option One, Accredited Home, OwnIt Mortgage Solutions and others grew from nothing to originating billions of dollars of mortgage loans almost overnight.

Their rush to lend and helter-skelter growth relied on the candor of the mortgagees and not on common sense, prudent lending or reasonable underwriting standards.

The growth in subprime-only originators was irrational, but the industry will now be rationalized and the marginal lenders will go bankrupt. And in the fullness of time, the more diversified lenders will benefit from their demise.

Culprit No. 3: The Wall Street brokerage community's packaging, warehousing and trading of mortgage securities is immense, with about a 60% share of the mortgage financing market.

After tax shelter abuses in the early 1980s, junk(y) bonds in the late 1980s, overpriced technology stocks and ludicrous IPOs and disingenuous research reports in the late 1990s, one would think that Wall Street had learned its lesson.

It has not.

The higher a market surges, the easier it is for Wall Street to peddle and package junk.

The magnitude of the potential gains are always too attractive and tempting, particularly as product demand swells into another cycle excess, as it did in subprime. Astonishingly, even the obligatory emergency conference calls intended to persuade investors that all is well were superficial and failed to disclose the inherent conflicts that each and every multiline brokerage has.

The major brokerages will be litigated against, again. They will pay large fines but will proceed in business until the next bubble, which they will also capitalize on.

Culprit No. 4: The little-known secret in the subprime market is that the principal ratings agencies have been lax in their downgrades of subprime paper and securitizations.

This should not be considered a surprise, because like their Wall Street brethren, they prosper from the rising tide of credit issuances. In doing so, similar to a teacher who has turned his back on a boisterous and disobedient class, those recalcitrant agencies (Moody's, Fitch, and S&P) have ignored the erosion in credit quality and abetted the rush and market share taking of subprime lending.

Importantly, until downgrades are issued by the agencies, investors routinely carry their investments at cost, or par—downgrades force investments to mark to market and sell.

The rating agencies will likely go unscathed because they always do.

Fed Is No Savior in Subprime Slide

3/15/2007

Bullish observers have increasingly been making the case that the growing fungus of subprime credit problems will force the Fed into a loosening of monetary conditions sooner rather than later.

These days, the private-equity put doesn't seem to be working, so it appears that the struggling bulls now must hold on to the notion of a Bernanke put to counter the currently troubling and tenuous stock market conditions.

After all, lower interest rates always reverse investor sentiment and adverse financial conditions, right?

My view is that with the level of inflation remaining stubbornly high, coming to the aid of a bunch of reckless and overly aggressive mortgage bankers is not necessarily seen by Chairman Ben Bernanke & Co. as an immediate responsibility of the Fed.

They might deem it too early in the crisis or think there is no crisis at all.

In fact, consider the cheerleading of Treasury Secretary Henry Paulson in Tokyo last week and remarks made recently by Federal Reserve Governor Susan Bies, both of whom have downplayed the subprime problems:

> "Credit issues are there, but they are contained. I don't think it (subprime) has, at this point, implications for the aggregate economy in terms of the ongoing expansion."
>
> —*U.S. Treasury Secretary Henry Paulson*

> "Based on some recent observations, mortgage lending certainly is an area in which we believe financial institutions and supervisors have learned some key lessons about risk management."
>
> —*Federal Reserve Governor Susan Schmidt Bies*

Also, consider this quote from another Fed official on what he sees as the Fed's true role.

Ultimately, though, ex ante judgments about leverage, concentrations and liquidity risk will continue to prove elusive. Our principal focus should therefore be not in the search for the capacity to preemptively diffuse conditions of excess leverage or liquidity, but in improving the capacity of the core of the financial system to withstand shocks and on mitigating the impact of those shocks.

And, as always, central banks need to stand prepared to make appropriate monetary policy adjustments if changes in financial conditions would otherwise threaten the achievement of the goals of price stability and sustainable economic growth.

—*Timothy Geithner, president of the New York Federal Reserve Bank, February 28, 2007*

Now even if the Fed did lower interest rates in March or April, the markets could interpret the move more negatively than the bulls realize by calling attention to the magnitude of the mortgage crisis and by fueling inflationary fears, serving to pull the capital markets into a tailspin.

As we move into the summer or fall, there will be better visibility of the subprime problems. By that time, it will be abundantly clear to even the bulls that an inventory-swollen housing market is back on the sick bed as the two most important marginal buyers—the first-time and trade-up buyers—have lost access to home-financing. And, by then, the multiplier effect of the housing downturn should be in full force, causing the economy to sputter and for corporate profit expectations to fall to more realistic levels.

The upheaval in the subprime mortgage industry is in its middle stages, but the broad impact on the U.S. economy is in its infancy. To paraphrase, Frankenstein's Dr. Waldman, the credit markets and Wall Street have created a monster—subprime—and it will destroy the economy.

The Simple Math of Subprime's Slide

3/26/2007

I am not looking for a depression in housing or for the economy, but those who look for housing to stabilize and for an increasingly restrictive mortgage credit market to be anything other than a substantive drag on 2007–2008 aggregate economic growth are just plain wrong.

It's worrisome to look at the state of housing demand and supply today.

The explosion in mortgage delinquencies in the second half of 2006 has only recently begun to be converted from delinquencies to foreclosures (and for-sale signs). Currently, the housing market's foreclosures stand at a 40-year peak.

Economy.com estimates that there were about 400,000 foreclosures in 2006. With signs of continued rising delinquency rates thus far this year, 2007 foreclosures should be considerably higher than last year's figures. I would estimate that foreclosures in 2006–2007 will add nearly 1 million units (or 26.5%) to the current level of 3.75 million homes for sale. Stated simply, most are underestimating the massive supply of homes that will be dumped on the market over the next year to two years.

While record foreclosures will assuredly lead to a rapid rise in the supply of homes available to be sold in 2007 and 2008, tougher lending standards (particularly in the subprime category that is the lifeblood of first-time buyers) will squelch housing demand. Historically, creative lending (option ARMs, interest-only, negative amortization, etc.) shored up the housing markets by allowing (indeed encouraging) otherwise unqualified borrowers to participate in the roaring residential market of the last few years.

First-time buyers and speculators, who, before delinquencies mushroomed, were qualified for high (95% or more!) loan-to-value mortgages at below-market interest rates (80% of subprime loans over the past three years were 2/28 ARMs) based on teaser interest rates are now being qualified increasingly by the mortgage interest rate charged after reset.

This is serving to effectively price out a major demand source for homes as they are no longer eligible for low down-payment, non-documented loans that were previously granted with below-market or teaser interest rates. Indeed, subprime mortgages have been the only source for a large amount of homebuyers in the last three years. No more.

I would conservatively estimate that about 55% of the subprime borrowers, 25% of the Alt-A borrowers and 15% of the prime mortgage lending borrowers will no longer be able to secure financing for new homes because of tightened conditions. (This will produce about a 25% drop in housing demand.)

Speculators and investors (who were responsible for nearly 20% of all home purchases in 2004–2006) also will find it more difficult to secure borrowings, and it is likely that this buying category will revert close to its historical demand role of about 5% of all homes. (This will result in another 10% to 15% drop in housing demand.) Finally, end-of-economic-cycle conditions (lower consumer confidence, slowing economic growth and moderating job growth) should contribute to another 10% drop in housing demand, which is as it has done historically.

Adding together the above three influences, new home demand should fall off by almost 50% (vs. the rolling 12-month average showing a 17% drop off in 2007) even before the effect of a market inundated by record foreclosures is considered.

Precipitated by the subprime mess, the entire daisy chain of home demand is deteriorating. With the first-time buyer out of the market and increased demands of higher collateral, better credit and loan documentation, the trade-up market is also in trouble. So is the Alt-A market. And in the fullness of time, as Nouriel Roubini surmises, a more general credit crunch remains possible.

Credit Suisse projects that about $500 billion of mortgages will reset this year (60% of these are subprime loans). According to First American CoreLogic's recent study, "Mortgage Payment Reset: The Issue and the Impact," resets will produce 1.1 million additional foreclosures (and more than $100 billion of losses) over the next six years. That's nearly another 185,000 homes per year coming into supply, on top of the nearly 1 million homes foreclosed on in 2006–2007!

What is particularly worrisome to me is that home prices remain inflated relative to household incomes (Merrill's Rosenberg did a good analysis on this topic last week; Today's home prices stand at the highest multiple to disposable incomes in history.) We have still not resolved the high price of homes by either prices moving lower or incomes moving higher. Affordability (or the lack thereof) will provide another headwind to the housing recovery.

There remains too much land and finished product inventory owned by the homebuilders. The publicly held companies are positioned to weather the storm, but the more levered private companies will be a continued liquidator of land and homes. Indeed, new home-price incentives look to be on the ascent, another headwind to supply.

With housing activity dropping and resets rising, consumer confidence should dive in the months ahead, construction employment will plummet and a cessation of mortgage equity withdrawals will further grease an already weakening slide in personal consumption expenditures.

From my perch, investing on the basis that the subprime carnage and exploding ARMs will not affect the consumer, the economy, and our equity market is a risky proposition.

Here is the economic equation as I see it: restrained mortgage credit plus reset mortgage rates equals more money needed to finance homes and less money available to purchase goods, which in turn equals a slowing economy.

The next down leg in housing is upon us. Employment, consumer confidence, and retail spending will be the next victims of housing's retreat.

Housing Red Ink Could Spell Recession

5/9/2007

The odds favoring a housing-induced recession are now increasing. My bearish preoccupation with the health of the housing markets appears to be justified by history.

The slow-motion drop in consumption seen in the last 12 months will likely accelerate, aided by growing evidence of a second housing downturn this year and possibly another downswing next year, which will be exacerbated by ever-increasing supplies of unsold homes served up, in part, by mortgage resets in 2007 and 2008.

The bullish crowd contends that there is no evidence that the real economy has been affected by the housing market and subprime collapse, rising energy prices or geopolitical threats. Nor, according to them, has the economy been affected by a host of other varied microeconomic and macroeconomic issues.

Today, liquidity is a catchphrase in support of continued economic growth and stock market appreciation, just at a time that collateral and interest rate terms in private-equity deals have begun to tighten.

The same things were said in the late 1980s.

During that period, unprecedented land and housing speculation followed the erosion in lending standards that were a byproduct of the deregulation of the savings and loan industry and the liquidity introduced by Michael Milken's Drexel Burnham, which brought an unprecedented increase in takeover activity.

Ultimately, the economic progress of the early and mid-1980s gave way to an implosion in the high-yield debt markets, an economic downturn and a horrific housing depression (and the loss of the previous decade's liquidity). In the early 1990s, the economic contraction was severe in both magnitude and duration (continuing for three years), even though the federal funds rate was reduced by 500 basis points, to 3%, and stayed there for over 20 months.

(As a result of the recession's severity, several money center banks, such as Citigroup and Bank of Boston, were almost insolvent and had to be saved by the Tisch family.)

Fast-forward to the present.

In 2007, the economy is nearly two-thirds larger than it was 16 years ago, a period in which the downturn in real estate produced nearly $300 billion in losses. But not only is the residential mortgage market much larger now but so are subprime delinquencies and the ultimate losses they will deliver.

Moreover, home mortgage borrowing, home ownership (69% of families vs. only 64% in 1991) and the impact of housing on aggregate economic activity have never been higher. Equally important, household debt as a percentage of GDP is dramatically higher, and home equity as a percentage of home market values has never been lower.

Once again, as in the late 1980s, lax lending standards have become the mainstay of our markets and now are a contributor to the real estate and subprime mess. Also, liquidity is the most often quoted term to explain the market's buoyancy, takeover activity and rising stock prices.

Given the extraordinary creation of wealth—in part because of the ongoing strength of the equity markets and, until recently, the large price appreciation in home prices and breathtaking mortgage equity withdrawals—one should not be surprised by a delayed or slow-motion response, particularly by consumers.

Nevertheless, there is an obvious chain of real estate-related jobs (mortgage brokers, landscapers, title searchers, real estate lawyers, mortgage bankers, realtors, contractors, etc.) that will suddenly be lost at breakneck speed over the near term.

The worst is yet to come—the housing's multiplier effect is starting to kick in.

The consumer has never been more levered, homeownership as a percentage of household net worth has never been higher, the issue of home affordability has yet to be resolved, the inventory of unsold homes is at record levels, homeowner vacancy rates are at an all-time high (2.8% vs. 1.2% in the early 1990s), foreclosures and delinquencies are skyrocketing, and mortgage interest resets are just beginning to further pressure household incomes.

The damage associated with the housing problems will be long-lasting—and, as in the early 1990s, lower interest rates will not readily jump-start growth and rescue the economy.

Hedge Funds' Dirty Little Debt Secret

6/26/2007

The downside of the leveraged and carried trade, mainly through the Bear Stearns High-Grade Structured Credit Strategies Fund, has been opened up like a Pandora's Box of inflated hedge fund valuations, impotent credit ratings and other risk issues.

It all started with the erosion in subprime credits, as delinquencies and foreclosures in late 2005 skyrocketed after housing affordability was stretched by a sustained period of low interest rates, which encouraged housing's speculative activity (the outgrowth of which was record buying of non-owner-occupied investment properties) and the insensibilities of lenders.

The culprits and sinners of this cycle are plentiful. They include a too-easy Fed, loosely regulated and heedless housing lenders, avaricious home speculators, funds of funds that encouraged hedge fund investors to leverage, greedy hedge fund investors—you would have thought that they learned from the demise of John Meriwether's Long Term Capital Management—irresponsible ratings agencies that were reluctant or ill-equipped to downgrade credits, brokerages that packaged these complicated products and, of course, hedge fund managers who have the temptation of large compensation incentives to take undue risk. (They participate in at least 20% of the fund's profitability.)

Reckless lending and the egregious use of leveraged capital have permeated our financial system, raising the risk that the subprime disaster is the leading edge of a deteriorating credit cycle and that its effect will be chilling.

The key to the ultimate impact will be the slope of the economic cycle. If the bulls are correct and a sustained period of economic growth (free of inflationary pressures) is in the cards, credit problems will likely be contained. If I am correct that we are moving toward a recession in early 2008, the subprime mess will be only the tip of the iceberg, and problems will move up the credit ladder.

On a different note, a lot of hedge funds are now trembling—and I don't mean because Congress wants to raise the tax rate on general partners' carried interest. The big hedge fund secret is that, barring credit downgrades, many leveraged and esoteric investments (such as the collateralized debt obligations that inhabited the Bear Stearns hedge fund) aren't marked to market.

This creates the illusion of profits in a hedge fund, until an outsized event (the subprime mess, Russia's refusal to pay its debt, a terrorist event) occurs. Then the proverbial excrement hits the cooling device.

Regardless, there is likely a large amount of undistributed senior risk sitting in dealers' hands today.

The lessons to be learned from this crisis are that:

- Market values matter for leveraged portfolios;
- Models sometimes misbehave and must be stress-tested and combined with judgment;
- Liquidity itself is a risk factor; and
- Financial institutions should aggregate exposures to common risk factors.

And portfolios should be marked to market.

Other stocks that may have mark-to-market issues include private equity funds turned public powerhouses Fortress Investment Group and Blackstone as well as other banks that mix their own proprietary trading with their banking services, including firms such as Goldman Sachs, Lehman Brothers, and JPMorgan Chase.

Loaded Up on Leverage

7/16/2007

The market is approaching an unprecedented and dangerous crossroads: not only is there enormous confidence in the notion of another long worldwide economic boom abetted by non–U.S. influences, but similar to in the late 1980s, there is a bubble in credit availability, credit costs and in investor activism—i.e., buy stock, make a 13-D filing (à la Icahn), make waves and make a boatload of money.

It can't be that easy. (Remember the aborted United Airlines takeover in the late 1980s that brought an end to the speculation surrounding junk-bond financings?)

Moreover, leverage, as in past cycles, is playing a much more active role in today's hijinks. But, leverage is always the monster that kills, and it will likely have a primary role in upsetting this cycle as it has had historically.

Of course, in the last stages of an accelerating trend in prices, the consensus view always seems to look smart. Think back to the last two bubbles: the housing bubble that was formed in the early 2000s, and the stock market bubble emanating from the late 1990s.

To paraphrase Broadway hoofer Ethel Merman in *Gypsy*, "everything was coming up roses" for home prices and for Internet stocks.

Rose-colored glasses were the fashion du jour as the investment community was convinced of the new paradigm and long boom in home prices (and activity), in the unparalleled prospects for technology/Internet and in almost a zombie-like trance in listening to the proselytizing by *Wired* magazine's Peter Schwartz and Peter Leyden that a long and uninterrupted economic boom was inevitable. "We're facing 25 years of prosperity, freedom, and a better environment for the whole world. You got a problem with that?"

In evaluating the past housing cycle, however, investors ignored, up until the very end, the growing mortgage credit abuses that would undermine the cycle by stretching affordability to unfathomable levels.

In the late 1990s, pie-in-the-sky valuations and day trading's speculative excesses were ignored because, in the long run, stocks always rose and a Dow Jones Industrial Average (DJIA) target of 36,000 was the exclamation point in James Glassman's book for all of us to read in late 1999— just prior to the Nasdaq's 75% decline.

In the prior two bubbles/booms, prices were extended and exaggerated by borrowed funds or excess liquidity. Subsequently, the bubbles' bursting of falling prices were exaggerated by the calling in of the credit-financed liquidity.

It is no different today. Credit availability is unprecedented, and activism and private-equity activity are bubbly. Deals are being executed using ever-increasing leverage as credit spreads remain narrow and disbelief has been suspended. At the same time, fundamentals are not as sturdy as is generally accepted.

Grandma Koufax used to say, "Dougie, forewarnings are on your forearm. But for the time being, the joke is on you."

Consider the following:

- *U.S. housing:* Housing's fall is accelerating and will weigh on economic growth for some time to come. No worries, the bulls say, as the bottom has to be near—still-low historic mortgage rates, household formations, demographics, migration, and job growth are supportive of a housing recovery.
- *Worldwide real estate:* The bubble that began in the United States and spread around the world is showing signs of being pierced in Europe. No worries, the bulls say—private equity is a buyer on any weakness.
- *Job growth:* The Bureau of Labor Statistics' birth/death adjustment overstates job growth when the economy is slowing down. No worries, the bulls say—the economy will recover from the tepid first-quarter 2007 growth, and so will jobs.
- *Consumer:* Department-store comps are in a free fall, and a 0.9% drop in retail sales (the largest decline since August 2005) is a further indication that the middle-income consumer is starting to spend less and that a general cooling in spending is on the horizon (as mortgage resets further pressure individuals). No worries, the bulls say—never bet against the consumer as high-end U.S. consumers are healthy

and the emergence of a consumer class in the emerging markets will more than fill in the gaps.

- *Business spending:* Even though business balance sheets are in terrific shape, a weakening consumer, lower home prices and subdued confidence will weigh somewhat on capital spending expenditures. No worries, the bulls say—businesses have been underspending in this cycle, and a catch-up should be anticipated. (It's 1997 all over again.)

- *Corporate profits:* Domestic profits are punk. No worries, the bulls say—international markets are the catalysts to growth.

- *U.S. dollar and earnings quality:* An accelerating drop in the U.S. dollar? No worries, the bulls say—45% of U.S. corporate profits are derived overseas (and will result in foreign-exchange sales/profits benefits), and, as a result of the dollar's schmeissing, U.S. corporations are getting to be ever-cheaper takeover fodder.

- *Inflation:* We now have $74 per barrel for crude oil, rising wage rates, sky-high food prices and a near-record headline CPI. No worries, the bulls say—core CPI, the price of laptops, cell phones, and flat-panel TV screens are all receding. Inflation is contained.

- *Credit cycle:* Credit availability is now being impacted by the subprime mess and a heavy inventory of product (bridge loans and takeover debt). No worries, the bulls say—the liquidity provided by the kindness of strangers will fill the void that is necessary to overcome the deteriorating domestic credit conditions.

- *Geopolitical:* Al Qaeda is gaining power, the United States' Iraq policy is in shambles, and Israel/Middle East is a powder keg. No worries, the bulls say—we have to get used to it (as it has been that way for thousands of years).

- *Political:* Increased evidence that the Democratic Party is moving toward a more onerous taxation policy? No worries, the bulls say—it's a 2010 issue.

- *Sentiment:* Margin interest at record levels, a bubble in optimistic sentiment? No worries, the bulls say—we are in a negativity bubble.

- *Private equity:* The pace of private equity deals has begun to recede as credit spreads begin to widen, borrowers become more circumspect and the supply of recycled private equity is queuing up to be taken public. No worries, the bulls say—liquidity remains an international event, and now foreign companies such as Rio Tinto/Alcan are getting into the act. And the almost endless supply of recycled takeovers poised to go public is a 2008–2010 event.

- *Valuation:* The Value Line Composite of the largest 3,500 companies trades at over 20✕ earnings, the S&P 500 trades at over 20✕ earnings, the Nasdaq trades at 28✕ earnings and the Russell 2000 P/E trades at around a 50% premium to the 2000 highs. No worries, the bulls say—the stated P/E of the S&P is at an historically reasonable 17✕.
- *Emerging markets:* Conspicuous individual investor day trading and speculation in markets such as China are eerily reminiscent of the stock market bubble of the late 1990s. No worries, the bulls say—it's early in the cycle of speculation.
- *Criticism:* Cynics deliver logical arguments regarding economic/ market conditions. No worries, the bulls say—the naysayers are perma-bears; their arguments not worthy of consideration.

In bubble-like market conditions, when many fundamental threats and headwinds are increasingly ignored, stocks tend to overshoot reasonable levels of value until the worriers are totally discredited.

That time might be growing near.

Don't Underestimate How Bad Things Are

7/25/2007

It's time to panic.

Why?

I'll tell you.

To be sure, the economic and investment world does not face Armageddon. But often—especially when market momentum takes over and new paradigms emerge—people simply ignore reality, and in this case the reality has been ugly, and stocks are finally wising up to that.

I've believed for some time that the leverage in the world's financial system would lead to the inevitable end of a halcyon period of plentiful and cheap money. After all, leverage is always the monster that kills and historically has upset the credit cycle.

We are now seeing the beginning of the downside to the mounting leverage in private equity, credit markets, and the consumer segments of our economy, creating the potential for a more volatile backdrop and, in all likelihood, unaccustomed market headwinds.

While the meltdown in subprime mortgage values has been the most publicized of jitters in the credit markets recently, concerns are now growing about risky loans everywhere.

The appetite for high-yield credit has begun to dry up, with issuance of low-quality debt staying below $1 billion for the third successive week.

Prices of bank debt, which is integral to the buyout boom, fell dramatically this week, as many segments of the credit market seized up on Thursday and Friday.

The spread between the average yield of the Lehman U.S. High-Yield Corporate Bond Index and Treasuries, which narrowed to a record-thin 2.33 percentage points in late May (or less than half of the average spread over the last 20 years), has recently widened to around 3.25 percentage points in the last one and a half months.

Other headwinds are mounting:

- Housing is undergoing another down leg, and does not appear to have a chance of recovery until 2009–2010.
- Non-U.S. central banks are raising interest rates in an attempt to rein in economic growth and higher inflation.
- The cost of insuring European junk-rated corporate debt against default (as measured by the iTraxx Crossover Index) recently surged to its highest level in two years.

Also, banking credit losses are expanding rapidly, private equity debt and bank loans are getting revised or are unsold, securitization losses are rising, the U.S. dollar is in a near-free-fall, and the rate of growth in June's headline CPI is at record levels.

The CRB RIND Index (a measure of industrial spot raw material prices) is at an all-time high, oil refinery bottlenecks around the country have pushed gasoline prices to 12-month highs, U.S. corporate profit quality is low (aided by foreign-exchange translation, lower tax rates and buyback benefits), and there is growing evidence of corporate profit margin vulnerability that has surfaced in second-quarter earnings releases.

Caught up in the momentum of price, investors have barely been concerned with the likely impact that a continued Democratic tsunami in 2008 would have on trade policy and on legislation raising individual and corporate tax rates. Moreover, investors seem little troubled by the mounting geopolitical tensions around the world.

Surprisingly, this eroding fundamental backdrop is occurring as worldwide equity prices are within 1.5% of multiyear highs.

Regardless, just as credit spreads have moved from being priced to perfection to being priced to reality since late May 2007, stocks will likely move lower as well.

Again, it's time to panic.

No Quick and Easy Fix for This Market

8/13/2007

Since the housing market's collapse, cheerleading government officials, audaciously bullish strategists, investment bankers, commercial bankers and money managers, extrapolating economists and even irresponsible ratings agencies have felt the economy would not be affected. Skeptics were discredited because, in large measure, worldwide share prices continued to trace a pattern of nearly uninterrupted advances. They were all wrong; the economy has not been unaffected.

Many of those same observers have felt that the subprime disaster would not infect other parts of the credit market. They were wrong there, too, as the credit markets around the world have seized up and have been forced to rely on the injection of liquidity by central bankers in order to temporarily halt a full-fledged credit crunch.

The bullish cabal is now again arguing containment—that a combination of potential policy decisions, such as allowing Fannie Mae and Freddie Mac to expand their lending ability, Fed easing and central bank liquidity adds, will be the ticket to a return to stability.

They will be wrong again.

The cleansing process will take time. There is no short-term fix. The pendulum of the credit cycle is only in its early stage in what appears to be a swing back to normalcy. And the magnitude of the leveraging of the worldwide economy and of hedge fund investors will not allow for normalcy overnight.

The worldwide helicopter drop of money last week (through central bank injections of liquidity) was in response to the banking industry's demand for cash. Over here, fed funds were boosted to a panicky 6.00% in early Friday trading, well above the target level of 5.25%. Over there, it was even worse as market participants have been late in responding to and understanding the magnitude of the subprime problem. (It was only last week that three European funds and Bank Paribas acknowledged losses.)

Unfortunately, these (de facto easing) moves will likely serve only as a Band-Aid to a system that has dined at the trough of leverage for years.

We have not even begun to feel the economic effects of rising delinquency and foreclosure rates, to say nothing of the broadening crisis in credit. It was only in late 2006 that these rates began to climb.

Consumer and, more importantly, business confidence is about to hit the skids as the credit event morphs into an economic event. And the private-equity model of leveraging up Corporate America is now in jeopardy. Consider the near-$300-billion backlog of nonsyndicated bridge loans and unsold junk bonds in the pipeline. With interest rates for levered transactions shooting up in recent weeks (if those sort of loans are even available at all), many of these deals are in jeopardy to be completed.

For example, how in the world does J. C. Flowers finance the more than $16 billion of debt to acquire Sallie Mae? The answer? It doesn't, and the company will likely cite the "adverse event" defense in an attempt to walk away from the near-$1-billion breakup fee obligation.

The commercial banking and investment banking industry is over-confident, overleveraged and under-reserved. And so, too, are the dominant investors of the new millennium (i.e., hedge funds and the fund of funds community). Recklessness will be replaced by conservatism in the months (and possibly years) to come.

The government-sponsored entities are still bruising from more than $10 billion of fraud/losses and the associated political fallout. Given the recent histrionics, Fannie Mae and Freddie Mac are likely to stay limited in their ability to support the housing markets outside of conforming mortgages.

What is needed is a more permanent fix, a comprehensive housing Marshall Plan aimed at clearing up the housing mess over the next one to three years. Unsold inventories, stretched affordability and reticent mortgage lenders seem unlikely to be importantly affected by a cut in the fed funds rate.

A full-fledged credit crunch will be the mainstay of housing for at least another year. In periods of stress, fear is amplified. This helps to explain why mortgage rates for jumbo loans (even to creditworthy borrowers) are skyrocketing without a concomitant rise in the general level of interest rates—in fact, the opposite is occurring—and why mortgages are so difficult to come by. The purchase and refinance mortgage market is effectively shut down.

What we have learned from the last month is that in a period in which nearly every asset class rises in unison, disbelief tends to be suspended. When all investors are doing the same thing and making money, the hard questions are never asked because skepticism goes on holiday. And, importantly, when risk is hijacked, models misbehave.

Investors should be looking less closely at put/call ratios and investor sentiment surveys and instead should be reading the investment books that intelligently put credit and speculative market cycles in perspective. They should be reading books like Roger Lowenstein's *When Genius Failed: The Rise and Fall of Long-Term Capital Management*, Charles Mackay's *Extraordinary Popular Delusions & the Madness of Crowds,* and James Grant's *Money of the Mind: Borrowing and Lending in America from the Civil War to Michael Milken.*

In our tightly wound and levered financial system, investors today might be advised to concern themselves with return of capital; it is likely too early to be concerned with return on capital.

With corporate profit margins vulnerable to a regression back to the mean, price-to-earnings multiples still high—until recently the median P/E on the S&P 500 was about 20x—and the many non-investment threats (political and geopolitical), the outlook for equities has turned sour.

We will have vicious rallies in the bear market that I envision, but they will be fake-outs. Buy on the dip? Not with my investors' money. Sell or short the rips, as (you can bet your bottom dollar that) "the sun will *not* come out tomorrow."

Brokers' Profits Riskier

8/14/2007

The longs view the brokerage stocks, at roughly 9× earnings and trading at historically modest premiums to book value, as statistically cheap.

Though the shares are oversold for the short term, both cyclical and secular forces are conspiring to put the brokerage industry's profits in jeopardy. A moderation or contraction in credit products, private equity and hedge fund industry growth, when combined with mark-to-market and prime brokerage liabilities, suggest that the risks of ownership of brokerage stocks outweigh the rewards.

As a result of these conditions, earnings expectations remain far too bold, and company profit warnings are expected to begin posthaste.

The brokerage industry's fortunes are joined at the hip with the bubbles in credit (and derivatives) expansion and private equity, two correlated and intertwined asset classes. Unfortunately, these two bubbles have recently been pierced, marking a clear first-half 2007 peak in industry profitability. (This peak will not likely be reversed for at least another two years.)

Over the past decade, brokerages have feasted at the trough of credit availability. The current credit crunch leading to a temporary cessation of private-equity deals, however, is clearly changing that tailwind into a headwind. Brokerages' returns on investments have been goosed by the rapid growth in all types of fixed-income (and derivative) products, and the cycle's reversal spells lower securitization packaging fees and lower secondary credit market trading volume of the many credit and derivative products.

Moreover, the $8 billion-plus in first-half advisory fees—principally merger and acquisition, which is importantly influenced by private-equity deals—will decline dramatically in 2007's second half and seems destined to moderate further into 2008.

The hedge fund industry's woes (i.e., poor results and disintermediation) will begin to weigh on brokerage industry profits in the current quarter. Similar to the explosion in credit products, the mushrooming of growth of hedge funds has been a key contributor to brokerage profitability.

For example, it has been estimated that nearly one-third of Goldman Sachs' income has been derived from the prime brokerage and trading with hedge funds. In a more choppy and trendless trading environment and a less hospitable credit market, hedge funds will be increasingly vulnerable to a contraction in the number of hedge funds and to a moderation in inflows, or even disintermediation. Prime brokerage and equity and fixed-income trading volume seems destined to moderate in the next few years.

Besides the loss of fee income from lower trading and prime brokerage, the industry is exposed to mark-to-market risks in collateralized debt obligations, continuous linked settlements, mortgage-backed securities and private-equity bridge loans (owned in fee) that it is obligated to fund. Moreover, many brokerage firms' money market funds exposed themselves to subprime packaged products in an attempt to enhance yield. This is the next big shoe to drop.

The proprietary desks at Goldman and at other brokerages have fueled earnings growth; they have been the gravy on top of the main course of credit and hedge funds. Importantly, they have benefited from a simultaneous and steadily trending move upward in almost every asset class (commodities, equities, bonds, and real estate).

The 2002–2006 prop desk profitability will not be replicated in a more uneven market in commodities, equities, and fixed income. (Consider that it is likely that Goldman's prop desks took some of the same risks as its customer-based and broken Alpha Fund.)

To this observer, it is clear that the Democratic tsunami of 2006 will likely be extended into 2008's presidential election. The Democrats' agenda and initiatives are clearly aimed at reducing the schism between America's haves and have-nots. It is being manifested in attempts to change the taxation of private-equity profits and in other challenges to Republican policy.

And in reading between the lines of President Bush and Treasury Secretary Paulson's responses to the credit crisis, it is clear that even the Republican Party is moving toward the Democrats on this issue, as they both seem to be saying that Wall Street and the mortgage-lending communities should take the hits to their income statements without the benefit of government intervention.

Private-equity players such as Blackstone are starting to develop a vertically integrated organization by building up their own in-house M&A capabilities so that they can bypass the brokerages' fee apparatus.

Or as Grandma Koufax used to say, "Dougie, why buy the cow when you can get the milk for free?"

Shaking Off the Credit Nightmare

9/12/2007

Over the past 5 to 10 years, a surplus of cash has led to a shortage of common sense in the credit markets.

The outgrowth has included the following:

- The emergence and funding of thousands of hedge funds, many of them levered;
- The proliferation of junk bonds and leveraged loans;
- The mushrooming of private-equity funds, with attendant high rates of returns;
- The new age of residential real estate, with the emergence of subprime lending, and nonresidential real estate, with cash yields or cap rates falling fast; and
- A soaring and unregulated derivative market characterized by opaque securitizations and investment tranches.

The ability to leverage in all facets of our economy and in financial instruments multiplied in a world where investors overreached for yield. As credit got easier and leverage was ever-more accepted, investors took their collective guards down by accepting abnormally low returns by taking abnormally high risks.

There was, until recently, an absence of risk-awareness, leaving few investors prepared for the morphing of the subprime mess into an early-summer black swan of credit as the aggregate leverage employed in our financial system provided little margin for error. In swift order, concerns of return on capital shifted to return of capital in many asset classes as risk aversion replaced risk taking.

Private equity's merger and acquisition activity stopped on a dime as hundreds of billions of bridge loans became hung and are still unsold by commercial and investment banks. Leveraged "quant" hedge funds reported awful returns, and many have gone or will go out of business.

The lack of availability of mortgage credit hit home sales, and those hedge funds/investment firms/money market funds that owned or inventoried mortgage-backed securities and collateralized debt obligations saw financing pressure intensify due to their dependency on the commercial paper market, and so on and so forth.

Stated simply, anyone who had previously bet that "the good times would (continue to) roll," with the status quo of low volatility and an increasing appetite for risk, suffered (and continues to suffer).

The list of victims of the credit unwind should grow longer in the months ahead.

I think it's unwise to believe that the summer of 2007 is simply a bump in the credit road. The excesses were long in the making, and given their magnitude, the ensuing unwind will not be resolved in short order—regardless of the Fed's actions.

Though it rarely pays to invest for a full-scale meltdown or disaster, at the very least, one should steel oneself for a mean regression in credit that will dampen growth for some time to come as markets typically swing for a longer period of time than is generally expected. They did so on the upside to credit creation, and they will likely do so on the downside of credit contraction.

The pendulum swing back to normalcy in the availability-of-credit market and in credit losses is by no means the only factor contributing to what I believe will be, at the very least, a limited upside to equities.

Away from a deteriorating credit cycle, an all-time high in oil futures, ripping grain prices, a plunging U.S. dollar and the likelihood of political change are some additional headwinds facing investors over the next few months.

My long-held view of a period of blahflation (i.e., uneven and lumpy economic growth that both investment managers and corporate managers will find hard to navigate) remains my investment mantra.

In such a setting, unpredictable roller-coaster moves should be the market's mainstay, not a sustained uptrend.

Blinded by the Derivatives Boom

10/22/2007

We live in a brave new investment world. With the explosion of hedge funds—the newest and most aggressive and dominant investor—riches beyond the highest degree of avarice can be only a year away.

The industries of America's business icons (Ford, Carnegie, Rockefeller, etc.) are no longer the leaders, nor are the kids of the dot-com boom (Bezos, Yang, Case, etc.); today, the masters of the universe are hedge fund managers (Ed Lampert, Stevie Cohen, Paul Tudor Jones, etc.).

And there are many hedgies who are, understandably, wannabes—and who sometimes (arguably) misuse other people's money by worshiping at the altar of momentum in the pursuit of happiness. In the process, negatives are also sometimes ignored or, even worse, dismissed.

As such, in the pursuit of George Soros–like riches, momentum has taken a peculiarly more important role than ever. It has been almost unbridled as investors have often taken abnormal risks for normal returns in the low-interest world of 2000–2007. This is true not only in the equity markets but especially true in the credit markets.

And, as a result, over the past five to seven years, following the stock market bubble of the late 1990s and the easing in monetary policy around the world in the 2000s, we entered a period in which a surplus of cash led to a shortage of good sense in the capital markets. Investors prospered in the ensuing synchronized advance in almost every asset class—equities, private equity, fixed-income, commodities, gold and real estate.

As a consequence of the broad-based financial and economic prosperity, another new paradigm emerged—namely, the notion that a long and uninterrupted economic boom was believed by many to lie ahead. That promise, abetted by the low cost of capital and interest rates, stimulated the straw that stirred the drink of growth and speculation—namely, the financial derivatives markets.

That market mushroomed, in an unquestioning atmosphere in which t's were not crossed and i's were not dotted, to the point where the derivative market eclipsed the actual size of the markets it served. (In a generally unregulated market, this was easy.)

The appetite for derivative products creation grew almost boundlessly and was brought to us by that wonderful brokerage community that brought us the dot-com IPOs and biased research, stoking all asset classes and revving up the real estate market in particular.

Layers of different sorts of assets were securitized by the Street and packaged into one, and the generally unregulated asset-backed securities, collateralized debt obligations, structured investment vehicles and so on were given their birth. The new securities gave way to their cousins; levered hedge fund pools of capital emerged to take advantage of the availability of borrowed money ("the carry trade") supporting those ABC and XYZ assets. They could, in theory, produce alpha (or excess returns).

In time, the need for speed had as its outgrowth the loss of common sense, particularly in lending. Subprime and no-/low-documentation lending gained share of the total mortgage market, and speculators/ investors, drawn to those riches of flipping and day trading homes, began to stretch home prices to levels well beyond affordability and reason.

In time, the unintended consequence was literally a very shaky foundation to the residential real estate market and to the derivative products into which the subprime loans were dumped.

Over in equities, a new breed of stocks (energy, infrastructure, metals, emerging markets, etc.) flourished and took center stage during the synchronized worldwide economic growth boom and personal consumption binge, and these sectors were capable of making the sort of broad and parabolic moves that rivaled the AOLs and Amazons of the last decade.

Meanwhile, other secondary deleterious influences were emerging, too. Although, prima facie, these influences were positive for the markets—that is, as investors easily marginalized the United States' loss of its competitive edge in producing goods for worldwide consumption— they were destined to hold some negative consequences down the road.

The most important was the emergence of India and China as world economic powers and the concomitant dive in the U.S. economy's currency and economic standing, which buoyed the demand for basic materials as those countries' infrastructure developments began to take hold.

That rising demand served to have the adverse consequence of raising commodity prices around the world—and with it, attendant inflation and higher costs for manufacturers. Other influences during this period, such as the U.S.'s reliance on imported oil, sowed the seeds for higher noncore inflation.

In summary, the momentum of asset-price appreciation and the rewards that were a byproduct of those gains have been intoxicating and virtually unquestioned, even as headwinds mounted, in a world in which the dominant investors (hedge fund managers) get a carried participation in their growth.

And so the cocktail of derivatives, leverage and credit creation buoyed consumption in both the industrialized and emerging economies. What has recently intensified the problem is recognition that the derivative markets have bypassed the traditional conduit—namely, the commercial banking system (governed by capital and reserve requirements and audits).

In the absence of oversight, accountability has been weakened and, at times, eliminated. And then, almost overnight, conduits worth tens of billions of dollars are revealed. And so are tens of billions of dollars of debt securities and loans the market is unable to value.

Surprise, surprise. It was especially a surprise to the money center banks, which are at the forefront of the dance of write-offs—a marathon, not a two-minute fast step.

The problem with the aforementioned momentum and the exuberance that follows is that it does not last forever. Equally important (and often enigmatic) is that you never know what should end it—nor what will end it.

Today, there are a number of obvious problems/casualties that suggest that a more problematic and uneven stock market might be surfacing.

I am not saying the end of the world is near. It appears, however, that there are solid reasons to be increasingly concerned.

Most of my concerns are fundamental not technical. I would add, however, that the negativity bubble you read about could not be further from the truth; just look at the *Investors Intelligence* sentiment studies, the high level of margin debt, and/or the consistent raft of uninterrupted bullishness in the media.

Importantly, a confluence of a number of events is occurring at or near the conclusion of mature economies in the United States, Japan, and Europe.

Without further ado, below are some (but not all) of my concerns.

The pile of levered pools of capital that hold the extraordinary (in size and quality) amount of derivative assets are now in disarray. Mark-to-market issues and an acceleration in nonearning assets run deep and are endangering large bodies of market participants and their capital bases.

This includes the domestic money center banks, investment brokerage firms, and, importantly, the unregulated and monstrous special interests vehicles, collateralized debt obligations and levered hedge funds that play in that water.

The destabilizing effect of the impaired financial institutions cannot be understated or underestimated; just ask those investors who have overweighted financials (20% of the S&P) on the basis of value, only to see the sector drop on a daily basis. Banking problems tend to have a long tail and historically are not resolved in a quarter or two (e.g., the less-developed-country debacle, the junk bond fiasco and the early 1990s housing depression, all of which crippled the banking community for years).

Arguably, the problems in housing and leveraged derivatives in 2007 run deeper than the prior adverse cyclical issues. Finally, we should not lose sight of the fact that the money center banks, which are this cycle's (and nearly every cycle's) dolt, entered 2007 ill-equipped to deal with losses. (They were at a historically low level of reserves as a percentage of earning assets.) The banks, too, were momentum players, believing in the new paradigm and believing (incorrectly) in their own credit standards and (lack of?) analysis.

Recognizing that the level of credit losses virtually hit an all-time low in 2006, only to be reversed markedly through the first three quarters of 2007, a likely mean-reversion-of-loss experience augurs poorly for a capital-depleted and off-balance-sheet-dependent U.S. commercial banking system that has experienced a two-decade drop in loan-loss reserves just as the economy matures and the consumer falters.

To an important degree, the Fed has lost control of the capital markets. These are situations that cannot be arrested by somewhat lower interest rates. Many problems reside abroad and outside of the Fed's influence. And much that is domestic lies in unregulated territory.

Capital-weakened financial intermediaries spell an important retardant to the financing of growth. The era of unbridled lending is over. Just try to get a mortgage for a second home. Just try to get a jumbo mortgage. Just try to borrow with little or nothing down—on anything. Or just try to get a nondocumented mortgage loan, motorcycle loan, furniture loan, or automobile loan today.

The next shoe to drop will be the failure of a public homebuilder and a private mortgage insurer. The latter concerns me more than the former, as the markets are not aware of the economic implications.

The domestic, nonexport economy is in recession. The Fed gets it and will likely lower interest rates by another 50 basis points next week. But the adoption of a Japanese solution of supporting bad debts will have, as an adverse consequence, further drops in our currency and competitiveness and higher prices for consumer products.

Based on my recent trip, I can assure you all that the western European economies are falling faster than is generally realized for many of the same influences behind the U.S. weakness.

The dual impact of a higher real rate of inflation and climbing oil prices are a tax on the consumer and will weigh on corporate profit margins, which will be hurt by slowing top-line growth. Importantly, these are occurring at a time in which the consumer's debt load has never been higher based on nearly any measure. With declining home prices, however, the burden on maintaining financial net worth has never been more on the shoulders of stock prices, and that's a slippery slope.

An all-time high in debt service and in the debt load of the consumer and, importantly, the message of the market from the Retail HOLDRs' (RTH) steady demise and the equally steady drop in bond yields are precursors to the obvious slowdown.

The excess capacity in housing holds far-greater economic import than the excess capacity in technology six years ago.

Meager job and income growth and the squeeze on the lower- and middle-income classes at the tail end of a maturing economic cycle bodes especially poorly as the consumer's dependency on asset appreciation (stocks and houses) remains elevated.

The next five years in the capital markets seem destined to be unlike the past five years. The most significant difference is that the egregious use, generation and packaging of debt will not be repeated, and the consequences of that leverage will be adversely seen in areas of the world economies that we had never contemplated.

There will always be winners in the markets, just as there are always losers in the markets. The winners appear to be narrowing in scope, however, representing a classic sign of a maturing equity market. And, in more difficult markets, those babies are often taken out with the bath water.

A Market on the Brink

12/17/2007

The equity market is now on the brink, as rising inflationary pressures and slowing economic growth have increased the possibility of stagflation, a condition that has historically led to a contraction in P/E ratios and poor equity returns.

The core of my concerns remains the U.S. housing market, the future of which is inexorably linked to the current credit bubble's piercing.

Economic bulls have thought that the housing market's problems would be ring-fenced. After all, residential housing activity accounts for only about 6% of GDP—somewhat less than the 12% to GDP role of business fixed investment, which was responsible for a shallow recession five years ago.

Economic bears, such as myself, focus on the more important role of consumer spending, accounting for a record 71% of GDP, and its likely retrenchment, which is the outgrowth of lower home prices (for the first time since the Great Depression), restrictive mortgage credit and the absence of the home as an ATM for consumption.

Importantly, the days (1995–2006) of relying on the asset appreciation of homes and equities as savings conduits have been reversed.

Since the mid–1980s, the Fed has sanctioned bubble after bubble by stimulating and then ignoring them. Fed members have, up until recently, ignored real inflationary pressures, preferring instead to recognize the artificiality of core inflation. In addition, the Fed has ignored the causality between the credit market's earthquake and economic growth.

Frankly, it is almost comical to watch free market capitalists complain that the Fed did not do enough last Tuesday. From my perch, the Fed is acting responsibly; the critics of monetary policy, on the other hand, are acting irresponsibly by asking for higher and higher concentrations of interest rate opiates.

The only hope for our domestic economy is a protracted downturn to break the accumulated economic excesses and the lethal chain of endless asset bubbles of the last two decades.

Morgan Stanley and Merrill Lynch are now calling for a recession.

I will touch on some of the factors that indicate a move toward recessionary conditions.

Growth Concerns

1. The current credit crunch is unlike anything we have seen in modern financial history. The availability of credit will be markedly reduced in the years ahead.
2. Fourth-quarter credit writedowns at the world's major financial institutions remain elevated, and the prospects look no better into early 2008. This permanent loss of shareholders' equity will have negative lending repercussions, and the infusion of high-cost equity at these institutions will do little to encourage the banks to lend more.
3. According to Merrill Lynch, the slope of the yield curve and the value of credit spreads point to a 100% chance of a recession.
4. Last week's trade report indicates that the rate of increase in imports is declining and now stands at the lowest level in over five years.
5. Housing's outlook remains clouded despite the government's patch-work attempt to deal with the reset problems. Publicly held home-builder cancellation rates are almost 50%, and the inventory of unsold homes is at multidecade levels—and it's growing not stabilizing. A 2010 industry recovery could now be in jeopardy.
6. Leading indicators such as durable goods and shipping rates (Baltic Dry Index) point to a domestic economy that might be moving in a southerly route posthaste.
7. Inventory growth is at a standstill, which is an early warning signal that a drop in business fixed investment is the next shoe to drop.
8. After adjusting last week's retail sales figure for the calendar year, food and gasoline inflation produces a lukewarm picture of retail. Same-store comparisons have now been relatively weak for six months, especially at the malls. Target, Sears Holdings, and others have recently exhibited disappointing guidance. Just look at a chart of the Retail HOLDRs (RTH) if you need a harbinger of continued

poor retail news. Last night, *SpendingPulse* provided a decidedly weak outlook for apparel sales during this holiday period.

9. Job growth is punk vs. one year, two years, or three years ago.
10. A Democratic presidential victory, indicated almost universally by the current polls, means higher corporate and individual tax rates, which will provide an unneeded break on business capital expenditures and personal consumption.

Inflation Concerns

1. Even the greatest works of fiction—that is, the Bureau of Labor Statistics' chronicling of headline CPI and producer price index (PPI) rates—are signaling inflation levels not witnessed in several years.
2. Inflation implied in the five-year Treasury inflation-protected securities (TIPS) market has moved up to close to 2.30%, a gain of 0.15% in only a week.
3. Some Fed governors and former Fed Chairman Greenspan are beginning to look at food and energy price inflation as recurring. (I am still looking for a core consumer.)
4. Crude's stubborn rise has resumed as the price of a barrel increased to over $92 last week.
5. The CRB Index rose to within 3% of its all-time high on Friday, as the growth in emerging economies continues to place pressure on commodity prices despite a weakening domestic nonexport economy.

Other Concerns   There are other problems to worry about as well, mostly emanating from the last decade of overconsumption (i.e., the lack of due diligence in lending and the disregard of risk in borrowing) and the structured products that permeate the markets today.

- There is no quick monetary or fiscal relief that will fix the deeply rooted credit problems that have translated into assets of mass destruction orbiting within (and sometimes off) the balance sheets of many of our world's financial institutions.
- The largely unregulated derivative markets, the size and variability (read: mortgage ARMs) of consumer debt, the hedge fund (and fund

of funds) communities and the world's housing markets grew too fast as common sense and due diligence were abandoned in the last credit cycle.

- Markets are beginning to accept the notion that the financial workout will take time and, in all likelihood, can only be relieved by the natural forces of a protracted recession.
- Technical conditions have deteriorated and seem to be confirming the aforementioned fundamental issues.

Too Volatile to Call   The outgrowth of the aforementioned variables suggests that corporate profit (and profit margin), business spending and personal consumption forecasts remain far too optimistic.

There are some offsets to my fundamental concerns, but they are principally statistical and/or sentiment-based. Most prominent:

- A relatively low trailing market P/E multiple;
- Historically low interest rates; and
- Rising acceptance of many of my fears.

It has become increasingly difficult to gain an edge on the short-term market outlook. Quite frankly, anyone who thinks that he has one is lying to himself and to others. The near term is too unpredictable and too volatile and contains too many crosscurrents.

I remain more confident than ever in my intermediate view that a period of uneven and disappointing economic and profit growth augurs for substandard stock market returns.

From that context, the market is on the brink.

Two Solutions to What Ails the Market

1/23/2008

Yesterday, the Fed cut its funds and discount rates by 75 basis points, the largest fed funds cut since October 1984 (when Volcker's Fed bailed out Continental Bank) and the largest discount rate cut since December 1991 (when Greenspan's Fed feared the failure of Citibank).

While the Fed's actions will have a salutary impact on the U.S. banking industry's net interest margins, throwing cheap money into the markets will do nothing to address a dysfunctional credit market and the dangerous systemic risks associated with the monoline insurance industry. Nor will dead-at-birth home mortgage market fiscal policy relief (the Paulson plan) and cheap money provide any meaningful short-term relief to the current housing depression—or to the foreclosed or delinquent mortgages providing much of the current pain.

Policy aimed at providing solutions to the deep-rooted problems of credit and housing must, by definition, be more imaginative—something that, to date, a timid and tardy Fed and executive branch seem unable to grasp. This is particularly true given the already levered state of our maturing economy, in general, and consumers, in particular.

The investment community remains hungry for a solution to the following:

- The imminent business downturn;
- The excessive inventory of unsold homes that has presaged the consumer-led recession; and
- The resolution of the counterparty payment obligations, stemming from the proliferation of structured investment products.

Historically, investors are experienced in economic/profit recessions and their impact on equities in terms of timing, magnitude and duration. Investors' experience with credit dislocations, however, is less clear, and it is the associated counterparty risk fears that seem to be the proximate cause for the pronounced weakness in world equities markets.

Solving the Monoline Insurance Crisis   The source of the financial system's Achilles' heel lies in the monoline insurance companies.

The bond insurers, MBIA and Ambac, were originally formed to insure bond defaults of municipalities. Though there would be a cost to that insurance, the municipalities saved more in interest expenses than the insurance cost as the insurance with which MBIA and Ambac provided those municipal bonds held the same AAA credit rating of the insurers.

So far so good.

But the bond insurers, intoxicated by the profitability of other instruments, diversified away from municipal bonds in the late 1990s into the real estate markets. Unfortunately, at the same time, mortgage originators began to make too many loans to homeowners and commercial owners who could not afford to pay in all but the most optimistic interest rate, economic and real estate assumptions.

And too many of those ill-fated loans were packaged into structured credit products: Residential mortgage-backed securities (RMBSs) and commercial mortgage-backed securities (CMBSs) begat collateralized loan obligations (CLOs) that morphed into collateralized debt obligations (CDOs) and CDOs-squared. In the fullness of time, even more complex instruments—including variable-interest entities, structured investment vehicles and qualified special purpose vehicles—entered the picture.

Many of these securities and the credit default swaps that fortified those credit markets were ultimately insured by the incredibly levered monoline insurance industry. The monoline insurance industry's top line grew exponentially coincident with the boom in structured finance. Wall Street embraced the shares of MBIA and Ambac, and in 2007 the stocks reached record levels.

The risks that MBIA and Ambac were taking on were clearly not recognized by investors or by the companies. Last week, for example, MBIA disclosed that it has over $30 billion of insured mortgage-backed bonds, which includes over $8 billion of CDOs that own other CDOs (i.e., CDO-squareds).

The private mortgage insurance companies such as PMI Group, Radian Group, and MGIC Investment took a similar route and have suffered as delinquencies and foreclosures have spiked.

The solution to the emerging failure of the monoline insurers that hold insurance on homes, mortgages, bonds and derivatives is straightforward but requires bold initiatives and imagination. It is a public/private permutation of a Resolution Trust Corporation–type facility that will somehow acquire the equity of the leading monoline insurers and will, with or without private-sector partners, retain their portfolios of financial asbestos and sell them over time.

This solution will, importantly, serve to retain the AAA ratings of the individual bonds—the U.S. government has the highest bond rating extant—and the portfolios insured by MBIA, Ambac, MGIC Investment, Radian Group and PMI Group. In turn, this would prevent the domino effect of bond and mortgage downgrades and further forced selling and price markdowns at the world's leading financial institutions.

This program will, however, require a degree of financial creativity that has yet to be apparent from a thus far noncreative executive branch nor from an equally timid and tardy Fed, which seems to be behaving like Milton Friedman's "fool in the shower." It will, if enacted, immediately alleviate the concerns with regard to counterparty risks that have cast a pall over the world's equity markets and wreaked havoc with some of the world's largest financial institutions.

I would note that I have already drawn a clear parallel between the S&L crisis of the 1980s and the current credit crisis. So, not surprisingly, the solutions could be similar.

Again, the equities of the monoline insurers have declined by an average in excess of 85% from 2007's highs. The existing industry equity value of under $4 billion is *de minimis* against the size of the problem and low relative to the cost of a government acquisition of these companies.

Suppose the government acquires these companies en masse at a 50% premium to current prices: At a cost of only $6 billion, the U.S. government will own the majority of the companies that insure mortgages, plain vanilla municipal bonds and structured investment vehicles. More importantly, the total value of the toxic portion of the structured products insured that the government would inherit is manageable and modest relative to the cost of acquisition. For example, MBIA, the largest bond insurer has "only" about $30 billion of insured mortgage-backed bonds.

Solving the Housing Depression   The credit problems facing the world started with housing and moved up the credit ladder. For more than a decade, the normal/historical rigor of lending was abandoned in the residential and nonresidential real estate markets. The problems were exacerbated by the ratings agencies, which abrogated their responsibility of providing accurate assessments of risk.

As such, the solution to our currently dysfunctional credit markets lies squarely on the shoulders of housing. Policy must be immediately enacted that provides the framework that will specifically allow homeowners who are now unable to service their mortgages to become current on that payment. We have to stop foreclosures and begin to whittle down the inventory of unsold homes. This will serve to begin to remedy what ails the RMBS, CMBS, CLO, and CDO markets and aid the monoline insurance companies as, in the fullness of time, banking industry financial writedowns could turn into write-ups.

As Punk Ziegel's Dick Bove reminded me over the weekend, the mechanism and solution for turning around the housing markets is already on the books and requires no new legislation: It is Section 8 of the Housing and Community Development Act of 1974.

The solution could take several steps:

1. The homeowner who can't currently service his debt and uses his home as a primary residence would refinance his mortgage at a bank with a new fixed mortgage at a subsidized rate of 1% to 2% guaranteed by the Federal Housing Administration (FHA).
2. The bank providing the new mortgage loan pays off the homeowner's previous mortgage with the proceeds of the new loan.
3. The bank gets the new loan off its balance sheet, allowing it to continue to lend, and sells the FHA-guaranteed mortgage to the Government National Mortgage Association (GNMA) at a modest premium to par, which incorporates a bank profit for originating the mortgage.
4. GNMA takes a sizeable loss—the aggregate cost would be only about $150 billion, which is not bad considering the magnitude of the problem and the solution it could bring—and sells the mortgage at market rates (5.75% to 6.25% fixed mortgage) to Fannie Mae and Freddie Mac.

Voila!

I am absolutely positive that these two solutions would have a momentous, immediate and profound impact on equities. Stocks would literally rise by 10% overnight.

Ready for the Bear Stearns Challenge?

3/17/2008

The sale of Bear Stearns at a price of $2 per share to JPMorgan Chase will have short-term negative reverberations around the world as the credit quality of the leading financial institutions will come into question. While it was an illiquid balance sheet and the lack of institutional

"But these waves we are battling, caused by the biggest hurricane in 20 years, had been pounding the shore relentlessly. Although I wouldn't admit it to George (Soros), it was very clear to me that something unusual was going on."

—Victor Niederhoffer, *The Education of a Speculator*

confidence that brought Bear Stearns down (as panic and margin clerks are today's voting machines), the price tag of $2 per share could raise more questions than it answers. After all, the general impression was that the company's headquarters were worth over $1 billion and that the prime brokerage business was worth at least $2 billion, or 4× last year's cash flow of $550 million. These factors suggest that there must be more to the story.

Nearing a Bottom? It's different this time. Stated simply, the housing and credit bubbles have been unprecedented in scope and duration—and so has the novel and astonishingly large increase in debt (especially of a consumer kind), as all elements of risk control and due diligence were abandoned in the quest for yield enhancement. Meanwhile, amidst these bent secular influences, the reckless proliferation of unregulated and unwieldy derivatives continued, seemingly limited only by the imagination of man.

There is no single policy that will politely eradicate the egregious and out-of-control buildup in debt and the proliferation of unregulated derivatives in our shadow banking system. The natural forces of a business downturn seem the only solution to what ails the equity and credit markets.

Piecemeal and oldfangled policy responses to newfangled problems will no longer work and, in many cases, will lead to adverse and unintended consequences. Deleveraging out of the most recent cycle will be a rabid bitch. There will be many more currency, economic and hedge fund casualties. The Fed can only do so much—any more could jeopardize the world's view of its creditworthiness, which would serve to put even more pressure on our currency.

Stocks are now tumbling back toward the lows established in mid-January.

At the core of the equity market's and economy's problems are:

1. The derivative issue; and
2. The increased role that leverage and credit have had on worldwide economic growth and on speculative activity in all corners of our financial system.

To get some sense of the complexity of the derivative threat, I strongly suggest that subscribers consider reading pages 12–14 of Warren Buffett's 2002 letter to shareholders of Berkshire Hathaway for a fuller understanding. I may continue to be short his stock, but, once again, his wisdom and insights run true—well before the issue became au courant.

> *"Charlie (Munger) and I are of one mind in how we feel about derivatives and the trading activities that go with them: We view them as time bombs, both with the parties that deal with them and the economic system."*
>
> —Warren Buffett, 2002 Berkshire Hathaway letter

Most of the time, it does not pay to invest on the basis of the view that "it's different this time"—after all, multiple sigma events are just that, and, by definition, they occur infrequently. Victor Neiderhoffer, who I quoted at the start of this column, devotes his website, *Daily Speculations*, to applying historic reasoning in order to understand the current state of the market—and how to respond tactically.

Unfortunately, a two- to three-sigma event occurred in the housing market by 2005–2006, when housing affordability was stretched to unfathomable levels, and a black swan event is now in full force in the credit markets, thanks to many of the aforementioned secular developments.

The ultimate question is whether a small cabal of ne'er-do-wells at the banks and brokerages have infected the entire financial system with such large amounts of toxic paper so that traditional analysis of business/market cycles, the stock market's historical role of discounting an economic upturn after a recession and other factors lose their relevance as issues of liquidity, contagion and solvency gain center stage.

If so, the 1930s could be repeated—and so could the Nasdaq's 75% swoon of 2000–2002.

But I doubt it.

Bear Stearns: The Failure of Not Diversifying   History might not repeat itself, but it sure rhymes. Or as Yogi Berra once said, "It's like déjà vu all over again."

The decade of the 1980s gave birth (and death) to an upstart brokerage firm, Drexel Burnham, which created, sold and traded high-yield junk bonds—the turbo debt and foundation of the previous decade of greed. After the insider trading indictment of Drexel's Denis Levine was followed by Michael Milken's demise, junk bond liquidity dried up, recession befell the U.S. economy, and, by 1990, default rates on high-yield debt more than doubled to over 10%. Drexel, forced to buy the bonds of its junk bond clients, depleted its capital and filed bankruptcy.

In much the same manner as Drexel did in the junk bond market, Bear Stearns emerged as a leader in a parabolic growing market—mortgages. As we are now witnessing at Bear Stearns (as we did during the Drexel era), a brokerage's well-being relies, in large measure, on the kindness and confidence of strangers to accept its collateral and accept counterparty risks. That confidence is impaired swiftly when price discovery unveils a diseased portfolio of assets, which is further exacerbated by a high degree of leverage employed. This is especially true when the brokerage's business is not diversified and is narrow in scope—Drexel (junk bonds) and Bear Stearns (mortgages).

Following the Drexel bankruptcy and a real estate-led recession, the equity market regained its footing in late 1990. It didn't take much time—the same could hold true in 2008–2009.

A One-Off Situation   The principal investment question at hand is whether Bear Stearns was a one-off situation—whether its business was so levered and narrow in focus (mortgages) that, with its revenue base collapsing, operating losses would quickly have eaten up its $85-plus per share book value.

I would argue that, in the main, Bear Stearns (similar to Drexel Burnham) is indeed a one-off situation—very similar to when Penn Central shocked the financial system 28 years ago.

While the credit conditions suggest that it is different this time, my investment conclusion is that we are likely at the beginning of the end. As was the case of the Drexel bankruptcy, however, we are not at the end of the current crisis (as the deleveraging process will take more time).

Buying into Panic   The infinity of political, economic and psychological factors that influence the investment mosaic overloads the senses—more so today than in most prior periods.

Following are some (weighing not voting) considerations that could buttress the markets and/or suggest that the current issues could be in the process of being discounted in the markets, forming the basis for the potential for a more constructive view in the days/weeks/months ahead after the panic subsides:

- The curative and clearing process, addressing many of the financial institution's capital issues, has been under way for months. Though the Three Stooges of 21st Century Finance (i.e., the executive branch, Fed and Treasury Department) have been timid and unimaginative, last week's actions by the Fed and the rescue of Bear Stearns are a start in the right direction. And even Bush, Bernanke, and Paulson are beginning to recognize the immediacy of the problems and the need for outside-of-the-box solutions (such as investment banks' access to the discount window).
- We are bottoming not yet recovering in housing. Some permutation of the Barney Frank/FHA proposal seems inevitable, particularly in an election year. Regardless, home prices are finally descending at an accelerating rate, and the more realistic prices will no doubt begin to attract buyers as credit availability stabilizes. I still do not expect a housing recovery until 2010, but the vision of stability is within sight by next year.
- Corporate balance sheets are in great shape and should buttress the current credit issues.
- Sovereign wealth funds remain flush (though relatively uncommitted) and stand ready to commit opportunistically to shore up capital of some of the U.S.'s largest financial institutions.
- The yield curve's steepening could, in the fullness of time, incent banks to take more risks.
- Corporate profit expectations, which were unrealistic until recently, are being pared quickly and are catching up to my downbeat projections. Fourth-quarter 2007 earnings (including financials) dropped by over 20% and are now anticipated to drop by nearly 10% in first quarter 2008. More importantly, unlike prior recessions,

the credit problems are not trickling into other market sectors. Taking out financials, fourth-quarter 2007 profits rose by about 11% and are estimated to expand by about 7% in the current period.

- Over the past 50 years, job losses (a lagging economic indicator) have coincided with economic stabilization and a positive turn for equities. For example, reports of midsummer 1990 job losses were followed by a recovery in stocks that began in October, only two and a half months later. Ten years previous to that recession, stocks stabilized a month before job losses began occurring.

- Stocks have declined by 20% within a six-month period for the fourth time in a quarter of a century (1990, 1998, 2000). In the 12-month period following the 1990 and 1998 corrections, stocks rallied by 34% and 39%, respectively. The 2000 correction, however, begot a full-fledged bear market.

- As I have noted, unlike previous bear markets, equities were not the subject of speculation at the top; commodities, residential and nonresidential real estate, and private equity were.

- If corporate profits avoid a major slide in 2008, stocks are inexpensive relative to short- and long-term interest rates. Indeed, with a seeming bubble in the bond market, a broad reallocation of assets out of fixed income and into equities seems possible.

- With the speed and momentum of the credit crisis intensifying coupled with a continued weakening in economic activity (especially of a job kind), the negativity bubble now appears so inflated that it could be ready to pop. For example, the equity-only put/call reached an all-time high on Friday, the *Investors Intelligence* (of market letters) survey showed bears rising to levels not seen in six years and demonstrated one of the sharpest weekly increases (to 43.6%) in years, the *AAII* survey (of individual investors) came in at the largest level of bears (at 59%) in nearly 20 years, and the consensus survey of futures traders were (only 23% bullish) at the lowest levels seen in over five years. These instances display a negative sentiment extreme rarely seen—even at bear market lows.

Intermediate-Term Opportunities Are Emerging Most should continue to maintain below-average sized positions in order to take advantage of what Mr. Market presents, as an opportunistic approach to trading/investing remains my mantra. Erring on the side of conservatism remains an appropriate strategy for individual investors.

Frankly, it's time to let the market do its talking, not the pundits. My guess is that we will know the answer sooner than later and that the outcome will be more positive than most appear to believe this morning.

I am now making the hardest decision—again, only for the most facile traders/investors—as I am getting more constructive (mildly bullish) on my intermediate-term market outlook on the basis that we are now at the beginning of the end of the credit crisis.

Investors Have Lost Their Innocence

6/23/2008

For over two decades, with the possible exception of the aftermath of the speculative bubble of the late 1990s, equity investors have been comforted by the notion that nearly every dip has been a buying opportunity, as the U.S. economy has typ

> *"I used to be Snow White—but I drifted."*
>
> —Mae West

ically recovered relatively swiftly from economic and credit, geopolitical, systemic and assorted exogenous shocks. And for over two decades, fixed-income investors have been comforted by the tailwind of disinflationary influences, which provided excellent absolute and relative returns in bonds.

Stated simply, stocks and bonds were no-brainers to most. After all, investors' intermediate- to longer-term experiences in the capital markets were universally solid.

The media insisted that investors buy stocks and bonds for the long run as the sky was the limit. Even James Glassman and Kevin Hassett's *Dow 36,000: The New Strategy for Profiting from the Coming Rise in the Stock Market* seemed within reach.

> *"Here's another fine mess you have gotten me into."*
>
> —Ollie (Laurel and Hardy)

As we entered the new millennium, the U.S.'s economic moorings became unanchored as unprecedented low levels of interest rates produced a second wave of speculation in housing and day trading in homes replaced the day trading in stocks. The generous availability of low-cost capital and debt formed the foundation of an unprecedented boom in consumer borrowing, a massive spending binge and a desperate institutional search for yields.

A shadow banking industry emerged as the helter-skelter move into derivative products (which were unregulated, unwieldy and intentionally seemed to circumvent banking capital requirements) rapidly materialized. And an eager hedge fund community joined the happy hour of leveraging while unquestioning investors seemed to sanction the generation of common returns that were produced by taking uncommon risks.

At the epicenter of the leverage was the housing market, which was confidently embraced by owner nonoccupied investors, who stretched housing prices and affordability (home prices divided by household incomes) to unsustainable levels. Expectations of a long, uninterrupted boom in residential real estate became the newest paradigm.

> *"All for one! One for all! Every man for himself!"*
>
> —The Three Stooges: "Restless Knights" (1935)

Generally speaking, the availability of cheap credit made the notion of debt more acceptable and institutionalized leverage, serving to enrich a small cabal of originators who sliced and diced housing mortgage products. With the benefit of hindsight, however, it is clear that the mass marketing of debt began to poison the world's financial system.

That was then and this is now.

Last week, we saw a tsunami of selling, which was in marked contrast to my expectations for some stability.

We now face the aftermath of a bygone credit cycle gone ballistic. The world's financial system is, to some important degree, crippled and in a workout mode now. In all likelihood, the pendulum of credit will swing to an opposite extreme, and availability (the lifeblood of economic growth) will become dear, which is in marked contrast to the free-wheeling decade of the past.

Regardless of short-term direction, we continue to be in an investing environment that argues in favor of erring on the side of conservatism. Most should maintain smaller-than-typical investing/trading positions and should keep conviction on the back burner.

The experience of the past 12 months has exacted a toll on investors. The average household net worth has taken a hit from the depreciation in stock and home values, confidence in our politicians and corporations (especially of a financial kind) have rarely been lower, and, importantly, investors' innocence has been lost.

While, at some point (maybe sooner than later), the equity markets will rally from the current oversold readings, an extended period of investor disinterest and apathy seems likely to follow.

Wall Street Has Sold Out America

9/22/2008

With so many cross-currents, it is hard to have a conviction regarding the short-term trends in the equity market, but it is easy to have an economic view. It is only with the benefit of hindsight that we will know whether Thursday's market lows will hold. At some point after the initial thrust higher from the new SEC ban on short-selling and our government's $700 billion rescue package, hedge fund and mutual fund redemptions and an uncertain profit picture could lead to an absence of buying power and a vulnerable equity market.

I feel safe in saying that the market has limited upside.

The frequency of the recent bailouts—Bear Stearns, Fannie Mae, Freddie Mac, and AIG—and the scale of the policy initiatives needed to plug up a seized credit market underscore the fragility of the world's financial system.

It will take years, not months, for the world's economies and financial system to adjust and normalize to more reasonable levels of risk taking.

There will be more casualties.

Last month, I made an op-ed contribution to the *Financial Times*, entitled "This Blame Game Is Short on Logic," in which I addressed why the blame being thrust upon the short-sellers of financial stocks is misplaced.

Today, I direct my energies toward exposing the true culprit— namely, the Wall Street firms and their executives.

The current nightmare has exposed the players on Wall Street, who, in their packaging, slicing and dicing of mortgage products, have proven themselves to be most destructive.

The words of a mentor of mine ring out loud: As he recently said in an interview, the way to riches on Wall Street is being a part of that community not by investing in Wall Street shares.

Aggressive use of leverage, the risks associated with short-term funding (and long-term lending) of brokerage balance sheets and the subpar level of secular profitability (return on assets) on Wall Street have combined to expose an over-rated industry whose engineers—namely, a small cabal of the firms' traders and executives—bear full responsibility for the credit fiasco and its economic ramifications.

It was an accident waiting to happen.

Wall Street firms take uncommon risk in producing normal returns for their shareholders.

In the process of leveraging up, the financial benefits were bestowed upon a privileged few, but the systemic risks were passed on to the many.

Let me frame the math: A broker/dealer index that includes Bear Stearns, Goldman Sachs, Merrill Lynch and Paine Webber demonstrates that the average return on equity for the industry has averaged 15.9% over the last 23 years. (Return on equity peaked in 2006 to 2007 at about 26% and, taking out the last year, troughed at about 5% in 1990 to 1991). During the same period, leverage has ranged from about 30× to approximately 15×, depending on where the industry is in the cycle.

In other words, Wall Street's return on average assets has averaged roughly 1% over several profit cycles! I don't use leverage in my partnership, but I am certain if I returned only the 1% that Wall Street has achieved on average, I would have very few (if any) investors left.

A "heads I win, tails I win" compensation culture on Wall Street extracts capital and necessitates continued high degrees of leverage and its attendant risk.

Over the past decade, Wall Street's compensation was no longer calculated on multiple years of contribution/performance but rather became a short-term (meritocracy) calculation based on a one-year profit-and-loss statement. The extraordinary compensation at hedge funds, private equity and in the investment and commercial banks became a "heads I win, tails I win" proposition, as a star system emerged that was based on contributions calculated within reduced time frames rather than an assessment of the value-added contributions over lengthy periods of time (subject to high water marks and claw backs).

Importantly, outsized annual compensation packages were typically not retained but rather were allowed to exit Wall Street every year—in part, helping to explain the appreciation in home prices between 1995 and 2005 on the East and West Coasts and the willingness to take risks.

Wall Street has sold out America.

Fortunately, for the U.S. economy, Wall Street will never be the same until these lessons learned above are forgotten.

Welcome to Dystopia

11/3/2008

As investors, we now face a dystopian future.

Our future has been purchased from the past. My vision of the future does not preclude a stable/better stock market over the next several months but it does make the argument that disappointing or substandard investment returns seem the most likely outcome over the next three to five years in an economy that has suffered a massive coronary and that lacks future clarity.

I expressed concerns regarding an imminent depression in housing three years ago, and then, two years ago, I began to cite the alarming use of credit that could have dire consequences. When the excrement started hitting the fan, I wrote that the outlook for the highly levered consumer (and for the economy as a whole) sat squarely on the shoulders of stock prices, which is the other significant household asset that, up to mid-2007, had held price. I opined that a dependency on steady or improving equities was a slippery slope because so much can and usually does go wrong in the stock market.

Unfortunately, my housing, credit, and stock market concerns were realized in the extreme.

Our hand has now been dealt, and it's a weak hand, with reduced promises and possibly even worse investment returns.

As we approach the next decade, our social, economic and political future has materially changed, owing to the deep and muddy financial ditch in which we are now squarely stuck. Moreover, the scope and duration of the financial meltdown has placed our economy well past the tipping point, and it will have an enduring and negative effect. Consider that U.S. home prices have dropped by over $5 trillion in the last one and a half years and that, during the month of October alone, nearly $10 trillion has been lost in the global equity markets. Quite frankly, that ditch is so deep right now that we are in big trouble if our policymakers get it wrong over the next 12 months. My concern is that we might even be in trouble for a long period of time if they get it right.

My secondary (but no less significant) concern, which has an important bearing on stock prices, is that our economic future can be seen with far less clarity than in past cycles when the United States has ventured out of recession. That future has been purchased by our past policies of overindulgence, disregard for risk, and lack of forethought.

Not surprisingly, the economic perma-bulls prefer dreams of the future to the history of the past, but the fault I see in using previous recessionary examples is that history (and those charts) fails to recognize that it is different this time on so many fronts but particularly as it relates to the accumulation of debt and credit. By contrast, the realists see the aforementioned past policies and argue (perhaps more correctly) that the past is gone, the present is full of confusion and that the future scares the hell out of them.

For decades, U.S. investors have seen the hereafter as an expected gift, but, in reality, the future is earned—it is based on achievement. Unfortunately, never has a generation spent so much of our children's wealth in such a short period of time with so little to show for it.

There will be broad-based social, political, credit, economic and stock market ramifications from the economic and market jolts of the last 18 months, some of which are enumerated below. Few of these are P/E-multiple-elevating developments, and the emerging trends (if accurate) will likely produce an uncertainty of outcomes that make it difficult to glibly conclude that the market's dramatic decline has now been fully discounted and almost certainly questions the market's intermediate-term upside.

Social Change

- We face a changing social fabric and a behavioral revolution. The financial meltdown and wealth destruction is not just a financial event; it will contribute to cultural and social change. New trends will emerge; most will downsize. For example, young adults will likely be living with their parents for longer periods of time, and consumers will be trading down from well-known (and more expensive) branded products to cheaper generics. Generally speaking, future expectations of all sorts will be reduced, and learning to live within one's means will become increasingly commonplace.

- Our educational system faces upheaval. Expensive private institutions will face a sharp falloff in admissions, while state institutions will flourish and admissions will grow more competitive. Losses in university endowments will result in larger classrooms and layoffs in personnel.
- Municipalities will offer fewer services, and our military will be downsized. Sanitation, post office, fire, police departments and our armed forces will contract in size, and less will be expected of them.
- Regulatory reforms will multiply. As a consequence of the most recent period of self-dealing and of unregulated, unbridled and often senseless growth (particularly through the use of credit), the laissez faire attitudes of the past are now over. The pendulum of regulation, similar to the pendulum of credit, will become exaggerated. Our society and our corporations will become burdened with a quantum increase in the cost of regulation that will not only impede profits but could also stifle creativity.

Political Change

- Populism will be on the rise. It is said that when the individual feels, the community reels. An understandable distrust toward the authority of our government and our economic institutions (especially of a financial industry kind) will create a fundamental backlash that favors the consumer over the corporation. This will have a significant impact on corporate tax rates (higher) and middle-class tax rates (lower).
- Isolationism will also be on the rise. Nicholas Kristof's Sunday *New York Times* op-ed column discusses how the Bush administration has "wrenched the U.S. out of the international community." I am afraid (for now) that the economic woes are simply too grand and Kristof is too optimistic about the United States rejoining the world community.

The United States must turn inward over the next few years, as dealing with our domestic financial problems will trump other priorities.

- A more youthful Democratic Party will gain and remain in power. The Congress will lean decidedly more Democratic, as there is growing recognition that our economic burden to finance our current tax cuts, war and bailouts will be immense and that the obligation and solution lies squarely on the shoulders of our children and our children's children. Younger voters will turn out in record droves in the years to come, as that constituency will seek greater representation, serving to turn our political leadership markedly more youthful and more liberal in its conscience.

Economic Change

- Credit will be dear for years. The pendulum of credit, which moved to the extreme (read: plentiful) prior to the recent travails has, not surprisingly, moved toward the opposite end of the scale (read: unavailable). When one combines the still-capital short position of the banking industry with a deteriorating loan-loss cycle that stems from the economic downturn, the suggestion is that credit will be dispensed gingerly for some time to come. Lending institutions will err on the side of prudence and conservatism in their pursuit of reaccumulating internally generated capital, leaving a recovery in credit availability several years away as well.
- Retail sales will remain sickly for an extended period. With stock and home prices dramatically lower, personal consumption will be diminished vis-à-vis past recovery cycles as personal savings rise back to historic levels.
- After stabilizing in 2010, annual home price increases will be modest and locked in a decade-long range. Deflationary forces will stay in place for a longer period than the consensus currently anticipates.
- Visibility of future corporate profit growth will be lost. Economic bulls, many of whom missed the unexpected drop in corporate profits that is now so apparent, still feel confident that S&P 500 earnings will trough at about $70 next year. Unfortunately, there is no clarity to that number; more important, there is even less clarity beyond 2009.

In the absence of hard and predictable corporate profit figures, it is very hard to have a sense of whether the market has discounted next year's profits, so volatility will likely continue to be high. The softness and lack of clarity to earnings and continued high stock market volatility remain P/E-diminishing developments.

Investment Change

- Investor disinterest and apathy lie ahead. As I have feared, the consequences of the credit morass (among other things) will likely be a growing distrust of Wall Street and of politicians, as well as a nearly unprecedented apathy and disinterest in investing, which could extend for years. For some time to come, inflows into mutual and hedge funds will no longer provide support to equities; in the absence of evidence of a strong marginal stock buyer, a period of substandard investment returns (at best) seems the most likely outcome.
- Wall Street and private equity will never be the same. Stock commissions will drop, capital market activity and volume will moderate in a secular sense, Wall Street employment will be cut to the bone (and will not rise for years), and industry compensation will be a shadow compared to the "good old days." Business school classes will drop materially in size as law schools and medical schools undergo a renaissance.
- The dominant investor of the new millennium will become less dominant. The hedge fund industry shake-out has only just begun. Fee discounting will become prevalent. The fund of funds industry will be nearly extinguished over the next few years, as additional layers of fees are almost impossible to rationalize during an extended period of historically weak investment returns.
- Investment conservatism will replace the hedge fund go-to strategies. Fixed-income strategies and new, more conservative investment vehicles will likely gain popularity.

In summary, my vision of the next three to five years is one of less economic clarity, more economic conservatism, rising populism, a more youthful government and muted investment expectations and returns.

It is a vision not of utopia but of dystopia.

Harder than the Average Bear

12/2/2008

The natural rhythm of the markets has been disrupted since, sometime in September 2008, investors came to the realization that the current economic downturn was not going to be of a garden variety.

It was at that point in time that the decline in equities gained speed in the face of the failure of Lehman Brothers, along with growing recognition of an abrupt deterioration in business activity around the world. As a result of Lehman's demise and the accelerating economic downturn, credit eroded, junk bond spreads widened further, and the price of bank loans plummeted.

The magnitude of policy relief that has been heaped on our current condition in order to reinflate the domestic economy underscores how different it was this time, as we attempted to deflate out of the previous credit binge.

In the old days, recessions were anticipated by the stock market. But in late 2008, as George Soros related in *The Alchemy of Finance*, market participants seem to be shaping the slope of economic activity as the decline in equities is serving to deepen the downturn. Indeed, the swift drop in stock prices on top (and into a continuation) of lower nationwide home prices has recently fed a negative feedback loop as the acceleration has had a materially adverse impact on consumer and business confidence. As a result, the outlook for personal consumption expenditures and business fixed equipment has dimmed over the balance of 2008 and into next year.

Though share prices seemingly discount anything short of a Great Recession, visibility remains ever more clouded and a wide range of S&P 500 profit outcomes from 2009 to 2011 seems, to this observer, to be an important contributor to an unprecedented degree of volatility not seen in our professional careers. And that volatility is being exaggerated by a trigger-happy and rapidly consolidating hedge fund community that seems to accentuate both upside and downside market movements.

A description of what has happened in the past and what is now happening is easy; how to respond tactically and how to adopt a reasonably accurate vision of the future are much more difficult.

Positives and Negatives   The largest positive is that most now believe that the Fed and Treasury are pushing on a string as investment, economic and profit expectations have begun to adjust to reality:

- The Cassandras—Nouriel Roubini has guest hosted CNBC's *Squawk Box* on three occasions in the past six weeks and is now touring the globe to standing-room-only crowds as an economic consultant!—are now out in force.
- The discredited Pollyannas—even "Steady Eddy" Ken Fischer and many other perma-bull managers are suffering and are getting redeemed!—are in hiding, however, nowhere to be seen, and, they, too, have turned their back to Goldilocks.

The largest negative is that stocks are still reacting poorly to weakening results, and those negative but lagging fundamentals will likely be with us for some time to come.

We all recognize that, in the fullness of time, an unprecedented amount of stimulus will, well, stimulate! The only question is when.

My view is that it is simply too hard to have conviction until we meet the following conditions:

- Stability returns to the hedge fund community, as redemptions slow down, some large hedge funds fail, and money is recirculated to other investment managers.
- The slope of the domestic economy's downturn is better understood, as the possible recovery is seen with better clarity.
- The volatility in the capital markets diminishes.

Until the above three conditions get resolved, we are likely to be stuck in a broad trading range of plus/minus 10% to 15% for the short term.

We remain in an exquisite backdrop for traders but a difficult and frustrating setting for investors, in which it may be too late to sell and too early to invest for the long term.

At some time in the future (possibly sooner than later), a historic buy-and-hold opportunity will be in front of us.

The current test for investors is to remain solvent until that time is near.

Recovery

Introduction

The lesson of history is that you do not get a sustained economic recovery as long as the financial system is in crisis.

—Ben Bernanke

While vocally bearish in 2007–2008, I changed my ursine view in the first week of March 2009, when, on CNBC and in pages of the *Wall Street Journal, Bloomberg,* and, of course, *TheStreet,* I called for a "generational bottom" for the U.S. stock market.

In this chapter, I explain the metrics I observed to make the call that we will never again see the S&P 500 sell at 666 in our lifetimes—a call I still believe in.

It is important to recognize, however, that the domestic economic recovery has been lopsided. A top-heavy and uneven recovery, induced by monetary policy's heavy hand of inflating asset prices and balance sheet wealth, has failed to promote real income growth and holds the potential for social, political and other risks never seen in our lifetime.

While monetary policy has been good for Wall Street, it has not trickled down to the benefit of Main Street. Consequently, the future remains uncertain and, in the fullness of time, possibly problematic to stock valuations down the road.

Finally, after a near trebling in the S&P 500, I advise why we should never lose sight that genius is a rising market and that in a bull market, it is often indistinguishable between being lucky and being smart.

The Parable of the Mustard Seed

12/4/2008

"It is like a grain of mustard seed, which a man took, and cast into his garden; and it grew, and waxed a great tree; and the fowls of the air lodged in the branches of it."

—Luke 13:18–19

Larry Kudlow is fond of bringing the financial world's attention to the mustard seed parable, which, in a religious context, is often interpreted as being a prediction of Christianity's growth around the world. Jesus compares the kingdom of heaven to a mustard seed. The parable is that mustard is the least among seed, yet grows to become a huge mustard plant that provides shelter for many birds.

In an economic context, Larry believes the mustard seed parable has some merit, as the "shock and awe" from the recent policy moves geared toward stimulating the economy could sow some good economic results in 2009. Given the painful market action over the past six months and the extremely negative sentiment, which seems almost antithetical to investors' enthusiasm a year ago, Larry feels a rich investment harvest might be reaped.

While Larry's optimism has some virtue, I have argued that we are not in a garden-variety business/market cycle, as the wealth destruction of lower home and stock prices will retard growth—similar to the notion held by some religious scholars that the birds in the mustard seed parable represent an undesirable presence capable of eating up any new seeds the farmer sows in his field and preventing the trees (Christianity and the stock market) from bearing fruit.

Moreover, I have opined that it is hard to have conviction until:

- Stability returns to the hedge fund community, as redemptions slow down, some large hedge funds fail, and the money is recirculated to other investment managers;
- The slope of the domestic economy's downturn is better understood, as the possible recovery is seen with better clarity;
- Credit improves;
- Stocks react more positively to poor news; and
- The volatility in the capital market diminishes.

I recognize that my concerns, which are currently weighing on our credit and investment markets and on the world's real economies, have now been fully embraced by the media and by nearly every investor and strategist and that, to some degree, stocks have reflected the gross economic and credit realities. This is in marked contrast with conditions a year, six months, or even three months ago, when I saw a plethora of short opportunities framed in a variant and negative view.

Time and (lower stock) prices cure all, so even before credit improves, hedge fund redemptions decelerate, and signs emerge that the current forceful policy measures are remedying the downside economic spiral and an engaged President-elect surrounded by an experienced and intellectually gifted corps of advisers enacts his own policies, the market's downside influences could recede as stock prices might advance well before the all-clear economic signal is embraced.

Given the above, my investment blueprint over the next several months is taking a more positive tint. We seem to be moving toward the following paradox:

1. Investments that are deemed to be safe (e.g., 10-year notes, 30-year bonds) are increasingly unsafe, and I am shorting.
2. Investments that are deemed to be risky (e.g., selected equities) are becoming safer, and I am buying them (gingerly, for now).

I have concluded that we have likely seen the year's lows, but the harder issue is trying to define the slope of the recovery in stocks. Given the

headwinds (especially in credit), it should be frustratingly modest at first—
we still seem to be in a very broad trading range—but the trajectory will
hopefully gain steam as the year progresses and clarity regarding the depth/
duration of the recession develops, the hedge fund redemption issue is left
behind us and stocks increasingly react more positively to bad news.

Already some of Larry's mustard seeds are being ignored. For
instance, take a look at housing, in which a combination of targeted
and aggressive policy efforts aimed at reviving this beaten down sector of
the economy, a marked reduction in home mortgage rates, better
affordability and an extended period of low production of new homes
(vis-à-vis population and household formation growth) argue that the
balance between housing supply and demand might move closer in
balance earlier than expected.

In conclusion, I am not yet in a rush to buy aggressively, but I am
increasingly confident that investments made in the next three to six
months will look terrific one to two years from now.

I am also convinced that the current negative groupthink on the part
of the hedge fund community (and others), which is manifest by their
current low invested positions amid fear of further investment losses and
additional redemptions, will cause them to miss the bulk of the early
advance in equities when it comes. As such, the potential is for hedge
funds to become the new marginal buyer that is capable of extending the
market's initial gains in 2009.

Shopping lists should now be made for both holiday gifts and for
stocks, as they are both being discounted.

On the Road to Recovery

12/8/2008

I am a realist. We are in difficult and challenging times.

I have learned over the course of my investment career that the quest
for delivering superior investment performance has grown more complicated, as it is accompanied by demands for permanent flexibility, a
more balanced view and, usually, a less extreme portfolio construction. I
am also of the belief that neither Pollyannas nor Cassandras are stock
market moneymakers; they are, more typically, only attention getters.

While I fully recognize that the road back to economic growth and stock market repair will not be orderly—it will be filled with potholes and detours—a number of factors are now conspiring to improve the chances for business stability and for a recovery in the equity markets. From my perch, some of these include:

- *We are on the cusp of a more engaged leadership.* It will take unconventional and bold remedies to solve unprecedented and complex economic and credit issues. It now appears that an engaged and new incoming administration recognizes the severity of our economic problems, however, and the new team is composed of a group of outstanding and intellectual leaders with practical experience in overcoming past difficult periods of crisis. In my view, President-elect Obama's appointees form the basis for high-quality policy responses capable of addressing our uncertain economic future.

- *Massive stimulation now appears on the way.* A more ambitious and focused stimulus agenda is forthcoming, as a new administration better understands the slope of the domestic economy's downturn. As such, a possible recovery can be forecast with better clarity and higher probabilities. By contrast, the markets remain in disbelief, as a possible buying climax in Treasuries and a likely selling climax in commodities (such as oil) seem to be signaling an extreme view that the economic spiral will never end. As the lynx-eyed Bob Farrell commented to me over the weekend, the recent 20-day rate of change in Treasury yields, which has fallen more than 30%, the fastest levels since 1980, is a classic indication of prevailing and extreme economic pessimism. Each time the rate of change has fallen more than 15%, yields have rallied hard, usually implying improved business conditions. Another manifestation of economic bearishness is seen in the price of crude oil, which dropped by over 70% from its 2008 high and, in only the past week, has dropped by more than 25%, the largest weekly drop since the 29% drop in 1991 when U.S. forces invaded Kuwait at the end of Desert Storm.

- *The housing industry's problems are finally being addressed.* As I have long argued, housing has been at the epicenter of the economy and credit market's woes. Fortunately, a combination of targeted and aggressive policy efforts aimed at reviving this beaten-down sector of the economy, a marked reduction in home mortgage rates, better affordability and an extended period of low production of new homes (vis-à-vis population and household formation growth) argue that the balance between housing supply and demand might move closer in balance earlier than is now generally expected.

- *We have reached an extreme level of negative investment sentiment.* High bullish sentiment on fixed income is being matched by high bearish sentiment in stocks. According to *Investors Intelligence*, equity bulls now stand at only 23%, a 20-year low. By contrast, *Market Vane's* survey on Treasuries was at a remarkably high 89% bullish last week. Not surprisingly (considering the backdrop), investor expectations for the U.S. stock market have been ratcheted down week after week. Hedge fund net invested positions are at low levels not seen since 2002, the disintermediation of mutual funds is now reflected in record-level individual cash positions, and the flight out of hedge funds has continued apace, but these are rearview conditions. During past cyclical market lows and economic troughs, fear, panic and sizeable job losses have been essential ingredients to recovery.

- *Stocks have shown early signs of reacting more positively to bad news.* The National Bureau of Economic Research's rearview recognition of a one-year-old recession should encourage investors. Stocks anticipate fundamentals, and stocks typically mount a 25% rise before recession's end. Already a number of stocks have moved smartly higher in the face of negative news, especially in sectors that typically presage improvement in credit and of the overall stock market. In banking, JPMorgan Chase; in real estate investment trusts, Vornado Realty Trust, Boston Properties, and SL Green Realty; and in asset managers, AllianceBernstein and T. Rowe Price.

- *Energy and commodities prices have plummeted.* While carrying negative implications for the current economic downturn, the remarkable drop in stuff also holds positive implications for the consumer (serving as a tax cut) and for corporate profit margins.

- *The marginal buyer has emerged.* I have long been concerned about where marginal demand for stocks would arise. The answer might be the hedge fund industry, which is poorly positioned for an advancing market at present, as the market's extreme volatility, large investment losses and the specter of redemptions have resulted in a mass exodus of hedge fund cash to the sidelines.

- *Market volatility might soon diminish.* Looking into early 2009, some stability could return to the hedge fund community, as redemptions slow down, some large hedge funds fail (and close their doors at year-end), money is recirculated to other investment managers and the rate of decline in economic activity moderates (as the stimulus takes hold).

With so many extreme sentiment readings (and a steepening in the price and yield declines) in commodities and fixed income, coupled with more substantive/coherent policy measures (and a more engaged leadership) and a market that has begun to respond more positively to bad news, an important change in stock market conditions could be imminent just when most investors have turned to the sidelines.

Color me more bullish, as it is my view that in the fullness of time, policy, sentiment, and value will trump corporate profit and credit issues.

Fear and Loathing on Wall Street

2/17/2009

Though initially criticized, Hunter S. Thompson's *Fear and Loathing in Las Vegas* has become required reading for students of American literature. *Rolling Stone* magazine's literary critic, Mikal Gilmore, wrote that the book "peers into the best and worst mysteries of the American heart" and that the author "sought to understand how the American dream had turned a gun on itself." The critic went on to write that "the fear and loathing Hunter S. Thompson was writing about—a dread of both interior demons and the psychic landscape of the nation around him—wasn't merely his own; he was also giving voice to the mindset of a generation that had held high ideals and was now crashing hard against the walls of American reality."

It all sounds familiar, doesn't it?

The "wave speech" at the end of Thompson's eighth chapter is considered by many to have most completely captured

> "I hate to say this, but this place is getting to me. I think I'm getting the Fear."
>
> —Dr. Gonzo in Hunter S. Thompson's *Fear and Loathing in Las Vegas*

the hippie zeitgeist of the 1960s. It is a metaphor for our economic state as well.

> There was madness in any direction, at any hour. If not across the Bay, then up the Golden Gate or down 101 to Los Altos or La Honda. . . . You could strike sparks anywhere. There was a fantastic universal sense that whatever we were doing was right, that we were winning. . . . And that, I think, was the handle—that sense of inevitable victory over the forces of Old and Evil. Not in any mean or military sense; we didn't need that. Our energy would simply prevail. There was no point in fighting—on our side or theirs. We had all the momentum; we were riding the crest of a high and beautiful wave. . . . So now, less than five years later, you can go up on a steep hill in Las Vegas and look West, and with the right kind of eyes you can almost see the high-water mark—that place where the wave finally broke and rolled back.
>
> —Hunter S. Thompson, *Fear and Loathing in Las Vegas*, "The Wave Speech"

Just as *Fear and Loathing in Las Vegas* became a benchmark in American literature about U.S. society in the 1960s and the early 1970s, the melodrama of the past five years is becoming a seminal economic and investment experience.

> "Sometimes I lie awake at night, and I ask, 'Where have I gone wrong?' Then a voice says to me, 'This is going to take more than one night.'"
>
> —Charles M. Schulz

Parallels can easily be drawn between the drug addictions in Hunter S. Thompson's book and the credit addictions in the new millennium, and the withdrawal from the most recent dependency on debt has had unrivaled implications. The unwind will continue to be painful for some time to come.

It took a while for our country to turn around from the 1960s. There are still those who have not left the decade of peace and love. Similarly, it will likely take time for our country to turn around from the abuse of credit and the consumption binge experienced in the 2000–2006 interim interval.

A moment last Monday, just after noon, in Manhattan. . . . I'm in the 90s on Fifth heading south, enjoying the broad avenue, the trees, the wide cobblestone walkway that rings Central Park. Suddenly I realize: Something's odd here. Something's strange. It's quiet. I can hear each car go by. The traffic's not an indistinct roar. The sidewalks aren't full, as they normally are. It's like a holiday, but it's not, it's the middle of a business day in February. I thought back to two weeks before when a friend and I zoomed down Park Avenue at evening rush hour in what should have been bumper-to-bumper traffic.

This is New York five months into hard times.

One senses it, for the first time: a shift in energy. Something new has taken hold, a new air of peace, perhaps, or tentativeness. The old hustle and bustle, the wild and daily assertion of dynamism, is calmed. . . .

Any great nation would worry at closed-up shops and a professional governing class that doesn't have a clue what to do. But a great nation that fears, deep down, that it may be becoming more Suley than Sully—that nation will enter a true depression.

> —Peggy Noonan, *Wall Street Journal* op-ed,
> "Is 'Octomom' America's Future?"

Nowadays, investors lead lives of noisy desperation.
The fear and loathing is palpable:

- It is palpable every time investors read their monthly brokerage, hedge fund and 401(k) statements.
- It is palpable in the loss of wealth in our educational institutions, corporate pension plans and endowments.
- It is palpable in the lost liquidity and lost confidence in the gating of some hedge fund investments.
- It is palpable in the obliteration of value in private equity.

Fear and loathing also abounds from the transparency and partisanship of our all-too-visible political process, which has served to further reinforce a negative feedback loop.

The headwinds working against an economic resolution this year seem cast in stone. Those few who still express confidence in a second-half recovery, similar to the characters Raoul Duke and Dr. Gonzo in *Fear*

And I don't know about you, but I've got a sick feeling in the pit of my stomach—a feeling that America just isn't rising to the greatest economic challenge in 70 years. The best may not lack all conviction, but they seem alarmingly willing to settle for half-measures. And the worst are, as ever, full of passionate intensity, oblivious to the grotesque failure of their doctrine in practice.

—Paul Krugman,
New York Times
op-ed, "Failure to Rise"

and Loathing in Las Vegas, are either taking too many drugs or are oblivious to the clogged transmission of credit, the steady drop in business and investor confidence and the general waning of business activity.

There are significant positive developments amid the tumult that are currently being ignored.

Investor return and economic expectations have been ratcheted down as business activity is reset lower. As illustrated above, even Peggy Noonan's normally optimistic prose in *WSJ* has disappeared; she is sounding almost Krugman-esque in the face of the current economic malaise. Today, there is almost unanimity that neither an aggressive monetary policy nor a massive stimulus program nor an unprecedented and large bank rescue plan will have any possibility of success. Another positive. And, with the exception of the few remaining perma-bulls, most now appreciate that the consumer is cooked and that the great unwind of credit will be a headwind measuring in years not months.

Some more optimistic signs can be seen in sentiment such as the growing popularity of Cassandras as well as the better price action of certain segments of the market. (Markets always lead fundamentals.) The emergence of this sort of performance is a positive market tell and is a growing contrast to the uniform and correlated drop in almost every asset class during the second half of 2008.

In and of itself, an extremely negative sentiment cannot be expected to be an overriding tailwind in a backdrop of uncertainty. Despite the poor market landscape, however, there are some early signs of stability/ revival, even before the stimulus is put in place. They are, admittedly, tentative signs but positive signs nonetheless.

Here is a partial checklist of signs that I and others are looking for (and their status in italics) as indications for a more favorable stock market:

- Bank balance sheets must be recapitalized. *We await a bank rescue package in the week ahead.*
- Bank lending must be restored. *Bank lending standards remain tight. For now, we are in a liquidity trap.*
- Financial stocks' performance must improve. *We are not yet there. Financials' performance is still dreck.*
- Commodity prices must rise as confirmation of worldwide economic growth. *There has been some recent evidence of higher commodities, but it's still inconclusive.*
- Credit spreads and credit availability must improve. *While credit spreads are improving, the yield curve is rising and interest rates have rebounded, the transmission of credit remains poor. Time will tell whether monetary and fiscal policies will serve to unclog credit.*
- We need evidence of a bottom in the economy, housing markets and housing prices. *The economy's downturn continues apace. Months of inventory of unsold homes are declining and so are mortgage rates, but home prices have yet to stabilize despite an improvement in affordability indices.*
- We also need evidence of more favorable reactions to disappointing earnings and weak guidance. *We are not yet there, but this will tell us a lot about the state of the stock market's discounting process.*
- Emerging markets must improve. *China's economy (PMI and retail sales) and the performance of its year-to-date stock market have turned decidedly more constructive.*
- Market volatility must decline. *The world's stock markets remain more volatile than a Mexican jumping bean.*
- Hedge fund and mutual fund redemptions must ease. *While I am comfortable in writing that most of the forced redemptions have likely passed, we will find out more over the next few months. Regardless, the disintermediation and disarray of hedge funds and fund of funds have a ways to go.*
- A marginal buyer must emerge. *Pension funds seem to be the likely marginal buyer as they reallocate out of fixed income into equities, but we have not yet seen the emergence of this trend.*

While sentiment and valuation are not the sine qua non in determining share prices, it should be underscored that the current bear market is the second-worst in history, both in terms of price decline and the erosion in price-to-earnings (P/E) multiples. This means that embedded expectations are low. While sentiment, as measured by hedge fund and mutual fund redemptions, remains acutely negative, individual, sovereign and institutional liquidity remains abundant and is growing swiftly.

On multiple fronts, equities appear to have incorporated the bad news and are undervalued both absolutely and relative to fixed income:

"The most common cause of low prices is pessimism. We want to do business in such an environment, not because we like pessimism but because we like the prices it produces. It's optimism that is the enemy of the rational buyer. None of this means, however, that a business or stock is an intelligent purchase simply because it is unpopular; a contrarian approach is just as foolish as a follow-the-crowd strategy. What's required is thinking rather than polling."

—Warren Buffett

1. The risk premium, the market's earnings yield less the risk-free rate of return, is substantially above the long-term average reading.

2. Using reasonably conservative assumptions (most importantly, a near 50% peak-to-trough earnings decline, which is over 3× the drop in an average recession), the market has discounted 2009 S&P 500 earnings of about $47.

3. Valuations are low vis-à-vis a decelerating (and near-zero) rate of inflation. Indeed, the current market multiple is consistent with a 6% rate of inflation.

4. Stock prices as a percentage of replacement book value stand at 1×, well below the 1.4× long-term average.

5. The market capitalization of U.S. stocks vs. stated gross domestic product (GDP) has dropped dramatically, to about 80%, now at the long-term average. Warren Buffett was recently interviewed in *Fortune* magazine and observed that this ratio was evidence that stocks have become attractive.

6. The 10-year rolling annualized return of the S&P is at its lowest level in nearly

75 years, having recently broken below the levels achieved in the late 1930s and mid-1970s.

7. A record percentage of companies have dividend yields that are greater than the yield on the 10-year U.S. note. At 46% of the companies, that is over 4× higher than in 2002 and compares against only 5% on average over the last 30 years.

Today's growing investor disaffection and apathy with regard to equities has, at its root, Hunter S. Thompson's fear and loathing. Both have given voice to the mind-set of a generation that had held high ideals and, as it relates to stocks in 2009, is now crashing hard against the walls of American reality in credit and finance.

If it all sounds familiar, it is, as both the 1960s and the 2000s were the decades of dopes.

After the speculative boom of the 1960s, the U.S. stock market fell into the early 1970s, but the extension of the popularity of the "Nifty Fifty" kept the market in gear for a few more years. After the Nifty Fifty bust in 1973–1974, the markets resumed a modest ascent in 1975, which petered out two years later. By 1982, 12 years after the close of the 1960s, the great bull market of the modern era began, despite loud chants that "the sky was falling" by the increasingly populated community of Cassandras.

> *"My pessimism goes to the point of suspecting the sincerity of the pessimists."*
>
> —Edmond Rostand

Most investors entered 2008 with a far too constructive market and economic view. I did not, and it seems as though this greybeard's historical perspective was precise, as most of my concerns were realized. To be honest, most of my concerns have been eclipsed in recent months.

As we move into the midway point of the second month of 2009, market participants generally now have the opposite point of view of 14 months ago. I respect the fear and loathing, but I do not share the prevailing pessimistic view that John Mauldin substantiates in his brilliant and peripatetic "Thoughts from the Frontline" this week, as he argues that world trade is falling off the cliff, the magnitude of the world's bank write-offs are daunting and unknown, leading economic indicators are deteriorating, job losses are intensifying, S&P earnings are being adjusted downward to unfathomable levels, Secretary Geithner's bank rescue package is vague and that the stimulus program might only be a Band-Aid over a broadening set of problems.

It's downright, well, maudlin.

Today, the doomsayers are far more visible compared to after the dissolution of the Nifty Fifty advance in the 1970s, but my sense is that we don't have to wait anywhere near seven years (2016) for a resumption of a new bull market, as policy is going to be aggressive and immediate.

Arguably, John Mauldin's (and others') issues are now being incorporated into market expectations.

My economic view remains materially unchanged. We are likely in the Great Decession, somewhere in between a garden-variety recession and the Great Depression of the 1930s. We will, in the months ahead, continue to find out the many whom have been swimming naked as the tide goes out. And to continue with the Oracle of Omaha's references, it might be too early to be greedy when others are fearful, but I suspect that we are not far off from there.

The average recession in modern financial history has lasted 10 and a half months. The longest recession was between 1929 and 1933—real GDP dropped by over 25%!—and lasted 43 months; the shortest (1980) lasted only 6 months. I expect the Great Decession, which began in November/December 2007, to end in early 2010, or about 12 months from now. If accurate, the current recession will be the second worst on record, having lasted about 27 months.

It's so bad out there that some are questioning whether the world's economies will ever recover from the current mess. In doing so, they seem to be ignoring not only an emerging valuation opportunity but a number of events that should conspire to bring us out of the abyss, including (but not solely) the magnitude of the monetary and fiscal stimulation, the consumer tax cut and corporations' margin benefit from lower commodities (particularly of an energy kind), improving investor liquidity, the lowered cost of credit and a sentiment extreme of negativity.

At the risk of going Gonzo or garnering allegations that I could now be suffering from a hallucinogenic flashback from the 1960s, starting to average into the U.S. stock market could begin to make sense sooner than later.

When I objectively weigh all the body of evidence (the positives and the negatives above), I conclude that we are likely at the lower end of a broad trading range for the S&P 500. Fourth-quarter 2008 lows should hold.

We almost certainly remain in an exquisite trading market but an unimpressive investing (buy-and-hold) market for numerous reasons, including the great unwind of debt, the hit to household wealth and psychology after the deep drops in home and equity prices, the unique nature of this cycle's synchronized world economic falloff and the uncertainty of policy. Thus, a sustained market advance remains a low probability.

While much economic and corporate ugliness can and will likely occur in the year ahead, if year-end 2009 does mark the beginning of the end of the Great Decession, as I have surmised, stocks over the next few months will likely begin to discount stabilization well in advance, especially given the reasonable levels of valuation addressed previously.

To conclude, the lowering of the bar could be closer than many think, but the path to reach it remains icy, so investors should still tread carefully.

Despite the fear and loathing on the part of investors, I am beginning to find value and, for the first time in several years, I am in a (slightly) net long position.

Gun to my head, my baseline expectation is that the S&P could end up with a mid- to high-single-digit return for the full year, or about 15% above current levels.

Many stocks will rise more dramatically.

Color me a bit more bullish.

Bottoms Up, Mr. Market

3/3/2009

For the first time ever, I spent nearly a full hour with my favorite host, Sir Larry Kudlow, on CNBC's *The Kudlow Report* last night.

From my perch, the feature of the show was my call that the U.S. stock market could make a 2009 low this week, a very tough call but a position that I have been edging toward over the past several days.

The lion's share of the last segment of *The Kudlow Report* was devoted to my analysis of Warren Buffett and Berkshire Hathaway, and my market bottom call is made near the end of the segment.

My contention, as discussed on last night's show, is that the serious problems have been more than fully discounted in the world's equity markets. Moreover, while many have grown increasingly impatient with the new administration's piecemeal strategy toward addressing the banking industry's toxic assets, a cohesive deal, under the leadership of Lawrence Summers, will soon be forthcoming and will be effective.

The investment pyramid consists of the three angles of fundamentals, sentiment and valuation. I made this market bottom call based on my expectation of an early-2010 stabilization in the economy (making the 27-month recession the second-longest in history) coupled with an extreme sentiment and valuation swing. (As Dennis Gartman is fond of saying, sentiment and valuation have moved from the top left of the chart to the bottom right of the chart in an historic fashion.)

I am fully cognizant of the magnitude of our economic and credit challenges and that the future is not what it used to be. Indeed, my expectation of the Great Decession remains intact and is my baseline expectation.

The difficult fundamental backdrop and rapidly descending stock prices have resulted in a particularly volatile period.

I am also fully aware that most forecasts (of a stock and economic kind), especially at inflection points, are inaccurate or difficult to time, and I know that I am catching a falling knife, which is often an expensive and painful proposition.

Two to three years ago, I had a variant view, and I made a bearish call on equities at a time when (prima facie) all appeared healthy. While I clearly saw the developing cracks in the foundations of credit, in the economy and in the world's stock markets, the media, investment strategists, and mutual fund and hedge fund managers wore rose-colored glasses as they were almost universally bullish. Today, most of the same group, many of whom have been destroyed by the bear market, can see no light at the end of the tunnel, and frankly, this bolsters my confidence in the call.

It is now time for me to adopt another variant view by espousing a more bullish opinion on the U.S. stock market.

Bottom Call (Part Deux)

3/9/2009

I remain firmly committed to the notion that we are in the land of Chicken Littles and that the world equity markets are now tracing an important bottom.

For the second consecutive week on CNBC, I reiterated my more optimistic message.

Last night on CNBC's *Fast Money*, Dylan Ratigan started my segment with a quote from *The Intelligent Investor*'s Benjamin Graham that underscored a still-expensive market. Essentially, Yale's Dr. Robert Shiller made the case that applying Graham's view that a 10-year period of smoothed corporate profits took out distortions and concluded that the S&P 500 index trades at 13× compared to a multiple under 10× at the bottom of the last three recessions, suggesting that U.S. stocks were about 25% overvalued.

> *"Most of the time, common stocks are subject to irrational and excessive price fluctuations in both directions as the consequence of the ingrained tendency of most people to speculate or gamble . . . to give way to hope, fear, and greed."*
>
> —Benjamin Graham

My response was that the investment mosaic has grown a lot more complicated and a 10-year period provides far too few empirical data points, and it is too linear to use only one model, as Shiller suggests.

I prefer to look at multiple models. As it relates to Graham's observation, I would prefer to look at normalized earnings (12% return on earnings) on the S&P's book value of $560—or earnings per share of about $67 a share. Over a lengthier and more statistically significant period—seven decades—stocks tended to trade at 15× normalized S&P profits (S&P equivalent of 1005) and bottomed at between 11.5× and 12.0× (S&P equivalent of 787). We are now at only 685 of the S&P, or at a 10× multiple, so rather than being overvalued—as Benjamin Graham/Robert Shiller might opine—stocks have overshot the downside valuation that has historically provided support and now appear undervalued.

In the *Fast Money* segment, I detailed multiple valuation models I use to assess the current value of U.S. stocks, all of which make clear that equities have incorporated a lot of bad news and are undervalued both absolutely and relative to fixed income.

It is also important to recognize the importance of the value of stocks relative to fixed income and inflation, as Zachary Karabell mentioned last night. I do:

- The risk premium—the market's earnings yield less the risk-free rate of return—is substantially above the long-term average reading.
- Valuations are low vis-à-vis a decelerating (and near-zero) rate of inflation; indeed, the current market multiple is consistent with a 6% rate of inflation.
- A record percentage of companies have dividend yields that are greater than the yield on the 10-year U.S. note. At over 50% of the companies, that is nearly 5× higher than in the peak of 2002 and compares against only 5% on average over the past 30 years.

Not only are there few who believe that we are making a bottom but there is virtually no one who thinks a sustainable market rally is possible.

Chicken Little has regained credibility.

Nearly everyone can explain why the market has gone down and why it is unlikely to rebound, but hardly anyone can find a reason to rally. The business and general media, in marked contrast to the past, almost refuse to consider factors that can contribute to a sustained advance in stock prices.

It is important to recognize that only a handful anticipated the current credit and economic travail, nevertheless, the alacrity and confidence of a dire outcome in the land of the Chicken Littles is something for me to behold.

Three years ago, cash was not king, the buying power of private equity dominated the investment landscape, and no takeover (regardless of size) was impossible. Endowments, pension plans, banks and hedge funds jumped headlong into the leveraged world of private equity.

Even two years ago, mutual and hedge funds were enthusiastically invested in equities (especially of a materials, commodities and energy kind) as the newest paradigm of economic decoupling gained credence.

Today, cash (and liquidity) is back on the throne as king, as the great unwind of debt and the liquidation of overlevered investments gains momentum as the hedge fund industry implodes further.

Take the advice of the Johnny-come-lately Chicken Littles if you will, but trust me, they will not anticipate recovery, nor will they (like the cagey fox) participate in feasting on the developing and unprecedented values.

Attractive valuations, a negative sentiment extreme and early signs (and expectations) of economic stabilization are moving closer to reality.

The sky is not falling, as value is on our doorstep and dinner is being served.

Printing an Important Market Bottom

3/11/2009

Last night I not only reemphasized my 2009 market bottom call on *The Kudlow Report,* I also suggested the possibility that a generational low is being put in place.

Yes, I said that.

The most vociferous bull on our segment, a nice fellow from Boston who has been bullish most of the way down, got weak in the knees because of the magnitude of yesterday's market ramp. He actually said investors are getting too optimistic in only one day.

My response was that considering that the hedge fund industry is at its lowest net long position in years and since individual investors have recently accelerated their account liquidations and redeemed their mutual funds, they are not even thinking about getting back in. There is plenty of buying power sitting on the sidelines to fuel a sustained market advance.

But both institutional and individual investors will get involved again—if the market can post several days/weeks of strength. And there remains a huge asset allocation trade back into equities from cash-rich pension plans whose portfolios are now materially skewed toward fixed income.

Most will miss the rally—it's not surprising since the pain has been so extreme in recent months.

The purists will point out to a bunch of indicators that have yet to fall into place such as a low put/call ratio. But my response is that most buy puts to protect longs, so with most investors being light on equities, there is less of a need to buy protection in puts. So it is not surprising if the put/call ratio stays historically low, as long positions are historically low and cash positions are historically high.

My best guess is that we'll rapidly move back up toward the typical bear-market trough valuation—12× normalized or trend-line S&P earnings of about $67 a share, or about 805 on the S&P 500. In the fullness of time I expect the S&P to test its 200-day moving average, which is currently about 30% above yesterday's close.

Yes, I said that, too!

It Ain't Heavy, It's a Bottom

3/16/2009

Nearly two weeks ago, I suggested that a 2009 market bottom had been put in, and last week, I surmised that, in the fullness of time, a generational market low might have been put in for the U.S. stock market.

At inflection points, gauging the market's technical bearings is often useful as is a history lesson, so let's travel that route.

A deep oversold, worsening sentiment and positive internal divergences almost always provide the foundation to stock market recovery.

The move from the October lows to the March lows indicated growing fear and gave way to rising cash positions and the loss of hope, but the market's internals were improving. November's Dow Jones Industrial Average low of 7,552 was nearly 11% below the October low of 8,451, and the March low of 6,547 was 22.5% under October's low.

While each new low was more frightening than the prior one, there were improving technical and sentiment signals. For example:

- New York Stock Exchange volume at the October low expanded to 2.85 billion shares;
- At the November low, volume dropped to 2.23 billion shares; and
- At the March low, volume was only 1.56 billion shares.

As well, new lows traced decreasing levels:

- At the October low, there were 2,900 new lows;
- At the November low, there were 1,515 new lows; and
- At the March low, there were only 855 new lows on the NYSE.

From a sentiment standpoint, the March low marked an unprecedented number of bears, according to the *AAII* survey.

Last week (and right on cue!), we witnessed conspicuous breakouts and strengthening momentum off of Monday's bottom. The combination of Tuesday's 12:1 ratio of advancing stocks over declining stocks coupled with that day's 27:1 up-to-down volume ratio has not occurred in almost 65 years. The 9% three-day rally and rising volume on two 90% up days were very encouraging. I was also inspired by the strength of financial stocks and the ability of many stocks (e.g., General Electric) to advance in the face of bad news. (In the case of GE, there was a Fitch downgrade late in the week.)

Most strong rallies don't let investors back in easily and get overbought quickly. I expect the current one to be sharp initially and to continue without much of a retest over the next week, creating a short-term overbought by month's end.

So, how now, Dow Jones?

As a template, I expect the 2008–2009 stock market price pattern to most resemble the 1937–1939 period, which holds a number of similarities to the current period:

> *"History doesn't repeat itself; at best, it sometimes rhymes."*
>
> —Mark Twain

1. The stock market decline followed a four- to five-year rally, after a three-year decline of greater than 80%, which is similar to the Nasdaq experience.
2. Worldwide industrial production collapsed in 1937.
3. Commodities crashed in 1937.
4. The markets spent five years consolidating the declines.
5. Massive government spending pulled the United States out of the Great Depression. (Back then, it was preparing for WWII; this time, it will be government stimulus/infrastructure.)

The 50% drop over a five-month period in 1937–1938 holds a similarity to the market's recent drop in that neither had a high-volume selling climax. The market's 1938–1939 recovery, perhaps like 2009's, had four legs and lasted about seven months.

Leg one of the 1938–1939 rally was brief and intense; it lasted only about 12 trading days, and the indices rose by 19%. Leg two was an approximate 60-day consolidation that corrected half of the initial gain. Leg three was about a six-week rise of 30%. Leg four consisted of another two-month consolidation and retracement followed by a 22% six-week rally, serving to mark a multiyear high in the averages.

I expect a similar pattern (as in the late 1930s) to be traced ahead in 2009.

In the months ahead, the fear of being in will be replaced by the fear of being out.

A poorly positioned hedge fund community, with historically low net long exposure and rankled by negative investment returns and the fear of continued redemptions, should provide the initial thrust to the S&P's 50-day moving average of about 810. Again, it is important to recognize that, historically, strong rallies that have durability (similar to 1937–1938) typically don't let investors in during the first advancing leg. With such a clear burst of momentum, the fear of being out could drive the S&P 500 as much as 15 to 40 points above the 50-day moving average, paralleling the 20% third-quarter 1938 move and producing a short-term top and a temporarily overbought market.

The spring should be characterized by backing and filling as the sharp gains are digested, similar to the September–October 1938 interval. Second-quarter warnings will weigh on the market during the April–May period, but the markets could move sideways, bending but not breaking. Signs of market skepticism, sequential economic growth and evidence of a bottoming in the residential real estate and automobile markets (after a sustained period of underproduction) could contain the market's downside, providing a range-bound market with a firm bid on dips. As well, the results from the bank stress tests and the release of a more coherent and detailed bank rescue package could provide further support to equities.

By June, economic traction should begin to take hold from the accumulated fiscal and monetary stimulation coupled with the large drop in energy prices. While it will be too early to demonstrate a broad economic recovery, evidence of stabilization will be clearly manifested in improving retail sales, and stocks will take off for their final advancing phase. With fixed income under increasing pressure, large asset-allocation programs at some of the largest and late-to-the-party pension plans (out of bonds and into stocks) could trigger an explosive rally in the middle to late summer. This move by July or August could close the October 2008 gap in the SPDR S&P 500 exchange-traded fund (SPY) at around $107.

The Little Market that Could

4/6/2009

Early in the week of March 2, I appeared on CNBC's *The Kudlow Report,* where I asserted that the U.S. stock market was within three days of bottoming for the year, and quite possibly for a generation. On Friday, March 6, following two days of further market weakness, I reaffirmed my prediction that the bottom was in.

A week later, on March 9, I reemphasized my generational low bottom call to a skeptical crew on CNBC's *Fast Money.* On that show, I cited multiple valuation models I use to assess the current value of U.S. stocks, all of which made it clear to me that equities have incorporated a lot of bad news and were undervalued both absolutely and relative to fixed income.

At the time, there were few who believed that stocks were bottoming and literally no one who thought that a sustainable market rally was even remotely possible.

The extreme negative sentiment that was associated with those conditions sowed the seeds for the bountiful harvest over the past four weeks.

With the benefit of hindsight, value was being put on our doorstep, and dinner was being served four weeks ago.

The first week of March marked the market bottom, and the performance of stocks over the past month has been the singular best four-week performance since 1933.

Many have now boarded the love train.

Once again in March, as has happened in prior cycles' inflection points, markets have discounted the worsening rearview mirror and have peered optimistically into the future. Importantly, it is abundantly clear that we now have enough domestic economic data to point to a bottoming of production declines. This is particularly true as it relates to an imminent recovery/stabilization in housing, which is being catalyzed by a Fed-induced reduction in mortgage rates, record gains in affordability, and a more favorable economic proposition of home ownership vs. renting.

Housing markets will bring us out just as they brought us in.

My month-old S&P forecast is materially on forecast. As a reminder, it was predicted on a parallel with the conditions that existed in the 1937–1939 U.S. stock market.

If the pattern of my prediction unfolds, the market will have only another 2% to 4% upside before a two-month price consolidation takes hold.

If the above consolidation expectation is on target, gaming the markets will likely hold the key to delivering superior investment returns, especially over the next two to three months.

Short term, the market outlook will be importantly influenced by investor psychology and the degree to which public policy translates into economic traction.

In marked contrast to early March, when we were in a bull market for pessimism, today many have recently come aboard the stock market's love train and have turned more constructive:

- Sentiment surveys indicate a pickup in bullish sentiment.
- The McClellan oscillator is way overbought.
- The downtrend line for the S&P from the November 2008 and January 2009 highs shows resistance at 850.

Importantly, my early March variant view is no longer so.

The consequences of worshiping at the altar of price momentum can be punitive to the recently converted. One has to look no further than the recent downturn in gold shares and in the metal commodities, both of which became overowned and overbought asset classes.

Several other fundamental and technical factors could conspire to contribute to a period of market uncertainty and a healthy several months of backing and filling.

- First-quarter earnings reports will be poor and guidance mixed to bad.
- The success of the Fed programs, which seek to ring-fence toxic bank assets, will not be known for a few months.
- A still-levered and tapped-out consumer could pause in its spending (after demonstrating sequential improvement in the first three

months of 2009), even despite the benefits of lower interest rates and massive fiscal stimulation. This could jeopardize GDP growth forecasts, delay the domestic economy's recovery and result in even lower-than-expected corporate profits in 2009.

- Capital raises (especially of a financial kind) may lie ahead. Already, the REIT industry has embarked upon an industrywide recapitalization.
- Interest rates are starting to rise, providing some competition to stocks.
- The always-present fear of an exogenous event.
- Volatility remains elevated.

Weighing against the near-term consolidation argument is the historically significant improvement in the market's internals and breadth of the rally, with six 90% up days in four weeks, reflecting an abrupt change from the fear of being in to the fear of being out and left behind.

Regardless of whether a near-term consolidation is in the offing, volatility will remain heightened, and my formerly implausible S&P forecast now seems plausible.

Similar to *The Little Engine that Could*, the U.S. stock market appears positioned for further progress, and my mid- to late-summer destination of S&P 1,050 remains on target.

I think it can . . . I think it can.

Against the Grain

Introduction

Extensive experience has taught me that there are many ways to be wrong about the markets: through shortsightedness, of course, but also through excessive farsightedness; through pride, ignorance, bad luck, impatience, imagination or sophistry.
—Jim Grant, *Minding Mr. Market: Ten Years on Wall Street With Grant's Interest Rate Observer*

The crowd almost always outsmarts the remnants (except at inflection points). It is human nature to feel most comfortable being part of a herd.

I prefer a different path—the path of a contrarian. This voyage holds risks but also provides rewards if one exercises strong analysis and patience.

A very good example of my contrarian streak is my bearish case for Apple in September 2012, when the investing world was universally bullish on the stock at $700 a share. The shares eventually dropped to under $400 a share in the months ahead. Another example given in this chapter is my reasoning as to why shorting bonds might prove to be the investment of the decade.

Read on.

Experts Agree, Recession Is Over

8/14/2009

Phew, I am now relieved!

I am comforted in the knowledge that on Tuesday a CNBC poll revealed that 90% of Wall Street economists believe that the recession has ended and that a *Bloomberg* survey (also this week) showed that the consensus sees real U.S. gross domestic product (GDP) expanding at annual rate of at least 2% for the next four quarters.

That's the same group of economists who failed to recognize the consequences of a bubble in stock prices in 1998–2000, the meaning of a three standard deviation event in rising home prices (and affordability), the fallout from a bubble in credit, the broad ramifications of a derivative market gone wild and an imminent recession several years ago.

And that's the same group of economists who interpret a statistical recovery as a self-sustaining economy that is incapable of double-dipping under the influence of numerous nontraditional headwinds.

The economists' conclusions must also be comforting to those Americans without jobs who don't count as unemployed because they have been dropped from the labor force and all the people getting foreclosed on in a housing market that has bottomed.

Yesterday's retail release was punk, though the markets again ignored it. Consumption remains weak, even with savings at lower levels than many feared at only 4% to 5%. I have wondered what is the downside to cost-cutting and productivity gains as the paradox of thrift (and its implications) could haunt us in 2010. One also has to wonder how far into the inventory restocking process we stand, as jobs, income, and consumption continue to move in a southerly direction. And one has to wonder what the downside to productivity is and how large the permanent reduction in employment will be as companies begin to realize that they can run on less.

Those surveyed economists apparently don't recognize the abnormality of the last cycle's leveraged and credit drivers, which occurred amid weakened job and income growth, and that their conclusion that the U.S. economy faces a normal or routine recovery seems more of a wish than reality (even in spite of the magnitude of the monetary/fiscal stimulation).

With the earnings-reporting period almost over, the cheerleading surrounding such a great earnings season has reached a crescendo, but in reality, with so many companies missing their sales guidance, there was not, as Gertrude Stein once said, all that much there there. The paradox of earnings is that an economy cannot cut its way to prosperity. From my perch, a more objective middle-ground reaction is necessary.

While the market participants once again wear their rose-colored glasses, the current conditions reading shows pretty clearly that, nine months after it happened, CEOs absolutely feel worse than they did in the immediate aftermath of the Lehman debacle. For instance, confidence among CEOs weakened to 63.0 in July from 74.3 a month earlier, according to *Chief Executive* magazine's CEO Confidence Index, which surveys 266 executives.

In the current bull market for complacency and cheerleading, investors are increasingly embracing almost any news in a positive if not promotional manner. Speculation, which always sows the seeds to its own destruction, is all too obvious, as there are more day traders and as IPOs triple and quadruple on their opening trades, which is all too reminiscent of the U.S. equity market in the late 1990s.

Market Has Likely Topped

8/26/2009

Back in early March, there were signs of a second derivative U.S. economic recovery, the PMI in China had recorded two consecutive months of advances, domestic retail sales had stabilized, housing affordability was hitting multi-decade highs (with the cost of home ownership vs. renting returning back to 2000 levels), valuations were stretched to the downside and sentiment was negative to the extreme. These factors were ignored, however, and the S&P 500 sank below 700.

To most investors, back in early March, the fear of being out was eclipsed by the fear of being in. Despite the developing less worse factors listed above, bulls were scarce to nonexistent in the face of persistent erosion in equity and credit prices.

It was at this point in time that I confidently forecast the likelihood that a generational low had been reached.

I went on to audaciously predict that the S&P would rise to 1,050, a gain of nearly 400 points from the S&P low of 666 during the first week of March, by late summer/early fall. I even sketched a precision-like SPDR S&P 500 ETF (SPY) trajectory that would reach approximately the $105 level (a 1,050 S&P equivalent) within about six months.

Yesterday, the SPY peaked at 104.20, within spitting range of my intrepid March forecast of 105, and the S&P nearly touched 1,040 in Tuesday's early-morning trading.

Arguably, today investors face the polar opposite of conditions that existed only a few months ago, with economic optimism, improving valuations, and positive sentiment.

To most investors, today the fear of being in has now been eclipsed by the fear of being out, as the animal spirits are in full force. Bears are now scarce to nonexistent in the face of steady price gains in equity and credit prices.

As if the movie is now being shown in reverse, the bull is persistent, stock corrections are remarkably shallow, cash reserves at mutual funds have been depleted, and hedge funds hold their highest net long positions in many moons.

Stated simply, in the current bull market in complacency, optimism, and a boisterous enthusiasm reigns.

The investment debate has morphed in a dramatic fashion from concerns as to whether U.S. economy was entering the Great Depression II to whether the current domestic recovery will be self-sustaining.

The primary question to be asked is: Will the earnings cycle dominate the investment landscape and cause investors to overlook the chronic and secular challenges facing the world's economies, particularly as the public-sector stimulus is eventually withdrawn and paid for and the economic consequences of the massive public-sector intervention manifest themselves in the form of higher interest rates and marginal tax rates?

Most now have accepted the notion that due to the replenishment of historically low inventories, extraordinary fiscal/monetary stimulation and the productivity gains from draconian corporate cost cutting, the earnings cycle is so strong that it will trump the consequences of policy. More accurately, most believe that they can get out of the market before the full effects of policy are felt.

I am less confident, as a decade of hocus-pocus borrowing and lending and 35-to-1 leverage at almost every level in both private and public sectors cannot likely be relieved in the great debt unwind over the course of only 12 months.

It is important to emphasize that when I made my variant March call, I expected many of the conditions that now exist—namely, a resurgence of economic and investment optimism during the summer to be followed by a multiyear period of weak investment returns. Specifically, I expected a mini production boom and an asset allocation away from bonds and into stocks to be embraced and heralded by investors, who would only be disappointed again in the fall as it becomes clear that a self-sustaining economic recovery is unlikely to develop.

My view remains that it is different this time. Again (now for emphasis), the typical self-sustaining economic recovery of the past will not be repeated in the immediate future.

Just as I looked over the valley in March 2009 toward the positive effects of massive monetary/fiscal stimulation within the framework of a downside overshoot in valuations and remarkably negative sentiment, I now suggest another contrarian view is appropriate, as I look over the visible green shoots of recovery toward a hostile assault of nonconventional factors that few business/credit cycles and even fewer investors have ever witnessed.

Yesterday, the Office of Management and Budget/Congressional Budget Office provided an exclamation point to the secular challenges that the domestic economy faces in forecasting an accumulated deficit of $9 trillion over the next decade (up $2 trillion from the previous forecast just two months ago), and public debt as a percentage of GDP is projected at an alarming 68% by 2019 (as compared to 54% today and only 33% in 2001). Thus far, the drop in the U.S. dollar (influenced, in part, by the mushrooming deficit) has been viewed favorably by the markets, but we must now be alert to a downside probe that becomes a threatening market factor. In other words, what has been viewed positively could shortly become negatively viewed.

A double-dip outcome in 2010 represents my baseline expectation. When the stimulus provided by the public sector is finally abandoned, it seems unlikely to be replaced by meaningful strength or participation by any specific component of the private sector, and the burgeoning deficit will ultimately require a reversal of policy, leading to higher interest rates, rising marginal tax rates and a lower U.S. dollar. My forecast assumes that the market's focus will shortly shift from the productivity gains that have been yielding better-than-expected bottom-line results toward these chronic and secular worries.

Even more important, my forecast of a 2010 market peak reflects that the aforementioned nontraditional influences (and the untoward policy ramifications) will, at the very least, yield a broad set of uncertain economic outcomes that (in consequence and in probability) tilt away from a self-sustaining economic scenario sometime in the following 12 months.

Stocks bottom during times of fear. With the benefit of hindsight, the March 2009 lows represented a dramatic overshoot to the downside.

Markets top during times of enthusiasm. I believe that the markets are now over-shooting to the upside and that the U.S. stock market has likely peaked for the year.

"It is the mark of an instructed mind to rest satisfied with the degree of precision to which the nature of the subject admits and not to seek exactness when only an approximation of the truth is possible."

—Aristotle

Bearish Arguments Are Roaring

9/14/2009

This column will address top-down market valuation, explain why I believe the price-to-earnings (P/E) multiple expansion beginning six months ago appears to be coming to an end and then go on to recap the forces that make me more bearish on corporate profits vis-à-vis the emerging and more bullish consensus.

Given that the *First Call* total of S&P operating earnings for the first half of this year was about $30.50 a share and is estimated at $15 a share for the third quarter ending September 30, 2009, it is safe to say that 2009 S&P operating profits will approximate $62 a share. *First Call* consensus S&P earnings forecasts for 2010 now run around $72 to $74 a share, for a gain of almost 18% year over year.

Many strategists (both bullish and bearish) assume that a fair value price-to-earnings multiple—based on interest rates and inflation—rests at about 15.5. Averaging the 2009 and 2010 S&P consensus forecasts produces a melded $67.50 S&P earnings per share (EPS), a year-end target of 1,045 and a mid-2010 S&P target of 1,130 on EPS of $73. (The current S&P level is 1,043.)

Bearish strategists such as David Rosenberg believe the current S&P level is discounting a 40% increase in 2010 earnings over 2009, but the consensus believes that about 10% growth is being discounted.

Bearish strategists expect real GDP growth of about 1% to 2% next year, but the consensus now anticipates 3% to 3.5% growth in 2010.

The market's P/E multiple is up by 5.5 points, or more than 40%, since equities bottomed in early March. So, even for the bullish strategists, the phase during which expanding P/E multiples contribute to the market's advance is largely over, and future stock market gains will be dependent on the achievability of a healthy growth in S&P operating earnings toward the consensus.

My Take Stated simply, my argument is that the earnings expectations for 2010— the level and growth rate—will disappoint,

"In poker terms, the Treasury and Fed have gone 'all in.' Economic medicine that was previously meted out by the cupful (pumping dollars into the economy) has recently been dispensed by the barrel. These once-unthinkable dosages will almost certainly bring on unwelcome aftereffects. Their precise nature is anyone's guess, though one likely consequence is an onslaught of inflation."

—Charles Munger, Berkshire Hathaway

and the expectation of disappointment has brought the market into overvalued ground.

Let's assume we can all agree that the full extent of the P/E expansion phase is about over and that further market gains will rely on the realization of the optimists' baseline expectation of relatively smooth and solid earnings growth for 2009–2011. Even on the consensus expectations, the market appears to be fairly valued now and somewhat undervalued (by about 9%) on a 12-month forward earnings basis.

While I accept that the baseline consensus expectation of S&P 2010 EPS of $73 a share is a possible and logical outcome, a double-dip would not be illogical considering the economic, credit and equity markets' heart attack. I would argue that there exists a wider range of economic and profit outcomes than is customary during a recovery phase, and that the certainty associated with today's consensus of a positive outcome could be tested.

There is always the need for rigor in the analysis of the economy and profits. We know history rhymes and that we must rely on past relationships, even after adjusting for the new reality/reset to frame our views. But, to some degree, the same set of economic series and charts that failed to appreciate the historically unique and shaky foundation of credit-driven economic growth in 2002–2006 might be underestimating the economic consequences of the great unwind of credit, the ramifications of the massive policy decisions that were necessary to counteract the building recessionary conditions in 2008 and the unfolding of numerous nontraditional headwinds.

Nontraditional Headwinds   Jim Cramer says the bears are "ignoring the good news at their own peril." I would argue that the bulls are ignoring the emergence of a number of secular headwinds. Here are 10 of them:

1. Deep cost cuts have been a mainstay of corporations over the past few years. Cost cuts are a corporate lifeline (like fiscal stimulus), but both have a defined and limited life. Ultimately, top-line growth is needed.

2. Cost cuts (exacerbated by wage deflation) pose an enduring threat to the labor force. The consumer remains the most significant

contributor to domestic growth. Unemployment should remain high, exacerbated by many retiring later in life because their nest eggs have been reduced.

3. The consumer entered the current downcycle exposed and levered to the hilt, and net worth (and confidence) has been damaged and will need to be repaired through time and by higher savings and lower consumption. The consumer is hurting. Last week I met with a midsized bank's lending team. The bank is seeing a big mix change toward rising use of their debit cards (where money is in the bank) at the expense of credit cards (where money is then owed).

4. The credit aftershock will continue to haunt the economy. The unregulated shadow banking industry is dead, as is the securitization market. All signs indicate that banks will likely remain reluctant to lend to individuals and small businesses. Just try to get a jumbo mortgage today.

5. The effect of the Fed's monetarist experiment and its impact on investing and spending still remain uncertain.

6. While the housing market has stabilized, its recovery will probably remain muted. More important, there are few growth drivers to replace the crucial role taken by the real estate markets in the prior upturn.

7. Commercial real estate has only begun to enter a cyclical downturn. It might not be as deep as many expect, but it won't provide much of a contribution to growth.

8. While the public-works component of public policy is a stimulant, the impact might be more muted than is generally recognized. There may be less than meets the eye—most of the current fiscal policy initiatives represent transfer payments that have a negative multiplier and create work disincentives.

9. Municipalities have historically provided economic stability during times of economic weakness—no more. They are broadly in disrepair. State sales taxes are being raised all over the country, and so are sin taxes (to shore up municipal finances) on cigarettes, booze and maybe even sugar products.

10. The most important nontraditional headwind is the inevitability of higher marginal tax rates. How will higher individual tax rates affect an already deflated consumer? How will corporations react to higher tax rates? Will rising taxes be P/E multiple benders?

How Now, Dow Jones?   The liquidity that grew out of the massive government stimulation and the growth in the monetary base is reaching the equity market and our economy. It has been greeted by cheers and almost unnoticeable, brief and shallow pullbacks in stocks, producing a degree of price momentum that is almost reminiscent of the good old days in 1999/early 2000. Market participants appear now to have embraced the notion that we are in an economic sweet spot and that a below-average but self-sustaining domestic recovery is being endorsed.

With the perspective of the large market rise and dramatic change in sentiment (from dire to positive), there is now little room for disappointment.

A Secular Reduction in Credit Creation and Financial Inventiveness Lies Ahead   Coming out of the last several recessions, aggregate economic activity moved quickly back to peak levels, but, consistent with the accepted shallow-recovery thesis, it won't be as quick to recover this time. David Rosenberg expresses in *Barron's* that the secular rise in credit expansion of the past several decades could be a thing of the past in the years ahead, producing a truly different experience this time. While we have to try, it's hard for me to be confident in the certainty and precision of a baseline view, especially within the context of the long and uncertain tail of all the nontraditional headwinds. With financial inventiveness being put on the back burner, unbridled, unregulated, and (sometimes) unsavory debt creation will no longer catalyze growth in a world where banks are reluctant to lend, the securitization markets are broken and the shadow banking system is nearly extinct.

While it's fortunate that our financial institutions have reduced the chance of systemic risk by decreasing their balance sheet debt, the U.S. government has taken the banking industry's place. And with that come challenges anew over the next decade.

Berkshire Hathaway's Munger argued that those challenges and the bills associated with policy are being ignored—or investors believe they can get out before they come due.

The credit and stock markets have been buoyed and dominated by the better-than-expected earnings cycle. The replenishment of historically low inventories, the effects of recent and extraordinary fiscal/monetary stimulation, a recovery in residential housing activity and the productivity gains from draconian corporate cost-cutting are favored in influence by Jim Cramer (and others) and have clearly trumped the potentially negative consequences and those due bills of policy.

But stimulation is by definition bringing sales forward, and Policy (with a capital "P"!) has its consequences. Some programs have the potential for borrowing from 2010 to 2011; others, such as mortgage credits and even monetary policy, have a finite life to them. They end and the artificiality of the stimulative initiatives is lost—and the economy becomes demand-dependent. Given the past shock, it's hard to see a solid view of that demand.

Consumer Remains the Achilles' Heel   Then there is the consumer, who remains particularly exposed in the period ahead. Private wages and salaries fell by a record 5.2% annualized rate in July. While some improvement from depressed levels can be expected, the labor market remains weak and jobless claims are still elevated. The possibility exists that the consumer will retreat from the decades-long aspirational spirit and turn back toward the legacy of the post-Depression mentality of maintaining the status quo. With this reset could come disappointing personal consumption expenditures and a higher level of savings that will likely match the post–World War II average savings rate of 7.5% and could even begin trending back toward the direction of double-digit savings rates that existed in the recession of the early 1980s.

Summary   In summary, the market has discounted favorable expectations and seems more certain of a self-sustaining recovery cycle outcome. Reflecting the gravity and weight of so many inhibiting factors, I see a much broader range of possible outcomes and less certainty than some of the newly printed bullish market participants.

The credit expansion of the last several decades has reversed, it will take time to reverse the damage to net worth and confidence, the consumer remains in a fragile state, corporations will make do with more productive but fewer personnel (job growth could continue to disappoint), there are no apparent drivers to replace the role of housing (2002–2006), and numerous nontraditional headwinds (most importantly higher marginal tax rates) will have an uncertain impact on aggregate growth.

Top 20 Signs How Bad the Economy Is

11/2/2009

Dave Letterman–style, below are the top 20 signs how bad the economy is:

20. The economy is so bad that Barack Obama changed his slogan to "Maybe We Can!"
19. The economy is so bad that Sarah Palin is only shooting moose for food, not for fun.
18. The economy is so bad that when Bill and Hillary travel together, they now have to share a room.
17. The economy is so bad that instead of a coin toss at the beginning of the Super Bowl in February, they will play "Rock, Paper, Scissors."
16. The economy is so bad that Angelina Jolie had to adopt a highway.
15. The economy is so bad that my niece told me she wants to dress up as a 401(k) for Halloween so that she can turn invisible.
14. The economy is so bad that I ordered a burger at McDonald's and the kid behind the counter asked, "Can you afford fries with that?"
13. The economy is so bad that I saw four CEOs over the weekend playing miniature golf.
12. The economy is so bad that I saw the CEO of Wal-Mart shopping at Wal-Mart.
11. The economy is so bad that Bill Gates had to switch to dial-up.
10. The economy is so bad that rapper 50 Cent had to change his name to 10 Cent.
9. The economy is so bad that the Pequot tribe built a reservation on the site of one of their casinos.
8. The economy is so bad that the Treasure Island casino in Las Vegas is now managed by Somali pirates.
7. The economy is so bad that if the bank returns your check marked "insufficient funds," you call them and ask if they meant you or them.
6. The economy is so bad that I bought a toaster oven and my free gift with the purchase was a bank.
5. The economy is so bad that the only company hiring this week is the one that sends people to scrape bankers off of Wall Street sidewalks.
4. The economy is so bad that I went to my bank to get a loan, and they said, "What a coincidence! That's just what we were going to ask you!"

3. The economy is so bad that a picture is now only worth 200 words.

2. The economy is so bad that Hot Wheels stock is trading higher than GM.

And the number one sign how bad the economy is . . .

1. The economy is so bad that the guy who made $50 billion disappear (Madoff) is being investigated by the people who made over $1 trillion disappear (our policymakers).

More Nuance Is in Store

1/25/2010

I aggregate an annual surprise list because outlier events (black swans) are occurring with greater frequency, uncertainties will persist, and the conventional view is often wrong.

Markets are never black or white, and the investment mosaic is growing ever more complicated. While the determination of market prices and valuation will always be dominated by traditional factors (interest rates, inflation, corporate profit growth, etc.), markets have become far more nuanced and susceptible to disequilibrium in the aftermath of the unparalleled credit-driven boom and in light of complicated political issues and rising geopolitical risks that, arguably, have been all but ignored.

"The best investors are like socialites. They always know where the next party is going to be held. They arrive early and make sure that they depart well before the end, leaving the mob to swill the last tasteless dregs."

—The Economist, 1986

It can be argued as we exit January 2010 that the prices on Wall Street remain somewhat ahead of the conditions of Main Street. While the market rally has exceeded all expectations that existed during the first quarter of 2009, a year later we find an economy that is expanding but still heavily reliant on government stimulation—even despite a zero-interest-rate policy (ZIRP) and a lower U.S. dollar that promotes more robust exports.

The unemployment picture remains weak as corporations do without more workers, so the general welfare of the all-important consumer is

"I fall back on the analogy of a stalled car (the economy) being pulled by a tow truck (government stimulus). The tow truck will want to let the car down one of these days and go on its way. Will the car be able to move on its own? We can only wait and see. I think it's more likely to sputter along than it is to move forward energetically. But at least we don't have to worry any longer about the analogy of 15 months ago: an airplane whose engine has flamed out. A powerless plane in mid-flight presents a far more troubling image than a stalled car."

—Howard Marks, Oaktree Capital Management (Tell Me I'm Wrong)

not much improved. Small-business confidence and expansion plans are low because of tax, regulatory uncertainty and limited access to bank credit, so new hires are weak. In contrast to a weak consumer and frozen small business community, large corporations are prospering from draconian cost cuts (but not much top-line improvement), strong (cash-rich) balance sheets and an ability to obtain credit.

Short-Term Outlook: Neither a Bump in nor the End of the Road   Whether the current market decline is a bump in the road, the end of the road or something in between can be debated. I would choose that the most likely short-term outlook is something in between a bump in and the end of the road. While I don't see last week's drop as the start of a meaningful correction in equities, I don't see much upside either. In other words, the short-term market might be disappointingly dull and range-bound, with a slight negative bias.

The election news in Massachusetts and strong corporate revenue and profits were ignored last week. The year-to-date decline in the S&P 500 is over 2%; a week ago the markets were up by over 3% year-to-date. Investors no longer seem complacent—the put/call ratio is rising after several distribution days—and there is an element of panic in the air. From Tuesday's top to now, we have dropped by nearly 5.5%. More important, many stocks have fallen much more from their recent tops to Friday's close: Just look at Caterpillar's drop of 10 points, to

$54 a share, or the similar drop for IBM's shares. There are many other examples.

2010 Outlook: A Challenging Year of Subpar Returns   If last year was the time to ride the remarkable values that grew out of the late-2008/early-2009 financial and market panic, 2010 could be a year in which stock pickers (of both long and short ideas) and opportunistic traders deliver the best investment performance—it might also be a great year to sell premium, straddles and strangles.

It remains my view that the consensus forecasts for GDP, corporate profits, interest rates and for targets on the S&P 500 have a reasonably high probability of occurring but that a number of less benign outcomes remain possible. By the last half of this year, or in early 2011, the consensus forecast of a self-sustaining economic advance could be in jeopardy as there are many potential factors that could contribute to slowing growth. Accordingly, a fully invested position in stocks (which most strategists are recommending) should be questioned. From my perch, a relatively conservative posture seems more appropriate.

It is also my view that the markets have materially discounted improving macro conditions, and I am holding to my baseline expectation that 2010 will bring a high-single-digit negative return in the major market indices (down 5% to 10%). Valuations are not stretched. We'll likely see an extended period of zero-interest-rate policy (and a curse on cash by the Fed), relatively tame current inflation and inflationary expectations, and a strong year-over-year gain in corporate profits. Plus, as an asset class, investors have not embraced stocks in this cycle—mutual fund stock inflows are negligible. These are among the factors that should cushion the current market fall. The generational low of March 2009 remains very much intact.

It's Different This Time   Regardless of one's short-term view, the nontraditional challenges facing the capital markets are multiple. Most of these factors are valuation deflating, serving to cap the upside to the U.S. stock market in 2010 and argue against the view that we are embarking upon a normal 40-month-plus upcycle:

- Populist policy means more costly regulation and higher marginal taxes for the wealthy and our largest corporations; it also means that small-business confidence will remain subdued, as will hiring and expansion plans.

- The imbalances between revenue and receipts at state and local finances means higher sales taxes and less service. Municipal employment rolls will contract, unlike in prior economic recoveries.
- A still-leveraged consumer facing wage deflation and higher inflation means higher savings and lower personal consumption expenditures. Decades of an aspirational consumer might be reversed—that is, the definition of a better life could mean more money in the bank and less stuff.
- The absence of job growth at small businesses in the face of regulatory and tax uncertainties and the reluctance of large corporations to take on new hires as they seek further productivity gains guarantees that unemployment will remain elevated. With our population growing and our manufacturing base declining (as our global competitiveness deteriorates), from where will the jobs be generated?
- The residue of the housing boom is an unprecedented large phantom inventory of unsold homes that will weigh on the slope of the residential real estate market's recovery. While commercial real estate could weather the downturn far better than the bears expect, it too will not be a driver to economic growth in the years ahead.
- The threat of due bills (higher interest rates and inflation) down the road remains an albatross around the neck of the market's P/E multiple. The U.S. fiscal house is in disorder: Deficits are ballooning, and our educational system, Medicare, and Social Security are severely underfunded. How long and at what cost can we expect foreign central banks to fund domestic growth?
- Geopolitical threats are rising.

The Populist Zeitgeist of Dissatisfaction   I have argued that among the most important challenges to the economy and the markets is a tidal wave of populism. The angry subtext and poor attitude toward big business and the wealthy has rarely been this bad.

We don't now know how this all pans out.

We don't know whether, after deteriorating approval ratings and the Massachusetts election upset, President Obama will move to a more centrist policy position.

We don't know how health care and energy reform will be written.

We do know that the depth of our country's fiscal problems could mean that gridlock and legislative inertia are bad this time for the capital markets.

We do know that there is a new sheriff in town for the Republicans as the newly appointed Senator from Massachusetts will likely replace Sarah Palin as an important spokesman, leader, and even potentially become the frontrunner for the Republican presidential candidacy in the next election.

No More Black Swans . . . Maybe a Peking Duck   The cause of a possible downside market move and the least benign outcome for the markets are clear.

When the policies of populism (higher taxes and more costly regulation) are mixed with a number of other nontraditional headwinds (municipalities' disarray, a still-wounded lending mechanism, etc.), the trajectory of economic growth will almost certainly be stunted. I believe these influences and policies could be reflected, contrary to consensus, in a weakening economy by the second half of 2010—one of the less benign outcomes I referred to earlier.

These two factors—(1) public policy that grows from populism; and (2) nontraditional headwinds—form a potentially toxic cocktail, especially within the context of the size of the market rally of the past eight months and under the possible setting in which higher interest rates begin to offer competition to stocks.

We Are the World

2/16/2010

More than any other time in history, we exist in a global platform that has permitted more people to plug and play, collaborate and compete, share knowledge and share work. But, the hidden hand and interlinked nature of the markets and economies almost never work without a hidden fist. A world as one has an upside and a potential downside as we have witnessed throughout the recession and most recently concerning Greece's sovereign debt issue.

> *"If you don't visit the bad neighborhoods, the bad neighborhoods are going to visit you."*
>
> —Thomas Friedman

Back in 2005, Thomas Friedman wrote the international bestselling book, *The World Is Flat: A Brief History of the Twenty-First Century*, which analyzed the trend in globalization in the early twenty-first century. The title was a metaphor for viewing the world as a level playing field in terms of commerce, where all competitors have an equal opportunity. The title also alludes to the perceptual shift required for countries, companies and individuals to remain competitive in a global market where historical and geographical divisions are becoming increasingly irrelevant.

It is abundantly clear that, over time, the world's markets and businesses have become increasingly connected and interdependent.

> *"No man is an island, entire of itself . . . any man's death diminishes me, because I am involved in mankind; and therefore never send to know for whom the bell tolls; it tolls for thee."*
>
> —John Donne

With advances in telecommunications infrastructure and the rise of the Internet, the process has been accelerating rather dramatically over the past 15 years as technological and financial innovations make it much easier for people around the globe to communicate, to travel and to participate in international commerce.

Interconnectivity in a linked world is not a novel concept. For example, from your high school days, you might recall the quotation above from late-sixteenth/early-seventeenth-century English poet John Donne.

With the world growing smaller (and flatter), U.S. financial institutions have been especially active in smelling opportunities outside our country. Whether, as suggested in Sunday's *New York Times*, Goldman Sachs and other investment banks have exported the problems associated with financial derivatives or it was a by-product of the search for yield as interest rates dropped to historic lows, the fact remains that the proliferation of unwieldy and unregulated financial derivatives around the world deepened the economic downturn, and it continues to produce financial aftershocks with unknown consequences.

I believe that Greece will be resolved and, in all likelihood, the solution will not be terribly disruptive to our markets. The situation is manageable and should be put into perspective. The fiscal problems facing Greece will likely be bandaged over the next few months and, hopefully, will be resolved in the fullness of time through financial assistance, austerity and, ultimately, a more disciplined fiscal policy. Also, I believe that China's tightening was preemptive.

Nevertheless, we cannot paint over the far reach and potential problems associated with financial interconnectivity. My general feeling has been that many strategists are paying far too much attention to previous economic cycles (and traditional economic series) without fully recognizing the many new and nontraditional challenges to growth.

As Thomas Friedman wrote, most of our political elite don't understand that the world is flat, so the chances of policy mistakes loom larger.

Though our domestic fiscal problems are shallower than the problems over there, they still run deep. Contrary to the traditional view that gridlock is good for stocks, equities have been on the descent since Scott Brown's surprise Massachusetts Senate win.

The reasons for the weakness are multiple:

- The likelihood that continued gridlock would fail to address our fiscal problems;
- The lack of patience on the part of both Americans and our legislators/administration to do the right thing; and
- That the odds favor inappropriate policy or weak policy to confront so many structural (nontraditional) imbalances and a number of other issues.

It remains different this time, as over here and over there become interchangeable. Austerity, from the states of California and New York to the countries of Greece and Spain, remains a common theme that will detract from growth.

I emphatically reject the notion of those who see the current cycle as no different than the previous ones—namely, one that is capable of dependable, smooth, self-sustaining and enduring growth. By contrast, I have argued (and continue to argue) that the aftershocks and deleveraging from the last steroid-aided credit cycle will have a long tail and will be with us for some time. The aftershocks will appear in numerous corners that will not only stunt economic growth but could produce headwinds to the benign consensus view of a shallow economic recovery. Under these circumstances, a lid is likely placed on P/E multiples.

In summary, we now must add the uncertainty of global connectivity (and the pesky critters that reside in dark and unknown corners) as a new influential factor to an already crowded list of unusual aftershocks that are byproducts of the earlier easy-money credit cycle:

- A multimillion phantom inventory of homes (over 7 million) that will disrupt the housing cycle over the next several years;
- Less credit available as the shadow-banking industry remains adrift and the securitization market is quiescent;
- Corporate profitability and the pattern of the domestic economy will be more unpredictable and inconsistent;
- Disappointing organic sales growth;
- With limited upside to stock and home prices, the aspirational consumer of the past few decades will demonstrate a renewed conservatism in spending and in savings;
- A retrenchment in services and an increase in taxes at the state and local levels; and
- Confidence will remain subdued and, as a corollary, so will capital expenditures and employment growth be weak by historic standards.

While investors should continue to assign the highest probability to a benign and durable economic advance, a fine balance will be required to thread the needle and produce a smooth and self-sustaining world economic recovery. The foundation of growth remains shaky, and the risks of continued aftershocks and economically deflating policies (both in the United States and abroad) in a world so interconnected are simply too high to support a heavy commitment or above-average weighting to equities in 2010.

The Decade of the Temporary Worker

8/2/2010

U.S. corporations have a renewed emphasis on temporary hirings at the expense of permanent job placements.

Years ago, inventory on-demand solutions arose at manufacturing companies around the world, resulting in improved returns on industrial invested capital and corporate profitability both in the United States and abroad.

Not surprisingly, today, the trend of a broader use of temporary workers is the next generation of return optimization in an age of broad uncertainty and a wider-than-usual set of economic outcomes.

Prior to the 2008–2009 Great Decession, temporary employment growth has signaled permanent hiring strength.

Out of the 1990 recession, temporary jobs first began consistent positive year-over-year growth in December 1991. Overall nonfarm employment turned positive four months later (April 1992).

Following the 2001 recession, the "jobless recovery" produced a sputtering in temporary job growth throughout all of 2002 and did not post positive percentage growth until mid-2003. Six months later, total employment exhibited year-over-year growth.

In the current recovery, temporary jobs crossed into the positive growth region in January 2010 and then surged into double-digit growth with gains of 19.4% in June, following year-over-year rises of 16.9% in May and April's 14.6%, but total nonfarm employment has yet to grow year over year, since the series first turned negative 26 months ago (May 2008). The job loss was under 1% in June, however, and total employment will likely cross into the year-over-year positive region soon. As of now, the lag is five months, still shorter than the six-month lag between temp jobs' and all jobs' year-over-year recovery in 2003. If the lead-lag relationship holds up this time, year-over-year U.S. job growth should become positive sometime in the second half of the year, but the growth will likely be modest relative to past cycles of employment growth.

In other words, a rise in cyclical unemployment appears to be morphing into structural unemployment in the United States.

We can trace a number of reasons behind the movement that favors temporary workers:

- The severity of the 2008–2009 downturn coupled with the reduced accessibility of credit has made small businesses cautious.

- The economic recovery of late 2009/early 2010 has been shallow (by historical standards), and growth expectations have diminished—slower growth in output translates to a reduced pace of hiring.
- As businesses deleverage and become more cost-efficient, temporary workers represent a way to avoid the higher costs of permanent employees.
- Temporary hiring enables a business to maintain staffing flexibility, allowing it to adjust more quickly to workload fluctuations and rapid changes in business conditions.
- Limited or no need for employer contribution to workers' compensation insurance or unemployment, no employer liability for Social Security or Medicare taxes and no need to provide job benefits, including health insurance or retirement plans.
- Increased economic and policy uncertainty.
- A wedge of political and regulatory uncertainty.
- Rising health care costs.
- The likelihood of ever more populist initiatives favoring employees at the expense of employers.
- The need for more specialized workers for shorter periods of commitment.

What are some of the ramifications of this new era of temporary job growth?

- Less buoyant and dynamic domestic economic growth;
- A less consistent rate and more unstable trajectory of domestic economic growth;
- Sustained and higher-than-historic corporate profit margins;
- Less of a potential corporate commitment to permanent growth initiatives in hirings and in new capital plans;
- Less inflows into the domestic stock market through 401(k) plans and other retirement programs;
- Dampened consumer confidence; and
- Greater demand for renting over home ownership.

While, historically, the rise in temporary job growth signals a broader improvement in the employment markets, I am less certain in the current cycle and, for that matter, over the course of the next few years.

Economic bulls have been incorrectly predicting stronger jobs growth since fourth quarter 2009.

They have been disappointed and are likely to continue to be disappointed in the decade of the temporary worker.

The Scale Tips to the Bullish Side

8/23/2010

The perma-bulls (who generally missed the 2008–2009 bear market Great Decession), until recently have called for a "V"-shaped domestic economic recovery and have been targeting about 1,300 on the S&P 500 as their objective. Some strategists,

> *"It is always darkest before the dawn."*
>
> —Proverb

like JPMorgan's well-regarded Tom Lee, remain steadfast in their views and are still holding on to this target despite the ambiguity of the current soft patch that has taken most perma-bulls by surprise.

By contrast, the perma-bears (who generally missed the near-60% upside move in stocks from the generational low and the sharp recovery in domestic GDP) have called for a double-dip in the U.S. economy and have been targeting about 900 on the S&P. Their mantra consists of "black crosses"; "Hindenburg omens"; and structural, fundamental, and nontraditional headwinds.

I think both camps are hyperbolic (the bears more than the bulls) and attention seeking, but their respective views will likely not provide investors with viable or profitable strategies.

The investment and economic truth likely lies somewhere in between.

The economic recovery will likely be uneven and inconsistent. At times it will appear that the economy is headed back into recession; at other times it will appear that the economy is reaccelerating its growth rate.

I expect the S&P 500 to trade between 1,020 and 1,150 (roughly between 11× and 13× 2011 S&P EPS forecasts).

While we can never have such precision, my forecast taken literally (at the current 1,075 level) indicates that there is approximately 55 S&P

points of risk and about 75 S&P points of upside. In other words, the scale
has now tipped back to the bullish side.

We are in this vortex of tax and regulatory traps. The uncertainty of
policy has resulted in what can be viewed as a fiscal tightening and a
paralysis of corporate indecision. Arguably, the continued weak series of
economic releases over the past week increases the possibility that, by
year-end, we will see a renewed sense of urgency from our politicians for
policy relief from the tax and regulatory logjam.

A catalyst to a tipping point of changing fiscal policy could also occur
as an outgrowth of a Republican win in November's elections, leading to
a decision to continue the Bush tax cuts or even institute a payroll tax cut
(or other outside-the-box initiative) in early 2011. (The market, as it
usually does, will likely react positively in advance of these possibilities.)

In determining market levels—as I did in calling for a generational
low in March 2009—the principal factors I use in establishing a fair
market value and range for equities are economic fundamentals, interest
rates, valuations, expectations and sentiment.

**Moderating Economic Growth Has Historically Provided a
Healthy Backdrop for the U.S. Stock Market** An easy Fed that
is content to maintain a zero-interest-rate policy indefinitely, coupled
with a cycle low in inventories, residential investment, automobile unit
and capital spending sales relative to their long-term relationship to GDP
and relative to their longer-term trends, argue strongly against a domestic
double-dip. Moreover, an expected mean regression of these four series
could provide important support for a moderate expansion in GDP
growth in the years ahead.

In other words, the current soft patch indicates a moderating
expansion but not a double-dip.

And history shows that that moderate economic growth typically
produces positive investment returns. Since 1950, quarterly real GDP
growth rates of 0% to 1% have produced a quarterly return in the S&P
500 of more than 2%. According to Miller Tabak's Dan Greenhaus:

> Equity returns needn't be negative in a slow growth environ-
> ment. . . . There's about a coin flip's chance of the S&P 500
> being down in any given quarter in which GDP contracts.

Viewed another way, 50% of the time the economy contracts in a given quarter, the S&P 500 increases in value and does so by more than 9%.

Stocks Are Extraordinarily Cheap Against Interest Rates   The low level of interest rates remains the single most compelling bullish argument for stocks—and there are many examples of a disconnect between stocks, interest rates and other metrics/markets of risk.

- For the first time since 1962, the yield on the DJIA exceeds that of bond yields.
- Risk premiums (the difference between the earnings yield of the S&P index and the 10-year U.S. note) are at the highest level since the beginning of the modern era's bull market that began in the early 1980s.
- Nearly four-fifths of the companies contained in the S&P 500 possess earnings yields that are greater than bond yields. And many have (growing) dividend yields that are similar to their own bond yields.
- In a Friday conference call, JPMorgan's Tom Lee observed that the performance between bonds and stocks over the past 10 years has never been as wide in any decade in history. Whenever stocks have a negative 10-year gap in performance relative to fixed income, the average yearly return in the following decade is approximately 13%.
- Stocks are moving contra to the improving risk metrics and risk markets. For example, two-year bank swap spreads are back down to April levels—when the S&P 500 traded at 1218.
- Stocks have also disconnected from the junk bond markets. The high-yield markets are economically sensitive and are not indicating a broad economic slide. Junk prices are only about 3% off their high and stand at nearly +9% year-to-date. By contrast, stocks are 14% off their highs and are down by 4% year-to-date.

Valuations Are Compelling   At under 12× 2010 estimates, equities seem inexpensive to a multidecade average of over 15× and at 17× when inflation is contained and interest rates are low.

Since 1962 the yield on the 10-year U.S. note has averaged about 365 basis points above the quarterly pace of real GDP growth. With the current 10-year yield of 2.58%, the fixed-income market is discounting negative real growth in the domestic economy.

As Omega Advisors' Lee Cooperman mentioned to me over the weekend, industrial companies are taking notice of the developing values—it is unlikely that BHP Billiton and Intel would propose spending $30 billion and $9 billion, respectively, for the acquisition of Potash and McAfee if they felt an economic apocalypse was on the horizon.

Economic/Stock Market Expectations Are Low   There is not a market participant extant who doesn't recognize that the slope of the recovery in the domestic economy will be different this time and that the ramifications of the administration's populist policy, the growing perception of a structural rise in U.S. unemployment, consumer deleveraging, concerns of deflation, the emergence of nontraditional (and intermediate-term) headwinds (e.g., fiscal imbalances, higher marginal tax rates, costly regulation, etc.) all will serve as a brake to domestic growth.

And what about the common view that the consumer is spent-up not pent-up? The bearish view that the consumer is the Achilles' heel to growth might be challenged.

Sentiment Weak . . . and Weakening   Much like 17 months ago, we appear to be rapidly approaching a negative extreme in market and economic sentiment.

The hedge fund industry has derisked. Net long equity positions remain low by historic standards and, increasingly, hedge-hoggers such as Stan Druckenmiller are leaving the business.

To some degree, Stan's decision reflects how difficult it is to deliver superior investment returns in a world driven by the uncertainty of policy and economic/investment outcomes superimposed by the destabilizing effect of an algorithm-based world of short-term momentum strategies and, perhaps even more importantly, short-term-oriented investors. His decision reflects an investment world that has grown increasingly less predictable, and the ability to deliver superior investment returns has been challenged, in part by some of the factors mentioned above. We're in an environment in which portfolio managers and investors are dually frustrated. To many, it is getting to the point where "it's no fun anymore."

Importantly, Stanley's exit yesterday is reminiscent of when value was out of favor and glittering hedge fund manager Julian Robertson quit in the early 2000s, so I suppose you can say that history rhymes. But remember, almost as soon as the ink dried and Julian closed shop, his beloved "value stocks" came back in vogue.

Such a shift could happen again, as a dysfunctional market moves back into a biased-to-the-upside trend—just at a time when some throw their hands up in the air in despair.

Also, retail investors have fled domestic equity funds in favor of yields in the bond market. Over the past year, there has been a record flow into bond funds compared to equity funds.

With the two dominant investor groups—hedge funds and retail investors—derisking, who is left to sell?

Summary   The U.S. stock market has already discounted a recession/double-dip. And the notion of secular headwinds has been recently adopted by the consensus and has contributed to a weak equity market.

Domestic economic and stock market expectations are low.

While a number of risk metrics and risk markets have improved, equities still lie near the bottom of a projected trading range.

Stocks are especially attractive relative to interest rates, and an extended period of underperformance against fixed income has soured both hedge funds and retail investors toward equities.

It is time to fade the growing negative consensus and adopt a variant view by becoming more constructive on stocks.

The Lost Decade Has Passed Us

9/2/2010

Bull markets are born out of distress—witness March 2009. Bear markets are born out of prosperity—witness 2007.

Liquidating/derisking out of equities and acquiring/rerisking into fixed income has been the mantra of most individual and institutional investors over the course of the last three years. Since early 2008, retail

> *Two roads diverged in a wood, and I—*
>
> *I took the one less traveled by,*
>
> *And that has made all the difference.*
>
> —Robert Frost, "The Road Not Taken"

investors have sold over $200 billion of domestic equity funds, while purchasing nearly $600 billion in fixed-income products. That gap of over $800 billion is unprecedented as is last decade's spread in performance of bonds vs. stocks the largest in history. But history tells us that the S&P 500 performs famously in the following decade and ultimately moves contra to a peak in flows.

I believe that it is time to take the road less traveled and to raise net long exposure at precisely the time when such a strategy is most unpopular.

In many ways, the sentiment toward equities today is as bad as the extreme experienced at the generational low 18 months ago. Indeed, at Tuesday's close, the market zeitgeist was eerily reminiscent of 1979 when *BusinessWeek* published its "Death of Equities" cover.

The fact is that most classes of investors now view U.S. stocks with distrust.

But who is left to sell, especially if the concerns regarding a double-dip prove unjustified?

I continue to view the double-dippers as on the wrong page.

Consider that the cyclical components of GDP, such as autos and housing, now contribute so little to aggregate GDP that the year-over-year impact in late 2010/early 2011 can only modestly impact output. Moreover, with inventories-to-sales so low and with auto and residential investments so far from their longer-term trendline relationship to GDP—ergo, demand is pent-up—a double-dip seems an unlikely event. Even the spent-up consumer's debt-service ratio is at its lowest level since 2000, and, owing to a generational low in mortgage rates, a refinancing boom is inuring further to the consumer's state.

Souring sentiment, reasonable valuations, an absence of inflation, the likelihood that monetary policy will remain easy and the unlikelihood of a double-dip continue to form the foundation of value-creation in equities.

In the fullness of time, there is almost an inevitability that a large reallocation trade out of bonds and into stocks is forming. If I am correct, many investors are now offside.

In summary, 10-year Treasuries yielding under 2.60% seem dear and should be shorted, while U.S. stocks trading at 12× reasonable 2011 S&P profits seem cheap and should be purchased.

Make no mistake—the road less traveled will continue to have bumps, and some of those potholes will be with us for some time:

- The securitization market and the shadow banking industry are shattered and shuttered and will no longer deliver credit anywhere to the degree they did in the last credit cycle.
- Residential and nonresidential construction will not serve as a driver to growth, and there is little to replace the void.
- Regulation will remain a costly burden on industry.
- It is increasingly obvious that there is a structural increase in unemployment in the decade of the temporary worker.
- A policy of populism geared against the wealthy and large corporations will have negative implications—higher marginal tax rates will weigh on growth/profitability.
- Fiscal imbalances at local, state and federal levels are unprecedented.

The good news is that most of these nontraditional headwinds are now recognized by most investors, so the vehicles traversing those bumpy roads seem to be reasonably prepared and relatively well equipped.

Tactically, I would be patient, and I would not chase yesterday's strength. The journey may well prove worthwhile over the balance of the year.

Looking further ahead, the lost decade has passed us, and a new decade is upon us.

Rerisk prudently.

Equities Edge toward a Top

10/19/2010

I find myself back to taking the (market) road less traveled once again as investors' unjustified blind faith in the success of the second round of quantitative easing (QE2) has increased the U.S. stock market's degree of risk relative to the reward.

Let me start by emphasizing that the precision of stock market forecasts in a market dominated by algorithms, momentum players and even mob psychology is an increasingly difficult exercise, but I will try nonetheless.

In early July 2010, when the S&P 500 was plummeting and closing in on the 1,000 level, I suggested that the scale had tipped to the bullish side and that equities were in the process of making the lows for the year.

Since then, buoyed by the notion that the prospects for an open-ended QE2, which would be aimed at lowering real interest rates, raising inflation rates and have a strategy that might even be targeted at the S&P 500 in order to elevate the U.S. stock market, equities have leapt forward for weeks in a routine and consistent fashion.

In light of what I expect to be a disappointing economic impact from QE2—I call it quantitative wheezing—and the negative consequences of that strategy on the majority of Americans, I now believe that equities are in the process of putting in the highs for the year.

After spending like drunken sailors during the Bush administration, Republican legislators have acknowledged that it will block even the most sensible stimulus programs, and the Democratic administration and its legislators have lost the will to fight their adversaries. As a result, the responsibility for turning around the domestic economy now lies squarely on the shoulders of the Fed.

The implementation of QE2 during the first week of November is now a virtual certainty. The general belief in its efficacy has vaulted stock markets around the world considerably higher.

The markets believe that unusual, definitive, and targeted monetary solutions will solve deep-rooted problems that, in the past, were put on the shoulders of fiscal policy.

On Wall Street, we too easily extrapolate trends. Whether it's company earnings or industry statistics or economic recoveries, policies and rescue packages, investors want to believe in the more or most favorable outcomes. So we are told by Wall Street strategists and most long-biased investors that if the liquidity infusion from the first round of quantitative easing worked in the United States, it has to work in QE2.

Throughout the market's rally over the past six weeks, I was reminded of something Milton Friedman once expressed, which I have taken the liberty of paraphrasing below to emphasize my concerns with regard to the efficacy of QE2: If you put the Federal Reserve in charge of the Sahara Desert, in five years, there would be a shortage of sand.

We have embarked on a slippery slope of policy, and, from my perch, there is too much confidence regarding a favorable outcome.

Is it really a good idea to put our investment trust in the successful policy of the Fed in its ability to fine-tune inflation and stimulate growth? After all, in the past the Fed couldn't find its way home and failed to identify the stock market bubble in the late 1990s, the housing bubble in 2003–2007 and the recent credit bubble.

In a recent interview with *Fortune* magazine's Carol Loomis, Warren Buffett said that he "can't imagine anybody having bonds in their portfolio." At the same time, Fed Chairman Ben Bernanke is hellbent on buying U.S. bonds ad infinitum. Who do you have more confidence in?

I don't believe QE2 will meaningfully move the needle of domestic economic growth and will only have a limited impact on:

- The jobs market, which is plagued by structural unemployment;
- Housing, which is haunted by a large shadow inventory of unsold homes and in which mortgage credit will likely be further reduced by the moratorium on foreclosures; and
- Confidence, which is still mired in uncertainty regarding regulatory and tax policy (and which is undermined by high unemployment).

Conditions are far different for QE2 than QE1. Interest rates have already fallen to very low levels, and the benefits have already been felt on mortgage rates and in refinancing. Also, unlike QE1, when the world's central banks were all-in, differing policies now dominate the global landscape.

Meanwhile, our fiscal imbalances multiply, our currency craters (as a worldwide rush to currency devaluation is offsetting some of the normal trade deficit benefit), and the bulls rationalize these concerns by suggesting that the consequences "are beyond our investment time frame."

Importantly, there are a number of other possible adverse consequences from the inefficient allocation of resources that is the outgrowth of the next tranche of monetary stimulation.

While the immediate response to the likelihood of QE2 has been to buoy asset prices, the domestic economy is stalling at around 1.5% to

2.0% GDP growth, and little improvement in the jobs market has been seen. This hesitancy makes the anemic slope of the current recovery vulnerable to the unforeseen (e.g., trade wars, policy errors, etc.) and could place the generally assumed self-sustaining economic cycle at risk. As well, the long tail of the last cycle's abusive use of credit looms large, as demonstrated by mortgage-gate.

My bottom line is that QE2 will have only a modest effect on the broad economy. Our largest corporations will fare better as interest rates drop and will profitably extend their debt maturities in a cheap and hospitable bond market, but, as commodities rise, some troubling consequences could emerge.

We are not on a road to the stagflation of the 1970s, but we may very well be on the road to screwflation.

Screwflation, similar to its first cousin stagflation, is an expression of a period of slow and uneven economic growth, but, its potential inflationary consequences have an outsized impact on a specific group. The emergence of screwflation hurts just the group that you want to protect—namely, the middle class, a segment of the population that has already spent a decade experiencing an erosion in disposable income and a painful period of lower stock and home prices. Importantly, quantitative easing is designed to lower real interest rates and, at the same time, raise inflation. A lower-interest-rate policy hurts the savings classes—both the middle class and the elderly. And inflation in the costs of food, energy and everything else consumed (without a concomitant increase in salaries) will screw the average American who doesn't benefit from QE2.

In summary, somebody holds the key to a self-sustaining domestic economy, but I doubt that it is a monetary maven, as some of the potential side effects of quantitative easing might be worse than the medicine. And the confidence and animal spirits that the markets have expressed since early September might just be blind faith.

The domestic economy remains in a contained recession, and, while containment efforts will continue with QE2, the efficacy of these efforts will likely disappoint and wane.

I continue to see the risks to 2011 corporate profit and U.S. and worldwide economic growth rates to the downside. It remains likely that secular and nontraditional headwinds will produce an extended period of inconsistent and uneven growth in the years ahead, which will be difficult for both corporate managers and investment managers to navigate. Arguably, given the sharp rise in equities, the downside risks might be growing ever greater, especially if I am correct that QE2 will be a dud.

The key to remedying today's low P/E multiples would be to apply the same amount of attention, brain power and solutions spent on short-term policy on the underlying structural problems that our country faces.

But, patience, more than policy, is something that investors, politicians and others have precious little of these days.

More on Screwflation

10/20/2010

We all recognize the intended theoretical benefits of QE2:

- Lower real intermediate- and long-term interest rates are expected to stimulate credit-sensitive spending. Authorities expect housing and refinancing activity to expand (through lower mortgage rates), and a rate reduction is forecast to reduce the consumers' debt service expense.
- Higher stock prices are expected to buoy personal consumption spending through the wealth effect and reduce the cost of capital to corporations.
- A lower U.S. dollar narrows our trade deficit.

"In my darkest moments, I have begun to wonder if the monetary accommodation we have already engineered might even be working in the wrong places."

—Dallas Fed President Richard Fisher

I am less certain than most that the theory behind QE2 will become the reality of QE2.

Below are some additional questions that should be asked in determining the ultimate efficacy and effect of QE2.

1. With regard to the transmission mechanism in respect to higher equity prices:

   A. Is there any physical method whereby the Fed forces equity prices up?

   B. Is it pure jawboning that does it?

   C. Or is it that painfully low rates force more people into equities? At this point, it can't be choice C given where yields already are, can it? If it's choice B, how much powder is left? If it's choice A, how do they do it? Or is there a choice I am missing?

2. For the wealth effect of equities to matter, how much does the equity market need to go up from here to get a real kicker? Then, does the slope of the line matter? Is there a difference in the impact of the wealth effect if we get a step-function 20% increase vs. a smooth 20% increase over next two years, for example?

3. Does the wealth effect of equities matter much? Are equities so widely held by enough of the population that they matter, or is their impact on spending much less meaningful than housing?

4. While QE2 makes bank lending more attractive, given the rep and warranties issue that has come to the fore (and the general regulatory climate toward strengthening capital ratios), is it reasonable to expect banks to leverage up their balance sheets now?

5. Then, importantly, to the extent that quantitative easing helps increase asset prices, by definition and in fact, this also means that it increases the price of commodities and other inputs as well. Shouldn't the benefit of the wealth effect be offset by an expense effect (not to mention the fact that now a huge portion of the population can't earn any interest on their savings, which is also a huge cost)? And is it possible that, for the average American, the expense effect hurts more than the wealth effect of equities helps? Why is the expense effect not considered in a lot of the analysis? Could it be the wealth effect may help in total (huge benefit for the wealthy) but when the expense effect is considered, 70%-plus of the population comes out on the short end of this trade? I think the expense effect is much greater than it has been in the past. What-ever quantitative easing does to increase equity prices now also flows directly into commodity prices. Do the new Fed models account for this increased expense effect? Do they account for screwflation?

A Contagion of Black Swans

3/14/2011

Black swans are occurring with greater frequency.

Last week's historic earthquake in Japan contradicts the notion and appearance of stability and is yet another black swan in a series that has (time and time again) threatened the order over the past decade.

The new normal is abnormal and is bound to haunt investors for some time to come.

I am not referring to Pimco's Mohamed El-Erian's notion that world economic growth will be lower; I am referring to the new normal of disproportionate, high-impact, hard-to-predict and rare events beyond the realm of "normal expectations in business, history, science and technology" that are occurring with startling frequency.

Risks of more and repeated black swans, previously perceived to be small by corpo-

> *"I'm astounded by people who want to 'know' the universe when it's hard enough to find your way around Chinatown."*
>
> —Woody Allen

rations, investors, politicians and regulators, should now be reassessed, owing to (among other issues) globalization, tighter correlations, advancements in technology, the growing/excessive complexities of interlocking supply chains and derivatives, the acceptance of greater/extreme risk taking, the greater connectivity of increasingly more complex systems and so forth. I see a greater and more dynamic instability as the new normal. Witness the increased regularity of economically, politically, and socially altering black swan events over the past decade (*Note:* three of the eight deadliest natural disasters of the past century have occurred since 2004):

- The September 11, 2001, attacks on the World Trade Center and Pentagon;
- A 75% decline in the Nasdaq;
- The 2003 European heat wave (40,000 deaths);
- The 2004 tsunami in Sumatra, Indonesia (230,000 deaths);
- The 2005 Kashmir, Pakistan, earthquake (80,000 deaths);
- The 2008 Myanmar cyclone (140,000 deaths);
- The 2008 Sichuan, China, earthquake (68,000 deaths);

- Financial derivatives roil the world's banking system and financial markets;
- The failure of Lehman Brothers and the sale/liquidation of Bear Stearns;
- A 30% drop in U.S. home prices;
- The 2010 Port-Au-Prince, Haiti, earthquake (315,000 deaths);
- The 2010 Russian heat wave (56,000 deaths);
- BP's Gulf of Mexico oil spill;
- The 2010 market flash crash (a 1,000-point drop in the Dow Jones Industrial Average [DJIA]);
- The broadening scale of unrest in the Middle East; and
- Thursday's earthquake and tsunami in Japan.

We can no longer turn the clock back to a simpler time. We must play the hand we are dealt. And our time is interconnected, interlinked and increasingly complex. And our hand has, at its core, a rising number of outlier or black swan events.

We shouldn't be overly paranoid nor should potential outlier events blind us to investment opportunity. But we must be mindful.

Throughout history, there have been times when it has even been more profitable for investors to bind together in the wrong direction than to be alone in the right one. The long-term direction of equities will likely always be higher, and the crowd of optimists will invariably outperform the remnants of pessimists.

Nevertheless, for years, investors seem to have been blinded to the uncertainty of the rare black swan event. We now know that these black swans are occurring with greater regularity and with greater overall impact— and, as such, we must recognize that the occurrences may not only hold the potential for reducing aggregate growth but that the uncertainty of these outlier events could conceivably cast a pall over stock valuations.

After all, the inability to predict black swan events implies a greater inability to predict the course of economic and market history—whether it is a natural disaster, a surprising geopolitical event, or an unexpected economic or credit outcome.

It is only obvious after the fact, as investors, in particular, seem to harbor a crippling dislike for the abstract. Perhaps the problem with experts is that they do not know what they do not know.

For some time, investors have been exposing themselves to the high-impact, rare event yet sleeping like babies, unaware of it.

But recent events might bring on some nightmares.

Our domestic economy faces numerous structural issues (the most important of which are the extreme fiscal imbalances at the federal, state and local levels), with governments (here and abroad) not necessarily up to the task of dealing with the complexities.

Given the newness of these and other nontraditional and secular challenges as well as the greater frequency of black swan events, P/E multiples might be pressured and could even contract as a comparison between today's valuations to those of history can be expected to lose some of its significance and relevance.

In summary, I marvel at the confidence of strategists in a smooth and self-sustaining economic recovery in such an uncertain world.

Strategists routinely make valuation comparisons based on it rhyming with historical experience. Similar to the belief in bell curves, these comparisons should be viewed with caution, because, in all likelihood, another black swan could appear on our investment doorstep—maybe sooner than later.

In this setting, a more conservative asset mix and higher cash position than normal seems to be a prudent strategy.

Apocalypse Soon

4/11/2011

Over the past 24 months, the cyclical tailwinds of fiscal and monetary stimulation have served to raise the animal spirits and investors' willingness to buy longer-dated assets such as equities and commodities (soft and hard).

The Bernanke Put (and a zero-interest-rate policy) replaced the Greenspan Put (but with a far more generous exercise price!), and market valuations have risen dramatically in the latest two-year period.

Since the market's low, as measured against trailing-12-month sales, equity capitalizations have increased as a percent of sales from 75% to 140%. And by my own calculation, stocks have risen from 13×–14× to

16X–16.5X normalized earnings. Nevertheless, bulls somewhat disingenuously argue that the doubling in stock prices is reasonable within the context of a doubling in corporate profits. But those same bulls conveniently (and selectively) dismiss the notion of normalized (not margin-inflated) earnings, while they liberally employed normalized earnings as justification for owning stocks when profits disappeared in the late-2008/early-2009 interim interval.

During the same time frame, fear has made a new low, and complacency has made a new high, as reflected a marked imbalance between bulls and bears in most investor sentiment surveys. To put it mildly and to state the obvious, market skepticism has not paid off. Indeed, the pessimists have been written off (and even ridiculed), similar to the zeal in which the optimists were written off 24 months ago.

The stimulation so necessary in keeping the world's financial and economic system from falling off the cliff has come at a cost (and with potential risks), as reflected in rising commodities and precious metals prices. The impact of policy has relieved us from the depths of the Great Decession but has arguably burdened the United States with large due bills, positioning the domestic economy with a potentially weak foundation for growth.

Consider these possible headwinds to a smooth and self-sustaining trajectory of growth:

- Higher energy costs remain the biggest risk to profit and worldwide economic growth—it is the greatest and most pernicious tax of all. The rapid rate of change in the price of crude oil has historically presaged weakness in U.S. stock prices. A world rolling quickly toward industrialization, with an emerging middle class and goosed by an unprecedented amount of quantitative easing has conspired to pressure commodity prices (especially of an energy kind). Moreover, Japan's nuclear crisis has likely further increased our dependency on fossil fuels. U.S. policy is on a slippery slope on which oil might be increasingly impacted by the outside influences of Mother Nature and political developments—all of which is beyond our control.

- Besides energy prices, a broadening increase in input prices also threatens corporate profit margins. While Bernanke is unconcerned with rising inflationary pressures and the CRB Index, as the

Economic Cycle Research Institute notes, the Fed runs the risk, once again, of being behind the inflation curve and, in the fullness of time, being faced with the need to introduce policies that could snuff out growth with errant policy. Hershey, Procter & Gamble, Colgate-Palmolive, McDonald's, Wal-Mart, and Kimberly-Clark have all announced sharp price increases (of 5% to 10%) in the cost of their staple products, running the gamut from chocolate kisses to diapers.

- The cost of 2008–2011 policy is a mushrooming and outsized deficit. Since the generational low in March 2009, the U.S. dollar has dropped by over 23% against the euro, as market participants have dismissed the notion that the hard decisions to reduce the deficit will be implemented. As Nicholas Kristof wrote in the *New York Times* yesterday, "This isn't the government we are watching, it's junior high school. . . . We're governed by self-absorbed, reckless children. . . . The budget war reflects inanity, incompetence and cowardice that are sadly inexplicable." At the opposite side of our plunging currency is the message of ever-higher gold prices. (*Warning:* Dismissing the meaning of $1,500-per-ounce gold might be hazardous to your financial and investment well-being.)

- The rich get richer, the poor go to prison, but everyone else is victimized by screwflation. Most importantly, policies have placed continued pressures on the middle class, with the cost of necessities ever-rising and wage growth nearly nonexistent. The savers' class has suffered painfully from zero-interest-rate policy and quantitative easing, policies that have contributed to the inflation in financial assets (and to an across-the-board hike, or consumer tax, in commodity prices) but have failed to trickle down to better jobs growth, to an improving housing picture or to an opportunity for reduced consumer borrowing costs and credit availability. Meanwhile, the schism between the haves (large corporations) and the have-nots (the average Joe) has widened, as best reflected in near-record S&P 500 profits and a 57-year high in margins. Corporations have feasted (and rolled over their debt) in the currently artificial interest rate setting, but the consumer and small business owners have not fared as well. Particularly disappointing has been overall jobs growth (as reflected in the labor participation rate) and the absence of wage growth (as the average workweek and average hourly earnings continue to disappoint).

It is my view that ultimately corporations' margins will be victimized by the screwflation of the middle class, as rising costs may produce demand-destruction and an inability for companies to pass on their higher business costs.

- Structural unemployment is ever-present. Globalization, technological advances and the use of temporary workers becoming a permanent condition of the workplace are all conspiring to keep unemployment elevated and wage growth restrained. The lower the skill grade and income, the worse the outlook for job opportunities and real income growth. (This is not a statement of class warfare; it's a statement of fact.)
- Meanwhile, the consumer's most important asset, his home, continues to deflate in value, despite the massive stimulus policies, a multidecade high in affordability, improving economics of home ownership vs. renting and burgeoning pent-up demand (reflecting normal population and household formation growth). Consumer confidence has continued to suffer from the unprecedented home price drop, which has been exacerbated by the aforementioned (and decade-plus) stagnation in real incomes. The toxic cocktail of weak home prices, limited wage growth and nagging upside commodity price pressures (particularly from the price of gasoline), will likely pressure retail spending for the remainder of 2011.

Reflecting the doubling in share prices and relative to reasonable expectations, most (except the most ardent bulls) believe that the easy money has been made in stocks. But expectations still remain buoyed, as 1,450–1,500 S&P price targets are commonplace.

I am less sanguine, as many of the factors I have mentioned provide us with what seem to be legitimate questions regarding the smooth path of growth that has underpinned the bull market.

Near term, the stabilizers are coming off, monetary easing and fiscal stimulation are being replaced by rate-tightening and austerity—first over there (across the pond, where I witnessed protests in Paris over the past weekend) but relatively soon to our shores by our Fed and by measures of budgetary constraint instituted by our local, state, and federal governments.

The intermediate- to longer-term shift back from the prior consumption-led, finance- and housing-driven domestic economy to manufacturing-led growth presents numerous challenges to growth that the bulls have all but dismissed.

I continue to see vulnerability to full-year 2011 GDP growth projections, corporate margins and profitability.

The prospects for a smooth and self-sustaining domestic economic recovery and the attainment of $95 a share in S&P 500 profits may be in jeopardy. While this favorable outcome remains possible, it might be challenged by cyclical and secular issues and is exposed, more than most recoveries, by any number of shocks or black swans.

Changing monetary and fiscal policy will be more restrictive, and recent worldwide events have provided renewed uncertainties and unforeseen dangers that cast more questions regarding the optimistic assumptions that underscore the bullish investment and economic cases.

To this observer, consensus corporate profit forecasts have become the best case and are no longer the likely case.

Downward earnings revisions now represent the greatest near-term challenge to the U.S. stock market, as I continue to hold to the view that, at the margin, upside S&P 500 earnings and domestic economic surprises have peaked and that the probability of more earnings warnings and downward profits and economic revisions are likely on the ascent. This trend is not only a domestic observation as the near-term global growth prospects have also moderated recently due to slower-than-expected strength in other parts of the world, the aforementioned price spike, and the Tohoku earthquake.

First-quarter 2011 business activity likely ended weaker than expected, with first-quarter 2011 GDP demonstrating about a 2.5% rate of growth (far less than the near 4% consensus expectation of a few months ago). As economist and friend Vince Malanga mentioned to me over the weekend, the forward economic outlook is not inspiring and is showing signs of decelerating growth: "March ISM manufacturing index showed notable declines in the growth rates for orders, exports and order backlogs. . . . And core capital goods orders were surprisingly weak in both January and February."

If businesses begin to treat the geopolitical crises and elevated oil prices as more permanent conditions, order cancellations and corporate-spending deferrals loom in the months ahead, and the 3.5% to 4.0% GDP forecasts will prove too optimistic. While job growth has recently improved, the absence of wage growth, a likely weakening in personal spending and the absence of a revival in home sales activity this spring could translate to a worse job and retail-spending picture in the months ahead (especially relative to the more optimistic consensus expectations).

I would note that not only is the near-term profit cycle at risk but, from a longer-term perspective, earnings cycles seem to be occurring with greater frequency and profits have been accompanied by more volatility and greater amplitude (peak-to-trough).

Earnings peaked in 1990. The brief recession that followed resulted in only a modest drop in profits and in share prices. The next peak in earnings didn't occur for another decade (in 2000). Both profits and stock values fell more considerably than in the early 1990s, and it took only seven years (2007) for earnings and stock valuations to rise to another higher peak. Should the pattern continue (10 years, 7 years, and now 4 years), it implies that 2011 could represent the next peak in stocks and in earnings.

There could be numerous reasons for this phenomenon. The timing of the Fed's tightening/easing actions and the role of financial innovation (and the proliferation of derivatives and growth in the securitization markets) are two possible explanations.

Nevertheless, I see nothing on the horizon that changes my expectations that the profit cycle is more mature and will demonstrate more volatility than most expect.

Just as the earnings cycle is experiencing more volatility over shorter periods of time, so are black swans and tail-risk events occurring with greater frequency. Consider that three of the eight worst natural disasters of the past century have occurred since 2004. Or that the U.S. stock market has encountered 21 drawdowns of more than 20% over the past 30 years.

Summary Though clearly not as extreme as at its polar opposite and oversold condition at the market's generational low in March 2009, today's overbought market holds a new and different list of fundamental, geopolitical, technical, sentiment, and valuation risks.

At the very least, in these uncertain times, hedge or purchase protection.

For, if not Apocalypse now, there is a risk of Apocalypse soon.

10 Reasons to Buy American

12/14/2011

I believe that the events over the past year highlight the likelihood that the U.S. stock market will be favored among most other investment markets in the world.

Europe's economies are moving in reverse—at best, a deepening recession is in the cards. Europe used to rule the world, but it no longer dominates. The U.S. stock market has become the best house in a bad neighborhood.

The U.S. economy is moving forward, with a 3%-plus real GDP for fourth quarter 2011 expected and growing signs that the domestic recovery will be self-sustaining (albeit, at a moderate pace).

I believe, more than ever, that the events over the past decade have highlighted the likelihood that the U.S. stock market will be favored among most other investment markets in the world.

Below are 10 reasons for my optimism:

1. U.S. relative and absolute economic growth is superior to global growth. The U.S. economy, though sluggish in recovery relative to past expansions, is superior to most of the world's economies (with the exception of some emerging markets) in terms of diversity of end markets, quality of global franchises, management expertise, operating execution and financial foundations.

2. U.S. banks are well capitalized, liquid, and deposit funded. Our banking industry's health, which is the foundation of credit and growth, is far better off than the rest of the world in terms of liquidity and capital. Our largest financial institutions raised capital in 2008–2009, a full three years ahead of the rest of the world. As an example, eurozone banks continue to delay the inevitability of their necessary capital raises. Importantly, our banking system is deposit funded, while Europe's banking system is wholesale funded (and far more dependent on confidence).

3. U.S. corporations boast strong balance sheets and healthy margins/profits. Our corporations are better positioned than the rest of the world. Through aggressive cost-cutting, productivity gains, external acquisitions, (internal) capital expenditures and the absence of a reliance on debt markets—most have opportunistically rolled over their higher-cost debt—U.S. corporations are rock-solid operationally

and financially. Even throughout the 2008–2009 recession, most solidified their global franchises that serve increasingly diverse end markets and geographies.

4. The U.S. consumer is more liquid and stable. An aggressive Fed (through its extended time frame of zero-interest-rate policy) has resulted in an American consumer that has reliquefied more than individuals that live in most of the other areas in the world. (Debt service and household debt is down dramatically relative to income.)

5. The United States is politically stable. After watching regime after regime fall in Europe in recent weeks (and given the instability of other rulers throughout the Middle East), it should be clear that the United States is more secure politically and from a defense standpoint than most other regions of the world. Our democracy, despite all its inadequacies, has resulted in civil discourse, relatively balanced legislation, smooth regime changes and law that has contributed to social stability and a sense of overall order.

6. The United States has a solid and transparent corporate reporting system. Our regulatory and reporting standards are among the strongest in the world. Compare, for example, the opaque reporting and absence of regulatory oversight in China vs. the United States. (It is beyond compare.)

7. The United States is rich in resources.

8. The United States has a functioning and forward-looking central bank that is aggressive in policy (when necessary) and capable of acting during crisis.

9. The U.S. dollar is (still) the world's reserve currency that is far more solid than the euro.

10. The United States is a magnet for immigrants seeking a better life. This and other factors have contributed to a better demographic profile in our country that has led to consistent population growth and formation of households. (Demographic trends in the United States are particularly more favorable for growth than those population trends in the Far East.)

In summary, conditions that have evolved over the near- and intermediate-term have conspired to favor risk assets in the United States over many other areas of the world.

In the period ahead, look inward (not outward), as I expect a powerful reallocation trade out of non-U.S. equities into U.S. equities.

Buy American. I am.

The Case for Shorting U.S. Bonds

3/12/2012

Bonds have achieved a near-50% total return since year-end 2009. With those outsized returns, shorting bonds has been a toxic strategy.

Over the past half-century, bonds have historically been considered a risk-free asset class.

Nevertheless, I believe bonds should now be seen as a return-free asset class that is very risky and long-dated fixed income should require a warning label for all potential buyers.

Historical Returns The great bull market in bonds has persisted during most of the last four decades.

Over the past 38 years (since 1974), the total return on the long bond registered negative returns in excess of 5% in only four years: 1987 (−6.3%), 1994 (−12.0%), 1999 (−14.8%) and 2009 (−25.5%).

The market landscape is littered with investors and traders who have unsuccessfully shorted U.S. bonds over the past two years.

It has been a painful experience, but often the hardest trades (and those that have been most unsuccessful) are the most profitable going forward.

So, before I outline the rationale behind the five key reasons to short bonds, given that the burden of proof lies squarely on the shoulders of the bond naysayers, I wanted to start with the five reasons not to short bonds.

Five Reasons Not to Short Bonds Above all, the U.S. economy faces powerful secular headwinds that weigh as an albatross around the neck of a trajectory of self-sustaining growth.

1. *The forecast? Muddle-through growth:* At best, muddle-through remains the baseline expectation for domestic economic growth for 2012.

2. *A feel-bad environment:* Deleveraging and caution associated with the pronounced economic downturn of 2008–2009, coupled with structural unemployment, represent a confidence deflator and act as a governor to personal consumption over the near term.

3. *The Bernanke put:* The Fed will likely anchor short-term interest rates as far as the eye can see. More quantitative easing will be on deck if the domestic economic recovery falters.

4. *A large manufacturing output gap:* Capacity utilization rates are nowhere near levels that are typically associated with demand-pull inflation.

5. *A negative demographic shift:* Aging Baby Boomers are ignoring stocks, preferring to buy risk-free fixed-income products. After two massive drops in the U.S. stock market since 2000 and a lost decade for equity investors, this rapidly growing demographic seems to continue to have an almost insatiable appetite for bonds.

In summary, the positive case for U.S. government (and corporate) debt is that there are numerous cyclical and secular factors that will weigh on domestic growth, serving as a significant hurdle against the short bond thesis.

Five Reasons to Short Bonds   It is my contention that even if domestic economic growth is constrained, a bond short can prosper, even under the baseline expectation of a muddle-through growth backdrop.

1. The flight to safety will likely have a diminishing half-life. With some progress being made in Europe (reflected in lower sovereign debt yields and sharp rises in European stock markets) and with confidence in the world's financial system improving, it is only a matter of time before the flight-to-safety premium in bonds dissipates.

   Bond yields are unusually low, and I would note that the current 10-year U.S. note (2.0%) is approximately one-half the yield of the recession of the early 2000s. Gold prices already suggest that the safety premium could disappear sooner than later. (I view gold as a fear trade, and the recent drop in gold prices should be seen as a forward indicator of less fear.)

   While U.S. economic growth remains subpar, a reacceleration is inevitable in the fullness of time. Demand for durables (housing and auto) is pent-up not spent-up, and continued population and household formation growth will serve to unleash latent demand at some point in time.

Over the past five decades, long-dated bond yields have tracked (and averaged only slightly under) the nominal growth rate in the United States—4.4% (2% real GDP estimate plus 2.4% current inflation) compared to the yield on the 10-year U.S. note of 2.0% and the 30-year U.S. note of 3.1%—in fact, long-dated yields often exceed nominal GDP.

2. Flows out of stock funds and into bond funds seem to be at a tipping point. Since 2007, nearly $450 billion has been redeemed from U.S. equity funds, and $850 billion has been placed into U.S bond funds. This swing of $1.3 trillion is unprecedented in history. In early 2012, the hemorrhaging of stock funds has stopped. It is my contention that, at some point, a massive reallocation from fixed income into equities is inevitable.

3. Confidence is recovering as economic growth reemerges and risk markets improve. The real yield on the 10-year U.S. note correlates well with consumer confidence, which is now recovering.

4. Inflation remains an issue. A steady increase in inflation and inflationary expectations has occurred as most inflationary gauges (Treasury inflation-protected securities [TIPS], etc.) are at six-month highs. I would not entirely eliminate the concern on demand-pull inflation as emerging markets grow more industrialized. Moreover, cost-push inflation is a growing possibility—particularly in light of geopolitical pressures that could create a black swan in the price of crude oil.

5. The failure to address our fiscal imbalances could come back and bite the bond market. The November elections might result in more gridlock. A Democratic president, and a Republican House and Senate imply that little positive progress should be expected in meaningfully resolving our burgeoning deficit in a still-divided Washington, D.C. This could encourage the bond vigilantes and further alienate foreign central bankers in their appetite for our bonds and notes. (Many are already diversifying away from the U.S. bond market.)

Strategy in Shorting Bonds I readily admit that, in all likelihood, with U.S. GDP growth of less than 2% in first quarter 2012, bond prices will be relatively range-bound in the weeks ahead.

But any evidence of a resumption of growth will have a dual impact: It will likely reduce the flight to safety (reflected in bond premiums) and, at the same time, produce the historically normal and natural upward pressure on interest rates associated with an improving economy.

When this happens, bonds will, once again, become certificates of confiscation.

Residential Real Estate Is Ready to Recover

3/28/2012

The housing market's shadow inventory of unsold homes is starting to clear, certain areas of the country are experiencing signs of more robust activity, and, despite low levels of new-home production (based on historical data), homebuilders are even regaining pricing power in several geographic regions.

Stated simply, the U.S. residential real estate market is about to launch a broad and sustainable multiyear recovery. And, from my perch, the share price strength in housing-related equities is telling the real story of an improving and self-sustaining home market that could continue through the balance of this decade.

As proof of my emerging optimism, I would suggest listening to Toll Brothers' last two earnings conference call presentations and the recent observations made by CEO Doug Yearley in the media.

- Spring selling season is strong. Over the past five years, Toll's early-spring selling season had sputtered out in late February/early March. In 2012, however, its sales activity is getting stronger as the year progresses.
- Homebuilder pricing power is returning. In fact, Toll Brothers is having its best-selling season since 2007. Orders are up "significantly" and nearly 30% of the company's communities have increased home prices. (A year ago, none had pricing power.)
- The sun shines in Florida. Miami, one of the epicenters of home speculation in the last cycle, which had been previously inundated

with foreclosures two to three years ago, has turned around meaningfully, thanks to an inflow of South American and Northeast U.S. buyers. This turnaround has been in place for 9 to 12 months.

- Shadow inventory is clearing. Surprisingly, even some areas of the country that have been adversely impacted by the weight of a large shadow inventory of foreclosed or soon-to-be-foreclosed homes, have improved measurably and are turning the corner. A good example is Phoenix, which had over 15 months of supply for sale 12 months ago but now has a developing shortage of inventory (under 3 months of supply).
- West Coast land prices are soaring. In certain areas of northern and southern California, the raw land market is regaining a speculative tone as prices have risen dramatically. The strength of land prices, while well ahead of the health of the home price market, is typically a leading indicator of industry pricing and activity.

It is my expectation that both new- and existing-home prices, which suffered price declines of close to 34% from 2007 to 2011, face a better year ahead in 2012 and over the balance of the decade.

While the housing recovery of 2012 to 2020 will likely start out slowly, owing to the large inventory of unsold homes, still-restricted mortgage credit and the current preference for renting, there is now ample evidence that residential real estate markets have already turned in a national market that has grown bifurcated. Areas of the country that are unencumbered by a large supply of foreclosed properties—for instance, the Washington, D.C.-to-Boston corridor—are doing better. Cancellation rates are down dramatically, and some pricing power is returning for the homebuilders. By contrast, areas such as inland California, Nevada, and the like continue to suffer in price and in sluggish transaction activity as a result of the indigestion of the last cycle.

In other words, the weaker regions are masking a developing national recovery in housing that has the potential to be more durable and healthier than the past cycle.

Below are the seven main reasons why (in conjunction with the Toll Brothers comments) I expect a durable recovery (in demand, activity/ transactions and in prices) in the U.S. housing market:

1. Housing affordability is at a multidecade high.
2. Reflecting normal U.S. demographic trends (household formations of 1 million-plus per year) and a low level of 2008–2012 new-home production, there is plenty of pent-up demand ready to be unleashed.
3. As rental prices have risen and as home prices have fallen, the economics of home ownership has improved.
4. We have seen a decisive improvement in the jobs market.
5. Mortgage rates are at historic lows.
6. Housing surveys have turned positive.
7. Confidence is improving.

The Bear Case for Apple

9/24/2012

Pride goeth before a fall—also publicity, handshakes and celebrity. The biblical injunction about the first and the last trading places often has literal truth. Thus, stocks and bonds, which fared poorly in the inflationary 1970s, excelled in the disinflationary 1980s. The country's most admired companies (as listed annually in the glossy business magazines) are frequently on their way to becoming among the country's least admired investments. When a cynical investor hears that there are too many optimists in the market, he will begin to worry. By the same token, an over-abundance of pessimists will give him courage. After all, he may ask, if everyone is already bearish, who is left to sell?
—James Grant, *Minding Mister Market: Ten Years on Wall Street With Grant's Interest Rate Observer*

Apple has been a once-in-a-century profit dynamo that has prospered and has expanded its market share by delivering innovative products and expanding its self-sustaining ecosystem.

The chart of Apple's shares since 1985 is remarkable.

In the 1960s and 1970s, the stock market was inhabited by the "Nifty Fifty," a small subset of one-decision stocks that had strong balance sheets, solid franchises (typically leaders in their field), relatively superior profit prospects and were generally credited with the bull market of that era. Some examples of the Nifty Fifty included Wal-Mart, Avon Products, Disney, McDonald's, Polaroid, and Xerox. The stocks flourished for a while but ultimately became overvalued and were weighed down by the bear market that continued until 1982.

Today there is no more Nifty Fifty, arguably there is the nifty one— and that one is Apple. The Wall Street analytical community and many money managers are unambiguously and unanimously optimistic about the company, but let's not lose sight of the fact that the sword is double-edged, as an investor who bought the Nifty Fifty at the end of 1972 would have had 50% less wealth by year-end 2001 relative to an investor who bought the S&P 500. (Sic transit gloria.)

Over the weekend, the *New York Times*'s Joe Nocera wrote an interesting article that speculated that Apple has peaked.

It got me thinking, and below I highlight a list of 10 concerns, fully recognizing the current quarter will be ahead of expectations.

Apple's significant role in the indices and its extraordinary relative and absolute performances have been an important determinant of investment returns. A portfolio heavily weighted to Apple has been a ticket to outperformance. By contrast, a portfolio dismissive of Apple's prospects and underweighted the stock has underperformed.

But the preceding paragraph modifies the past; it does not necessarily hold for the future.

Investment history shows that when there is such unanimity of good will bestowed toward a corporation's equity, when the very share price performance of only one security has such a profound impact on aggregate investment returns, when a record amount of analysts (53) follow an individual company with enthusiasm and optimism and when a company's total capitalization is mentioned in the media constantly and throughout the trading day, resonating throughout the investment community, it is time to be on guard if not concerned.

Surprise No. 10: Despite the advance in the U.S. stock market, high-beta stocks underperform. Though counterintuitive within the framework of a new bull-market leg, the market's lowfliers (low multiple, slower growth) become market highfliers, as their

P/E ratios expand. With the exception of Apple, the highfliers—Priceline, Baidu, Google, Amazon and the like—disappoint. Apple's share price rises above $550, however, based on continued above-consensus volume growth in the iPhone and iPad. Profit forecasts for 2012 rise to $45 a share (up 60%). In the second quarter, Apple pays a $20-a-share special cash dividend, introduces a regular $1.25-a-share quarterly dividend and splits its shares 10-1. Apple becomes the AT&T of a previous investing generation, a stock now owned by this generation's widows and orphans.
—*Doug Kass, "15 Surprises for 2012" (December 27, 2011)*

I have written positively about Apple this year.

While I recognize that valuation and concept shorts are usually a free pass to the poor house, Joe Nocera's editorial to me was a reminder that, as Grandma Koufax used to tell me, "trees don't grow to the sky."

There is no better time to consider the negative case for Apple given its marked outperformance and its recent penetration of the $700-a-share mark.

Principal Short-Term Positive: A Blockbuster Quarter The upcoming quarter will be big for Apple. The fastest ever rollout for iPhone 5 will be accompanied by higher-than-expected margins, as there are two separate cost-reduced models now. Soon everyone will know that, and if not fully in analyst numbers, it will be in buy-side expectations. (See the recent rise in the stock even after what was viewed as a somewhat me-too product launch.)

10 Concerns

1. *Quality vs. price:* Apple is now selling less or equal for more money. The company used to sell a better product for more money, which is a great strategy. Its products were simply market defining, and competitors were not close. Recently, however, things have changed, and competitors have caught up. Now Apple is selling an equal to worse product than the competition for more money (both phones and tablets). That strategy cannot work forever. This is the biggest issue.

2. *Delivering a more complicated product:* Products are also getting more complex and Microsoft-like. Apple's challenge is to deliver ever more complicated products (with a lot of new components) in sufficient quantities. See most recent Foxconn issue. Previously, we would never have seen such a story because there were never issues and nobody would dare voice them.

3. *The Oracle of Cupertino:* Steve Jobs is no longer around to convince consumers that his products are magical. There is no longer a single visionary voice, especially with the vision of Steve Jobs. There are stories floating around about internal disagreements and power struggles given the unique void created by the loss of a single dominant figure in an unusual corporate structure that he controlled.

4. *Increasing product homogeneity:* Apple no longer has a huge ecosystem advantage. Most if not all the apps that consumers care about are available on Android and Microsoft, which can also run Office apps such as Excel that Apple doesn't. The first-mover advantage might be lessened or lost if Apple continues to try to do everything on a proprietary basis—for instance, maps (and who wants a smartphone with bad maps?).

5. *Economic headwinds:* Some of the markets served by Apple are saturated, and in a worldwide economy facing strong headwinds, consumers may balk at a product that can be purchased at much lower prices from competitors. Until last quarter, Apple never missed consensus expectations during a product transition. There is more to last quarter's miss than transition.

6. *Poor economic proposition for Apple's partners:* Apple's carrier partners do not like the economics they give to Apple. Apple's partners have shown that they can and will shift to the good alternatives that consumers seem to like (e.g., Samsung Galaxy).

7. *Roadblocks to new initiatives:* Potential business partners in general do not like or trust Apple relative to other initiatives. The music industry and AT&T have not had great experiences with Apple, and the company might find it hard to sign deals for new initiatives.

8. *Product cannibalization:* The iPad mini may cannibalize the higher-margin iPad—or just be a neutral at best.

9. *Growing size mandates delivery of more product blockbusters:* An investor better believe in a huge new blockbuster product next year. TV is complex due to relationships with cable companies, set-top box manufacturers and channel guide programmers. Google may one-up Apple in the space, as it owns Motorola's set-top box division and has Google Voice already. If it comes to integrating more complex solution for TVs with content, cable companies and other media partners have learned not to trust Apple given the poor outcomes other Apple partners have had (e.g., music industry, AT&T, etc.).

10. *Valuation:* Apple's stock is cheap on a P/E basis but arguably very expensive on price/sales (4.4×) and total absolute market capitalization basis ($625 billion).

A House Divided against Itself

1/28/2013

Today, there is an almost unanimous view that the strength in housing will be the most important factor (or one of the more important factors) in offsetting the fiscal drag associated with the spending cuts and tax-rate increases (necessary to pare down the burgeoning U.S. budget).

To many, a booming housing market seems to be an almost single justification for ambitious economic growth targets and for an enthusiastic view of the U.S. stock market.

Optimism surrounding the housing market wasn't the case 18 months ago—indeed, back then there was a great deal of skepticism (that I didn't share).

Over the past year and a half I have consistently made the case that the housing market's upside would surprise most investors over the near term and that the U.S. residential market is likely to embark upon a durable and multiyear recovery.

The key points I made in my prior analysis were that the benefits of historically low mortgage rates, vastly improved home affordability and pent-up demand (once the U.S. economy and jobs market stabilized) would yield higher home prices and rising sales turnover. Some of these factors remain in force, but other depressing factors have been introduced that could produce a halting consumer, uneven housing activity and less certain home pricing over the course of 2013.

While I remain of the view that a durable housing recovery is in place, I am less optimistic about the next 12 to 15 months.

The housing recovery may not be steady in progress, smooth in growth and uninterrupted in its trajectory.

The fact is that housing as a series (in activity and prices), more often than not, exhibits volatility—even when it's on the way toward recovery.

In early 2013, the U.S. consumer faces uncommon hurdles that could adversely impact the housing markets and lead to disappointing personal consumption trends.

Specifically, given the backdrop of higher individual tax rates, reduced government spending, a possible trend toward higher interest rates and a still-chastened single-family homebuyer (who has recently faced an unprecedented 30% drop in home prices), I do not anticipate a smooth recovery in housing over the next 12 to 18 months in the face of these macro and consumer headwinds.

The single-family housing market lacks durable leadership—repeat buyers are carrying the housing market. The more important first-time homebuyers are out of firepower and peaked in May 2012, investor buyers peaked in June 2012, and all-cash existing sales volume turned flat in December 2012.

I worry that the Fed's stimulus, which induced a housing recovery over the past 18 months, might have even pushed forward home activity and demand and could conceivably produce a 2013 hangover.

Even if housing continues to recover and exhibits something more than a stimulus-related bounce, it would take a hell of a rise in construction activity to impact aggregate U.S. economic growth given construction's relatively small role in GDP. For illustrative purposes, let's presume the consensus is correct and that the residential housing market will continue to exhibit strong growth. Construction represents only about 3% of GDP. Therefore a 20% increase in construction activity will only positively impact GDP by 0.6% (before the multiplier effect takes hold). This compares against a likely 1% to 2% headwind from spending cuts and higher taxes. (I am using a larger multiplier than most.)

Bottom line: The future outlook (in both home sales activity and for home prices) is principally a function of three variables (and I hold to a less-than-optimistic view of all these factors).

1. *Economic conditions:* Strength in the domestic economy, wage growth and the status of the jobs market are the historic pillars of the housing market. I am less sanguine than most regarding these variables.
2. *Credit conditions:* The availability of mortgage credit and the level of interest rates are also important ingredients to the health of housing. A further rise in interest rates could grind purchase and refinancing applications to a crawl (as housing demand has been pushed forward), even though mortgage rates are low by historic standards.
3. *The propensity for home ownership:* The desire to own vs. rent is cyclical. The pendulum has swung from the speculation of the last cycle, in which homes were day traded, to a more conservative view of home ownership (likely to be with us for several more years).

These three categories are not setting up to provide steady growth in the U.S. housing market over the near term—there are numerous question marks.

Economic Conditions   My baseline expectation is for (at best) 1.5% real GDP growth in 2013—this is below consensus expectations. And I believe there is further risk to the downside.

I remain particularly cautious on the consumer (and homebuyer), who, despite a slightly improving jobs market, faces numerous headwinds.

Credit Conditions   Over the past week the yield on the 10-year U.S. note rose from 1.82% to 1.95%. The consensus appears to be that the 10-year will rise no higher in yield than 2.25% to 2.50% in 2013—based in part on continued deleveraging, slow growth and a friendly Fed (which will effectively repress long rates). Homebuyers have become accustomed to low mortgage rates, but I would caution that given housing's historic rate sensitivity, any rise in interest rates above consensus expectations could immediately provide a headwind to the U.S. housing market. Indeed, I expect refinancing and purchase applications to suffer in the near term if rates continue last week's rise.

The Propensity to Own a Home   The average middle-class U.S. consumer is beaten up.

Faced with two large stock market drawdowns in the last decade, a flash crash, screwflation (in which income has not kept pace with the costs of necessities of life: insurance, education, food, etc.), the largest economic recession since the Great Depression, continued jobs insecurity and a 30% drop in home prices, consumer behavior has changed and is not likely to revert to the historical spending patterns exhibited in the last few cycles.

A very good example of this is the evidence that individuals failed to purchase domestic equities until January 2013, as buying stocks took a backseat to making ends meet. As it relates to housing, the stunning drop in home prices in 2007–2010 will probably continue to be associated with a more conservative view toward home ownership and with a greater desire to rent. This helps to explain the continued lackluster single-family home market.

We can see this phenomenon demonstrated in the continuing dominance of multifamily starts relative to single-family starts throughout 2012. It will be interesting to see how the enormous supply of apartments will impact rents and home prices in the coming year.

Summary   In summary, while a real estate recovery is under way, a full-blown housing recovery is probably a few years away.

I can see several factors (fiscal drag and higher interest rates) negatively impacting the consumer and serving to cause unevenness or even a pothole in the current housing recovery.

The housing market will not save the U.S. economy, and growing optimistic expectations for the residential real estate market are not likely to be met in 2013–2014.

Even if I am understating the recovery in housing, construction activity represents a relatively small fraction (3%) of GDP, and, as such, its aggregate impact on domestic economic growth is probably being overstated by many.

Beware the Interest Rate Cliff

5/29/2013

Since early May, the yields on 10-year U.S. Treasury notes and 30-year U.S. bonds have risen abruptly, by a bit more than 50 basis points. Yesterday was the worst day for U.S. fixed income in years, with a 6.5% increase in yields (10-year). Stated simply, the markets are running ahead of the Fed's tapering.

The bullish argument on interest rates is that as long as rates don't rise too fast, the optimistic outlook for the economy and the equity market will remain intact. I am less certain, as I see a false economic dawn in the United States and around the world.

The bottom line is that interest rates are an important raw material of the U.S. economy. As they rise, it will affect everything (profits, capital spending, hirings, etc.), and stock prices will likely have to adjust (and the adjustment won't be upward).

Addicted to Low Interest Rates   U.S. corporations, consumers and even our government are addicted to lower interest rates.

- Corporations have benefited from lower rates (and lower taxes). The combined impact has contributed to nearly a third of the profit margin expansion over the last decade. (*Remember:* This series is among the most mean-reverting extant.) It should be noted that despite the large amount of debt refinancing over the past few years, there remains a lot of corporate floating rate debt outstanding (e.g., in recently IPO'd private companies).
- Consumers have benefited from lower rates. Borrowing costs of all kinds facing the individual are variable. Most important of these are mortgage rates. (*Note:* Even before the recent rate rise, mortgage purchase applications fell by near double-digit rates.)
- The U.S. government has benefited from lower rates. Consider that with our $18 trillion deficit, every 100-basis-point interest rate rise translates into $180 billion of additional interest costs. (Note: The current U.S. debt load has about a five- to six-year maturity.)

No Great Rotation Expected   What about the widely anticipated great rotation out of bonds and into stocks?

We haven't seen it yet, and I suspect we won't. Even if interest rates rise, given the still-uncertain fate of the consumer (screwflation, the aftermath of the Great Decession, the second large stock market drawdown in a decade, the still-elevated unemployment rate as corporations rerate their full-time job needs in the face of the costly burden of Obamacare), my guess is that the yield-deprived consumer/retiree will grab higher-yielding fixed-income instruments that they perceive to be safer than stocks.

Rising Rates Will Disproportionately Impact the U.S. Housing Market   What impact will higher interest (and mortgage) rates have on the all-important U.S. real estate markets?

In my view, plenty.

Already, a small rise in rates has adversely impacted mortgage purchase applications. After falling by 9.8% two weeks ago, applications dipped by another 8.8% in the past week. This is especially true if not only mortgage rates climb but if home prices continue to firm; this is a toxic cocktail that is already showing signs of pricing first-time buyers out of the market.

Making matters worse and housing markets tighter are (on the supply side) recent regulations' impact on a slower pace of foreclosure sales as well as (on the demand side) the aggressive push by hedge funds and other institutional buyers to purchase homes (to rent out).

Rising Japanese Government Bond Yields Could Cause a Rate Contagion   Then there is Japan and its bond market where the recent rise in Japanese government bond (JGB) yields could threaten Japan's recovery (as the country's debt-to-GDP ratio is 200%) and, arguably, is beginning to impact U.S. bond rates. Indeed, one can argue that the price movement in JGBs is having more of an impact on our fixed-income market than the prospects and perceived timing of Fed policy (and tapering).

> *"What hath Kuroda wrought? JGB yields a bigger influence on Treasuries than tapering potential."*
>
> —Pimco's Bill Gross

Stock Valuations Are Adversely Impacted by Rising Interest Rates Finally, every discounted dividend model utilizes interest rates in calculating fair value. Higher interest rates reduce the theoretical value of the market and individual stocks.

As well, higher Treasury yields will not only continue to hurt the rate-sensitive segments of the U.S. stock market (utilities, staples, etc.), but they will also likely result in fixed-income products becoming more appealing to yield hounds.

Summary A 50-basis-point rise in U.S. note and bond yields in just three weeks is being ignored by the market participants. This might be a mistake in judgment as the seeds of slowing economic growth accompany the planting of higher interest rates.

The bottom line is that as interest rates rise, it will affect everything; prices will have to adjust, and the adjustment won't be upward.

Beware of the interest rate cliff—the addiction to low interest rates runs deep.

Housing Faces a Credit Event

7/8/2013

The sharp two-month climb in interest rates represents a significant credit event.

The rate rise will have reverberations for housing, on the general economy and for the U.S. stock market.

I remain of the view that many areas in both public and private sectors are far more vulnerable to the recent rise in interest rates than most market participants recognize.

Among the areas most impacted by a ratcheting in interest rates is housing.

Back in early 2012, I adopted a variant view and suggested that housing's recovery would surprise most to the upside. And while housing's momentum has been impressive over the past year and the sector appears to have entered a long-lived recovery, I now suspect that a surprising pause (of consequence) could occur over the next six to 12 months.

I would now avoid most housing-related stocks.

A possible slowdown in the U.S. housing market will have broad economic implications, and some second-half domestic economic forecasts might prove to be too optimistic. I expect no better than 3% nominal GDP growth (1.5% real) over the last two quarters of this year. Importantly, this well-below-consensus projection is a big departure from the Fed's official forecast of over 4% nominal GDP, which provides a guideline to monetary policy.

My more sobering economic view incorporates the recent improvement in the jobs market but recognizes the continued weakness in business capital spending and the drag from lower government expenditures combined with the anticipation of moderating retail sales and personal consumption (given a five-year low in the savings rate and the anticipated loss of refinancing-aided household cash flow).

Let's consider the ramifications of the sharp climb in interest rates since early May on the U.S. housing market. A slowdown in the residential real estate markets will pose a threat to existing- and new-home sales, home prices, builders and bank earnings and the home improvement market.

1. *Existing-home sales will suffer.* A surge in new-age purchases made by institutional investors (hedge funds, private equity, etc.) has buoyed the U.S housing market. These purchases have pushed up prices to above-consensus low-double-digit increases, sowing the seeds for a housing slowdown.

   It is important to recognize that only a handful of inflated sales prices can buoy a community of homes. We can already see the pressure in a marked reduction in the participation in first-time buyers (to under 30% of national sales from 40% a year ago). Real estate maven Mark Hanson has estimated that first-time buyers' volume is down 60% to 70% in the last two and a half years.

   Almost as significant as higher home prices is the accelerated rise in conventional mortgage rates—almost unprecedented in terms of percentage off the lows but still low by historical standards.

   But it is important to recognize that the absence of exotic loans available in this cycle compared to the previous cycle means that purchasing power has been markedly lowered. (The traditional housing affordability indices don't properly take this into account.)

It takes nearly $100,000 of income in 2013 to purchase a $523,000 home compared to only $66,000 needed in the 2000s.

Year-to-date, these two factors have reduced the purchasing power of buyers by more than 20%. Organic buyers' ability to move up has also been diminished, as it will grow more difficult to sell the first house and/or buy the new home.

2. *New-home sales will falter, putting pressure on homebuilder profits.* Some portion of the previously contracted homes that have failed to lock in a mortgage rate at the time of sale will be canceled. And, given the changing complexion of the mortgage market, it will be difficult for builders to make up the lost sales in the second half of 2013. The market has already looked through better-than-expected home-building earnings and pummeled merchant builder shares. More weakness may lie ahead.

3. *The rate of appreciation in home prices will be down-trending by year-end 2013.* It is important to remember that Case-Shiller's pricing index lags real prices by at least four months. It is my view that all other measurements of prices will indicate weakness/deceleration in the rate of growth in home price appreciation by the end of the year, maybe sooner.

4. *The home improvement market will be weakened over the balance of 2013.* Shares in the well-regarded remodeling sector—including Home Depot, Lowe's and the like—remain particularly vulnerable. Refinancings have historically been an important increment to household cash flows and, in turn, remodeling activity. Refinancings have collapsed, and, as a result, the outlook for durable spending is diminishing. With wage growth still moribund and the savings rate at a five- to six-year low, forward-looking personal consumption expenditure growth will likely be lethargic.

5. *Mortgage-centric banks face headwinds.* Many mortgage-dependent banks (which have been operating as little more than government mortgage brokers and refinancing machines) will be put to the test. Refinancings will likely be down by over 70% in third quarter 2013. Second-half new mortgage loans will disappoint. Despite optimism surrounding bank stock net interest margin improvement, mortgage banking will produce a hole in bank profits.

Summary

- The speedy rise in interest rates will likely interrupt the strong momentum in the U.S. housing market.
- A deceleration in the rate of growth in residential real estate activity/turnover and in home prices lies ahead.
- U.S. economic growth will be adversely impacted by a slowdown in the recovery in the real estate market.
- Sell housing-related stocks.
- Similar to housing, the U.S. stock market may sour.

The sharp climb in interest rates since early May points to some prospective weakness in the U.S. housing market (measured both by sales activity and prices) and is conspiring to reduce overall domestic economic growth to levels likely unforeseen by policymakers and by most forecasters.

The drag of fiscal austerity, tax and regulatory policy will also weigh on U.S. growth. Non-U.S. growth remains subpar. Inflation will continue to be more of a threat than deflation.

Though the global financial condition is greatly improved from four years ago and the ECB, Bank of England and Bank of Japan are on the same ZIRP page, in this slow-growth backdrop, policy risk (of premature tapering) is heightened and represents an ever-present threat to the U.S. stock market.

Housing, in particular, seems exposed to the quick climb in rates. It remains my view that prospective homebuyers—still shaken from an unprecedented 34% drop in home prices from the peak and in the face of stagnating wages and salaries—are far more sensitized to costs (home prices and mortgage rates) than many believe. The fence-sitter argument (i.e., that buyers will appear as rates rise) seems to have been debunked by the recent decline in purchase applications. And given the lack of opportunities available today in the creative, no-/low-documentation mortgages of yesteryear, affordability trends in 2013, though still attractive measured by history, are becoming a stronger headwind to housing.

I would avoid housing-related equities and mortgage-centric banks in the months ahead, and I would be skeptical of the consensus forecast of a meaningful acceleration in domestic economic growth (from second-quarter 2013 estimates for real GDP of less than 2% to nearly 3% in the second half of 2013).

As to tying this all into the overall stock market's outlook, an abrupt rise in interest rates as we have just witnessed—Friday's rate rise was the largest one-day increase in nearly five years—need not necessarily spell doom if profits are on a strong trajectory.

Unfortunately, this is not the case, as an unsettled and volatile fixed-income market is being accompanied by a less-than-stellar profit backdrop. Second-quarter 2013 earnings (excluding financials) are forecast to drop by about 1% while top-line sales increase by only 1.5%.

Second-half earnings are being projected at nearly 10% growth.

Similar to the ambitious housing projections for 2013–2014, the U.S. corporate profit outlook seems too optimistic as well.

QE's Growing Impotence

7/23/2013

The massive rally in the U.S. stock market has increasingly ignored that quantitative easing has become an ineffective stimulant to domestic economic growth.

Second-quarter 2013 real GDP now looks to be under 1%, well below expectations when the quarter started. This follows only 0.4% in fourth quarter 2012 and 1.8% in first quarter 2013—both of which were well under forecasts as well. In nominal terms, the GDP growth rate will likely drop from 3% in first quarter 2013 to 2% in second quarter 2013.

As a result of weak nominal GDP, sales growth in both the first and second quarter of this year has been nonexistent.

Second-half growth expectations for the domestic economy (as well as the forecast by the Fed) remain in the area of 2%. Recent economic data suggest that these projections may also fall short.

Optimistic second-half forecasts incorporate the view that fiscal drag is receding, job growth is improving, the wealth effect should take hold (and trickle down) and that the U.S. housing market will continue to strengthen. I am less certain that fiscal drag will moderate and that the housing recovery will continue to be strong.

Moreover, a favorable analysis of the jobs market fails to take into account the rising percentage of part-time (and low-paying) jobs and a generally anemic wage growth outlook. As well, the trickle-down theory fails to recognize that this effect is far less important than the income effect on overall spending. With the personal savings rate at a five-year low, it is unlikely that personal consumption expenditures will be strong enough to generate inventory rebuilding at the corporate level and, thus, a virtuous or self-sustaining economic cycle.

Of course, second-half projections also have to incorporate the non-U.S. picture. Unfortunately, the global economy still lacks an engine for meaningful recovery. China may no longer be the engine of growth that it has been in the past, and the eurozone's economy remains strained.

Finally, there is the issue of interest rates and our addiction to their low levels. Tapering appears around the corner, and we shall see if the equity market will be tolerant or if rising interest rates act as a headwind to growth and the expected rebound in second-half growth fails to materialize.

While second-half 2013 S&P 500 earnings have exceeded expectations (with year-over-year growth of close to 5%), much of that improvement has been confined to the financial sector, where share buybacks, and reserve reversals have buoyed results.

Importantly, if we exclude financials (which benefited from buybacks and lower loan-loss provisions or reserve releases) from overall results, both first- and second-quarter earnings growth are barely expanding and are likely to be flat to down.

In other words, the quality of earnings growth and the absolute rate of growth in profits (excluding financials) thus far in 2013 have been poor.

Rather than take down valuations reflecting this poor earnings quality, the weak absolute level of nonfinancial earnings and tepid sales growth, to my surprise, market participants have elevated valuations.

In fact, the year-over-year change in the S&P 500's P/E multiple has been roughly 4.2× the average year-over-year increase in the last 35 years.

I now believe that 2013 S&P profits will total about $107 a share and 2014 S&P profits will fall in the range of $109 to $110 a share. These estimates, though slightly higher than I expected when the year began, are about $1 to $2 below 2013 consensus projections and $5 to $6 below 2014 consensus projections.

The previously mentioned domestic economic growth dynamic calls into question whether the United States is in a self-sustaining recovery or whether our economy is still, four years after the end of the recession, dependent upon continued and unprecedented easing in monetary policy and the maintenance of zero interest rates.

Based on the dialogue over the past two months, it is clear that both the Fed and other central banks are fearful of spooking the markets. Nevertheless, it is also clear that global bond rates have likely completed a three-decade decline.

Given these conditions, it is increasingly clear that the benefits of quantitative easing have been diminished with each round.

Flawed Case for a Bull Market

11/19/2013

The cornerstone of the bull market case is that valuations are reasonable and not excessive by historical standards. It is further argued by the bulls that given the low rate of inflation (and inflationary expectations) and very low interest rates, the current level of valuation is justified and even inexpensive.

The conventional method of calculating P/E multiples based on stated or raw earnings is, arguably, a fundamentally flawed approach that assumes currently elevated profit margins and profits are sustainable. Indeed, measures that normalize margins have almost always correlated better to U.S. stock market performance over history.

It is only the cyclical (and elevated) position of profit margins that prevents recognition that equities are richly valued.

I would argue that to utilize earnings that reflect profit margins that are more than 70% above the norm (over a documented span of over 65 years) is an aggressive assumption and fails to adjust for the unique and changing conditions that contributed to the sharp improvement in margins since 2009—all of which are deteriorating and likely putting renewed pressure on margins.

Investors should consider evaluating current valuations from the context of normalized earnings not based on today's elevated (raw) profits and profit margins.

How Will the Variables that Produced High Profit Margins Trend Going Forward? There are three important factors that have contributed to unusually high corporate profit margins—all of which have begun to reverse.

1. Corporate interest expenses have experienced a marked reduction. Generational low interest rates have boosted margins dramatically. In all likelihood, interest rates will rise over the next several years, perhaps materially, driving corporate interest expenses higher.
2. Effective corporate tax rates have undergone a steady decline. Through offshore tax havens and other methods, corporations have consistently lowered their taxes. The reduction in corporate interest expenses combined with lower effective tax rates have contributed to more than one third of the improvement in corporate profit margins. In all likelihood, tax rates will climb over the next several years, as our leaders in Washington, D.C., address the ballooning deficit.
3. Corporations have reduced their fixed costs by cutting overhead, shedding jobs and making temporary workers a more permanent part of the workforce. Year-over-year productivity growth in third quarter 2013 was zero compared to 0.2% in second quarter 2013 and as contrasted to significant gains over the past five years. Productivity growth has slowed steadily over the past year, as year-over-year unit labor costs are now 1.9%. Corporations have cut to the bone, and productivity gains are in the process of reversing now.

Over history, profit margins are among the most mean-reverting economic series extant.

Raw P/E and raw price-to-forward-operating-earnings look reasonable only because profit margins are about 70% above their long-term norms.

Other Valuation Metrics Yield Extreme Readings Every ounce of my cynicism and analysis is supported by historical precedent.

With the assistance of Dr. John Hussman, the elements of my overvaluation case are underscored by the following seven items that look beyond raw earnings:

1. The median price-to-revenue ratio of the S&P 500 is now at an historic high, eclipsing even the 2000 level.

2. The Shiller P/E is above 25, exceeding all observations prior to the late 1990s' bubble except for three weeks in 1929.

3. Market cap-to-GDP is already past its 2007 peak and is approaching the 2000 extreme.

4. The implied profit margin in the Shiller P/E (denominator of Shiller P/E divided by S&P 500 revenue) is 18% above the historical norm. On normal profit margins, the Shiller P/E would already be 30.

5. If one examines the data, these raw valuation measures typically have a fraction of the relationship to subsequent S&P 500 total returns as measures that adjust for the cyclicality of profit margins (or are unaffected by those variations), such as Shiller P/E, price-to-revenue, market cap-to-GDP and even price-to-cyclically-adjusted-forward-operating-earnings.

6. Because the deficit of one sector must emerge as the surplus of another, one can show that corporate profits (as a share of GDP) move inversely to the sum of government and private savings, particularly with a four- to six-quarter lag. The record profit margins of recent years are the mirror image of record deficits in combined government and household savings, which began to normalize about a few quarters ago. The impact on profit margins is almost entirely ahead of us.

7. The impact of 10-year Treasury yields (duration 8.8 years) on an equity market with a 50-year duration (duration in equities mathematically works out to be close to the price-to-dividend ratio) is far smaller than one would assume. Ten-year bonds are too short to impact the discount rate applied to the long tail of cash flows that equities represent. In fact, prior to 1970 and since the late-1990s, bond yields and stock yields have had a negative correlation. The positive correlation between bond yields and equity yields is entirely a reflection of the strong inflation–disinflation cycle from 1970 to about 1998.

Slow Growth and a Challenging Profit Landscape Lie Ahead   My argument might be rendered moot if global economic growth would begin to accelerate meaningfully—in that case, corporations would achieve operating leverage—or if interest rates would stay abnormally low.

These are not my core expectations.

The profit landscape remains challenged, and interest rates, in the fullness of time, will be rising.

For 2013, I expect a below-consensus forecast of between $107 and $109 a share for S&P profits (the consensus is for full-year profits of $109 a share). For 2014, the consensus estimates that the S&P 500 will achieve profits of about $116 to $120; my base case estimate is for $112 to $114, a gain of under 5% (year over year), which is, again, below consensus.

Slowing sales, a contraction in margins, the reduced influence/ benefit from aggressive monetary policy and political uncertainties are some of the reasons why my baseline earnings expectations are for below-consensus 2014 S&P profits.

Optimism Swells with Higher Stock Prices   The strength in stocks throughout most of 2013 has been consistent and spectacular, and arguments such as what I have expressed have fallen on deaf ears.

The reality is that shorts have been a hedge against profits.

That said, most people get interested in stocks when everyone else is, but the time to get interested is when no one else is.

This is certainly not the case today, as investor sentiment and higher stock prices have turned almost universally optimistic these days.

But a public opinion poll is no substitute for thought.

Near the end of enormous upside moves such as we have experienced since the generational bottom in March 2009, analysis often goes unquestioned as new-era thinking is embraced.

We all know how badly the dot-com/technology era ended a few years after the misguided view of a long boom.

My argument today is that using raw earnings to justify current valuations might be misplaced logic, as, from my perch, the irrational is being rationalized.

At the least, the reward vs. risk remains unattractive in the U.S. stock market.

At the worst, a Minsky moment may lie ahead in the not too distant future in which asset values drop following a lengthy period of prosperity and increasing value of investments.

Everybody in the Pool

12/2/2013

Investors of all sizes and shapes are nearly all in the pool now.

Investor sentiment (in most surveys) is tilted very bullish, mutual fund investors hold near-record-low cash reserves, hedge funds are at multi-year highs in terms of net long exposure, and retail investors (though not at the extremes of 1999–2000) have plowed money into domestic equity funds en masse since the beginning of the year.

Importantly, margin debt reached another high in October of $413 billion (up 3% month over month after rising 5% in September). In fact, margin debt is approaching the March 2000 and July 2007 highs as a percentage of GDP. Currently, margin debt is about 2.4% of nominal GDP vs. 2.6% in July 2007 and 2.8% in March 2000.

Monetary Policy Trumps the Real Economy   The many potential headwinds (e.g., Washington shutdowns, geopolitical risks/uprisings, a probable taper, rising interest rates, tepid corporate sales and profit growth, signs of ineffective Fed quantitative easing policy, the vulnerability of corporate profit margins, the growing schism between the haves and the have-nots in a failure of trickle-down economic policy, the consequences of financial repression done for the greater good on the savers class, etc.) have, to date, been ignored and dismissed by stock market participants.

Importantly, the disconnect between the real economy and the stock market has grown more pronounced, as the markets continued their ascent in recent months.

The most recent leg of the bull market started at about 1,670 on the S&P 500. Since then, the S&P has rallied by over 8%.

The joyous swimmers have returned to the investment pool in numbers during the munificent climb from the market depths of 2008–2009.

Not only have traders and investors ignored the potential investment headwinds, but they have rewarded the S&P 500 with a quantum increase in valuation. Though P/E ratios have risen on average only 2% a year since 1990, valuations have climbed by nearly 25% in 2013.

Where Are the Bubbles?   There has been a lot of bubble talk of late. That talk (and the very existence of those questioning bubbles) seems to many as a rejection that there is a stock market bubble at all.

The problem with bubbles is that if you sell stocks before the bubble bursts, you look foolish, but you also look foolish if you sell stocks after the bubble bursts.

The market is not yet a bubble; it is simply overvalued (maybe by as much as 10%).

If I were pressed, however, to express if and where the bubbles reside today, they likely exist in the extraordinary faith in the Fed and central bankers around the world to shoulder the responsibility of catalyzing economic growth and in the general notion that corporate profit margins (and thus the outlook for future corporate profits) are inflated and in bubble territory at about 80% above the long-term average over the past six decades.

Too High   To date, the aforementioned headwinds have been seen simply as opportunities for investors to buy more stocks on weakness.

Grandma Koufax used to say, "Dougie, investment trees don't grow to the skies."

To a rising chorus of self-confident and almost boisterous bulls, fueled by a nearly unprecedented and continuing market rally, the investment trees indeed appear to be rising into the sky.

The argument, gaining credence with every 10-handle move in the S&P 500, is that with short-term interest rates anchored at zero, there is no alternative. But as Tennessee Williams wrote, "There is a time for departure even when there's no certain place to go." For, at many points in history, regardless of yield, cash has been king.

One day, perhaps in the near future, our investment pool will be drained.

When that will happen (tomorrow, in two weeks, in two months or in two years) is anyone's guess.

While the catalyst to the first meaningful market correction (in some time) can never be known for sure, it could come in the form of poor forward profit guidance, recognition that profit margins will mean revert or, more likely, it might just be that buyers have been sated when they all are in the same pool.

In less than five years, we have moved from a generational market low to a generational market high, and investors (many of which started 2013 in a sour mood) are now anticipating a sequel in the year ahead.

Expect the Unexpected in 2014

12/9/2013

Stock market history teaches us to be mindful and respectful of patterns but also to recognize the influence and importance of the unexpected.

Today, investors, strategists, and the business media seem to have a singular focus.

They are currently obsessed with forecasting when a taper will be introduced and are attempting to interpret its impact on the bond and stock markets.

When it is universally agreed that one factor (tapering) holds the key to the market, it likely means that that determinant is priced in (and so, I might add, is the likelihood of very dovish forward guidance coincident with the inevitable tapering).

According to a *Bloomberg* survey of economists, there is a 34% probability of a December tapering, a 26% probability of January and a 40% probability in March.

My view is that a December tapering has almost a zero probability, as there will be insufficient economic data to make the decision and it could potentially disrupt year-end funding and confidence (during the important holiday sales season). A more likely January tapering would encompass three full improving jobs reports, incorporate holiday sales results and there would be greater visibility of the outcome of fiscal debate in Washington.

As to interest rates (the second part of the riddle), that's a more interesting question.

Specifically, what level of interest rates would pose a risk to stocks (defined as a 5%-plus correction)?

Most view 3.25% or higher in the 10-year note yield within three months (indicating that yields have broken out of a two-and-a-half-year range and that forward guidance is not sufficient to hold down rates), 3.75% or higher within six months, 4.25% or higher within nine months or 4.5% or higher within 12 months as threshold points. My view remains that 3.5% or higher will be surprisingly negative for housing, the mortgage-backed securities market and potentially for the stock market.

Thus far, the capital markets have not been impacted by somewhat improving economic data.

In all likelihood, what will really move the markets over the next six to nine months isn't priced in at all right now. As mentioned previously, the consensus on tapering (it's schedule and market impact/importance) is more or less all the same—that is, January or March in timing (67% chance) and basically not impactful and essentially irrelevant to the markets.

This is likely the natural outgrowth of a forgiving market with a strong degree of momentum to the upside that has ignored any potential headwind (economic, interest rate, geopolitical, political) throughout 2014.

Nevertheless, at this point in time, it remains probable that the market's consensus will prove wrong on its almost singular focus on tapering—in the same way the crowd has been wrong in assessing the outlook for interest rates, the stock market and for asset classes over the past 12 months.

What a Difference a Year Makes   The rush to risk over the past 12 months and the performance of numerous asset classes have been noticeably at odds with consensus expectations and different than what nearly anyone expected a year ago. At year-end 2012: The markets were closer to being oversold; they are now severely overbought.

The outflow out of stock funds was at the highest level since the 2009 generational low. Throughout 2013, we have seen steady inflows into equity funds.

Wall Street strategists were well grouped to expect a modest rise in stocks (of 5% to 10%). Stock returns were 4x that this year. They were, as it is written, cautiously optimistic. Today strategists, though still relatively muted in forecast, have begun the one-upmanship of who has the highest S&P 500 price forecast. At the very least, the bearish are being ridiculed, causing massive changes in expectations from strategists and, to be sure, the late exit/capitulation of nonbelievers and short-sellers.

Investor sentiment, cautious a year ago, has been replaced with sentiment being as positive as at any time in the five-year advance (based on the various sentiment surveys). Indeed, at a ratio of 4:1, the bull-to-bear ratio is at the highest level in nearly 25 years.

Technicals were unimpressive/uneven throughout the last half of 2012. Transports were in a downtrend that started in mid-2011, there were numerous breadth divergences that began in second-quarter 2012, and utilities were recovering nicely from a late-summer fade. Today, the technicals, a reflection of strong price momentum, are universally seen as the world's fair and supportive of continued market gains.

The 10-year U.S. note was yielding about 1.60% vs. nearly 2.90% today. Inflows into bond funds in December 2012 were at near-record levels. Today those funds are being disintermediated in accelerating fashion.

Emerging markets were at 18-month highs. In 2013, emerging markets have been conspicuous underperformers. The price of gold was near an all-time high (at $1,750 an ounce). The price of gold has crashed this year.

Most important, there was little attention paid to the Fed's intention to continue QE/ZIRP ad infinitum. Today we are unduly attentive to Fed monetary policy and interest rates (nearly held hostage), which seem to weigh in all our decisions and in the market narrative.

Expect the Unexpected   A surprising influence (other than tapering or interest rates) will likely impact the markets in the year ahead.

I don't have a crystal ball, but it could take many forms.

On the negative side, it could be an unforeseen black swan event that no one is now considering or growing evidence that corporate profit margins are vulnerable to a regression toward the mean or it could just be that the market sells off because the demand has been sated.

On the positive side is that the forgiving nature of the market could lead to an upside blow-off sometime in 2014. Though sounding like a two-handed observer, I, not surprisingly, would say that reward vs. risk justifies a more cautious stand.

The great investors survive on that which is unpredictable—the unexpected courses through their investing veins.

In conclusion, I would search for factors other than tapering that will shed light on the performance of equities next year.

Expect the unexpected.

Climbing a Wall of Complacency

1/21/2014

It has been nearly five years since the Great Decession and the ensuing generational bottom in the U.S. stock market.

The S&P 500 has risen from 666 to almost 1,850. At 58 months, the current cyclical bull market advance is the second longest on record and is quickly approaching the 60-month expansion that occurred from 1982 to 1987.

Nevertheless, aggressive monetary stimulation has arguably (ex-inventory accumulation) failed to ignite escape velocity for the domestic economy, and the U.S. is yet (in my view) in a position to forge a self-sustaining recovery.

The single most important reagent to higher stock prices last year has not been better corporate profits—rather it has been an upward adjustment in P/E ratios.

In 2013, P/E ratios on the S&P 500 rose by 25% vs. the average annual increase in P/E ratios since 1990 of only 2% per year.

Twelve months ago, there were virtually no Wall Street strategists that anticipated such an acute upward adjustment in valuations. Today, there are virtually no Wall Street strategists that are skeptical of current valuations.

In fact, bullish investor sentiment has been elevated to levels rarely seen. The lowly VIX is a sign of complacency, a wall that the market has climbed over the past 18 months. The market bears are ridiculed by the business media, and the short community is a species that is on the verge of extinction.

I would argue, therefore, that the market has climbed a wall of complacency.

There Isn't a "Real Worry"   A growing consensus is finding it difficult to conceive of any negatives or headwinds to more gains in the global markets in 2014. "The only thing people are worried about is that no one is worried about anything. . . . That isn't a real worry," wrote Morgan Stanley Chief U.S. Equity Strategist Adam Parker recently.

I have learned over my stock market career that investors would far prefer to buy on price strength than on price weakness—and that the crowd of investors typically outperforms the remnants, as trends generally stay in place for extended periods of time.

In its later stages, however, a sustained market advance inevitably brings (or sucks in) money managers, Wall Street strategists (who face career risk in missing out) and investors (who are overcome by similar emotions).

Maturing bull markets grow forgiving, and the rigor of analysis gets diluted by the joy (and ownership) of the advancing shares of market leadership. In time the lens of the microscope that inspects the quality of earnings (growth) as well as the one that gauges the future outlook breaks and is tucked away in a closet underneath reams of critical analysis.

The strength in global stocks over the past few years has been resounding in force and duration. Earnings, however, "the mother's milk of equities" (hat tip Sir Larry Kudlow), buoyed by share buybacks and the paring back of fixed costs, have been lackluster, as top-line sales growth continues to be punk. And forward guidance has been disappointing, with the ratio of lower guidance to higher guidance at near-record levels.

A Weak Start to the Earnings Season   For those looking unsuccessfully for reasons to be cautious, we need only to look at the loss of momentum in corporate profit growth as we enter the new year.

It is still early in the earnings season, and at the risk of negative data mining, thus far there have been a number of high-profile misses, including Citigroup, Wells Fargo, CSX Corporation, Royal Dutch Shell, Intel, Fastenal, Best Buy and many other retailers, Capital One, Ford, General Motors, United Parcel Service, Elizabeth Arden, and so forth.

Profits and Margins Are Vulnerable   The reduction in fixed costs is more or less behind corporate America. Interest rates have seen generational lows and, in the fullness of time (2015/2016?), will be rising along with interest costs. The lower effective corporate tax rates will also likely be a thing of the past, as one day, our fiscal issues will have to be addressed by responsible policy and with the implementation of higher taxes to generate more revenue to the government. Profit margins are also vulnerable to a rising U.S. dollar, as a large percentage of S&P profits are the outgrowth of overseas sales.

Profit margins (one of the most mean-reverting economic series extant), at over 70% above multidecade averages, are exposed. Utilizing raw, stated, and nominal earnings (and inflated margins) in looking at where valuations might reside in an historical sense (in other words, not normalized profits and margins) could prove to be a fool's errand.

There Is a Near-Universal View that Stocks Will Outperform Bonds in 2014 Individual investors and portfolio managers (who are paid to worry) should always be concerned whether lying within consensus or outside of consensus.

As we begin 2014, there rarely has been such a consensus with regard to the direction of the major investment asset classes—namely, stocks up and bonds down.

As well as equities delivering roughly a 10% return and bond yields rising modestly, there is a strong consensus about nearly everything else. The following views have been overwhelmingly embraced by the majority:

- There is risk to the upside for global economic growth.
- European stocks will outperform their U.S. counterparts.
- Japanese equities will outperform both Europe and U.S. markets.
- Developed equity markets will outperform emerging markets.
- The U.S. dollar will be among the strongest currencies.
- The Fed's tapering has been fully discounted.
- Industrial, technology, and financial stocks will be among the strongest market sectors.
- Utilities, consumer staples and energy stocks will be among the weakest market sectors.

I believe that there is a lot of room for disappointment to the consensus, and I have adopted the opposite view regarding some of the above items.

Specifically, I expect bonds to outperform stocks in 2014 as the rate of growth in domestic (under 2%) and global GDP growth (under 3%) decelerates as the year progresses.

Against the backdrop of a high-single-digit decline in the U.S. stock market, the return on long-dated, taxable U.S. bonds could be between 5% and 10% in 2014.

I also anticipate that interest rates will decline from 2013's year-end levels and that the yield on the 10-year U.S. note will spend most of the year between 2.5% and 3.0%.

Price Is Truth, but Reward vs. Risk Has Grown Unattractive   Many argue that Mr. Market is climbing a wall of worry. I contend that Mr. Market is climbing a wall of complacency.

There are numerous reasons for my downbeat market view this year—one of my greatest concerns is that massive central bank liquidity has obscured price discovery. Each tranche of quantitative easing has resulted in a reduced effectiveness in fostering growth. Even Federal Reserve Bank of New York President Bill Dudley has recently stated that he has no idea what QE has accomplished. One has to wonder what will happen to the stock market in the process of bond purchases moving from $85 billion a month to zero.

Below are a few additional concerns (in no order of importance):

- Corporate profit margins (70% above historical averages) are stretched to 70-year highs, so earnings are exposed.
- Second-half 2013 strength in domestic economic growth has been boosted by nonrecurring inventory accumulation. Some more recent signs (e.g., automobile sales, retail spending and housing data) suggest a deceleration in growth may lie ahead.
- The baton exchange from Ben Bernanke to Janet Yellen could be unkind to the markets. On average, a change in the Fed chair has resulted in about a 7% drop in the major stock indices.
- Quantitative easing may not be a continued tailwind for stocks.
- Sentiment measures are elevated to historically bullish levels. This is seen not only in the disparity between bulls and bears (in the popular surveys) but also manifested in the third-highest margin debt to GDP in history.
- Valuations (P/E ratios) rose by nearly 25% in 2013 vs. only 2% annually since the late-1980s.
- The Shiller P/E ratio is at or near historic highs (excluding the bubble of the late-1990s).
- According to JPMorgan, the S&P 500 is now more expensive on a forward P/E basis than it was at its previous peak in October 2007.

- Interest rates might pose more of a threat than is generally viewed. The rose-colored glasses being worn by investors might be cleared in the year ahead, as the withdrawal from QE and low rates might be harsher.
- A year ago, market enthusiasm was muted. Today there are no cautionary forecasts for the S&P for the next 12 months.

I recognize fully that the market's phenomenal advance is what it is. It is often said that price is truth—it is all that matters.

Market trends stay in motion until they are disrupted, but (honestly) neither I nor anyone else knows when a stock market correction might occur, or, for that matter, what the catalyst will be.

Tops tend to be more elusive than bottoms. Tops are more of a process while bottoms are typically quicker and more obvious.

Rather than predict a top, I often find it helpful to establish upside/downside objectives in individual stocks and in markets in order to ascertain reward/risk and appropriate market exposure.

To me, the S&P 500 has no more than a 5% upside and has about a 12.5% downside over the balance of this year.

In other words, the downside to the U.S. stock market exceeds the upside by a factor of 2.5×.

In conclusion, we shouldn't lose sight of the big picture, which suggests, to this observer, that there is much more downside than upside in the markets and that risk, increasingly alien to many investors inured to the market's rewards since 2009, will likely happen fast and when few expect it.

Turn, Turn, Turn

6/11/2014

Over the past few weeks, many money managers and strategists have made the following observations in support of their market optimism:

- There is no or limited complacency in the capital markets.
- Valuations are elevated but remain reasonable.
- There appear to be few economic excesses and, as such, no boom from which to bust.
- There is no alternative to stocks.

- The U.S. economy is well positioned to return to average to above-average growth, with low-cost energy, manufacturing cost advantages, and the wealth effect of higher home and stock prices.

The meme above is consistent and pervasive. After all, the crowd usually outsmarts the remnants (except, of course, at inflection points), so it rarely pays to be proactive. Play the trend, don't fight the tape or question the market's rise. And, above all, stay fully invested—if not, you will face career risk.

I would argue that:

We are in a bull market in complacency. Complacency means, "self-satisfaction, especially when accompanied by unawareness of actual dangers or deficiencies." Bulls have rarely been more self-confident in view, but there are numerous dangers to the bull market in stocks that are being ignored by many.

For instance:

- Subpar economic growth, which is still (five years after the Great Recession) dependent on exaggerated and extreme implementation of monetary policy;
- A growing schism between haves and have-nots after the failure of QE;
- Weak top-line growth;
- Vulnerability to corporate profits and profit margins; and
- A consumer that is spent-up, not pent-up.

And the list could go on, but we'll stop it there.

Arguably, valuations are stretched. I would repeat for emphasis that while P/E ratios (against stated or nominal profits) are only slightly above the historic average, normalized profits are well above the historic average, as profit margins, which are at a near-60-year high, are now exposed to a reversal of the factors that contributed to the 70%-plus six-decade average.

For instance:

- Interest rates will rise;
- Productivity will fall; and
- Reversals of bank industry loan-loss provisions will moderate.

Looking at nominal or stated profits (projected at $117 to $120 a share for the S&P 500) rather than normalized earnings (to account for degradation in profit margins) could prove to be a fool's errand, just like the mistake that was made back at the generational bottom (when trailing earnings of only $45 a share understated normalized corporate profitability). At that time in 2009, investors were as reluctant to buy as they are emboldened to buy in 2014.

There are bubble-like pockets of extreme overvaluation. Above all, there is most definitely a bubble in the belief that central bankers can guide the economy higher and into a self-sustaining trajectory of growth absent fiscal and regulatory reform. (It's been five years, and we are not yet there.) Importantly, bubbles are not the mandatory starting point to corrections, as stocks often fall from excessive valuation rather than bubbles.

Equities are less frothy than fixed income. I don't feel stocks are inexpensive or compelling buys at the margin. I don't buy the either/or argument, as cash is an asset class. At numerous times in history, not losing money (and being in cash) is a reasonable alternative to being in risk assets.

The domestic economy is unlikely to kick in and gain escape velocity in 2014's second half. Though it has maintained its second-half optimism recently, I expect that the Fed will end up lowering its official economic forecast. The recovery and wealth effect has been lopsided, favoring the wealthy. It is not broad based. This is clear in the U.S. housing market's pause since last summer. The consumer (the average Joe suffering from stagnating wages and higher costs of the necessities of life) remains the Achilles' heel of U.S. economic growth. And the growing savings class is an important constituency that will continue to be penalized by zero-interest-rate policy. Most economists have predicted escape velocity for the U.S. economy since 2011. They have been wrong-footed and might continue to be.

In summary:

- Fear has been driven from Wall Street, and there is no concern for downside risk.

- Global economic growth is falling short of earlier forecasts, while a number of regions are flirting with deflation.
- While the shoulders of economic growth have relied on central banker policy, in the absence of regulatory and fiscal reform, QE's impact is now materially moderating.
- S&P 500 profits are estimated to have risen by only about 10% in 2013–2014, against a 38% rise in the S&P 500 index. (The difference is the animal spirits' impact on rising multiples, something everyone now accepts but none anticipated 18 months ago).
- Though fundamentals remain soft (with sales and profit growth muted), bulls are self-confident in view as share prices propel ever higher.
- Bullish sentiment (measured by *Investors Intelligence* bull/bear spreads, etc.) is at an historical extreme.
- Shorts are an out-of-favor, endangered and ridiculed species.
- There is less to valuations than meets the eye.

I would strongly consider reducing exposure to the U.S. stock market.

Wall Street Personalities

Introduction

If stock market experts were so expert, they would be buying stock, not selling advice.

—Norman Ralph Augustine

Stock market talk is cheap; investors and traders are inundated by information flow on the markets these days.

Rigor is the sine qua non, however, and the common thread of value-added investment analysis and superior portfolio management.

Reading everything you can is important but so are your relationships. Contacts steer us in the right direction of potential investment ideas that must be followed up by hard work and analysis.

I have had the good fortune of rubbing elbows, working and being friends with some of the most fascinating personalities—some of them the brightest and wealthiest money managers on Wall Street. Initially in my career, "Scarsdale Fats" (a.k.a., Bob Brimberg) introduced me to many of these iconic figures when I was just starting out in the investment business.

But some of the most interesting personalities are not that well known. For instance, Boca Biff, the quintessential odd lotter, who gets trapped into every possible fad. In the process, he has made and lost tens of millions of dollars. See also the Bearded Prophet of the Apocalypse, who, afraid of the world as we know it, left the hedge fund business to reside on a farm in New Hampshire.

In this chapter, I profile not only one of the greatest hedge-hoggers ever, George Soros, but I also write about *Barron's* Alan Abelson, our country's journalistic treasure, who became an important influence on me over the three-decade period before his death, as well as Jim Cramer, my friend/buddy/pal who resides at the epicenter of *TheStreet*.

A Soros Story

6/11/2001

In its online edition Saturday, the *Wall Street Journal* reported that "after a year of turning his back on the risky game of hedge-fund investing . . . legendary investor George Soros is actively looking for a chief investment officer to replace Stanley Druckenmiller and take the helm at Mr. Soros's firm, Soros Fund Management."

This news got me to thinking about something that happened between George Soros and me in the early 1980s.

This anecdote (or should I call it my nightmare?) is true.

And, above all, remember the poor judgment that I exercised 20 years ago, when you consider my stock recommendations and market strategy. In 1981, George Soros's hedge fund empire was flailing. His partner, Jimmy Rogers, had left, and George seemed out of sorts. His main investment vehicle, the Quantum Fund, was down measurably. He needed help, and one day I received a telephone call from him to discuss the possibility of joining him in the big job. I mean "Soros big."

In my infinite wisdom I turned him down—not once, but twice that year. You see, I asked George to show me his portfolio. And he did, showing me a computer printout of his holdings during a leisurely walk we took through Hyde Park in London, England.

I thought it was far-flung and bereft of any central themes (from 13-D filing positions in American technology stocks to sizeable, esoteric commodity holdings), and I concluded that it would be near impossible for him to turn Quantum around.

That, my friends, was the single dumbest decision (investment or otherwise) I, or nearly anyone else, have ever made.

After I turned down George, he ultimately offered the job to a well-known money manager who, rumor has it, accepted the job and lasted one week, earning an amazing $500,000 for his week's efforts.

Months later, George began to parcel out his hedge fund's money to several outside managers. I was the recipient of one of the earliest Soros distributions.

I remember asking George if he wanted a diversified portfolio, or only my "foremost five or 10 picks." In a husky voice, laced with his unmistakable Hungarian origins, George replied, "I want your single best idea. Just one stock, Douglas." (George rarely minces words).

So I put millions to work, in one stock: First Charter Financial, the largest publicly traded savings and loan in the United States. At that time, the yield curve was inverted, loan originations were low, and industry capital and surplus were dwindling. As a contrarian, that's just the time to buy the sector (something like buying technology stocks in early April).

Several weeks later, George called me and said that he was having a Quantum board meeting at his West Side apartment in New York City. He asked whether I could attend and make a presentation regarding my First Charter Financial investment. It was my pleasure, and a few nights later, I was talking thrifts to a bunch of London- and Geneva-based bankers at George's dinner table.

To put it mildly, the members of the Quantum board of directors didn't agree with my premise that things would turn around for First Charter and the savings and loan industry. Nor did they understand American accounting conventions that did not mark mortgages to market.

The next morning I received a call from George Soros ordering me to liquidate the First Charter Financial investment, which I did.

I had purchased the stock for about $9.50, and sold the position for about $8.75.

Five weeks later, Charlie Knapp's Financial Corporation of America bid $35 per share for First Charter Financial. Two months later the acquisition was completed.

And, now, as radio commentator Paul Harvey would say, "you know the rest of the story."

The Bearded Prophet of the Apocalypse

12/23/2002

Let me explain how I first met the Bearded Prophet.

After leaving Boston's Putnam Management in 1977, I joined a New York-based firm, Glickenhaus & Company, where I, along with two others (including the legendary Seth Glickenhaus), started an equity management business that became quite successful over time.

About six months after my return to New York City, I and a couple of my buddies formed an investment group in which ideas were exchanged, the First Tuesday of the Month Club.

This wasn't your grandmother's ordinary investment club, as it included a number of up-and-coming money managers who would become quite well known over time.

Included in the First Tuesday of the Month Club were Omega Advisors' Leon Cooperman (he was running Goldman's institutional research product at the time), Rocker Partners' David Rocker, Gabelli and Company's Mario Gabelli, Westwood Management's Susan Byrne and Fran Bovich (now at Morgan Stanley), Lou Margolis (who headed up Salomon Brothers' options business), Kynikos's Jim Chanos and several other equally talented investors, including the Bearded Prophet of the Apocalypse (who at the time was the head trader of the best hedge fund extant).

This was some brilliant and stimulating group—almost 25 years ago!

Fast-forward to May 2002, and an interview by Morgan Stanley's chief investment strategist, Barton Biggs, in his weekly Global Investment Research piece.

In that May interview, Biggs pointed out the Bearded Prophet's strength in some amazing long-term calls, which included predicting the acts of terrorism two years ago, recognizing that a developing and pervasive streak of corruption and corporate greed (CEO compensation has risen from 40× average workers' income to over 530×!) falsified corporate profits, predicting that bond yields would decline from 15% in the early 1980s to less than 5%, and forecasting that when the Dow was selling at only 9×, it would rise to more than 30×. The Bearded Prophet shorted the Nifty Fifty in the early 1970s, he argued correctly that President Reagan's policies spelled disinflation and said that the price of oil would plummet in the early 1980s.

Biggs ended his interview with the Bearded Prophet (he used the name Jimmy) with the declaration that Jimmy is an imaginary composite who does not resemble anyone he knows.

I know for a fact that the Bearded Prophet is a real person. His name also has two syllables, like Jimmy, and ends with the same letter. And he is not Greek, as Barton Biggs suggested, in an obvious attempt to conceal his identity—rather he was born in Italy.

I originally met the Bearded Prophet through one of my great pals who passed away many years ago, the legendary Bob Brimberg (who was given the moniker Scarsdale Fats in Adam Smith's wonderful book *The Money Game*).

The Bearded Prophet never went to college. He is a warm and compassionate friend and father, eccentric, iconoclastic and, at times, a bit mysterious.

And he practices what he preaches. A while ago, fearing terrorism and an economic apocalypse, the Bearded Prophet moved out of a tony neighborhood in Long Island to a rather secluded area of New England. He left the investment business (though he still manages a hedge fund that consists mainly of his own wealth).

I rang up the Bearded Prophet on Wednesday to get his view of the world and following are the things that he told me.

The valley between the haves and have-nots in this country and around the world sow the seeds for social and financial change that has only just begun.

The first serious blow to the bow of social, financial, and geopolitical change occurred on September 11, 2001. There will be others that will transform the world's social order. (The Bearded Prophet is best in looking at the big picture.)

There is an inevitability to the world's intemperance and much more dramatic change, reflecting, in part, the technological advances in communication (Internet, advancements in television in less developed countries). And more extensive and timely communications systems demonstrate to those have-nots that the schisms between the wealthy and the indigent have grown wider and wider.

The Bearded Prophet believes that the bear market and the corporate corruption and greed have contributed to a lost generation of investors. Trust will be slow to rebound.

The rebound in the economy will also be most disappointing. Growth will be kept in check by a leveraged consumer, the absence of confidence in our institutions and social unrest.

The Bearded Prophet's portfolio has 91% of his assets in Treasury bills (with less than a one-month maturity) and the balance in a couple of speculative dollar stocks and short index positions—it's been that way for about three years.

To summarize the Bearded Prophet's specific forecasts:

1. The highest the Dow Jones Industrial could be at the end of the bear market is 1,200, but there is a distinct possibility that the markets will be closed for an extensive period of time.
2. Bonds will ultimately rise by more than 50% from current levels.
3. We will go to war with Iraq, and that engagement will be much longer and more tragic than many believe possible. The war will "make it very hard to sleep at night, as terrorism acts will occur regularly. The unimaginable will happen, with a distinct possibility of a nuclear confrontation."
4. Our capital markets and economy will end up in worse shape than Japan. All the Japanese debt is held with Japan; U.S. debt expands all across the globe.
5. Housing prices will collapse, paralleling the decade-long drops in Japanese residential real estate.
6. Most U.S. corporate pension plans will be bankrupted.
7. In time the U.S. mutual fund industry will consolidate by over 75%.
8. Some of his favorite shorts include the Diamonds, Fannie Mae, Freddie Mac, Microsoft, Morgan Stanley and Cisco. "Brokerage stocks will decline to book value," he says.

On Being Jim Cramer

6/12/2003

I am not a suck-up. Indeed, in the past, Jim and I have disagreed on a host of subjects regarding the markets and individual stocks. We have frequently debated each other.

Back a couple of years ago, our disagreements were ugly. Then we got to know each other, and a mutual respect for our differences emerged.

We certainly disagree on the market and economic outlook today. But after our disagreements—when each of us cogitates over the other's view—we learn from each other. (I know this is sappy, but it is true.) Our relationship is symbiotic. On occasion, we will alter our views as a result of the polemic.

Just ask Jim when he stopped selling Toll Brothers at my suggestion in April. And Jim was influential in my decision to cover some AOL Time Warner two months ago. And we have agreed on many other issues, like on the duct-tape bottom.

Because of his extraordinary and documented investment successes, Jim's views are important—and to me, will always require scrutiny.

I would much rather consider and dissect Jim Cramer's views on the basis of his real-time investment successes than consider the views of any other investment strategist, who has not been in the trenches like Jim and has not achieved his accomplishments and material wealth.

Jim is a public persona with a personality that is unique and at times defies description. He is, however, no more idiosyncratic than other successful hedge fund managers I know. He is just a bit more visible, as his views are articulated with frequency over many platforms. That is unusual in our field.

As such, criticism against him is rampant. And the temptation for his critics to selectively bring up his failures is understandable but wrong.

It is also wrong to consider Jim's bullish market outlook as a contrarian indicator.

Look at the *Investor's Intelligence* figures or Merrill Lynch's internal put/call ratio, but don't use Jim Cramer as a contrary tell.

If you do, it might be dangerous to your financial health.

Defending Cramer

4/2/2007

Late last week, I asked Jim Cramer for permission to write a column in response to what I would describe as an abusive and ad hominem attack on him, "Cramer vs. Cramer: Will His Crazy Confession Destroy His Career?" written for *Slate.com* on March 22 by former Merrill Lynch Internet analyst Henry Blodget.

Though I did send a draft of today's column to him last evening, Jim gave me permission to respond to Blodget on my own terms. I give Jim credit for being willing to have me resurrect a story I am sure he is very angry about and wishes was never written. Nevertheless, he provided no input for today's opening missive nor was he given the opportunity by me to edit or make recommendations for this column.

Before I respond specifically to Henry Blodget's article, I would like to make some general observations about disseminating one's views in the public arena and lay out the reality of Jim Cramer's decision to take the road he has taken.

- Being in the public eye has its rewards and its liabilities. While the financial rewards in the media are considerable, they pale in comparison to the renumeration of running a successful hedge fund. That said, a media presence and acclaim provide celebrity and other satisfaction. In the case of Jim Cramer, he is sacrificing the likely prospects for the generation of enormous income in favor of trying to educate investors. Moreover, it is generally known that Cramer gives all his portfolio profits to charity.
- Being in the public eye vividly reveals one's mistakes and blemishes, especially in the fickle and the ever-changing and unpredictable equity markets. Jim Cramer does not hide from his investment picks. He quantifies the investment performance of his *Action Alerts PLUS* portfolio and his recommendations on *Mad Money* in a unique and precise manner for all to see. His results are impressive—consistently so.
- Being in the public eye also exposes one to jealousy and ad hominem attacks. As the subject of a cover story in *BusinessWeek*, as the author of three books and in his ubiquitous presence on CNBC, Jim is an easily identifiable target for his critics.

According to Blodget's own pen, he writes a column "about bad investment advice." As such, Blodget felt compelled to write about Cramer and "to comment on what just might qualify as the worst financial counsel ever offered." The author refers to an interview on *TheStreet.com*'s "Wall Street Confidential" between Aaron Task and Jim Cramer three months ago that Blodget says "can be read as recommending that hedge funds boost returns by orchestrating stock prices and spreading false information." Quoting Cramer as saying that "this is the way the market really works" and those who don't do these things "shouldn't be in the game." Blodget notes that "it raises questions not only about Cramer's activities as a hedge fund manager, but about his judgment. It also, I think, threatens Cramer's career."

Blodget specifically argues that "Cramer endorsed the idea of creating a level of activity before the market opened that could drive the futures down. Similarly, if I were long, and I wanted to make things a little bit rosy, I would go in and buy a bunch of stocks and make sure that they were higher . . . I would encourage anyone in the hedge fund game to do it. Because it's legal. And it is a very quick way to make money." Blodget goes on to describe how Cramer would hit offers (if he wanted a stock to go down) and take bids (if he wanted a stock to go up) in Research In Motion and quotes Cramer "that it might cost me $15 to $20 million to knock RIMM down to beleaguer the longs." Then Blodget reiterates Cramer's comments made in *TheStreet.com* interview in which he states that hitting RIMM down will "get the Pisanis (CNBC) of the world" to say something lousy about RIMM, reinforcing its price decline. In other words a "vicious cycle" develops in a stock and "we now know where some of it (his hedge fund record) came from."

Blodget concludes that Cramer (1) is "giving terrible advice" because "his practices might be illegal"; (2) could be interpreted as "orchestrating a price decline"; (3) "is undermining everything he says" on *Mad Money* because he is suggesting that small investors take his advice; and (4) is "putting his employers (*TheStreet.com*, General Electric, and CNBC) in a bind."

Blodget ends his *Slate* column with the following observation, "Jim Cramer has committed professional suicide."

I disagree with nearly every point made by Blodget in the *Slate* piece, and some of the allegations show limited knowledge of investing. But before I do, let me frame the context under which Jim operates on *Mad Money, Real Money*, in his publications and in his interview with Aaron Task that is attacked by Henry Blodget.

I view Jim as a good, colorful teacher (of investment advice). Jim is the polar opposite of Ben Stein's role as the colorless and boring economics teacher in *Ferris Bueller's Day Off* ("Bueller? . . . Bueller? . . ."). In contrast to Stein's character, a good teacher (in order to get the attention of his students)—like Jim Cramer—tells a good, entertaining and memorable story. By communicating an interesting and animated story, often using hyperbole (and even exaggeration), his students (including the television audiences, book readers and *TheStreet.com* subscribers) more readily get the message of his lecture (or investment advice). Cramer's interview with Aaron Task was filled with exaggeration, as his storytelling was clearly designed, in part (as Jim is always wont to do), to provoke Task and make the piece more memorable. It is in this context that the "Wall Street Confidential" interview should be viewed and judged.

1. Orchestration and manipulation of share prices? Blodget seems to think Jim Cramer, who was the general partner of a $400 million to $500 million hedge fund could create enough activity to drive futures lower or higher (depending on his core position) in premarket trading. Blodget fails to recognize that the markets are far too deep for Cramer's hedge fund to materially affect futures trading. It's just plain dumb to think otherwise. His illustration in trading of Research In Motion is equally ludicrous. To think that Jim would spend $20 million, or about 4% to 5% of his hedge fund's assets, to create the impression that Research In Motion has problems is equally stupid. And Jim Cramer ain't stupid.

2. Spreading false information? I am almost certain that Jim Cramer has never spread false information to reporters, analysts or anyone else for that matter. Information is routinely shared by money managers and the press. Blodget seems to have little respect for the media who are more informed that he realizes. Jim's reference to spread fictional stories to the "Pisanis of the world" is simply hyperbole and exaggeration, made to create a captivating story. Nothing more, nothing less. Bob Pisani is no fool. He is not an automaton who parrots what a hedge fund guy says, even when that someone is Jim Cramer.

3. Putting CNBC, *TheStreet.com,* and General Electric in a legal bind? His constituents—CNBC, *TheStreet.com,* and GE—have remained silent because they, too, recognize the hyperbole of Jim's storytelling and messages.

In conclusion, Henry Blodget is far off base on most of his accusations, and he loses sight of the context of how Cramer differentiates his message from the generally uninformative universe of market gurus. His *Slate* column is nothing more than an ad hominem attack on a very visible, often excitable, entertaining and value-added Cramer. Indeed, the game works differently than Henry Blodget seems to believe. Jim Cramer's capacity and reservoir of investment knowledge (manifested in his Lightning Rounds on *Mad Money*) are almost unparalleled and unchallenged. He is providing a value proposition for many investors. And being able to call on his investment knowledge base while on his feet—and on the fly (again, like in *Mad Money*'s Lightning Round)—is a particularly unique quality that gets the message across crisply, succinctly and entertainingly. His body of knowledge and history in the hedge fund business makes him especially qualified to educate investors as host of *Mad Money,* as an author of three books on investment techniques, as a contributor to *Real Money* and *TheStreet.com* and as an adviser of an *Action Alerts PLUS* portfolio (which likely mimics what he would be doing if he still operated a hedge fund). His informed, animated, hyperbolic, and humorous style segregates him from any other commentator extant. And in the course of his peripatetic and exaggerated style of delivery, Jim extols sound advice that is not only memorable but whose principles and tenets should not be forgotten—they should be memorized.

There is a constant thread in Henry Blodget's "Cramer vs. Cramer." It is a tempest in a teapot probably provoked for the purpose of disgracing Jim Cramer. It is also a blatant attempt to receive publicity. From my perch, Henry Blodget continues to be an expert on bad advice, just as Jim Cramer is an expert on good advice.

Defending Cramer (Part Deux)

2/9/2009

In the past, I have come to the defense of Jim Cramer against a host of media attacks. I do this not because I write for *TheStreet.com*—I view myself as an independent person who speaks his mind regardless of the consequences—rather, I have defended Jim because I strongly believe that he provides a value-added contribution to the individual investor in navigating an increasingly difficult investment terrain.

Jim does this not only on CNBC's *Mad Money* but, importantly, in the publication of his books, *Jim Cramer's Mad Money: Watch TV, Get Rich, Jim Cramer's Stay Mad for Life: Get Rich, Stay Rich (Make Your Kids Even Richer),* and *Jim Cramer's Real Money: Sane Investing in an Insane World,* which provide more pensive analytical tools and recommendations in approaching one's investment portfolio.

Bullish media and Wall Street analyst hype are legendary and, to some degree, represent the proximate cause for many investment miscues on the part of individual investors whom have historically behaved in a Pavlovian fashion in their reaction to perma-bullish pablum, so, when someone like Jim Cramer provides a more thorough and objective educational outline to navigating the market, it should be welcomed by the media, not criticized.

Over the weekend, *Barron's* published the story, "Cramer's Star Outshines His Stock Picks."

The thrust of the article is that "Jim Cramer's celebrity is bigger than ever," but the "stock picks featured on *Mad Money* don't live up to the host's hype." The *Barron's* article is critical of his opinions on an enormous number of stocks and suggests that "in the days leading up to their mention on *Mad Money,* stocks start to move in the direction of his recommendation. Post-mention, they revert to their previous trend, short-changing investors." The piece goes on to suggest that Jim's staff is "heavy-footed in their research" and the subject matter of many shows appear to be leaked because of that process.

As I have defended Jim Cramer from attacks by the media in the past, I will do so again today, hopefully as an impartial and independent observer.

My basic point has been that, above any other media pundit, Jim provides a value-added educational experience for the average individual investor.

He does this in several ways:

• He goes belly-to-belly with company managements on *Mad Money.* He typically doesn't serve up the easy pitch but rather usually goes to the root of the valuation/fundamental controversy.

- His Lightning Rounds give his quick and abridged impression of a stock's outlook.
- He develops investment themes and strategies that are easily understood and developed reasonably well on *Mad Money* and in his books.
- Most important, on *Mad Money,* he provides an educational handbook on how to analyze a company/sector, with a focus on the development of the principal determinants of future stock market behavior.

Jim qualifies almost every investment recommendation with the caveat that investors should not take, prima facie, his word on a stock. He says that every investor has an obligation to do his own homework.

Jim qualifies almost every investment recommendation with another caveat: Don't buy on the spike or strength following his mention. Wait until things calm down, he says.

As to potential leaks, that is an occupational hazard if one is going to carefully research an idea and cover multiple sources. A more comprehensive research approach by *Mad Money* staff is far more preferable than superficial preparation. The same phenomenon occurs in *Barron's,* the source of this weekend's criticism, as trading desks often hear about rumors of *Barron's* cover stories. Most are specious, but now and again, they are accurate.

The *Barron's* article analyzes "650-odd" Cramer recommendations and concludes that "his bullish picks underperformed the S&P by about 3.5 percentage points over the 45 trading days after each show."

To that, my response is: So what? Not only is the statistical error broad vis-à-vis the underperformance and the degree of underperformance modest within the context of the volume of recommendations but this analysis presumes a buy-and-hold strategy, which, particularly in today's volatile times, is plain silly and not the intention that Jim necessarily recommends.

Finally, many of Jim's investment recommendations are indeed nuanced and qualified. Treating every investment recommendation as the same and compiling an investment performance is, to some degree, comparing apples to oranges.

In my final analysis, individual investors are better served listening to Jim Cramer, both with regard to his recommendations and his methodology, than any other business commentator extant. His body of investment knowledge is remarkably broad and lacks the superficiality of most of his brethren.

Jim is an investment populist who, unlike many in my hedge fund cabal, has forsaken that financial rainbow for a greater cause—namely, helping out the individual investor.

Jim is an easy target, but from my perch, he should not be vilified; he should be admired.

Leon Cooperman and James Brown: The Godfathers of Hard Work

12/26/2006

While James Brown never captured the zeitgeist of the Beatles, Rolling Stones, or Elvis, he bettered them all in volume (100-plus albums), originality, endurance, and breadth of influence. Only Elvis Presley has sold more records, and Brown holds the distinction of selling the most rhythm and blues records ever. Interestingly, none of the singles ever recorded by James Brown got to No. 1, and only two were in the top five on *Billboard's Top 40*. This arguably reflects worse on the pop audience than it does of his music.

Remembering the Godfather of Soul   Most remember James Brown (who died two days ago on Christmas Eve), as the Godfather of Soul who sang "Living in America" in the movie *Rocky IV*.

I remember James Brown as something more than a great recording artist; I remember him as the hardest-working performer in show business and one who overcame adversity (much of which was self-imposed).

The Hardest-Working Performer in Show Business   I first heard of James Brown when I was 19 years old and listened to his album, *Live at the Apollo*. He was brought up by his Aunt "Handsome Honey" Washington, a madam in a Georgia brothel. He rose above poverty, jail, drug addiction, and a world's changing view of the type of music that was to be in vogue—especially in the 1970s with the popularity of disco—and worked tirelessly, breaking numerous records of singing performances (recordings and live concerts). Nothing, it seems, could keep him down or keep him from his appointed task of entertaining.

For obvious reasons (somewhere over the hedge fund rainbow can be a huge payday), competition is keen in the hedge fund industry, just like the entertainment biz. While many hedge hogs are well schooled in the country's leading business and finance programs, I have learned from some of the best hedge hogs that the way to differentiate one's performance is through really hard work, which was characterized by most of James Brown's career. As evidence of his peers' view of his talent, Brown is the most sampled entertainer in R&B history.

The Hardest-Working Hedge Hog   The best example of a superior work ethic that I have personally experienced (and one of the best hedge fund practitioners extant) is Leon Cooperman, my old boss at Omega Advisors. Prior to forming Omega, Leon ran the institutional research department at Goldman Sachs for many years before he established his hedge fund in the early 1990s.

If James Brown was the Godfather of Soul, Leon has become (over the following 15 years) the Godfather of Stock Picking, and (like James Brown) the best single example of hard work in the investment business that I have ever met. No doubt Leon would cringe about my observation that his work ethic parallels that of the King of Soul!

Leon would routinely be the first in the office at Omega (almost always by 6:00 A.M.), and inevitably, he would be one of the last to leave. When things went wayward—as occasionally happens to the best of them—he would sleep in his office in a roll-up bed!

In *Hedgehogging*, Barton Biggs writes that "great investment managers are intense, disciplined maniacs." And in Chapter 14, I believe, though I could be wrong, Biggs writes about Leon's remarkable work ethic in his thinly veiled discussion of "Greg, who runs Mega."

Don't believe me? Just ask Jim Cramer, who worked with Leon for several years at Goldman Sachs.

The Agony and the Ecstasy of Hard Work   James Brown, like today's hedge fund managers, underwent a stressful life filled with intensity, dedication, foibles and insecurities. Throughout his life, Brown experienced the ecstasy and elation inherent in his craft, as do hedge hogs who deliver sustained and superior investment performance. He also experienced the agony and despair of his personal demons, similar to hedge hogs who are on the wrong side of Mr. Market.

Though honored by the Kennedy Center in 2003, James Brown's loss will be conspicuous this evening, but his legacy of perseverance and hard work has not been lost by me. Nor will his constant rebounds from the jaws of defeat be lost on this observer.

In Leon Cooperman and James Brown—the Godfathers of Hard Work—we can learn from the best.

Ben Stein Whistles Past Mortgage Mess

8/15/2007

From my perch, one of the most astonishing features of the recent decline in stocks and rise in credit spreads is the smug rejection of the notion that things have changed—particularly of a credit nature.
No better view of the ostrich-in-the-sand mentality was delivered than by warm and cuddly actor/lawyer/columnist/comedian/economist/

Clear Eyes shill Ben Stein in this weekend's business section of the *New York Times*, and then again on CNBC Monday evening.

In the past, I have admired the common sense and logic of argument in Stein's writings. Maybe Stein was acting this week, as he did in the role of the economics teacher in the classic movie *Ferris Bueller's Day Off*. After all, on Sir Larry Kudlow's show, Stein suggested that the mortgage lenders will "end up fine," and he concluded that the subprime mess is a media hoax in an attempt to "talk America into a panic." Excuse me?

Tell that to Thornburg Mortgage, which is temporarily ceasing loan production, Countrywide Financial, American Home Mortgage, Accredited Home Lenders or the millions of individuals who are about to lose their homes and those that can no longer get a mortgage. Or tell it to the investors in the Bear Stearns hedge funds and the Sentinel Cash Management Fund.

Tell it to the homeowners who live next to foreclosed homes who are about to rein in their own spending for fear that they might be the next foreclosure. Or tell it to the Wal-Mart customers and mall customers who are no longer buying. Or tell it to the U.S. banks that are caught with hundreds of billions of dollars of illiquid bridge loans. Or tell it to the foreign banks that are taking multibillion-dollar write-downs and are reining in their credit activity. Or tell it to the employees at brokerage firms, banks and retailers who will soon be laid off.

The subprime market is not an isolated problem as suggested by Stein; it is only the beginning of the chain.

The global credit bubble of leveraged financial engineering (and ownership of risky assets) has been pierced. Wall Street sold arcane and illiquid products with promises of limited risk and fat profits.

Our financial and investment world is so tightly wound and levered that the likely fallout is going to be far broader than almost anyone expects. What had been a liquidity problem is now morphing into a solvency problem in a wide and surprising array of assets and companies, including money market funds, Canadian trusts, cash management funds, mortgage companies, investment bankers, and so on.

The price discovery in the credit markets will inevitably result in further wealth destruction, bankruptcies and an ever-increasing risk aversion, regardless of central bank behavior. The excessive use of cheap, mispriced credit is the source of the problem, and providing more liquidity (as central bankers do) can hardly be considered a healthy solution.

Stein seems to endorse the ludicrous notion that there remains a negativity bubble. Many were wrong three months ago, and Stein is wrong today, as stocks and credit don't fall in the manner that they have in the past month if there is broad-based pessimism. Rather, with the benefit of hindsight, it is now clear that there was a bubble in optimism, as disbelief had been suspended on the part of buyers of credit, buyers of homes and buyers of stocks.

In his now-famous interview with Erin Burnett, Jim Cramer went on a rant in which he expressed his idea that certain members of the Fed didn't understand the severity of the current credit problem.

Jim Cramer knows how bad the situation is.

Ben, pardon my French (and my reference to *Ferris Bueller's Day Off*'s Cameron Frye), but on the subject of credit, you are clueless.

The credit event that you dismiss is already morphing into an economic event.

Curb Your Enthusiasm, Ben Stein

9/10/2007

What follows is an e-mail I sent to Ben Stein yesterday after reading his column in Sunday's *New York Times* Business section, "It's Time to Take a Deep Breath."

Dear Ben,

Well, the first days are the hardest days,
Don't you worry anymore
When life looks like Easy Street
There is danger at your door.
Think this through with me
Let me know your mind
Wo-oah, what I want to know
Is are you kind?

—*The Grateful Dead, "Uncle John's Band"*

I read with interest your *New York Times* column in the Sunday Business section.

It might be time to take a deep breath. But for another reason, to recognize the dramatic and the cumulative impact of excessive debt/leverage creation on our citizenry (especially the consumer kind) and to consider the ramifications of the black swan credit event that awaits the unwind.

In your article, you have basically recounted the same argument that you have used in prior columns. You write that "the percentage of those who have defaulted is still fairly small." In other words, all will be well, as market participants are overreacting to an isolated credit situation, and the Fed will pull us out of this limited mess.

Disappointingly, you added Cramer to your criticism, using him as a symptom of the overzealous media. Jim is an easy target, too easy, and you take advantage of it in a derisive comment. I, too, have been at odds with Jim but, quite frankly, have defended him over the last few years because he is generally well informed; he educates the individual investor (who believes too much of what he hears in the media) and has actually walked the walk (not just talked the talk) in running a successful hedge fund.

Not lost is the irony that you are critical of Jim Cramer for making a negative market comment, whereas most in the press have derided him for being too bullish.

Quite frankly, Ben, the media is imbalanced almost universally on the side of optimism. They, to quote Cramer, generally (like administration cheerleaders who "know nothing") are "talking" from their platforms in the press box; they are not on the field. And the "field players," like the CEOs at YRC Worldwide, AutoNation, and many others know the real truth. Economic conditions are a lot worse than you suggest as even our mutual friend, Larry Kudlow, had reduced the usage of his "greatest story never told" line because he, too, recognizes the direction the economy is taking.

You have consistently dismissed the notion that the subprime credit event would morph into an economic event. And, based on Sunday's column, you continue to hold to this view. Quite frankly, I am surprised that the recent signs of broader economic weakness (like Friday's job number) are so readily dismissed by you.

If you don't believe this ursine grey-beard, I would suggest that you sit down with Howard Marks, the head of Oaktree Management (a $30 billion hedge fund). He is out on the West Coast with you and has written some succinct pieces on the pendulum shift of credit, the lemming-like search for yield, and he has chronicled a number of other financial abuses of the new millennium. His firm's telephone number is in the Los Angeles yellow pages, and I am sure he will take your call.

Finally, you also appear too quick to dismiss the alternative of "ice" in your column, claiming "Some strict disciplinarians want to let the markets go through hell and let borrowers and investors suffer," which suggests that the Fed can reignite the economic "fire." And, with the

Some say the world will end in fire,

Some say in ice.

From what I've tasted of desire

I hold with those who favor fire.

But if it had to perish twice,

I think I know enough of hate

To say that for destruction ice

Is also great

And would suffice.

—Robert Frost, "Fire and Ice"

exception of your reference to a dollar crisis, you don't seem to think that too much can go wrong in our overlevered and unregulated (derivatives) financial world.

Apparently, you have missed some news out of Barclays, Deutsche Bank, Citigroup, all of the leading U.S. investment bankers and others who are up to their eyeballs in structured investment vehicles, bridge loans to private-equity deals and unsold junk bonds.

I could not disagree more with your conclusion that "If I were the editor of the business section for just one day, I would run one immense headline: 'Everything Is Going to Be Fine. Go Back to Work.'"

Ben, the world has changed—and not for the better. Arguably, the Fed might be pushing on a string.

Curb your enthusiasm, Ben, because many of our friends in the financial and banking communities will not have a job when they return to work in the months ahead.

With Respect,
Doug Kass
Seabreeze Partners

> *These traders, not economists or securities analysts, can turn the world upside down, make governments tremble, give central bankers colitis and ruin the lives of ordinary men and women saving for their children's college education or their own retirement. In America today, it is the traders, not the politicians or the generals or the corporate bosses, who have the power.*
>
> —Ben Stein, *New York Times*, "Can Their Wish Be the Market's Command?"

Ben Stein Blames You

1/28/2008

My Sunday morning routine is usually cast in stone. I typically wake up at around 5:00 A.M. and spend an hour or so writing my opening missive for Monday. Then, I read the obituaries—I am, after all, still a short-seller!—and then the Sports, Week in Review, and Business sections in the *New York Times*. Thereafter, I work on solving Sunday's *New York Times* crossword puzzle. (I am proud to say that I have completed the last five in a row.) Next, I watch NBC's *Meet the Press,* ESPN's *Sports Reporters,* and ABC's *This Week with George Stephanopoulos.*

Finally, my regular day starts, and these days, it is filled with thoughts about the stock market, cogitating over the week that was and what to do next and why, in addition to calls or e-mails between other hedge-hoggers.

Yesterday morning, I was prepared to write a column preliminarily entitled "The Case for a Bull Market: What Could Go Right and How." I was going to emphasize the latent buying power of sovereign wealth funds and make the case that the equity market might be discounting a far deeper recession than might occur. I had planned to underscore that interest rates remain subdued, that the curative process of restoring capital bases at leading financial institutions continues apace and that a negative sentiment bubble seems to be emerging coincident with lower share prices. I was even going to highlight that there might be some light at the end to the tunnel of housing as fiscal and monetary stimulation is moving into overdrive.

That is, until I read Stein's column—"Can Their Wish Be the Market's Command?"—in Sunday's *New York Times* Business section. No one has the concession on the truth, especially as it relates to investing. But rigorous analysis, logic of argument, power of dissection, weighing sentiment, and modeling remain good ways to try to find that truth.

I have chronicled Stein's general lack of realism in his series of *New York Times* articles, in communicating and recognizing growing economic problems and in improperly isolating and laying blame on the stock market's poor showing to his list of imaginary ne'er-do-wells.

- Six months ago, Mr. Stein blamed the market's weakness on the media's hysteria.
- Seven weeks ago, he blamed the market's weakness on Goldman Sachs and its economist, Dr. Jan Hatzius. (*Note:* Not even the Dr. Evils at Goldman Sachs benefited in the aggregate from the subprime melt-down, as suggested by Stein. Sure, Goldman shorted mortgage debt, but, in the main, the broker/dealer is long the economy/markets. Proof positive is Goldman's weak performing common stock, the source of how most Goldman principals make their incomes.)
- Yesterday, Stein blamed the market's weakness on traders.

From my perch, Stein's assertions have been consistently wrong and continue to be poorly reasoned.

I even submitted one of my columns to the *New York Times'* editorial staff as a rebuttal to Stein's articles. Rejected!

My Grandma Koufax taught me to be nice, though she was a killer in her children's wear business (and in her stock market trading). She used to regularly say, "Dougie, he is a nice boy, and he is good to his mother." And I am sure Ben is and was.

> *"In the short run, the market is a voting machine. In the long run, it's a weighing machine."*
>
> —Benjamin Graham

I have tried to respond to Mr. Stein's words in a professional and respectful manner—I even share my columns with him via e-mail—and I have avoided anything that resembled an ad hominem attack on him by addressing, point by point, his misguided observations and underlying assumptions of economic causality and his views regarding the stock market's outlook.

Stein and I both agree that statistics show, in the long run, stocks rise and economies prosper—though that was not the subject of yesterday's column. And, yes, daily market volatility of 2% to 3% is occurring because of trigger-happy hedge fund traders' buying and selling. But it is a broad list of economic uncertainties (and daily headline risks) that generate indecision and lack of confidence in their trading actions that seem to be producing this volatility.

Traders influence volatility, but they cannot control stock prices over any reasonable time frame. Investors do.

Wild intraday price moves are unsettling to most investors, but the history of stocks shows that yearly market moves more often than not do produce meaningful price changes. Though sometimes impacted by an exogenous event, outsized changes are dependent upon the degree of confidence or certainty in economic outcomes. When uncertainties exist, stock prices and economies can stall for years (and sometimes even for a decade or more) and vice versa.

The view of a favorable long run is all well and good, but in the highly competitive world of hedge funds/personal money management, properly identifying and navigating monthly and yearly trends/moves (as well as finding superior individual stocks) can result in superior and differentiated investment performance.

Just ask investors who have prospered and outperformed and money managers who have demonstrated a consistent ability to time buying/selling and identify value in markets, sectors and stocks—namely, Ken Heebner, Stanley Druckenmiller, Leon Cooperman, George Soros, and Steve Cohen.

Back to Ben's vision of our economy and the markets.

Over the past two months, many previously bullish economic/market commentators have incorporated the reality of the economic, credit market and stock market situation by scaling back their optimism. Brokerage firm economists and strategists at Morgan Stanley, Goldman Sachs, Merrill Lynch et al. have adjusted their extrapolations of prosperity toward more realistic goals and assumptions.

While Stein has questioned the motivation of some of this (especially at Goldman Sachs), we all know that massive capital and people commitments are made to insure accuracy of those predictions. And, if wrong, again, as my Grandma Koufax used to say, "Dougie, they'll have less bread to be buttered."

Even Dr. Arthur Laffer did an about-face on CNBC's *Kudlow & Company* and has turned cautious, and several other of Sir Larry Kudlow's Band of Merry Men have grown less cheery.

At Wharton, I learned that the basis for determining market valuation lies at the foot of security analysis and modeling—as delivered by Benjamin Graham and David Dodd in *Security Analysis*—not on the part of the whims of traders.

As Ben Graham wrote, in the fullness of time, stocks move toward the weight of value. Investors use many rigorous and disciplined methodologies in valuing stocks and in determining fair market value:

1. Many strategists and investors use top-down, discounted cash flow and dividend models to determine the fair market level of equities. These models are not static; they change as the underlying model assumptions change. The most theoretically sound stock valuation method is called income valuation or the discounted cash flow method, involving discounting the profits (dividends, earnings or cash flows) the stock will bring to the stockholder in the foreseeable future and a final value on disposition. The discount rate normally has to include a risk premium, which is commonly based on the capital asset pricing model.

2. The Gordon model is the best known of a class of discounted dividend models. It assumes that dividends will increase at a constant growth rate (less than the discount rate) forever.

3. The P/E method is perhaps the most commonly used valuation method in the stock brokerage industry. By using comparison firms, a target price-to-earnings (or P/E) ratio is selected for the company, and then the future earnings of the company are estimated. The valuation's fair price is simply estimated earnings times the target P/E.

4. Some feel that if the stock is listed in a well-organized stock market, with a large volume of transactions, the listed price will be close to the estimated fair value. This is called the efficient market hypothesis. On the other hand, studies made in the field of behavioral finance tend to show that deviations from the fair price are rather common, and sometimes quite large.

5. In addition to fundamental economic criteria, market criteria also have to be taken into account for a market-based valuation. Valuing a stock is not only to estimate its fair value but also to determine its potential price range, taking into account market behavior aspects. One of the behavioral valuation tools is the stock image, a coefficient that bridges the theoretical fair value and the market price.

Today, the aforementioned underlying dependent variables that support some of the model assumptions above are either being downgraded or are uncertain in their outcomes, and this is pressuring stocks.

> Because I usually write about finance, I have come to believe in the theory of what I would call "financial realism," or what might more accurately be called "trader realism." Under this theory, on which I have an imaginary patent, traders can see masses of data any minute of any day. They can find data to support hitting the "buy" button or the "sell" button. They don't act on the basis of what seems to them the real economic situation, but on what's in it for them.
>
> —*Ben Stein*

Stein's major assertion is that what his brother-in-law Melvin (a Harvard Law School graduate) taught him about legal realism applies to the stock market and to the traders running the stock market. Mr. Stein cites the following:

> What really happened (in the legal system) at the appellate level and probably at the trial level, too, was that judges made up their minds based on their predilections, their biases, which lawyer was their friend, what they had for breakfast that day.

He gives little rigorous documentation to his assertion. It is simply his feel that the traders set prices, as suggested in the following quote from his article, based on the magnitude of the stock market damage inflicted relative to his view of the economic damage that has occurred.

It is simply more B.S. from B.S.

> Note that the losses in United States markets alone are on the order of about $2.5 trillion in recent weeks. How can a loss of roughly $100 billion on subprime—with some recoveries sure to come as property is seized and sold—translate into a stock-market loss 25 times that size? The answer is trader realism.
>
> The losses in the stock market since the highs of October 2007 are about 14%. This predicts—very roughly—a fall in corporate profits of roughly 14%. Yet there has never been a decline of quite that size for even one year in the postwar United States, and never more than two years of declining profits before they regained their previous peak.

And earlier in the article, he provides a synopsis of his almighty trader theory:

> More than that, they trade to support the way they want the market to go. If they are huge traders like some of the major hedge funds, they can sell massively and move the market downward, then suck in other traders who go short, and create a vacuum of fear that sucks down whatever they are selling.
>
> Note what is happening here: They are not figuring out which way the market will go. They are making the market go the direction they want.

The above demonstrates such a degree of naïveté that I am really shocked that the *New York Times* published the article.

For example, when a company misses its earnings guidance by a penny or two, the same disproportionate impact occurs on its share price. The equity capitalization loss is vastly in excess of the miss to profits. That is because, generally speaking, the miss to expectation can sometimes be seen as a warning of larger misses to come.

The same observation is true with regard to the economy or to the credit markets.

More broadly, the subprime problem (originally expected to be contained) has metastasized into a global credit crisis that neither Ben (Stein or Bernanke) nor any of us mere mortals have ever experienced. With it has come hundreds of billions of dollars of permanently lost capital that has disappeared.

What concerns investors is that it has occurred at the time that the financial system (and the U.S. consumer) has never been more levered. The multiplier effect is unknown, though they have been accompanied by massive write-downs at the world's largest financial institutions, and markets hate the unknown.

Stein continues to dismiss the all-too-obvious economic and stock market problems that litter the world, many of which I have detailed ad nauseam. Rather than recognizing those risks, Mr. Stein prefers to simply place the blame on the body of avaricious and self-motivated traders who control and overwhelm the markets over the very short term.

I respectfully suggest to Ben that he listen to the Coach and Target conference calls—they are still available on replay—and read the MBIA, Countrywide Financial, and Merrill Lynch 10-Qs in order to get out of the fourth estate's ivory tower.

Moreover, who are these "traders" that Stein blames? (Honestly, he is beginning to sound like Senator Clinton in 1998, with her "vast right-wing conspiracy" argument.) The traders I know are getting killed these days—sometimes on both their long and short positions.

The dedicated short community manages less than $5 billion in total—that's under 10% of the size of the Fidelity Magellan Fund—and most long/short managers, an asset class that dominates today's investment landscape, are substantially long-biased. (According to Ed Hyman's ISI surveys, they are about 55% net long.)

For Stein to be correct that the market's drop is simply a conspiracy of traders, test his hypothesis in reverse. Is the market ever dear?

When it goes up, is it only a conspiracy of buyers as most traders are long-biased?

My conclusion? Stein is simply suffering from a conformational bias of the worst order.

Not surprisingly, I prefer the more substantive economic reality portrayed in other pieces in Sunday's *New York Times*—those written by Gretchen Morgenson, Dr. Robert Shiller and Jim Grant—to Stein's nonrigorous assertions regarding the power and culpability of the trading community.

In summary, one thing is certain to me: Ben continues to fiddle in the *New York Times* while the world's equity markets burn.

The answer to the investment mosaic is always complicated. (I certainly don't possess the answer.) Market prices are based on numerous influences, generally grounded in market psychology, corporate profit expectations, and the term structure of interest rates.

Investors are staring into a financial abyss caused by real-world problems, yet Stein pooh-poohs it all, almost dismissing the issues out of hand by blaming the whole thing on "traders"—the definition of which I don't really understand, and Ben has not explained who exactly they are.

If Stein has only influenced one single investor to ignore today's market and economic headwinds, he is doing a disservice to that reader and to the *New York Times*.

I expect more.

Eat My Shorts, Ben Stein

2/15/2008

Last night, Ben Stein blamed the drop in equities on the short-selling community.

I simply can't let Stein's comment go unanswered. My intention is not to make an ad hominem attack on him but rather to set the record straight.

I have responded to Ben Stein's blame game over the past eight months with

> *"Short-sellers can push the market down forever."*
>
> —Ben Stein on last night's "Kudlow & Company"

facts not opinions. In the interim interval, Stein has alternatively blamed the media, Goldman Sachs and its economist, traders and, now, short-sellers.

I admire analytical acuity, investment rigor and logic of argument, but Stein's recent diatribe is astonishingly naïve, nonrigorous and materially incorrect.

The dedicated short community is small, estimated to be less than $6 billion, which is down dramatically over the last decade's bull market. To put this into perspective, the dedicated short pool is less than 10% the size of Fidelity's Magellan Fund.

As to the short portion of traditional long/short managers (which, according to Stein, is capable of exerting huge downside influence on stocks), it is completely overshadowed by the long portion.

On last night's show, Stein specifically mentioned the Citadel Investment Group, founded by the lynx-eyed Kenneth Griffin, as one of the funds capable of committing massive amounts to the short side in an attempt to impact stocks to the downside. I spoke to several people close to Citadel, and their short-selling exposure (and return attribution) is dwarfed by their long-biased investments.

Maybe it was inevitable that the short-sellers would be blamed for the egregious use of debt/leverage in the world's financial system. After all, why blame the entrenched ratings agencies (which, cycle after cycle, fall flat on their analytical faces), Wall Street firms (which exist to sell product) or the buyers of junk credit like the commercial banks (which abandoned their due diligence and common sense) when there is such a convenient scapegoat?

Quite frankly, if more investors and politicians had listened to Gary Shilling's pronouncements on the housing industry, Nouriel Roubini's dire analysis of the world's credit system, Pershing Square's William Ackman's comprehensive admonition of the monoline insurers or, even back in time, Kynikos's Jim Chanos's keen analysis of the shady accounting at Enron, billions of dollars in losses could have been avoided, and public policy solutions to systemic problems would have been encouraged before it was too late.

I am a hard worker and motivated by the opportunity afforded me by our capital system. Professionally, I labor for analytical truth for the sole purpose of delivering superior returns to my investors. If my investment theses are founded on faulty premises, I will perform poorly and my investors will flee.

That being said, I outlined (ad nauseam) my specific concerns on housing two to three years ago, subprime one and a half years ago and the emerging credit problems one year ago with clarity and rigorous analysis well before they entered the court of popular opinion.

My forecasts were largely ignored on my many appearances on "Kudlow & Company," and, even up until the fall of 2007, those concerns were roundly dismissed by some of Larry's Band of Merry Men.

So, Ben:

Blame the market's decline on the Bossa Nova.

Or blame the market's decline on the fundamentals.

But don't blame the market's decline on the short-sellers.

My Q&A with Nouriel Roubini

7/19/2010

Yesterday afternoon, Nouriel Roubini was the speaker at the Summer Institute lecture series at the Jewish Center of the Hamptons.

"I am ugly, but I have a beautiful mind."

—Nouriel Roubini

I attended Nouriel's talk on Sunday, having previously presented my own talk at the Temple's Summer Institute lecture series exactly a year ago in the same forum and on the same subject: the economy and the stock market.

In the interests of full disclosure, I have been critical (perhaps, at times, too critical) about:

1. The way in which the media have embraced Nouriel;
2. Nouriel's apparent inflexibility and dogma; and
3. Nouriel's inaccurate stock market forecasts.

In keeping with his reputation, Nouriel was escorted by a young, attractive girl, with a skirt nearly up to her *pupik*. (She was clearly not a congregant at the Temple!)

After that entrance, things went downhill, as there was little in the way of added value (at least to this observer) extracted from his presentation, since I have heard all of it before.

Nouriel gave his standard talk: The United States is entering either a "U" (at best) or a "W" (at worst), while over there, he estimates 0% growth in the eurozone over the next 12 months.

Reduced fiscal and monetary stimuli, the cessation of temporary benefits (inventory build, Cash for Clunkers, homebuyer's tax credit, etc.) and diminished confidence (consumer and corporate) spell subpar growth (1.5% estimated second-half domestic growth). Deflationary pressures remain the mainstay in the aftermath of the last economic and credit cycle and in the face of tax policy (higher January 2011) and the obliteration of the shadow-banking system and securitization markets.

In the United States, Nouriel says we are kicking the can down the road and that we face a fiscal train wreck with no visible exit strategy in sight.

The one part of his talk that stood out to me was in the section of his speech in which he talked about some possible solutions to our fiscal imbalances. Specifically, he feels that we, as a nation, have been overly preoccupied with housing-central policy. He argued that housing provides little in the way of sustained productivity and growth and that many of the benefits of home ownership (such as the mortgage-interest deduction) should be reassessed.

In the Q&A session, I asked Nouriel three questions:

1. How can he explain the schmeissing in U.S. equities when, at the same time, certain risk measures (lower bank swap spreads, LIBOR, junk bond yields, a higher euro, etc.) and risk markets appear to have stabilized?

2. Could the U.S. stock market be attractive in light of generally reduced economic expectations and lower corporate profit assumptions?

3. Could the U.S. stock market be attractive with markets selling at less than 12× realistic 2011 S&P 500 profits vs. an historical average of 15.5× and at 17.0× when interest rates and inflation are quiescent?

On the first question, Nouriel agreed with my observation that, unlike the May swoon, risk metrics had stabilized. I was delighted to hear that he said he now recognizes that his principal role is as an economist, as he has learned over the past few years that there are other influences that affect the equities market and that the stock market and the economy are often (especially on a short-term basis) out of sync. On the second and third questions I asked, he felt that the stock markets were still discounting higher and unrealistic economic growth and corporate profits. I responded that my impression is that economists have ratcheted down economic and profit forecasts—many of whom are not materially higher than him now. On question three, he admitted that, absent another dislocation, stocks might be cheap relative to history.

Before Sunday, I had never met Nouriel Roubini. I came away from yesterday's lecture not learning more than when I entered but thinking that he is more well intentioned and perhaps even more studious than I previously thought. He is an engaging speaker, and he seems to be a very nice guy.

So, in the future, I plan to go easy on the guy—perhaps in the hope that he will invite me to one of his infamous parties!

Party on, Nouriel!

The Orchid Indicator

2/8/2011

Here we are, with 91% of all equity holdings in the U.S. held by the top 20% income group in the country. The top 1% own 38% of all the equity valuation. The lower 80% of the income strata own the asset class that the Fed wants so desperately to reflate (and with unmitigated success to be sure!). That same 80% are now being crushed by the indirect impacts of monetary policy—the ones that Bernanke dismisses—and are also ones that are seeing their cash flow drained by the surging gas and grocery bill. Geez—real wages deflated 0.5% in November, by 0.1% in December, and by what looks like at least 0.3% in January. The last time real work-based income fell three months in a row was when the economy was plumbing the recession's depths from April to June of 2009.

—David Rosenberg, Gluskin Sheff

I have been raising orchids for more than 20 years, ever since I began studying them while I was recovering from a harness racing accident in 1990. As a result, I know many of the local growers in South Florida.

I had a long conversation with one of my main guys, Orchid Bob, on Saturday morning at a local green market.

An orchid is a generally disposable purchase and, as such, is a reasonably good gauge of the state of consumers' discretionary spending patterns.

Orchid Bob's business has taken a dramatic turn for the worse over the last few months.

Bob did about $15,000 of business in November 2009 and approximately $20,000 in December 2009.

His business starting weakening three months ago: He did only $8,000 to $10,000 in November 2010 (down nearly 40% year over year). In the following month, the seasonally strong December 2010 period, Orchid Bob only sold $5,000 worth of orchids (down by an enormous 75% year over year).

Orchid Bob's business has continued to weaken, as during last month (January 2011), he sold a measly $3,000 during the first 30 days of this new year.

Bob's business is a local one, so he would have been unaffected by the Northeast and Midwest snowfalls and by the numerous flight cancellations. His clientele are generally not fancy Palm Beachers but rather middle classers.

Orchid Bob's business weakness has been confirmed by poor sales at the other growers I met with or spoke to over the weekend; I plan to stay on top of my orchid channel checks in the months ahead.

This highly anecdotal and small sampling may be meaningless or it might be meaningful. My suspicion is that many small businesses face a fate similar to Bob's.

Time will tell whether screwflation will or already is starting to take hold.

What I do know is that Bob the Orchid Man has met screwflation head-on and his orchid business is now in a depression.

We should be closely monitoring the relative and absolute performance of the Retail HOLDRS in the weeks ahead to judge whether, as I continue to suspect, the consumer will be the Achilles' heel of the current domestic economic recovery.

Look out the window. More and more Americans are being left behind in an economy that is being divided ever more starkly between the haves and the have-nots. Not only are millions of people jobless and millions more underemployed, but more and more of the so-called fringe benefits and public services that help make life livable, or even bearable, in a modern society are being put to the torch. . . .

Standards of living for the people on the wrong side of the economic divide are being ratcheted lower and will remain that way for many years to come. Forget the fairy tales being spun by politicians in both parties—that somehow they can impose service cuts that are drastic enough to bring federal and local budgets into balance while at the same time developing economic growth strong enough to support a robust middle class. It would take a Bernie Madoff to do that. . . .

The U.S. cannot cut its way out of this crisis. Instead of trying to figure out how to keep 4-year-olds out of pre-kindergarten classes, or how to withhold life-saving treatments from Medicaid recipients, or how to cheat the elderly out of their Social Security, the nation's leaders should be trying seriously to figure out what to do about the future of the American work force.

Enormous numbers of workers are in grave danger of being left behind permanently. Businesses have figured out how to prosper without putting the unemployed back to work in jobs that pay well and offer decent benefits.

Corporate profits and the stock markets are way up. Businesses are sitting atop mountains of cash. Put people back to work? Forget about it. Has anyone bothered to notice that much of those profits are the result of aggressive payroll-cutting—companies making do with fewer, less well-paid and harder-working employees?

For American corporations, the action is increasingly elsewhere. Their interests are not the same as those of workers, or the country as a whole. As Harold Meyerson put it in *The American*

Prospect: "Our corporations don't need us anymore. Half their revenues come from abroad. Their products, increasingly, come from abroad as well."

American workers are in a world of hurt.

—*Bob Herbert, "A Terrible Divide"* (New York Times *op-ed*, Feb. 7, 2011)

The schism between the middle class and flush corporations is growing ever more conspicuous. This is not meant to be a statement of class warfare or a political view; rather, it is meant as an accurate economic statement.

The market has clearly looked through and dismissed this issue and is ignoring its potential consequences, as it focuses on more constructive developments (corporate profit growth, an expansion in merger and acquisition activity, positive stock price momentum, etc.).

Stay tuned to see whether screwflation plays out and challenges the self-sustaining recovery thesis that has provided the foundation for the current bull market.

The Most Important Book

5/9/2011

> *"When I see memos from Howard Marks in my mail, they're the first thing I open and read. I always learn something, and that goes double for his book."*
>
> —Warren Buffett

Howard Marks has recently produced a tour de force, an exceptional and seminal book on behavioral finance (and investing) entitled *The Most Important Thing: Uncommon Sense for the Thoughtful Investor* (Columbia Business School Publishing, 2011).

Just published this month, it is the single-best investment primer I have read since the two classics:

1. Graham and Dodd's *Security Analysis* (1934); and
2. Benjamin Graham's *The Intelligent Investor* (1949).

And, similar to the aforementioned investment classics, it is likely that Howard's book will find its way, in the fullness of time, to the classrooms of the leading business school and MBA programs.

Among the many extraordinary features of his book is that it will likely appeal both to investment novices as well as investment experts.

In a manner, *The Most Important Thing* is much like reading Warren Buffett's annual letters to Berkshire Hathaway's shareholders, but it takes Buffett's witticisms several steps further in developing a broad framework and investment philosophy of how to think about the markets and how to differentiate one's investment performance especially during times of uncertainty.

I have learned over my career that there is no surefire recipe for investment success; there is no magical elixir. Those who simplify investing in how-to books or list glittering generalities in the business media do their audience a great disservice.

Howard recognizes that the investment mosaic is a complicated one when he writes, "In actuality, successful investing requires thoughtful attention to many separate aspects—all at the same time. Omit any one and the result is likely to be less than satisfactory."

And it is that complexity that Howard Marks embraces with 20 chapters of most important things.

Above all, Howard recognizes the importance of having an investment perspective:

One's investment philosophy is formed and accumulated over lengthy periods of time—it is not only a combination of nuts and bolts and qualitative and quantitative educational instruction received but it includes life's lessons and, most importantly, the willingness to go through one's investment life with your eyes open. You must be aware of what's taking place in the world and of what results those events lead to. Mark Twain once said and Warren Buffett has often repeated the phrase that "history may not repeat itself but it rhymes." Only in this way can you put the lessons to work when similar circumstances materialize again. Failing to do this—more than anything else—is what dooms most investors to being victimized repeatedly by cycles of boom and bust.

And Howard has formulated his perspective after having seen most, if not all of it, over his career:

> Living through the 1970s was especially informative, since so many challenges arose. It was virtually impossible to get an investment job during this period, meaning that in order to have experienced the decade, you had to have had a job before the decade started. How many of the people who started by the sixties were still working in the late nineties when the tech bubble rolled around? The answer is not many as most professional investors had joined the industry in the eighties or nineties and didn't know a market decline could exceed 5%, the greatest drop seen between 1982 and 1999. It also helps to explain why so many got caught so badly in 2008.

Investment perspective and lessons aplenty are weaved with terrific anecdotes and powerful prose throughout Howard's work:

> A wise friend once said to me that: "Experience is what you got when you didn't get what you wanted." Good times teach only bad lessons: that investing is easy, that you know its secrets and that you needn't worry about risk. The most valuable lessons are learned in tough times. In that sense, I have been "fortunate" to have lived through doozies: the Arab oil embargo, stagflation, nifty 50 stock collapse and the death of equities in the 1970s. Also, Black Monday in 1987, when the DJIA dropped by 23% in value in one day; the 1994 spike in interest rates that put rate-sensitive debt instruments into free fall; the emerging-market crisis; Russian default and the meltdown of Long Term Capital Management in 1998; the bursting of tech stock bubble in 2000–01; the Enron accounting scandal in 2002; and, of course, the worldwide financial crisis of 2007–08.

Howard lists 20 most important things:

1. Second-Level Thinking
2. Understanding Market Efficiency and Its Limitations
3. Value
4. The Relationship between Price and Value

5. Understanding Risk
6. Recognizing Risk
7. Controlling Risk
8. Attentive to Cycles
9. Awareness of the Pendulum
10. Combating Negative Influences
11. Contrarianism
12. Finding Bargains
13. Patient Opportunism
14. Knowing What You Don't Know
15. Having a Sense of Where We Stand
16. Appreciating the Role of Luck
17. Investing Defensively
18. Avoiding Pitfalls
19. Adding Value
20. Pulling It All Together

Of all the most important things, I thought Howard's chapter on the ingredients of developing a variant view (or edge) was possibly the most informative and useful.

The author underscores that investment approaches cannot be routinized—to succeed, we have to be less mechanistic and more adaptive. When the environment changes, so must we as investors.

To this observer, above all, the investment lessons in *The Most Important Thing* were what Howard describes as "second-level thinking":

> You must think of something others haven't thought of, see things they miss or bring insight they don't possess. You have to react differently and behave differently. In short, being right may be a necessary condition for investment success, but it won't be sufficient. You must be more right than others, which by definition means your thinking has to be different. Let's call this second-level thinking.
>
> First-level thinking says, "It's a good company: let's buy the stock." Second-level thinking says, "It's a good company, but everyone thinks it's a great company, and it's not. So the stock's overrated and overpriced: let's sell."
>
> First-level thinking says, "The outlook calls for low growth and rising inflation. Let's dump our stocks." Second-level

thinking says, "The outlook stinks, but everyone else is selling in panic. Buy!"

First-level thinking says, "I think the company's earnings will fall; sell." Second-level thinking says, "I think the company's earnings will fall by less than people expect and the pleasant surprise will lift the stock: buy."

In other words, first-level thinking is simplistic and superficial—second-level thinking is deep, complex and convoluted. The difference in workload between first- and second-level thinkers is massive.

Finally, second-level thinkers ask the following questions:

- What is the range of likely future outcomes?
- What outcome do I think will occur?
- What is the probability I am right?
- What does the consensus think?
- How does my expectation differ from the consensus?
- How does the current price for the asset comport with the consensus view of the future and with mine?
- Is the consensus psychology that's incorporated in the price too bullish or bearish?
- What will happen to the asset's price if the consensus turns out to be right and what if I am right?

Post Script   When I received a copy of *The Most Important Thing* two weeks ago, it came with a personal note from Howard Marks that said, "We think so much alike, you could have written this (see p. xii)." I proceeded to p. xii in the book's Introduction to find the following passage:

> I've also benefited from my association with Peter Bernstein, Seth Klarman, Jack Bogle, Jacob Rothschild, Jeremy Grantham, Joel Greenblatt, Tony Pace, Orin Kramer, Jim Grant and Doug Kass.

While I don't deserve that reference (and certainly don't deserve to be included in the class of such brilliant investors), I wanted to, in the interest of full disclosure, point out the mention.

That said, I can honestly say that his reference (to me) had nothing to do with the praise and effusive comments I have for his wonderful book—a book that I literally could not put down and one that I have already read twice!

Run, don't walk, to purchase Howard Marks's *The Most Important Thing: Uncommon Sense for the Thoughtful Investor.*

The Gospel According to Barton Biggs

5/2/2012

Barton Biggs is a former creative writing major at Yale University, a former Morgan Stanley head strategist and research director—he was responsible for the formation of the investment management business at Morgan Stanley—author of *Hedgehogging* (my personal favorite book on the hedge fund industry) and founder of hedge fund Traxis Partners.

Barton is an iconic figure, similar to Peter Lynch, Lee Cooperman, George Soros, Stanley Druckenmiller and Jim Chanos. But unlike Omega's Lee Cooperman and ex-Fidelity's Peter Lynch, whose strength is (and was) going belly to belly with company managements in an intense bottom-up approach, Soros Management's George Soros and Duquesne's Stanley Druckenmiller, whose wheelhouse is speculating in foreign exchange and interest rates, and Kynikos's James Chanos, whose strength is on the short side, Barton's turf is in macroeconomic investing and in asset- and geographic-allocation strategy.

Barton is incredibly smart, his investment knowledge base is broad, and he doesn't suffer fools gladly. He can be daring in market view and aggressive in portfolio structure, but he has learned over the years to be disciplined in controlling risk and respectful of Mr. Market.

I have routinely communicated with Barton over the years, and he is nice enough to send me his irregular commentary about the investment turf. That commentary is usually a combination of investment philosophy

> *"We must base our asset allocation not on the probabilities of choosing the right allocation but on the consequences of choosing the wrong allocation."*
>
> —Jack Bogle

and a view of the markets rooted in macroeconomic investing. His most recent essay, "It's Never Easy," crossed my desk last week, and I want to summarize his comments, as they represent true pearls of wisdom.

- "Good information, thoughtful analysis, quick but not impulsive reactions, and knowledge of the historic interaction between companies, sectors, countries, and asset classes under similar circumstances in the past are all important ingredients in getting the legendary 'it' right that we all strive so desperately for."
- "[T]here are no relationships or equations that always work. Quantitatively based solutions and asset-allocation equations invariably fail as they are designed to capture what would have worked in the previous cycle whereas the next one remains a riddle wrapped in an enigma. The successful macro investor must be some magical mixture of an acute analyst, an investment scholar, a listener, a historian, a riverboat gambler, and be a voracious reader. Reading is crucial. Charlie Munger, a great investor and a very sagacious old guy, said it best: 'I have said that in my whole life, I have known no wise person, over a broad subject matter who didn't read all the time—none, zero. Now I know all kinds of shrewd people who by staying within a narrow area do very well without reading. But investment is a broad area. So if you think you're going to be good at it and not read all the time you have a different idea than I do.'"
- "[T]he investment process is only half the battle. The other weighty component is struggling with yourself, and immunizing yourself from the psychological effects of the swings of markets, career risk, the pressure of benchmarks, competition, and the loneliness of the long distance runner."
- "I've come to believe a personal investment diary is a step in the right direction in coping with these pressures, in getting to know yourself and improving your investment behavior."
- "As I reflect on this crisis period so stuffed with opportunity but also so full of pain and terror, I am struck with how hard it is to be an investor and a fiduciary."
- "The history of the world is one of progress, and as a congenital optimist, I believe in equities. Fundamentally, in the long run, you want to be an owner, not a lender. However, you always have to bear

in mind that this time truly may be different as Reinhart and Rogoff so eloquently preach. Remember the 1930s, Japan in the late 1990s, and then, of course, as Rogoff said once with a sly smile, there is that period of human history known as 'The Dark Ages and it lasted three hundred years.'"

- "Mr. Market is a manic depressive with huge mood swings, and you should bet against him, not with him, particularly when he is raving."

- "As investors, we also always have to be aware of our innate and very human tendency to be fighting the last war. We forget that Mr. Market is an ingenious sadist, and that he delights in torturing us in different ways."

- "Buffett, a man, like me, who believes in America and the Tooth Fairy, presents the dilemma best. It's as though you are in business with a partner who has a bipolar personality. When your partner is deeply distressed, depressed, and in a dark mood and offers to sell his share of the business at a huge discount, you should buy it. When he is ebullient and optimistic and wants to buy your share from you at an exorbitant premium, you should oblige him. As usual, Buffett makes it sound easier than it is because measuring the level of intensity of the mood swings of your bipolar partner is far from an exact science."

- "Fifty some years ago, Sir Alec Cairncross doodled it best:
A trend is a trend is a trend
But the question is, will it bend?
Will it alter its course
Through some unforeseen force
And come to a premature end?"

- "Nations, institutions, and individuals always have had and still have a powerful tendency to prepare themselves to fight the last war."

- "[W]hat's the moral of this story? Know thyself and know thy foibles. Study the history of your emotions and your actions."

- "At the extreme moments of fear and greed, the power of the daily price momentum and the mood and passions of 'the crowd' are tremendously important psychological influences on you. It takes a strong, self-confident, emotionally mature person to stand firm against disdain, mockery, and repudiation when the market itself seems to be absolutely confirming that you are both mad and wrong."

- "Also, be obsessive in making sure your facts are right and that you haven't missed or misunderstood something. Beware of committing to mechanistic investing rules such as stop-loss limits or other formulas. Work very hard to better understand how you as an investor react to both prosperity and adversity, and particularly to the market's manic swings, both euphoric and traumatic. Keep an investment diary and reread it from time to time but particularly at moments when there is tremendous exuberance and also panic. We are in a very emotional business, and any wisdom we can extract from our own experience is very valuable."

- "Understanding the effect of emotion on your actions has never been more important than it is now. In the midst of this great financial and economic crisis that grips the world, Central Banks are printing money in one form or another. This makes our investment world even more prone to bubbles and panics than it has been in the past. Either plague can kill you."

> *"Serving on the front lines of this investment discipline for the past forty years with some of the most influential investors of our time, Deemer provides a front-row seat on some fascinating history, rich with insights and anecdotes and, of course, loaded with wisdom. His true gift is making the arcane world of technical analysis accessible and relevant to all investors. If Warren Buffett is the Oracle of Omaha, Deemer is the Prophet of Port St. Lucie."*
>
> —Sandra Ward, senior editor, *Barron's*

Walt's Wit

5/31/2012

In Port St. Lucie, Florida, lives a longtime friend of mine, Sir Walter Deemer, a technical analyst par excellence who recently authored an excellently written new book, *Deemer on Technical Analysis: Expert Insights on Timing the Market and Profiting in the Long Run* (McGraw-Hill, 2012).

I am proud to have endorsed the front cover of Walt's book.

But first, some details on how I met Walt.

Back in the mid-1970s, I was working for Larry Lasser (who was then director of research) and Jerry "The Chief" Jordan (who ran the aggressive funds) at the Putnam Management Company in Boston. Larry and The Chief were tough to work for, but never in my career did I learn so much as under their tutelage. And I will forever be grateful for that.

At that time, Walt Deemer was the technical analyst at Putnam. He was deeply respected, having learned his craft from the best there ever was, Bob Farrell, Merrill Lynch's legendary technical analyst.

> *"I'm glad General Motors stock didn't go down in vain."*
>
> —Walt Deemer, technical analyst for The Putnam Management Company (1975)

My favorite story about Walt was back in 1975, when General Motors (GM) cut its dividend, and two of Putnam's portfolio managers in total panic wanted to sell the stock. In fact, they were apoplectic after the announcement. Walt, a man of dry wit and strong technical moorings, remarked in the halls of Putnam that morning (repeatedly so that all could hear), "I'm glad General Motors stock didn't go down in vain."

Walt turned out to be very right on General Motors' shares. (He usually turned out right!) After the dividend cut, the shares subsequently doubled in 1975 and added another 47% in 1976.

Now back to Walt's new book!

To me, *Deemer on Technical Analysis* is not only an informative tour (of 25 Chapters and 300 pages) through Technical Analysis 101 but it is filled with lively and witty anecdotes and investing lessons that are invaluable, even to the fundamental investor!

My favorites include a discussion of Bob Farrell's 10 lessons (plus one!) of investing and the fable of the fishing boat. (Readers will relish the appendix, which lists free Internet sources of information on technical analysis and some valuable and free charting sites.)

Farrell's 10 Rules   Here are Bob Farrell's official 10 rules as related by Walt:

1. Markets tend to return to the mean over time.
2. Excesses in one direction will lead to an opposite excess in the other direction.

3. There are no new eras—excesses are never permanent.
4. Exponentially rapidly rising or falling markets usually go further than you think, but they do not correct by going sideways.
5. The public buys the most at a top and the least at a bottom.
6. Fear and greed are stronger than long-term resolve.
7. Bull markets are strongest when they are broad and weakest when they narrow to a handful of blue-chip names.
8. Bear markets have three stages—sharp down, reflexive rebound, and a drawn-out fundamental downtrend.
9. When the experts and forecasts agree, something else is going to happen.
10. Bull markets are more fun than bear markets.
      And Walt offers a new rule from Bob:
11. Though business conditions may change, corporations and securities may change and financial institutions and regulations may change, human nature remains essentially the same.

The Fable of the Fishing Boat   Then there was the time in 1978 when the bear market was taking its toll on Putnam's holdings. Walt just couldn't make the portfolio managers understand that bear markets trump even the best fundamentals.

So he circulated the following memorandum to Putnam's investment department, which he considers the best thing he ever wrote:

Once upon a time, there was a big fishing boat in the North Atlantic. One day the crew members noticed that the barometer had fallen sharply, but since it was a warm, sunny and peaceful day, they decided to pay it no attention and went on with their fishing.

The next day dawned stormy and the barometer had fallen further, so the crew decided to have a meeting and discuss what to do.

"I think we should keep in mind that we are fishermen," said the first to speak. "Our job is to catch as many fish as we can; that is what everyone on shore expects of us. Let us concentrate on this and leave the worrying about storms to the weathermen."

"Not only that," said the next, "but I understand that the weathermen are ALL predicting a storm. Using contrary opinion, we should expect a sunny day and, therefore, should not worry about the weather."

"Yes," said a third crew member. "And keep in mind that since this storm got so bad so quickly, it is likely to expand itself soon. It has already become overblown."

The crew thus decided to continue with their business as usual.

The next morning saw frightful wind and rain following steadily deteriorating conditions all the previous day. The barometer continued to fall. The crew held another meeting.

"Things are about as bad as they can get," said one. "The only time they were worse was in 1974, and we all know that was due to the unusual pressure systems that were centered over the Middle East that won't be repeated. We should, therefore, expect things to get better."

So the crew continued to cast their nets as usual. But a strange thing happened: the storm was carrying unusually large and fine fish into their nets, yet at the same time the violence was ripping the nets loose and washing them away. And the barometer continued to fall.

The crew gathered together once more.

"This storm is distracting us way too much from our regular tasks," complained one person, struggling to keep his feet. "We are letting too many fish get away."

"Yes," agreed another as everything slid off the table. "And furthermore, we are wasting entirely too much time in meetings lately. We are missing too much valuable fishing time."

"There's only one thing to do," said a crew member. "That's right!"

"Aye!" they all shouted.

So they threw the barometer overboard.

(*Editor's Note:* The above manuscript, now preserved in a museum, was originally discovered washed up on a desolate island above the north coast of Norway, about halfway to Spitsbergen. That island is called Bear Island and is located on the huge black-and-white world map on the wall in Putnam's "Trustees Room" where weekly investment division meetings took place.)

What differentiates Walt's book and sage advice is that he was on the front line—he walked the walk in leading Putnam Management's technical analysis effort when Putnam was one of the premier money management firms extant.

I want to close by repeating what I view as my buddy/friend/pal Walt Deemer's most famous words of wisdom—these words are always relevant, perhaps even more so in today's markets.

"When the time comes to buy, you won't want to."

—*Walt Deemer*

Alan Abelson and Me

5/13/2013

It was early 1992.

I was still recovering from a July 1990 harness racing injury that left me in a wheelchair and in a full-body cast.

I was going stir crazy at home and I decided to write a research report on Marvel Entertainment Group, a recently minted initial public offering (IPO) that was majority owned by Ron Perelman.

I spent a few weeks calling comic book retailers, distributors, Marvel's competitors and even some comic book writers who worked at the company and elsewhere.

I had been reading Alan Abelson's column in *Barron's* since the early 1970s, when I was an MBA student at the Wharton School. I dutifully read *Barron's* by 7:00 A.M. each Saturday, and I have been running to buy it every Saturday since. My first stop was always "Up and Down Wall Street," Alan's signature page.

I decided to show my critical analysis of Marvel to Alan Abelson.

Upon its completion and when I could physically leave my New York City apartment, I ventured into a van with my full-time nurse to Alan's office on the sixteenth floor of the Dow Jones building in downtown Manhattan.

I had never met Alan—I had no appointment.

I wheeled up to the receptionist (with exterior fixation rods in my left leg and still in a full-body cast) and asked if I could meet with Alan Abelson. I had a critical analysis on Marvel Entertainment, I told her.

The receptionist asked if I had scheduled an appointment, and I replied no.

She told me that Mr. Abelson only sees people by appointment and most certainly wouldn't see someone who had come in off the street and who he didn't know.

Fortunately for me, Alan was walking out of the men's room near the elevator bank and was walking by us on the way back into his office.

I appeared to be in rough shape—I suppose I was—and I imagine that this elicited some pity for me from Alan. He asked, annoyed and rather briskly, what did I want.

He actually didn't use those words. I don't know if it was just with me or with others, but this most erudite writer, had, well, a colorful vocabulary. I don't remember so many expletives in one question! (Those curse words often infiltrated his conversations with me over the next 21 years.)

Alan said he would give me 10 minutes (no more) and to proceed into his office.

I started by praising him, telling him how devoted a reader I was, but he summarily cut me short. "Get down to the [expletive deleted] reason you are here; I don't have all day," he admonished me.

I said that I had written an analysis on Marvel Entertainment Group. Marvel, I explained to Alan, was the comic book industry leader, accounting for 57% of the entire market. Second-place D.C. Comics has 17.6%; nobody else topped 10%.

Marvel, was a famously successful IPO several months earlier, majority owned by Ron Perelman's MacAndrews & Forbes Holdings. The stock (trading at nearly $70 a share) was riding the wave of comic book collecting—it was a huge winner after being taken public at $16.50.

I asked him if he had ever heard of Marvel. He grinned and pointed to the prospectus for the Marvel IPO on his office table. It was clear he was already doing work on the company.

Our meeting was less than 10 minutes. He asked me for my home telephone number and said that he would get back to me.

It was a Wednesday afternoon. At nine that evening, Alan called my home and said that he thought it would be an interesting cover story for that weekend's *Barron's*.

I was in shock. I mean, are you kidding? Alan Abelson from *Barron's* likes my idea? I am going to be published in *Barron's!*

The next morning, I received a call from a *Barron's* fact checker, and the rest, as they say, is history.

On Saturday morning, my column, "Pow! Smash! Ker-plash!—High-Flying Marvel Comics May Be Headed for a Fall," was featured in *Barron's,* and that article marked the beginning of my relationship with Alan and with his magazine.

The thrust of my column was that Marvel's growth was about to stall, the debt load would weigh on the company's future returns and that the company's comics "increasingly resort to gimmickry to break down consumer resistance" to price increases. I also cited the likelihood that independent comic books that took more risks were beginning to gain market share and to attract mainstream comic book writers. Indeed, I suggested that some high-level defections from Marvel were imminent. On cue, the following week after my column was published, eight top Marvel artists and writers defected to rival Malibu Graphics (with an industry market share of only 4%), where they were given unprecedented editorial and financial control over the characters they created and formed their own imprint, Image Comics. Going to Malibu were Rob Liefeld (who worked on *The New Mutants, X-Force* and *Youngblood*), Jim Lee, Chris Claremont (*X-Men*), Erik Larsen and Todd McFarlane (*Spider-Man*).

The following Monday was a federal holiday, and when the market opened on Tuesday, Marvel's shares went into a tailspin, dropping by over $11 a share, to $54.65, and Perelman lost nearly $100 million on paper.

Marvel lashed back at my article, calling its assertions "inaccurate and highly misleading." Terry Stewart, the company's CEO said my *Barron's* feature had a lot of "erroneous conclusions." The company sued me for a great deal of money for authoring such an "inflammatory article." Marvel lost the suit and paid my incurred legal expenses.

Alan was angry about the suit. Soon after I won the judgment/verdict, he wrote a column that Marvel's listing on the New York Stock Exchange gave Perelman a sense of entitlement and the notion that he was immune to criticism (or something to that effect).

Within a year, Marvel bought Fleer baseball cards, which had also benefited from the interest in collecting.

Soon thereafter Alan interviewed me, and I reported that the acquisition would be Marvel's downfall—adding more corporate debt and owning two businesses (comics and baseball cards) was a huge mistake. Moreover, there was no synergy between the two businesses, both of which appeared to be peaking in popularity. I said in the interview with Alan that in real life my cousin was Dodgers' Hall of Famer Sandy Koufax. Did that mean I could play baseball? No. Indeed, baseball was one of my worst sports!

In early 1993, Marvel purchased 46% of ToyBiz, which possessed the right to sell Marvel toys. In the meantime, Perelman upstreamed huge dividends to his companies, and he sold $500 million of bonds secured by Marvel's shares. In 1994, Marvel purchased an Italian sticker company (Panini), and the following year it bought SkyBox International.

Throughout these events, Alan kept on writing, with me as the source, about what a mess Marvel was getting into, and each time he supported my original analysis on the company.

In December 1996, the debt-laden Marvel filed for bankruptcy, and my reputation as a short-seller was cemented.

Later, Ike Perlmutter and Avi Arad snatched the company from Perelman and from Carl Icahn, who had accumulated a large position in Marvel's bonds.

In 1997, a lawsuit claimed that Perelman and Marvel's board of directors diverted $550 million to MacAndrews & Forbes prior to the company's bankruptcy. A decade later, Perelman agreed to an $80 million settlement.

In 1998, Marvel came out of bankruptcy. Eleven years later, a much different Marvel Entertainment was acquired for over $4 billion by Disney.

Alan and I would routinely talk on the telephone almost every Thursday afternoon. He would often fall back on the Marvel article and how marvelous and prescient the conclusions were.

When he wasn't around, I spoke to Shirley Lazo. Throughout the week, Alan and I routinely exchanged faxes and calls. (It has only been over the past few years that Alan has used e-mail.)

Alan was to interview me another 20 to 30 times in his column over the next two decades—way more than any other Wall Streeter during that period.

As most are aware, Alan Abelson passed away on Thursday.

I wrote a tribute to Alan for next weekend's *Barron's*, in which I said that Alan was a national journalistic treasure—I hope they publish it.

Alan was a wordsmith and dear friend who championed the individual investor.

My condolences to Reed Abelson and the other members of Alan's family.

I will miss him very much.

An Open Letter to Sir Larry Kudlow

3/8/2014

> *"We believe that free market capitalism is the best path to prosperity!"*
>
> —The Kudlow Creed

Dear Sir Larry,

I just read the CNBC announcement that you are retiring from *The Kudlow Report* at the end of March.

I wanted to write to you and say that you have been a beacon for me and many others throughout nearly a decade and a half (on *The Kudlow Report, Kudlow & Company, Kudlow & Cramer,* and *America Now*).

You are bigger than just a commentator and host of *The Kudlow Report;* you are a man who has faced headwinds and adversity and has conquered them all.

You are among the handful of beautiful people I have been associated with who have known trials, known struggles, have known loss and have found their way out of the depths to rise to new heights.

My Grandma Koufax used to say, "Dougie, it's not where you start that counts; it's where you end up. If the road was smooth, you have likely taken the wrong route. And, remember, never to suffer would never to have been blessed."

Hardship either makes or breaks people. It made you.

To me, you have ended your role as host of *The Kudlow Report* at your professional apex.

You have been a forerunner in the integration and analysis of politics, policy and markets in the media.

Your delivery has always been fluid, your point of view always substantive, not easy tasks.

You are by far the best dressed in the Fourth Estate.

You have had the rare ability to bring out the best in investment debate and from experts with markedly opposing viewpoints. Despite spirited debates, you managed to end every segment on high, courteous and respectful notes.

I will forever treasure my many appearances on *The Kudlow Report*. Most were filled with exciting sparring against the bullish cabal. Some even ended up with a historic calculus, like my early-March 2009 "generational bottom" call I made on your show.

You also brought me back together with old friends during that period, like with Uncle Vinnie Farrell, Joe Battipaglia, Mikey Holland and many others.

On a more personal note, your mentoring of my son Noah will never be forgotten by me, him, or my family.

Now with Noah getting his doctorate at the University of Pennsylvania, I am sure he is on the way to an even more exciting career than when he originally met you that first time over dinner at Nicolas Restaurant in New York City. You, in part, are responsible for some of Noah's great successes in print (*Huffington Post* and *TheStreet*), on television (MSNBC) and in his important role in addiction treatment.

To myself, Noah, and so many others that you have helped, you are a personal role model.

I am a former "Nader Raider"; you are a former member of the Reagan administration. Our politics are diametrically opposed, but our debates have always been lively and respectful of view.

You are my favorite Republican, ever.

I call you Sir Larry because of the esteem I hold for you.

Like members of my family, I like to think that you call me Dougie because of the fondness you have for me.

Wherever you are and whenever you call, Sir Larry, Dougie is there for you.

With Love and Fondness,

Dougie

More Remarkable Tales of Boca Biff

12/16/2013

> *"Those who do not remember the past are condemned to repeat it."*
>
> —George Santayana

In January 2004, Boca Biff made his debut in my diary.

Boca Biff is a real person. He is not a composite of individuals I have met over the years.

Boca Biff's investments, both in name and in dollar size, were all actually made by him.

It is fair to write that Boca Biff lives by the investment credo that man's greatest glory is not in never falling, but in rising every time we fall, because fall is Boca Biff's middle name.

No character (and there have been many characters) I have written about has elicited such a response from so many subscribers and contributors.

Over the past 15 years, Boca Biff has embodied the mentality of the day trading and speculative community who worships at the altar of price momentum in the church of what is happening now. As such, Boca Biff has become a better market/sector/asset class barometer than the put/call ratio, *Investors Intelligence*, mutual fund/hedge fund exposures or any other sentiment indicator.

The Boca Biff indicator has become a wonderful measure of the very embodiment of speculation during Mr. Market's frequent speculative bouts.

I suppose we can say is that what Boca Biff has learned from history is that he hasn't learned from history.

But let's begin by framing Boca Biff's speculative diary of trading over the past 15 years.

1998–2000: The Day Trading Orgy   It all started with that once-in-a-generation orgy of speculation in the late 1990s as a new class of investors emerged on the market's stage—namely, day traders.

The 1997–2000 time frame held a historic precedent that took day trading to a new art form. As most recall, the bubble began to burst in the first half of 2000—almost, it seemed, as quickly as it surfaced. In time, the Nasdaq fell by about 75% from its highs.

Over nine years ago, I introduced readers to the true story about my favorite day trader, Biff Marksman. I subsequently changed his name to Boca Biff in order to protect his anonymity better and in order to protect our innocent subscribers from him.

Biff is an old acquaintance—we have had a love/hate relationship over the years. He operates out of his home in Boca Raton, Florida. You can almost see his dwelling from the entrance of the Boca Raton Hotel, a locale that former Securities and Exchange Commission (SEC) Commissioner Breeden once described as a town where there are more sharks on land than in the waters surrounding it. The city's name comes from *boca de ratones,* a Spanish term meaning "rat's mouth," that appeared on early maps and referred to hidden, sharp-pointed rocks that gnawed or fretted ships' cables. It is a town where the Ferraris, mansions and over-the-top conspicuous consumption are known to sometimes run wild.

As significant, Boca Raton has always been the capital of the day trading community and ground zero for brokerage boiler rooms—many of the sons and daughters of Stratton Oakmont found their way to the area (e.g., Biltmore Securities, LH Ross, and the Harriman Group)—that inhabit the resort area.

Boca Raton is Boca Biff's home base.

Biff Makes $15 Million in 1997–1999, Then Loses $20 Million in 2000 As I mentioned previously, I first wrote about Biff in 2004.

I hadn't heard from Biff since 2000, as I thought that he was cured from the leveraged day-trading influence that took the United States and the markets by storm in the mid- to late 1990s, contributing to a mushrooming in margin debt, the ultimate speculative rise in our markets and the eventual—or should I say inevitable?—piercing of that bubble. Of the day traders, there were few that played as intensely as my friend Biff.

Biff's first plunge into day trading was in early 1996 with Iomega. Biff became a certified Iomegean, as Iomega became the "it" stock back then with a market capitalization that peaked at $6 billion as investors believed it was the future of digital storage. The shares peaked out at over $100 a share in 1996 and sold down to $2 a share by January 2000. Biff didn't play hard at that time, but he clearly got the speculative fever.

Unlike most day traders in the late 1990s, Biff had a real job—he owned a high-end window and door company—but as stocks mounted their speculative (but short-lived) ascent in 1998, his primary gig took a back seat to trading stocks.

Biff operated out of his den office and turned about $500,000 into almost $15 million in a matter of 24 months by day trading the most speculative stocks extant and by purchasing and trading dot-com IPOs.

During that period (1998–2000), I spoke to Biff 5 to 10 times a day. In most of our conversations, Biff ridiculed me for not getting on the bandwagon and trading the most speculative four-letter stocks on the Nasdaq. Our conversations were one-way, as Biff did the talking or, in most cases, the gloating, as his disinterest in the companies' business models was legion.

Coherence of investment thought and clarity of expression were not Biff's forte.

After Biff made the first $10 million day trading Internet stocks and playing the IPO market, I suggested that, after all our conversations, he had absolutely no knowledge of his trades/investments and that he should stop trading and book his profits and place them into municipal bonds. His response to my recommendation is not suitable for these pages, and off on his day trading merry way he went, adding another $5 million or so of profits into late 1999–early 2000. His original trades of 5,000 to 10,000 shares in size quickly turned into investments of 150,000 to 200,000 shares in some of the most speculative stocks extant.

His investment vocabulary and stock holdings included such beauties as eToys, Pets.com, e.Digital, theGlobe.com, Kozmo.com, Boo.com, Exodus, and Xcelera.com, a group of companies that quickly disappeared from sight and caused a generation of day traders and speculators to return to their original professions.

In time, Biff lost not only his $15 million of profits but an additional $5 million, leaving him in a deep financial hole. He also had a tax problem as he received extensions on his tax returns because he wanted to defer paying taxes on his short-term gains in order to "have more capital to play with."

Humbled and broken, he went back to his old day job on a full–time basis—that is, after selling a minority interest in his company to a well-to-do relative in order to raise funds for federal taxes he owed.

Though at one time he was up $15 million, his cumulative loss from 1997 to 2000 now stood at $5 million (before federal tax penalties and interest charges).

From Iomega to Taser: Biff Repeats His Mistake in 2004 In 2004, I received a telephone call from Biff, as if nothing had happened and as if we had maintained a dialogue over the previous four years. (We had not.) Biff was back day trading in force, seduced back by the emerging speculative forces (and his animal spirits) and the rewards he reaped from them.

The emergence of "worldwide liquidity" and low interest rates were the watchwords of his faith in the U.S. stock market.

Back was Biff, touting those four- and five-letter stocks sans business models and purpose—except possibly to briefly enrich the day traders and reward the insiders who were selling their holdings to the day traders. At that time, in my numerous conversations with Biff, it was almost as if he believed that the 1990s was a dress rehearsal for the mid-2000s.

In 2004, his stock du jour, Taser, replaced his infatuation with his original spec venture in Iomega in 1996–1997 and then the Internet stocks back in 1999. (Most of his holdings back then went to zero.) He more doubled his money in Taser, which climbed from $15 to $35 in 2004 only to fall back to $5 a share later that year.

From Taser he parlayed his profits into a package of homeland security stocks. Here is what I wrote in 2004:

> [I] just picked up the telephone to hear the shrieking, hysterical voice of Boca Biff, who is all over the homeland security rage. . . . His stocks (IPIX, Mikron Infrared, and Mace Security International) all sounded like he was bellowing about his speculative choices of yesteryear.

Unfortunately, the outcome was the same. The air fell out of Biff's speculative homeland security universe as the year came to a close. Very soon thereafter, all of these plays disappeared from the face of the stock pages.

Biff made a slight recovery in Google's shares after the homeland security debacle, but forays into crude futures, Overstock.com's shares and a large investment made in Pulte Homes and some other tertiary homebuilders were his undoing. By the end of 2005, he was wiped out again.

His cumulative loss from 1997–2004 now stood at about $15 million.

2006: The Return of Boca Biff   By December 2006, an unrepentant Boca Biff returned to the markets in force for the third time in nearly a decade.

During that time, I wrote the following on these pages:

He's back! Last night, here I was, minding my own business on the cold linoleum floor, drinking cheap tequila, when the telephone rang. It was Boca Biff!

Boca Biff has been licking his wounds. . . .

He promised his family, which apparently could no longer tolerate the ups and downs, that he wouldn't again venture into the stock market. Nor would he speculate in homes and land. After casually responding to one of those spam e-mails to refinance his home, however, from an eager mortgage broker that was about to go out of business—he's got a beautiful old Mizner-style home in Boca—he found himself very soon thereafter (in early 2006) with about $1.5 million of loose change.

His wife forced him to give the proceeds of the refinancing cash out to a mutual friend (Baron Von Broker) who dutifully put these monies in a money-market account and far from the hands of Boca Biff. When the market bottomed in the spring, Baron Von Broker turned bullish and encouraged Boca Biff to buy conservative oil and large gold mining stocks (two sectors that he correctly felt had promise). True to his promise to his wife, Boca Biff demurred and kept his monies in the money-market account.

As Boca Biff related in our telephone conversation last night, he watched and watched the market's unrelenting rise through the summer and into the fall until he couldn't take it anymore and finally made the plunge last week (on margin). Stated simply,

Boca Biff is trying to make back his accumulated $15 million-plus loss—this is the truth!—by purchasing a package of out-of-the-money calls on a group of high-beta stocks that recently have made a 52-week high, including Apple Computer, Goldman Sachs, Merrill Lynch, Google, First Marblehead, Fairfax Financial, Research In Motion, Allegheny Technologies, U.S. Steel, Baidu.com, and Las Vegas Sands.

He tells me the notional value of his calls (if exercised) exceeds $30 million! When asked why now, Boca simply said, "Don't be a moron, Dougie: It's global liquidity. Don't you get it?" And then he actually said to me that he heard from his driver that General Electric will receive a bid by a private-equity firm sometime in the next six months.

I should add that Boca Biff transferred all his money from the money-market fund from Baron Von Broker (who being a conservative and intelligent fiduciary, refused to accept Biff's aggressive strategy) and purchased the call positions from a newly formed, Boca Raton, Florida-based brokerage, Penny, Shark & Oakmont.

I should also add that Boca Biff is currently being divorced by his wife.

While this venture back into stocks (and call options) proved profitable, he recaptured only about one fifth of his losses as his capital base had been depleted and limited his exposure.

Fortunately, sales at his window and door business collapsed a few months before the Great Decession of 2008–2009 became a reality, and with that warning sign, Biff cashed out well before the collapse in the U.S. stock market.

His cumulative loss from 1997–2007 now stood at about $11.5 million.

After the 2009 Generational Bottom: Boca Biff Returns   With more lives than an alley cat, Biff, the ultimate plunger and that paragon of speculation, was back, resurfacing in the early winter of 2009 as the markets rallied off of the generational bottom in March and began to stabilize.

Biff and I hadn't spoken in a while; I think he was embarrassed to call me. He had been licking his wounds, which included unprofitable forays in the stock market, large losses from speculating on homes in South Florida, a collapse in his window and door business and, after all of this, a failed marriage.

As Boca Biff related in a telephone conversation with me, he got remarried in 2008 to a woman who had received a reasonably large divorce settlement. Biff went on to say that he watched and watched the market's unrelenting rise through the summer and into the fall until (again) he couldn't take it anymore and finally made the plunge last week—(again) on margin.

Boca Biff was back in the game.

"I asked, "Why now?"

He responded, "Don't be a moron, Dougie. It's global liquidity. Don't you get it? Moreover, I am getting 11 basis points currently in my cash reserves at my brokerage account with Baron Von Broker." He went on. "Importantly, I have remarried, and my new wife not only comes with some money but she has no clue regarding my investing mistakes of the past. I managed to keep my Mizner home in Boca. She loves it here, and she adores me."

His favorite stock? AIG.

"Why?" I asked.

"Are you nuts?" he replied. "I heard from my new brokerage firm, Kennedy, Fitzpatrick and Gould [a Boca Raton–based brokerage named after the first three commissioners of the SEC] that AIG has normalized earnings power of $40 a share. And FMG (my brokers) tell me the government will be forced by Hank Greenberg (who is coming back to the board of directors) to help renegotiate their debt with the company."

"What qualifies them to make that analysis?" I asked.

"I'll tell you what, dope. Two of the guys still have their Ferraris, so they've gotta be smart. And they have tripled my accountant's brokerage account with them in the last three months after buying the private mortgage insurers, PMI Group and MGIC Investment. That's why! Oh, they had been out of business until seven months ago; they had a little problem with the authorities and were barred from doing brokerage business for a couple of years, so they are hungry and aggressive and need to make their new clients some ca-ching. I forgot to tell you that they are so confident that they will make me money that they didn't even charge me commissions for the trades; they said all they wanted was 10% of the profits."

I told Boca that was illegal. His response? "Whatever, loser. They've gotta live."

"What else?"

"Fannie Mae and Freddie Mac are going into double digits on the heels of a 'V' recovery in housing. And they have huge short positions. The government is saving everybody. You can't lose."

"Anything else?"

"Yeah," said Boca Biff, "but my brokers told me they would break my legs if I mentioned them. They haven't finished buying yet."

"Come on, Biff," I said, "Give at least one name up."

"There's one, Kennedy bought me 4 million shares at $2.12 last week. He has a lot of confidence in it. I think he put over three-quarters of my account in it. It's run by Kennedy's niece. She's young (I think 28 or 29), but she was a really big mortgage broker in Delray Beach in the day, and the company she runs is now buying subprime mortgages from a bunch of banks in South Florida. After the housing markets blew up, she went to Nova Southeastern University in Ft. Lauderdale and got an associates' degree in real estate in May. She's a smart one, I tell you."

"What's the name of the company and the symbol?" I asked.

"It's called Boca Industries; I don't know the symbol. It's on the pink sheets or something. I can only get a quote from Kennedy, my broker. I think his firm owns most of the float, so he has to know something."

Suffice to say, Boca Industries was a total fraud and soon went belly up, and it turns out that Biff was buying his brokers' stock position that they had received to promote the company. Biff was forced to liquidate his other stock holdings after once again blowing up, and Kennedy and his broker partners along with the management of Boca Industries all went to jail as they were convicted of a three-year pump-and-dump scheme.

Biff lost another $8.5 million on Boca Industries plus another $5.0 million in the other trades/investments.

His aggregate losses in day trading and investing over the course of the 12-year period (1997–2009) were back up to about $25 million.

Boca Biff Finally Makes a Score   I hadn't heard from Biff again until late 2010. I thought that perhaps his last unprofitable foray from 2004 to 2009 (and the credit crisis that stamped out his profits) coupled with a near $9 million loss from an investment in Boca Industries that he purchased in late 2009 were enough to rid him of his stock market jones.

After yet another divorce, however, Boca Biff, who obviously has a way with the opposite sex, married the young daughter of a well-known New York City real estate magnate who owns a professional sports team.

In [another telephone] conversation, Biff told me that he has been purchasing out-of-the-money calls in his new wife's name (and with his wife's money) on only two stocks: Netflix and Apple. For a total investment of "only" $4 million, Boca Biff tells me he has calculated that when the securities rise by another 50%, he will recoup his entire losses since 1997.

When I questioned the wisdom of putting all his eggs into two baskets, he laughed at me.

"Moron, these stocks go up every day whether the market rises or falls. An idiot can see that these stocks will go up another 50% in the next few months. And maybe I am too conservative; they could double. Jim Cramer hasn't even put the symbols on his knuckles the way he used to do with Google on his *Mad Money* show! Just you wait for that!"

"How do you know for sure that they will continue to rise, Biff? Isn't holding out-of-the-money calls on only two stocks very risky?" I asked.

"My stock broker is my new stepson. Do you think he would hurt his mother? Dougie, don't you read Warren Buffett's rules of investing? He says that wide diversification is only required when investors do not understand what they are doing. I know what I am doing! Anyway, how else can I get my money back?"

He advised me to tell you that he is, "laughing all the way to the bank with his Netflix and Apple out-of-the-money calls." With his profits he bought Amazon out-of-the-money calls and made some more money.

On a roll, Boca Biff was getting more and more cocky.

He suggested that if I have a blog, then his recent picks should entitle him to his own blog next to Jim Cramer's.

I told him that it was a good idea and that it should be labeled, "Over the Cliff with Biff."

He hung up on me!

Biff made back $11 million in the call foray—he would have made more, but a health scare forced him to cash out (profitably).

His cumulative loss since 1998 now stood at slightly under $14 million.

Biffy the Angel   Let's fast forward to March 2012 when I caught up with Boca Biff as his guest at a lavish dinner at Trump's Mar-a-Lago Club in Palm Beach, Florida.

Twenty months ago, Biff and The Donald became new BFFs and Biff became a new member of Mar-a-Lago; they initially became friendly when Biff's company provided the 145 doors and windows in a renovation of Trump's palatial estate.

Our conversation went something like this:

"My cancer is licked now, but it has been a rough road," Biff said. "Between the hospital visits and a debt restructuring at my window and door business [he had expanded too aggressively and couldn't withstand the South Florida construction drop], I had no time for the markets, which kind of sucked.

"But my new stepson is this genius who attended the California Institute of Technology. He and his pals started some kind of company—I am still not sure what it does—that I invested only $400,000 in. They sold it to Google late last year and I cleared $9 million! I put $1.5 million into three new Silicon Valley startups with my stepson. (He is running one of them.)

"I am a Silicon Valley angel now. I go out to the West Coast twice a month, and I am part of a group that listens to these 25-year-olds talk about their startups. They call me Biffy the Angel.

"And I am now back in the game, Dougie."

"Please don't tell me you are speculating in pinksheet tech stocks now or in the latest craze in the stock market." I implored.

"What, do you think I am an idiot? This venture stuff is 'free money.' It's hard to lose; the appetite for these companies is growing exponentially!

There is one and only one stock I want to invest in: Apple! But this damn stock is a money burner at almost $600 a share, so I have been buying these weekly call options. I trade thousands of 'em every day. A lot of action. The premium hurts and I haven't made any money yet, but

I am feeling more confident in this play than any other I have done in the last few years. I know 'cause I even read Walter Isaacson's biography on Steve Jobs.

Well, maybe there are two stocks to invest in. To be conservative and diversify a bit, I am buying a few thousand out-of-the-money Priceline calls."

You just can't make this stuff up.

With his venture capital score (the sale to Google) and some modest gains in his Apple call play, Biff's cumulative loss was reduced to only $2.5 million—after losses of about $25 million three years ago.

Boca Biff's Silicon Valley startups didn't do as well as his original $9 million score, but he only had a relatively small amount of money invested in them.

September 2012 Biff had made another $9 million in Priceline and Apple options, remarkably bringing him back into the black after losses of almost $25 million by early 2009.

While the bottom fell out of Apple's shares in late September, Biff lost about $7.5 million in Apple calls. After the big swings (in profits and losses), he was now dead even from his crazy trading since 2004.

Biff called me sporadically in the interim interval, just to shoot the breeze, though we did have a serious conversation in early October 2012 to discuss my bear case for Apple—at the time he was long thousands of Apple calls.

Boca Biff was now about flat in his investment account from 1997 to present—but what a ride (up and down) it had been.

Boca Biff Does Bitcoin   We didn't talk investments at all until I spoke to him last Thursday night.

His door and window business he told me was expanding rapidly—he was rolling up competitors through stock acquisitions (under the promise that he will go public), but he had recently decided to make the single largest speculation in his life.

Boca Biff, he explained to me, invested $15.5 million in bitcoins. And he invested another $3 million to $5 million in a San Francisco-based company called Coinbase, a bitcoin wallet company that recently raised $25 million (led by the well-regarded venture capital firm, Andreessen Horowitz).

As Biff reasoned, central bankers are debasing all currencies, and with real interest rates rising, gold has little interest for him. Bitcoin will, according to Biff, become the only peer-to-peer payment network of digital currency in the world. "This is the ground floor," exclaimed Biff.

He has not only done a great deal of work on his theory, but according to Boca Biff, "Satoshi Nakamato" (the pseudonymous developer of bitcoin) has been his houseguest over the past few months in Boca Raton, Florida.

During one weekend, Nakamato explained the "blockchain" to Boca Biff, a transaction ledger that assured the integrity of bitcoin as a digital currency. And that bitcoin has first-to-market mover advantage over other crypto currencies such as litcoin, peercoin, namecoin, quarkcoin, megacoin, and feathercoin.

Citing his new consultant on his bitcoin investments, economist Dr. Tyler Cowen, the future of bitcoin, Boca Biff explained, was in China, where the digital currency provides an easy path to avoid strict capital controls and the exportation of currency out of their country.

Our conversation was cut short, as Boca Biff was off to have dinner at the Four Seasons Hotel in New York City with Cameron and Tyler Winklevoss and his daughter. His daughter, let's call her "Boca Lilly," in real life is currently a second-year student at Harvard Business School. She was introduced to the Winklevoss twins after they gave a lecture at Harvard.

Eighteen years later, Boca Biff's investing saga continues.

If a cat has nine lives, Boca Biff might be on his twelfth life.

Boca Biff has become one of my most reliable market/asset class tells.

I personally can't wait for the next chapter of "The Tales of Boca Biff."

It is probably coming sooner than we think.

Buffett Watch

Introduction

Dougie, Warren Buffett is the greatest investor of all time. He is also a mensch.

—Grandma Koufax

While watching Becky Quick interview Warren Buffett on CNBC's *Squawk Box* in March 2013 I learned that the Oracle of Omaha would invite me to be the "credentialed bear" at the 2013 Berkshire Hathaway annual shareholders meeting and to share the dais with him for the better part of six hours.

I was shocked and flattered.

In preparation over the next two months, I and two of my analysts, Nick Pollari and Kelley Hopkins, embarked on a research project aimed at asking Buffett and Charlie Munger 10 to 15 questions that were hard-hitting, respectful and that never had been asked before. Considering how well researched the Oracle and Berkshire Hathaway are, this was no easy task. In the process, I learned quite a lot about my subject, some of which is contained in this chapter and had never been previously disclosed.

In thinking about all of my experiences on Wall Street, none compares to that Saturday in May 2013 in Omaha, Nebraska, which is fully documented in this chapter. As well, I uncovered some little-known facts about Warren Buffett and some terrific stories such as the one about Rabbi Kripke.

The chapter also explains why I have shorted Berkshire Hathaway's stock in the past and why I am skeptical that the company can continue its remarkable performance going forward.

11 Reasons to Short Berkshire

3/10/2008

> *"The investor of today does not profit from yesterday's growth."*
>
> —Warren Buffett

I have worshiped at the altar of Warren Buffett since the late 1970s—ever since an investor and acquaintance, Conrad Taft, introduced me to his investment methodology and style at Berkshire Hathaway. Indeed my writings over the past seven years have often been punctuated with Buffett-isms. I have repeatedly objected to, scoffed at, and refuted criticisms of Buffett's strategy.

That said, the rationale behind avoiding/shorting Berkshire Hathaway's common stock must be segregated from my respect/worship of the greatest investment icon of the past half-century.

Berkshire Hathaway's beginnings were as humble as Warren Buffett has remained today. Its birth took place when he began to acquire the shares of Berkshire Hathaway (nee Berkshire Spinning and the Hathaway Manufacturing Company) in the early 1960s. His initial investment performed poorly but provided a platform for unprecedented growth through a series of well-timed acquisitions of publicly held companies. Berkshire stands, with a market value of about $200 billion, as the sixth-largest company in the United States—behind ExxonMobil, General Electric, Procter & Gamble, Microsoft, and AT&T.

The insurance business line represents the most important contributor to Berkshire—both as a percentage of aggregate earnings as well as the all-important generation of cash flow for Buffett to invest in companies that are perceived to sell at a meaningful discount to estimated intrinsic value. Berkshire's shares have compounded in excess of a 21% annual rate—or at twice the rate of growth for the S&P 500. Last year, Berkshire's shares rose by over 25% against a 3% rise in the S&P 500.

"The future is never clear, and you pay a very high price in the stock market for a cheery consensus. Uncertainty is the friend of the buyer of long-term values."

—Warren Buffett

As discussed below I have concluded that Berkshire's shareholders face a number of headwinds. Value will be more difficult to add than ever before, reflecting (among other things) the company's size, fiercer competition in the search for undervalued investments and a potentially more hostile economic and stock market backdrop. As well, the issue of Buffett's stewardship could weigh on the shares over the near term. In the extreme, the company could (without Buffett at the helm and in the fullness of time) be viewed as just another diversified conglomerate without a "moat."

1. There will never be another Warren Buffett. In part because of lucrative hedge fund compensation, however, the investment landscape is now inhabited by a lot more smart and aggressive managers combing for value—far more than 5, 10, 20, or 30 years ago. Over time, Buffett has been increasingly willing to guide investors through his strategy by providing investment insights. It is said that imitation is the greatest form of flattery, and, through the years, a number of managers have imitated Buffett's strategy of "stepping over one-foot bars" and buying at a discount to intrinsic value (making, in cases, the search more of a science than Buffett's art by even computerizing his process). Importantly, newer hedge fund managers such as Duquesne's Druckenmiller and SAC's Cohen have become the new Buffetts by developing more aggressive multistrategy styles that have produced returns far in excess of Berkshire Hathaway. Others (particularly private-equity firms such as Kleiner Perkins Caufield & Byers) have realized more ebullient returns by embracing the technology sector, an integral growth driver in which Buffett refuses to invest. As a result of the above developments, the degree of outperformance of Berkshire's shares vis-à-vis the market has been narrowing over the past decade (12.5% vs. 4.7%) from the prior two decades (31.7% vs. 15.0% and 36.8% vs. 9.7%). I expect that outperformance to continue to narrow. Not only is the value approach becoming a more efficient proposition, as it is today littered with more participants, but many more smart investors (activist hedge funds, longer-term Buffett-like investors such as Edward Lampert and private-equity firms) are armed with large and ever-growing war chests, putting them on the same level playing field today as Buffett. This leaves fewer rocks for Buffett to uncover. Finally, the timely and comprehensive dissemination of information is vastly superior in 2008 vis-à-vis the past. As a result (and in regards to investing in Berkshire), Mae West might have been wrong when she said, "Too much of a good thing can be wonderful." To paraphrase Buffett, the future holds less "cinches" and finding investment "fish in a barrel" will likely grow more difficult.

2. Investors will likely immediately dump shares if Buffett is no longer at the helm. Warren Buffett will be 78 years old in August 2008 (Charles Munger is 84). I am not signaling that he plans to step down even though his diet apparently consists almost entirely of unhealthy Cherry Cokes and cheeseburgers! (His actuarial life expectancy is another nine years!) Buffett has said that he intends to split his job into two positions, a CEO and a CIO—he has already announced that a search is on—but should he decide to begin to delegate responsibilities (sooner than later), it can be expected that many long-term investors in Berkshire will likely consider cashing out. Considering the shares' liquidity—the average daily trading volume is roughly 1,000 shares— and the disproportionate role that Berkshire has on many individual and institutional Buffett-devotee investors' portfolios, this could put pressure on the stock.

3. Growth has slowed recently. Berkshire has achieved compounded annual investment returns of 24% over the past 40 years, but returns have been less over the last five years. The market values the company at a premium to its peers, as it appears to many that the historic outperformance and Buffett's investment alchemy can be duplicated. By implication, the $40 billion cash hoard at Berkshire is assumed to be a shore of latent investment value upon employment. By contrast I would argue that a combination of a more difficult stock market and economic backdrop when coupled with fiercer competition from other investment managers might render that $40 billion as having a value not much more than that $40 billion figure. In a recent *Barron's* column, Andrew Bary suggested that another conglomerate, Loews, could provide more value as (at that time) its shares sold at only 12× projected earnings and at a discount to its net asset value.

4. Buffett says the salad days for insurance, the cornerstone of the Berkshire complex, are over. After several years of no catastrophic experience it is inevitable that "the winds will roar or the earth will tremble . . . and results could be worse" in Berkshire's insurance segment. Regardless of 2008 catastrophic experience, profit margins will be under pressure in the face of a more competitive landscape. (Buffett expects insurance industry profit margins will shrink by about four percentage points in 2008—even barring a catastrophe.)

5. An outlook for substandard investment returns and uneven economic growth will provide a headwind to Berkshire's growth. My baseline view is that we are in a period of blahflation (blah and inconsistent economic growth coupled with stubbornly high inflation)—a difficult environment of headwinds for even the Oracle.

6. Berkshire Hathaway's premium valuation has seemingly been a byproduct of the credit crisis and the perception of the company as a safe haven. Its shares trade at a large premium to similar financials and have increased in value by about 12% over the past six months (compared to an 11% decline in the S&P 500). Since March 5, 2007, Berkshire's shares are up by 26% vis-à-vis an 8% drop in the broader indices. Should stock market conditions improve, Berkshire's shares might underperform as deflated financial company shares regain their footing.

7. A sum-of-the-parts analysis, relative EPS and price-to-book comparisons of peers suggest that Berkshire's shares are overpriced relative to the market. A sum-of-the-parts analysis that compares Berkshire to its peers produces and assumes a 12× P/E multiple on projected 2008 profits of $9,750 a share and a $121,000 a share price target. A similar methodology, assuming a melded price-to-book on insurance and other businesses at 1.6× and on finance and financial products of 1.25×, yields a fair market value of about $125,000 a share.

8. Buffett's contribution of (85% of his) Berkshire's shares to charity could create an imbalance between demand and supply as stock is sold in the marketplace. Starting in 2006, Buffett began distributing Class B shares (602,500 shares at first and then declining by 5% a year). A shares convert into 30 Class B shares (1/200th voting rights), but not the other way around.

9. Some of Berkshire's most significant stock investments seem vulnerable to a post-credit-bubble crisis and may not recover for years. The company is substantially exposed to not only financials but also to a weakening housing market and to pricing competition in insurance. While American Express ($9 billion investment market value), Coca-Cola ($9 billion investment) and Wells Fargo ($7.8 billion investment) represent historically valuable business franchises, one can argue that they no longer will represent outstanding future value. They certainly have been a meaningful paper drain over the past 12 months. For now, Buffett's favorite holding period is forever, but Buffett's replacement could decide to sell any of these core positions (not likely, but always possible), and Berkshire would incur large capital gains taxes.

10. The law of large numbers works to Berkshire's disadvantage. Buffett admits in this year's letter to shareholders that "our base of assets and earnings is now far too large for us to make outsized gains in the future."

11. Berkshire's disclosure is weak and opaque. There is little information on Berkshire's noninsurance operations contained in the company's financial statements and large forays into reinsurance/derivatives are not materially explained. There can always be negative surprises, especially considering the current seizure in the derivatives market and in light of the possibility of a more problematic and volatile future market environment. Over the years, investors have given Buffett a mulligan when he has made mistakes (e.g., General Re). When Buffett leaves Berkshire's helm, I expect investors to be less forgiving.

Buffett Veers Off His Investment Path

5/13/2008

Since February, the shares of Berkshire Hathaway have consistently fallen. And despite the recent market rally, the company's common shares hit a new 2008 low yesterday.

I believe the principal reason is Warren Buffett's investment style drift, which was reflected in a large derivative loss in first quarter 2008.

Let me explain.

As a dedicated short-seller, I often take a variant view of a company's prospects through logic of argument and analytical dissection, mocking conventional wisdom and the associated popularity surrounding certain investments that, in my view, created an unwarranted degree of optimism in the marketplace.

"Risk comes from not knowing what you're doing."

—Warren Buffett

"You can observe a lot by just watching."

—Yogi Berra

Indeed, some of my best investment shorts—including Ron Perelman's Marvel Entertainment in the early 1990s, after which it filed bankruptcy; America Online, coincident with its 2001 acquisition of Time Warner; homebuilding companies, a favorite of the momentum crowd in 2004; or private mortgage and credit insurers in 2006—initially triggered ridicule by many market participants as my targeted stock market icons (and shorts) were typically seen as Teflon.

If one reads some of the great investment books that chronicle legendary traders'/investors' successes—such as Jack Schwager's *Market Wizards: Interviews with Top Traders*—there is a common thread to the successes of Soros Fund Management's George Soros, Duquesne's Stanley Druckenmiller, Fidelity's Peter Lynch, Capital Growth Management's Ken Heebner, Omega Advisors' Leon Cooperman, SAC's Steve Cohen and Steinhardt Partners' Michael Steinhardt: They consistently stick to their knitting and avoid style drift.

Not surprisingly, when I initially explained the rationale behind shorting Berkshire Hathaway in March 2008, I received a lot of criticism, particularly from some of my hedge fund heavyweight friends who I respect immensely. Frankly, it was hard for me to write that piece as I have worshiped at the altar of Warren Buffett over the years.

Nevertheless, I stood by my analysis and initiated a short, and I even shorted more Berkshire several weeks later.

The night before Buffett's Woodstock of Capitalism, Berkshire Hathaway reported horrible first-quarter 2008 results, weighed down by derivative losses and disappointing results in the company's insurance operations.

> *"Even Napoleon had his Watergate."*
>
> —Yogi Berra

> *"Derivatives are financial weapons of mass destruction, carrying dangers that, while now latent, are potentially lethal."*
>
> —Warren Buffett

There was little coverage of Berkshire's weak first-quarter performance, though Citigroup's research analyst downgraded the stock a week or so later, as it occurred on the eve of the company's annual shareholders meeting (and pilgrimage to Omaha)—a much ballyhooed event, which was covered widely by most business news networks.

There was even less coverage of Buffett's recent foray into derivatives. Berkshire's exposure to derivatives increased by $16 billion, to $40 billion, in the last year.

Over the past five years, Buffett frequently called derivatives "financial weapons of mass destruction," comparing derivatives to "hell . . . easy to enter and almost impossible to exit." Yet, he has, very much out of character, immersed himself in a large and, thus far, unprofitable derivative transaction. His investment successes have not been in speculating in the market (something he has been critical of) but rather by purchasing easily understandable companies with dependable cash flows that sometimes seem imperiled by an exogenous event and are available on the cheap.

It immediately occurred to me after gazing at Buffett's style drift (manifested in Berkshire Hathaway's large first-quarter derivate losses) that he might be increasingly viewed as the new millennium's Ben Franklin, a man who wrote "early to bed and early to rise" but spent many of his evenings in France, philandering all night and showing up to work after noon (to the massive frustration of John Adams). I concluded that Warren Buffett was getting a free pass and had drifted away from an investment process that had rewarded both him and Berkshire's shareholders so dramatically over the years.

"He hits from both sides of the plate. He's amphibious."

—Yogi Berra

Buffett is not only a great investor but, in recent years, he has become an even better marketer, with the benefit of his image accruing to Berkshire. For example, he has cultivated an image of someone who started with nothing, even though he was the son of a well-to-do stockbroker who became a U.S. Congressman. Everyone thinks of him as America's business grandpa, but remember, he grabbed control of a textile firm and promised not to change anything. He did make changes, though, eventually using the textile company's cash flow for acquisitions, shutting down the factory over time.

In essence, Buffett has sold himself as a savior, or investor of last (or often first!) resort. As such, he has positioned himself to prosper in the form of getting beneficial terms in acquisitions, a positive but still a marketing technique. As an example, Berkshire contributed over $4 billion of subordinated debt in the recent Mars deal. But what didn't get much press—and it should have—was that on top of the debt, Berkshire invested over $2 billion of equity in the Wrigley/Mars transaction at a discount to the price that Mars eventually will pay for Wrigley's common shares.

"The future isn't what it used to be."

—Yogi Berra

I am staying short Berkshire Hathaway. Enough said.

Warren Buffett Has Lost His Groove

11/12/2008

The unprecedented market decline has hobbled some of the most successful investors and industrialists of our generation, proving Warren Buffett correct when he wrote, "Over time, markets will do extraordinary, even bizarre things. A single, big mistake could wipe out a long string of successes."

Legg Mason's Bill Miller, Citadel's Ken Griffin, Viacom's Sumner Redstone, and Las Vegas Sands' Sheldon Adelson have suffered sharp reversals from their previous successes. No doubt many others will be revealed by year-end.

The market decline is now even hurting Berkshire Hathaway as, arguably, Warren Buffett has lost his groove.

Style drift. In the process of establishing a large derivative position on the S&P 500 by shorting puts, Buffett has deviated from his long-established investment discipline of avoiding "market plays" and of avoiding "financial weapons of mass destruction" (derivatives). This play has led to continued, multibillion-dollar losses over the past few quarters. According to the recently released 10-Q, Berkshire has lost a total of $9 billion on Buffett's short put position.

Recent share acquisitions of Goldman Sachs and General Electric have been ill-timed. Buffett has convinced Corporate America (and Corporate Europe!) that he is a kind, avuncular sort, an easy and quick-to-deal-with investor of last resort. Toward that end, Buffett recently came to the rescue of General Electric and Goldman Sachs, investing $8 billion in both issues combined. While both investments were made on favorable terms—they are both seriously underwater—not too long ago Buffett purchased $5 billion of 10% preferreds in Goldman Sachs, with five-year warrants struck at $115 per share. At the time, Goldman was trading at $125; it now trades at $74 per share. Buffett also picked up $3 billion in 10% perpetual preferreds in General Electric, with warrants at $22.25 per share. At the time, GE was trading at $22; it now trades at $17 per share.

Buffett's notion of long term is now becoming a convenient shroud to poorly timed investments. A recent *Forbes* article outlined most of Berkshire's largest investments. Berkshire's list of longer-term holdings includes a great many successful positions based on relationship to cost, but the cost/market gap is rapidly closing. Importantly, over the past few years, the performance of many of these investments—including Comcast, Coca-Cola, Kraft and U.S. Bancorp—have underperformed the market dramatically. And some of the largest holdings—such as American Express, CarMax, Conoco-Phillips, Gannett, Ingersoll-Rand, Moody's, USG, WellPoint, and Wells Fargo—have been unmitigated disasters in 2007–2008.

Over time, Warrant Buffett has been the greatest investor extant. His long-term investment performance is unparalleled, but his performance over the past five years, and especially over the past year, is beginning to trail off badly.

In support, Buffett devotees and apologists cite his time frame. They universally say that Buffett's strategy is for the long term—that Berkshire's short-term underperformance is irrelevant.

But is it?

Is the notion of long term now irrelevant, particularly given Warren Buffett's age and the likelihood that sooner than later he will be succeeded by one or several new individuals at Berkshire's helm? Is it irrelevant in our present and future dystopia, in a possible multiyear bear market or in an economy that faces headwinds we haven't seen in decades? Or is it just one of those tautologies that it is safe to buy in the long term?

Buffett's investment strategy, which served him so well over the years, has begun to noticeably sour and might not be suited for the future.

Warren Buffett has lost his groove. The question is whether he will get it back any time soon.

Buffett Brought Down to Earth

1/23/2009

On Sunday evening, Warren Buffett sat down with NBC's Tom Brokaw for a marvelous and straightforward interview.

Early in 2008, I took a controversial and negative view on Berkshire Hathaway's stock. During the late summer, I profitably covered a short I put on Berkshire at approximately $140,000 per share.

Based on the recent deterioration of Berkshire's investments, I might have been premature. (Berkshire's common now trades for under $89,000 a share.)

In the last 60 days, Berkshire's investment portfolio has plummeted in value. Buffett has lost over $4.5 billion alone on

"It's never paid to bet against America. . . . We come through things, but it's not always a smooth ride. . . . This is an economic Pearl Harbor."

—Warren Buffett, Dateline interview on NBC (Jan. 18, 2009)

his 300-million-share investment in Wells Fargo since Dec. 1, 2008, and another $1 billion loss on U.S. Bancorp's shares; both stocks have been halved in less than two months. His most recent investments in Burlington Northern Santa Fe, General Electric, and Goldman Sachs have deteriorated markedly in value from his cost basis.

Equally important, I have repeatedly uttered the notion that Berkshire's large derivative position—namely, short puts on the S&P 500—was evidence of investment style drift. Regardless of that view, Berkshire has now likely recorded an unrealized loss in excess of a $10 billion on the index short put position. A loss on that scale, whether realized or unrealized, is large even for Warren Buffett.

In 2008 and (so far) 2009, the Oracle of Omaha has been wrong; it has paid to bet against America.

Moreover, the U.S. "economic Pearl Harbor" has humanized and brought down to Earth many of the smartest investors in the world (e.g., Warren Buffett), as well as the entire private-equity universe, many well-regarded hedge funds and investors (e.g., Marty Whitman and Bill Miller), and some masters of the universe in residential and nonresidential real estate, among others.

Many industrialists, including Aubrey Kerr McClendon, Kerkor "Kirk" Kerkorian, Sheldon Adelson, and Sumner Redstone, have been thrown under Mr. Market's bus, as have financiers Dick Fuld, James Cayne, John Thain, and even Bank of America's Ken Lewis.

While the downfalls of a widening list of investment, financial and industrial icons have historically been associated with a market and economic bottom, the lesson remains the same: The average individual investor should continue to err on the side of conservatism in a market that provides a wonderful setting for trading but a not-so-exquisite setting for investing.

Is This the End of Warren Buffett?

1/27/2009

Last week, I suggested that Warren Buffett's star was crashing back to Earth.

Barron's senior editor, Andrew Bary, penned a similar piece over the weekend.

Armed with some additional information, I have made tentative conclusions regarding the intrinsic value of Berkshire Hathaway's common shares.

At year-end 2007, Berkshire's investment portfolio had a cost of $39.2 billion and a market value of $75 billion. Since the end of third quarter 2008, the value of Berkshire's investment portfolio has experienced a pronounced drop.

"All good things must come to an end, but all bad things can continue forever."

—Unknown

Berkshire's six investments listed below have fallen by over $16 billion in value; this is more than just a bump in the road:

1. Wells Fargo closed at $37.53 on September 30, 2008. Last week, it closed at $15.87. Berkshire owns 290 million shares, a drop of $6.3 billion dollars.

2. American Express closed at $35.43 on September 30, 2008. Last week, it closed at $16.00. Berkshire owns 151 million shares, a drop of $2.9 billion dollars.

3. Coca-Cola closed at $52.88 on September 30, 2008. Last week, it closed at $42.20. Berkshire owns 200 million shares, a drop of $2.1 billion dollars.

4. Burlington Northern Santa Fe closed at $92.43 on September 30, 2008. Last week, it closed at $63.32. Berkshire owns 63 million shares, a drop of $1.8 billion dollars.

5. ConocoPhillips closed at $73.25 on September 30, 2008. Last week, it closed at $48.10. Berkshire owns 60 million shares, a drop of $1.5 billion dollars.

6. U.S. Bancorp closed at $36.02 on September 30, 2008. On January 20, 2009, it closed at $15.34. Buffett owned 73 million shares, a drop of $1.5 billion dollars.

Note: These losses do not include the recent purchases of General Electric and Goldman Sachs preferreds and Berkshire's large and so far unprofitable foray into shorting puts on the major stock indices.

If one triangulates Buffett's comments in his annual reports during the late 1990s, he seems to view Berkshire's intrinsic value as the sum of its investments per share plus approximately 12× pretax profits, excluding all income from investments.

Given many of my concerns expressed initially in March 2008, I am increasingly coming to the conclusion that the above calculation of intrinsic value is too liberal. Considering the high cost of Berkshire's investment style drift into derivatives (massive short put positions), Buffett's refusal to sell and his apparent lack of recognition that investment moats no longer exist in some of his largest investments (especially in banking), I now feel that Berkshire's valuation will steadily suffer, despite the long-term allegiance of its investors who are geared toward evaluating the company over decades not years. Indeed, Berkshire, in the fullness of time, might suffer the same fate of many other listed closed-end equity mutual funds; its shares could trade at a discount to its investment value per share—plus some multiple to pretax profits.

Warren Buffett is justifiably revered by investors around the world, and I consider myself one of those who have worshiped at his investing altar over the past three decades. Nevertheless, from my perch, Buffett's salad days seem to be over; the only question that remains is the timing and to what degree investors will abandon the Oracle of Omaha.

Reflecting some of the above concerns and since late September 2008, Berkshire's shares have fallen from $145,000 a share to $85,000 a share. There is no apparent end to the decline in sight.

All good things, it seems, in markets and life, must come to an end.

One of the Worst Beatings Ever

3/2/2009

From the hallowed halls in Omaha to the masters of the hedge fund universe in New York City, Mr. Market is humbling the greatest investors in history.

Many asset management franchises and investment managers with outstanding long-term track records are currently on their knees and cornered into risk-averse mode for fear of further investment losses or investor redemptions.

There are numerous reasons attached to the drubbing, including but not restricted to the major issues below:

- Economy—a spiraling downturn in the world economy;
- Credit—a still-weak and clogged transmission of credit;

- Populism and political change—an anticapital President Obama;
- Structural—ultra-bear exchange-traded funds (ETFs) and momentum-based quant funds; and
- Structural (part deux)—hedge and mutual fund redemptions.

In turn, the net worth of households, endowments, pension plans, and other institutions have been caught by the dramatic descent in world share prices, contributing to the negative feedback loop for the economy.

Almost no asset class in the equity universe has been spared in a synchronized downturn that has hit nearly every strategy, even value investing.

Over the weekend, the single most successful investor over the past five decades, value investor Warren Buffett, issued his annual letter to Berkshire Hathaway shareholders, but what has transpired since year-end is even more interesting than what was contained in his annual missive.

But first, let me regress.

For nearly a year, I have outlined issues that I have had with the Buffett way. Many of my concerns have been realized and have arguably contributed importantly to the recent drop in Berkshire Hathaway's book value and the halving of the company's share price since early 2008.

If current trends continue over the balance of the year, 2009 will mark the third annual drop in book value at Berkshire Hathaway since 2001.

It has never been my intention to overly dramatize Warren Buffett's investment miscues nor was it my intention to understate his remarkable long-term investment achievements. Rather, it was my intention to underscore that his massive move in shorting the market (through a put derivative position on the world's major indices) represented a drift in style.

As suggested in the analysis that follows, I estimate that Berkshire Hathaway has lost approximately $15 billion, before counting back the premium of $4.9 billion, on the sale of puts on the major indices.

It was also my intention to question Buffett's analysis of the value of the assets that comprised the asset side of many of his investments in the financial sector and question, in turn, the foundation to his value-investing style that seemed to rely so importantly on his perception of a discrepancy between inherent value and real book value relative to market value.

From my perch, the moats (so dear to Buffett) perceived to have been protecting the businesses of some of his largest investments (especially of a financial sector kind) were, at the very least, threatened and, worst-case scenario, those moats have been breached.

Stated simply, Buffett's investment strategy over multiple decades could either:

- Have been abandoned by the Oracle of Omaha, owing to his reluctance to alter/sell off his strategic and principal holdings and maintain a tax-efficient portfolio approach; or
- Have been influenced by his mistaken analysis of the changing competitive landscape facing some of his portfolio companies. (In other words, the moat has been breached.)

Now back to the present.

According to Berkshire Hathaway's fourth-quarter release, book value dropped by $11.5 billion, or 9.6%, in 2008. According to my pal, Ram Partners' Jeff Matthews, this was the largest annual drop in book since Buffett began investing other people's money in 1956 and only the second year in which Berkshire Hathaway experienced a decline in book value.

What is surprising, though, is that through only the first two months of 2009, Berkshire Hathaway has already suffered its second worst drop in book value in history ($9 billion-plus).

At year-end 2008, Berkshire's investment portfolio had an unrealized gain of about $12 billion, with a market value of $49 billion compared to a cost basis of $37 billion. As recently as year-end 2007, Berkshire Hathaway had an unrealized gain of $35 billion in its investment portfolio.

No more.

Stated simply, the potholes that began to appear in Buffett's investment portfolio in September 2008 have worsened during the first two months of 2009. Indeed, by my calculation, the market value of Berkshire's investment portfolio—excluding recent preferred investments in General Electric, Goldman Sachs, Harley-Davidson and so forth—is down by almost 25%, or by an additional $12 billion, this year. So, despite decades of investing, the market value of Berkshire's investment portfolio has astonishingly returned to Buffett's cost basis of approximately $37 billion.

Below are my 2009 year-to-date estimates of the decline in value of some of Berkshire's largest individual equity holdings since the end of 2008:

- Wells Fargo—$5 billion loss;
- American Express—approximately $1 billion loss;
- ConocoPhillips—approximately $1 billion loss;
- Procter & Gamble—approximately $1 billion loss;
- U.S. Bancorp—approximately $1 billion loss;
- Coca-Cola—approximately $1 billion loss; and
- Kraft—approximately $1 billion loss.

In addition to the losses in Berkshire's investment portfolio, I calculate that the unrealized loss from the liabilities associated with the company's equity index put options ($35 billion notional), if the put options expired on Friday, would have produced an additional decline (and noncash charge) of over $5.5 billion this year. This places the aggregate losses associated with Berkshire's foray into equity index put options at approximately $15 billion (before the $4.9 billion premium received).

In summary, that's a total theoretical pretax loss of about $17.5 billion on Berkshire's investment and derivative losses in only two months of 2009 vs. a consolidated shareholders' equity of $109.2 billion as of Dec. 31, 2008, down from $120.7 billion at year-end 2007. It should be noted, however, that the estimated $17.5 billion loss must be adjusted for taxes in order to develop a projected GAAP loss to Berkshire's book value. Using a 45% effective tax rate produces a $9.6 billion book loss for the first two months in 2009, not materially less than the full-year $11.5 billion hit to book value experienced by Berkshire for all of 2008.

On page 77 of his 2008 annual letter, Buffett estimates that consolidated shareholders' equity has taken an additional $8 billion after-tax loss since the end of 2008. I suspect that the $1.6 billion difference (from my $9.6 billion estimate and Buffett's $8 billion estimate) reflects the difference in the timing of Berkshire's calculation last week as its portfolio losses Thursday and Friday were sizeable.

This all speaks to my conclusion last year that Buffett's strategy miscues and style drift would, in the fullness of time, result in investors assigning a less-than-premium valuation to the investment component of Berkshire Hathaway, making the stock's valuation move closer toward most closed-end equity funds, which trade at a discount.

This already seems to be occurring as the $9 billion-plus reduction in book value year-to-date (excluding gains from operating businesses) compares to a $28 billion reduction in the market capitalization of Berkshire Hathaway.

Away from the dual impact of investment and derivative losses, it should only be fair to mention that Berkshire's operating results featured record fourth-quarter 2008 insurance and investment income. As well, 2008's noninsurance income was the best yearly toll ever; it represented one of the best relative years of performance in Berkshire Hathaway's operating divisions.

Bear markets end when investors give up hope.

Despite the market carnage in general and at Berkshire Hathaway in particular, I have grown increasingly more bullish over the past two weeks.

Two years ago, few saw the cracking foundation of credit, of the economy and our stock markets.

Even fewer will see the seeds of recovery and anticipate a resumption of growth.

Similar to everyone else, I am terrified by the spiraling down in stock prices, but I have to make a judgment as to what degree of economic activity and what level of corporate profits the markets are now discounting.

My conclusion is that there are developing investment bargains, or, to borrow a phrase contained in Buffett's letter on Saturday, I am beginning to "feel like a mosquito in a nudist colony."

Nevertheless, regardless of my view, in an environment where the big boys are being annihilated and almost every investment strategy is being questioned, redefined and readjusted, we remain in a setting where most should err on the conservative side by keeping investment and trading positions at well-below-average sizes and maintaining that precious commodity called cash.

Buy American? I'm Damned!

3/9/2009

Today's column parodies Warren Buffett's October 16, 2008 *New York Times* op-ed, "Buy American. I Am."

The portions in italics are meant to represent what Mr. Buffett's updated thoughts might be if the editorial were rewritten today, four and a half months after its original publication:

New York Times
Op-Ed Contributor
"Buy American. I Am."
"At Some Point, Investors Should Buy American. I Already Did, but I Got in Way Too Early."

By WARREN E. BUFFETT
Published: October 16, 2008
Omaha
By DOUGLAS A. KASS
Published: March 9, 2009
Palm Beach

The financial world is a mess, both in the United States and abroad. Its problems, moreover, have been leaking into the general economy, and the leaks are now turning into a gusher. In the near term, unemployment will rise, business activity will falter, and headlines will continue to be scary.

I grossly underestimated the scope of the world's economic problems in October. I suppose when ignorance is combined with leverage, I, in particular, should have better anticipated the consequences we now see today. No longer have the leaks turned into a gusher; they have become more like a hurricane or a tornado in proportion. The accumulated loss of business and consumer confidence coupled with an acceleration in the declines in stock prices have translated into a classical negative feedback loop, which has worsened the fundamental backdrop well beyond what I and most others had expected. Indeed, I expressed a more cautious view in my letter to Berkshire Hathaway investors last Saturday.

So . . . I've been buying American stocks. This is my personal account I'm talking about, in which I previously owned nothing but United States government bonds. (This description leaves aside my Berkshire Hathaway holdings, which are all committed to philanthropy.) If prices keep looking attractive, my non–Berkshire net worth will soon be 100% in United States equities.

While I expanded my personal holdings of U.S. stocks during the fall and increased Berkshire Hathaway's exposure to equities since October 2008, over the short and maybe even intermediate term, I was clearly premature in going all-in. In retrospect, back in October I bought too many expensive suits that, at the time, looked cheap to me. I failed to recognize the scope of the world's economic weakness and the depth of the problems in our financial system.

Why? A simple rule dictates my buying: Be fearful when others are greedy, and be greedy when others are fearful. And most certainly, fear is now widespread, gripping even seasoned investors. To be sure, investors are right to be wary of highly leveraged entities or businesses in weak competitive positions. But fears regarding the long-term prosperity of the nation's many sound companies make no sense. These businesses will indeed suffer earnings hiccups, as they always have. But most major companies will be setting new profit records five, 10 and 20 years from now.

What I have learned from my investment experience over the past few months is that public opinion poll is no substitute for thought; sentiment is always trumped by fundamentals. In my October editorial, I expressed an investment strategy—namely, being fearful when others are greedy and greedy when others are fearful—that had worked brilliantly for me and others in previous cycles. It was a simple principle that has resulted in profits well beyond my wildest dreams, but this time the strategy ended up being more of an act of a simpleton! Buying the dip, at least at the level that I identified as providing me (and Berkshire) with value, proved wildly unsuccessful against the backdrop of a black swan event in equities. With the benefit of hindsight, this time the fear on the part of seasoned and unseasoned investors had validity, and the economic damage incurred over the past six months will have a lasting impact.

Let me be clear on one point: I can't predict the short-term movements of the stock market. I haven't the faintest idea as to whether stocks will be higher or lower a month—or a year—from now. What is likely, however, is that the market will move higher, perhaps substantially so, well before either sentiment or the economy turns up. So if you wait for the robins, spring will be over.

My October entry point in buying stocks was poor. I failed to consider what I had previously written in the past about market timing and investment strategy. Firstly, "Don't try to catch a falling knife until you have a handle on the risk." Secondly, I paid too high a price for the value I received in buying stocks and the degree in which I went all-in is another example that I should have practiced what I preached (and wrote!)—that is, "short-term market forecasts are poison and should be kept locked up in a safe place, away from children and also from grown-ups who behave in the market like children." Thirdly, I forgot my first rule of investing, which is "not to lose," and I also forgot the second rule, which is "not to forget the first rule."

A little history here: During the Depression, the Dow hit its low, 41, on July 8, 1932. Economic conditions, though, kept deteriorating until Franklin D. Roosevelt took office in March 1933. By that time, the market had already advanced 30%. Or think back to the early days of World War II, when things were going badly for the United States in Europe and the Pacific. The market hit bottom in April 1942, well before Allied fortunes turned. Again, in the early 1980s, the time to buy stocks was when inflation raged and the economy was in the tank. In short, bad news is an investor's best friend. It lets you buy a slice of America's future at a marked-down price.

It is clearly different this time. I should have heeded my advice that "if past history was all there was to the game, the richest people would be librarians." I should have paid attention to my Depression reference because there is a growing risk that the current economic downturn might morph into just that! In the past, stocks have anticipated an economic upturn in advance; in this cycle, stocks may not respond positively until it is clear that public policy has gotten traction and is reflected in better visibility of economic stabilization/recovery.

Over the long term, the stock market news will be good. In the twentieth century, the United States endured two world wars and other traumatic and expensive military conflicts; the Depression; a dozen or so recessions and financial panics; oil shocks; a flu epidemic; and the resignation of a disgraced president. Yet the Dow rose from 66 to 11,497.

Chains of habit are too light to be felt until they are too heavy to be broken. In the investment world, the rearview mirror is always clearer than the windshield. I have to begin to reassess whether my favorite holding period should still be forever. Maybe my investment relationships should no longer last a lifetime.

You might think it would have been impossible for an investor to lose money during a century marked by such an extraordinary gain. But some investors did. The hapless ones bought stocks only when they felt comfort in doing so and then proceeded to sell when the headlines made them queasy.

My stock selection has been poor and I have been too concentrated. I, too, have been exposed as swimming naked when the market tide went out over the past six months. I failed to properly analyze the risks of a number of my investment purchases. This is particularly true in my large involvement in financial stocks, as the moats I envisioned that protected their business franchises have been breached, reflecting the commoditization of financial products. Equally important, I materially miscalculated and overestimated the values of my financial holdings' assets, including American Express, Wells Fargo, and U.S. Bancorp, to name a few. To borrow from Gertrude Stein, "There was little there, there." Stated simply, in my investments, I thought that I had found 1-foot bars that I could step over, but they turned out to be 10-foot bars that I couldn't leap over!

Today, people who hold cash equivalents feel comfortable. They shouldn't. They have opted for a terrible long-term asset, one that pays virtually nothing and is certain to depreciate in value. Indeed, the policies that government will follow in its efforts to alleviate the current crisis will probably prove inflationary and therefore accelerate declines in the real value of cash accounts.

I should have been more risk averse. The depth of the world's economic problems suggests that deflationary forces will be with us for some time to come. Inflation has been delayed.

Equities will almost certainly outperform cash over the next decade, probably by a substantial degree. Those investors who cling now to cash are betting they can efficiently time their move away from it later. In waiting for the comfort of good news, they are ignoring Wayne Gretzky's advice: "I skate to where the puck is going to be, not to where it has been."

Perhaps in recent years I enjoyed the investment process more than the proceeds and rewards. Maybe I should not have made some of these decisions on my own. Maybe I should have sought advice from industry specialists or from analysts who had expressed concerns that the foundations of our credit markets, our economy, and the world's stock markets were increasingly on shaky ground.

I don't like to opine on the stock market, and again I emphasize that I have no idea what the market will do in the short term. Nevertheless, I'll follow the lead of a restaurant that opened in an empty bank building and then advertised: "Put your mouth where your money was." Today, my money and my mouth both say equities.

I have put both my foot and my money in my mouth. I went on investment "tilt" and ended up being the patsy at the poker table. I should have taken my own advice when I said that "it takes 20 years to build a reputation and five minutes to ruin it. If you think about that, you'll do things differently."

—Warren E. Buffett is the chief executive of Berkshire Hathaway, a diversified holding company.

—*Douglas A. Kass is the president of Seabreeze Partners Management, Inc. the General Partner of Seabreeze Partners Short LP and Seabreeze Partners Long/Short LP.*

Burlington Bet Could Derail Berkshire

11/4/2009

Unquestionably there will never be another Warren Buffett, and yesterday's deal will not be a "train wreck," but elements of yesterday's Burlington Northern Santa Fe acquisition go against some of his previous tenets.

Let's delve deeper into the Burlington Northern deal and its ramifications.

- *Not Ben Graham-like:* Unlike the Goldman Sachs transaction and a number of other timely deals over the past year, in which Buffett extracted blood through hefty warrants issuance, Buffett paid up for Burlington Northern (a 30%-plus premium), and he paid a full price of about 20× earnings.
- *Offering Berkshire stock:* A hefty portion of the acquisition of Burlington Northern was funded by exchanging Berkshire Hathaway stock. Buffett has in the past held his equity dear and has criticized himself for how expensive early stock acquisitions were.
- *Stock split:* To accommodate the large portion of the exchange of stock, he split Berkshire Hathaway's shares 50-1. Splitting his shares is something he previously cautioned against ever doing. Though the company introduced a lower-priced Class B share in 1996, in a letter to Berkshire shareholders in 1983, Buffett stated that investors should be "focused on business results, not market prices." He wanted owners, not renters, in his stock, but the split is likely to result in an intrusion of renters and in great fluctuations in Berkshire's shares.
- *Berkshire's cash hoard is now materially depleted:* This closes the bullish chapter during which Buffett, through a series of well-timed and

well-priced deals, had converted a low-yielding $45 billion-plus cash position into accretive and higher earnings yields through portfolio acquisitions. For the time being, there is little more that can be done to buoy Berkshire's returns; it's now up to the world's economies.

One of the clear positives to yesterday's announcement is that Berkshire's shares will become more liquid, and an entry into the S&P 500 now seems inevitable. That said, it should be emphasized that a steady supply of stock will counter the better liquidity offered up through a split and lower share price. The Bill and Melinda Gates Foundation will likely accommodate the renewed interest by stepping up their sales of Berkshire Hathaway stock. As it has previously announced, the Gates Foundation has been selling at a steady pace; the Foundation sold approximately 17,000 "B" shares in each of the last several months.

On to the negative side of the ledger, given his age (and the growing possibility that Buffett might hand over running Berkshire to his successor sooner than later), the size of the Burlington Northern deal relative to Berkshire's cash position and the scope of the deal (and the need to consolidate Burlington Northern's operations into Berkshire), this is likely the last meaningful deal that Warren Buffett will make.

My conclusion?

As there arguably still remains a Buffett share price premium, I would now make the case that the interaction of the above factors will lead investors to valuing Berkshire Hathaway more like a closed-end fund (selling at a discount to its underlying or intrinsic value) and less like the premium and prized possession that it has been over the past 40-plus years.

Omaha, Here I Come!

3/4/2013

Wow!

This morning I was surprised, honored, and flattered to have Warren Buffett invite me to be the "credentialed bear" on a panel at Berkshire Hathaway's annual meeting in Omaha during the first week of May.

The Oracle offered me this role on CNBC's *Squawk Box* this morning.

Let me explain the events that led up to the invite.

As I have done over the past few decades on a certain late-winter Saturday morning (ever since I was a graduate student at Wharton), I woke up this Saturday and read Warren Buffett's letter to Berkshire Hathaway shareholders.

In that letter Mr. Buffett wrote:

> Finally—to spice things up—we would like to add to the panel a credentialed bear on Berkshire, preferably one who is short the stock. Not yet having a bear identified, we would like to hear from applicants. The only requirement is that you be an investment professional and negative on Berkshire. The three analysts will bring their own Berkshire-specific questions and alternate with the journalists and the audience in asking them.

Upon reading this, I e-mailed CNBC's Andrew Ross Sorkin and Becky Quick and asked them if they would be kind enough to forward a letter I wrote on Saturday that basically threw my hat in the Oracle's ring as that "credentialed bear."

I included in the e-mail to Mr. Buffett my curriculum vitae and a column I wrote in March 2008 that explained the rationale behind why I was short Berkshire's shares back then almost five years ago. (It turned out to be a successful short and, surprisingly, for the right reasons.)

As well, I included references for Mr. Buffett of four hedge-hoggers and investment managers who were acquaintances of his, whom I knew he respected and were familiar with my body of work.

Andrew and Becky were really nice and forwarded my e-mail to Mr. Buffett over the weekend, and the rest, as they say, is history.

I had absolutely no idea the invitation would be forthcoming and found out like everyone else while watching *Squawk Box* with Joe and Becky this morning.

I am going to Disneyland—I mean, Omaha!

And in Omaha I will be Daniel in the lion's den, wading in a sea of Warren Buffett's strongest admirers.

But I will be up to the challenge.

Stay tuned.

My Pilgrimage to Warren Buffett's Omaha

4/29/2013

Becky Quick: Let's talk a little bit more about your letter and some of the things you put out in it. You mentioned that you were going to be doing some things a little differently this year at the annual meeting. Last year you added a panel of analysts who asked a lot of questions at the annual meeting—along with three journalists who asked questions and all the questions that come from the audience. You say you are going to have one insurance analyst but you've added another analyst who will be looking at the other Berkshire companies and that you are looking actively for a bear on Berkshire Hathaway. Why did you add that?

Warren Buffett: To make it more interesting. The crowd can hear somebody that thinks the stock is overpriced or that it's a house of cards or whatever it may be. And we want the media to be interesting. So that person will get six questions, and we now have that person because I said it had to be a credentialed bear, preferably one who was short the stock. Doug Kass is certainly a credentialed investor, and he said he is short the stock and he'd like to do it. Doug, you are on!

Becky Quick: Does he know this?

Warren Buffett: No, he just knows this now. . . . Doug, think of some tough questions. See if you can drive the stock down 10%!

Becky Quick: Why, so you can buy more shares?

Warren Buffett: Yes, that would be OK!

—*CNBC's* Squawk Box *(March 4, 2013)*

I was shocked, surprised, honored, and flattered to have been invited and selected as the "credentialed bear" to ask questions at the annual meeting in Omaha during the first week of May.

As I mentioned in a recent *New York Times* article, my initial response was one of elation. Similar to the quarterback who wins the Super Bowl, I told the author of that article, Peter Latham, that "I am going to Disneyland—I mean, Omaha!"

After all, similar to so many, I have worshiped at the altar of Warren Buffett since the early 1970s.

As the weight of the invite to ask questions of Buffett/Munger about Berkshire on Saturday, May 5, sunk in, I became reflective.

I quickly recalled that, at 20 years old, I experienced the Woodstock Music & Art Fair in August 1969 on Max Yasgur's farm in Bethel, New York, and now, 44 years later, I am going to ask Mr. Buffett questions at "the Woodstock of capitalism" in Omaha, Nebraska.

Going to the two Woodstocks in a half a century to me seems right, almost symmetrical, and pretty cool.

Over the next week, I will be memorializing my pilgrimage to Omaha, Nebraska, to the Woodstock of capitalism, Berkshire Hathaway's annual shareholders meeting.

Today, I am going to chronicle how I went about doing my research on Warren Buffett's Berkshire Hathaway as well as outline what I expect to accomplish on Saturday (and what Mr. Buffett likely expects of me).

Daniel in the Lion's Den   Let me start by making an observation.

Inviting a bear to an annual shareholders meeting is unusual; it might even be unprecedented.

But, to me, it shows the uniqueness of Warren Buffett.

As personae non grata, bears are more apt to be quarantined from earnings calls and conferences, let alone be invited to ask hard-hitting questions in front of legions of admirers that descend upon the auditorium in Omaha.

Both Berkshire Hathaway and Warren Buffett already have been scrutinized thoroughly by analysts, journalists, pundits and biographers—there is little unknown about both.

The difficult challenge I face is to ask original questions (some that have never been asked) that might divulge new information and insights about Berkshire and Buffett.

I approached my research assignment as an investigative reporter. Fortunately, I had some background in this, as, while getting my MBA at Wharton, I was one of Ralph Nader's "Raiders." I coauthored *Citibank* (along with Ralph Nader and the Center for the Study of Responsive Law), which was published in 1974. This background and my analytical history and experiences have helped me discover some facts that others have failed to find.

Part of my research was spent in interviewing people who were familiar with the business of Berkshire Hathaway and/or personally knew Warren Buffett.

In addition, I prepared for next Saturday by rereading many of the more important books written about the Oracle of Omaha.

I found the best books to include Roger Lowenstein's *Buffett: The Making of an American Capitalist*, Jeff Matthews's *Pilgrimage to Warren Buffett's Omaha* and Alice Schroeder's *The Snowball: Warren Buffett and the Business of Life*. Importantly, I read everything that *Fortune*'s Carol Loomis (who has edited and assisted Mr. Buffett in the preparation of his annual letter since 1977) ever wrote on Buffett and Berkshire—*Tap Dancing to Work* was particularly rich in information.

Without revealing too much before Saturday's meeting, my research underscored that Buffett is more than an iconic figure in investments, in philanthropy, in humor and in storytelling. He is complex. His interests are more varied than many know. He has an enormous amount of energy.

He is a loyal friend. But he can be controlling.

I was surprised to find out how much time he puts into preparing for Berkshire's annual meeting.

He is resilient. I was especially surprised by how many investment obstacles he faced and endured over his remarkable career—whether it was the general market or specific problems in portfolio holdings.

Warren Buffett likes people to ask for things, rather than the other way around, and that helps to explain the manner in which the invitation for a "credentialed bear" was delivered in his letter. As evidence of this, in his 2002 letter he invited shareholders who thought they were qualified to send him a letter to nominate themselves to Berkshire's Board of Directors. Again, in 2006 in the Chairman's letter to investors, he advertised for a successor to Geico's investment manager, Lou Simpson. "Send in your resume," he wrote.

What Do I Plan to Accomplish at the Meeting?   I take Warren Buffett on face value.

I like to think that he selected me for the purpose of having me ask hard-hitting, pointed, thoughtful, original, perhaps even uncommon questions in order to spice up the Q&A session of the annual shareholders meeting.

My plan is to ask a series of unique questions on a variety of topics. I plan, in the process, to be courteous and respectful. I also plan, at times, to approach the questions with the same sort of levity and wit that Mr. Buffett writes in his letters to shareholders. I am certain that my humor will pale in comparison to the Oracle, but I will try!

So, my primary objective is to go where no questioners have previously gone and to elicit responses to some important questions facing the company that have never been asked.

To say that I face an uphill fight is an understatement. It is fair to say that the odds are stacked up against me.

I am prepared for derision, some raspberries and even several Bronx cheers from the fans of Berkshire Hathaway and Warren Buffett. And I am prepared to have Charlie Munger call me a chump.

Nevertheless, I am up to the challenge.

Finally, in the interest of total honesty and disclosure, I am very excited. And my biggest thrill will be to take a picture with the Oracle and my son, Noah, who I am lovingly taking along on my pilgrimage to Warren Buffett's Omaha.

Warren and Me

4/30/2013

I was surprised how many things Warren Buffett and I have in common, though it certainly isn't our net worths!

- *Prostate cancer:* Both Warren Buffett and I were diagnosed with cancer in 2012. I had my prostate removed in a robotic-assisted laparoscopic prostatectomy in December 2012. (I am now cancer free.) Warren Buffett underwent successful radiation treatment last year.
- *Wharton School:* We both attended Wharton. After graduating from the Woodrow Wilson High School in Omaha in 1947, Warren Buffett entered the Wharton School at the University of Pennsylvania. He studied at Wharton for two years, and in 1950, he transferred to the University of Nebraska–Lincoln where he graduated with a bachelor of science in business administration. I attended Wharton in 1970 and received my MBA in finance in 1972.

- *Horse tip sheet:* We both published and sold a horse tip sheet. Handicapping horses combined two traits that Warren Buffett was good at, collecting information and mathematics. With his friend, Bob "Russ" Russell, Warren hawked a tip sheet, *Stable-Boy Selections*, at Ak-Sar-Ben racetack. At $0.25 apiece, his tip sheet undercut the *Blue Sheet*, a staple at racetracks. I hawked a tip sheet, *Wharton's Picks*, an independent study project in which I regressed variables in a computer and delivered the output in a computer-generated print-out, for the same $0.25 cents at Liberty Bell Park racetrack, competing against *Lawton* and the *Orange Sheet*, while attending business school.
- *"Stoopers":* A "stooper" is someone who collects thrown-away betting tickets from the floor of a racetrack. Often, bettors make mistakes, either by throwing out valuable tickets that haven't been cashed or when they discard tickets from disputed races whose order of finish is often changed. Warren, again with "Russ," was a stooper at Ak-Sar-Ben racetrack. I was a stooper at harness racetracks all around the country. (I would later breed, own, and drive harness horses with some success.)
- *Early interest in the stock market:* At the age of 12, Warren Buffett started buying stocks—with his sister Doris as a partner, he purchased three shares of Cities Service preferred stock for about $38 a share. The stock tanked to $27 a share, and Doris reminded him every day that they were losing money. When it recovered to $40 a share, he sold, netting a $5 profit. Cities Service eventually soared to $202 a share, teaching Buffett several important investing lessons—namely, don't fixate on your cost basis, be patient in your investments and not to take responsibility for anyone else's money unless you're sure you'll succeed. My Grandma Koufax taught me the stock market when I was 15 years old. I spent my vacations as a teenager "watching the tape" in a small brokerage firm in Rockville Centre, Long Island. I bought my first stock, Teledyne, in 1967. I did better on my Teledyne investment than Warren Buffett did with Cities Service. But, well, he did better subsequently.
- *Northwestern Wildcats:* Warren Buffett's wife, Susan, and his sister, Bertie, both went to Northwestern University. My son recently received an MFA in playwriting from Northwestern.

- *Baseball:* Warren Buffett loves baseball—it is likely his favorite sport. He is good friends with Omaha-born St. Louis Cardinals' pitcher Bob Gibson and his wife Charlene. Bob Gibson entered the Baseball Hall of Fame in 1981. I love baseball. My cousin is Sandy Koufax—don't forget my Grandma Koufax!—and I count as good friends Susan and Jim Palmer, former Baltimore Orioles pitcher and Hall of Famer (1990).
- *Palm Beach:* Warren Buffett experienced the snobbiness of Palm Beach, Florida, in 1970, when, at an excursion with his investment minions, he stayed at the Colony Hotel, which he called "a friendly family hotel that is friendly if you were the Kennedy family." I spent many nights at Palm Beach's Colony Hotel when I attended board of directors meetings at both DMG—now named Danaher—and for the Home Federal Bank of Palm Beach located on South County Road in Palm Beach. I currently reside in Palm Beach.
- *George McGovern and Allard Lowenstein:* Warren Buffett supported George McGovern for President in 1972. Buffett also contributed to liberal Democrat Allard Lowenstein's Congressional campaign. I, too, supported McGovern. And I once babysat for Lowenstein's children—he was a Long Island congressman (in the fifth district in Nassau county).
- *Penicillin allergy:* We are both allergic to penicillin. (Warren Buffett had a terrible allergy incident in 1970.)
- *Paperboys:* We both delivered newspapers as youths—he in Omaha, Nebraska, and I on Long Island, New York (*The Long Island Press* and *Newsday*).
- *Train sets:* We both had train sets in our homes.
- *Harmonie Club:* Warren Buffett's pal, Walter Schloss's grandfather, was a member of Harmonie Club of New York City. I joined Harmonie in 1982, and I remain a member.
- *Television appearances:* Warren Buffett has appeared on *The Office* (2011) and on *All My Children* (1992 and 2008). I appeared on the quiz show *Tic-Tac-Dough* when I was in fourth grade.
- *Nicknames:* Warren Buffett has been known, alternatively, as "The Wizard of Omaha," "The Oracle of Omaha," and the "Sage of Omaha." In fourth grade, I was known as "The Professor."

Note: I want to emphasize that this exercise was for fun. In no way do I want to imply that I am comparable to Warren Buffett, the greatest investor of all time.

Little-Known Facts about Warren Buffett

5/1/2013

Warren Buffett, his investment cabal of Ben Graham et al. and Berkshire Hathaway have been under a microscope for years but here are a few little-known facts.

- The first stock Warren Buffett purchased was in 1942—he was 12 years old. The stock was Cities Service—he purchased three shares at $38 a share. It immediately fell, and he sold it for $40 a share. He learned three lessons: be patient, don't fixate on price and don't be responsible for others.
- His first crush was on an eighth grader, Dorothy Hume.
- In Warren's *Stable-Boy Selections* horse racing tip sheet (distributed at Ak-Sar-Ben racetrack, Nebraska spelled backwards), he favored speed over class.
- Warren learned ping-pong at the University of Pennsylvania.
- He called the city of Philadelphia "Filthy-delphia."
- When he left the University of Pennsylvania, he called himself "Ex-Wharton Buffett."
- Ben Graham was born with the name Benjamin Grossbaum.
- Ben Grossbaum's family lost most of their wealth when he was 9 years old in the market panic of 1907.
- Ben Graham started as a runner on Wall Street.
- Ben Graham's partnership was originally funded by the Rosenwald family.
- Howard Buffett's middle name is Graham.
- Ben Graham was a philanderer. He once proposed to live half the year with his mistress, Marie Louise Amingues ("Malou"), and half with his wife, Estey.
- Ben Graham was initially rejected from Columbia Business School. Graham believed that the rejection occurred because of a "secret

deformity" that he thought the school had discovered: "For years I had been struggling against something the French call *mauvaise habitudes*" (bad habits, a euphemism for masturbation).

- Buffett Associates was funded by seven people, including Warren Buffett. The investments were between $5,000 and $35,000, but Warren only contributed $100.
- Larry Tisch sent Warren Buffett a check for $35,000 to invest in his partnership but incorrectly made out the check to Charlie Munger.
- Carol Loomis's husband was a stockbroker. In Loomis's first reference to Buffett in *Fortune* magazine, she incorrectly spelled Warren's last name.
- In 1968, Buffett tried to buy *Variety*. He failed and purchased the *Omaha Sun* newspaper instead.
- The year I was born, in 1949, Warren Buffett worked at J.C. Penney as a salesman.
- He went on Vornado's board of directors in 1973.
- Buffett's relationship with Salomon's John Gutfreund was solidified when the firm underwrote a Geico convertible offering.
- Berkshire spent $46 million for the first 48% of Geico and $2.3 billion for the next 52%.
- Leo Goodwin Jr., the son of Geico's cofounders, sold his Geico stock at the bottom and died penniless.
- Warren admired Walter Annenberg and likely got some of his protective moat theory from his lessons on "essentiality." (Annenberg: "There are three properties in the world that have the quality of 'essentiality.' They are the *Daily News*, the *TV Guide*, and the *Wall Street Journal*. And I own two out of three." Note: My, has the world changed, as protective moats sometimes dry up.)
- Walter Annenberg's father, Moe, had mob connections. He was sent to prison for tax evasion and running a telegraph wire with horse race results to bookies around the country.
- Were it not for a glitch in the contract, Berkshire would have purchased Long-Term Capital Management's assets. (Goldman incorrectly wrote that Berkshire was to buy the management company at LTC.)
- Meriwether's Long-Term Capital Management hedge fund was shorting Berkshire stock as a hedge against an overvalued market before it got into trouble.

- Problems arose when Long-Term Capital Management had only $4.7 billion in capital to support $129 billion in assets.
- I loved this Buffett quote aimed at Long-Term Capital Management's derivatives portfolio. "Derivatives are like sex. It's not who we're sleeping with, it's who they're sleeping with that's the problem."
- Coca-Cola's Ivester resigned his role as CEO—he wasn't fired. (Herb Allen and Warren Buffett lacked the authority to fire him.)
- Warren Buffett grew a beard after surgery on his colon.
- Bill Gates and Warren Buffett were ushers at Kaye Graham's funeral.
- Warren Buffett said he has made the most money in his career "by sitting on my ass."
- As Coca-Cola's stock fell and technology stocks lifted, a *Barron's* cover story on Buffett/Berkshire, "What's Wrong, Warren?" was critical, but Warren didn't respond to them. (Boy, was *Barron's* wrong, as very soon after the Internet got unplugged: 112,000 dot-com employees were fired. Amazon's Bezos was named "Person of the Year" by *Time*, and Amazon's share price subsequently fell from $113 a share to $17 a share.)
- At the Sun Valley Conference in 2001 Warren exhibited a slide that depicted and underscored the inevitability of the Internet stock boom of the late-1990s. ("Anything that can't go on forever will end," Herb Stein.)
- Jimmy Buffett and Warren Buffett are not related!

Conversing with the Oracle

5/5/2013

Let me summarize my once-in-a-lifetime experience.

Upon landing in Omaha on Thursday night, I immediately went to meet Lindsey Bell and *TheStreet* crew at the Omaha Hilton, right across from the convention center where the Berkshire Hathaway annual shareholders meeting would begin the next morning.

Lindsey did a nice job in the interview, seeking out not only my emotions but also the main subjects on which I planned to grill the Oracle on Saturday.

I spent the rest of the evening at 801 Chophouse, having an unbelievable steak and editing my questions at the bar and a bit later back at the hotel room.

Friday morning I was on CNBC's *Squawk Box* with Becky Quick and my buddy/friend/pal Mario Gabelli. It was a fun interview on the stage of the convention center that was later to be the locale of the annual shareholders meeting.

Becky asked me how I felt, and I said that I felt like a journeyman pitcher facing my Hall of Famer cousin Los Angeles Dodgers pitcher Sandy Koufax. What is worse is that I faced two terrific hitters. In the No. 3 position in the batting order was Charlie Munger, with a lifetime batting average of .390, and in the cleanup spot was the greatest hitter in the history of Major League Finance, Warren Buffett.

Nevertheless, in my questions on Saturday, I had hoped to throw the duo a few tough curveballs.

I now know why this weekend is called "The Woodstock of Capitalism." The action all day in the lobby of the Omaha Hilton was like being at a rock concert for capitalists.

I not only saw numerous business leaders milling around—including the chairmen of numerous large corporations such as Geico, Coca-Cola, Microsoft, and others—but numerous celebrities, too, such as filmmaker George Lucas.

The pals that accompanied me on the trip to Omaha were no slouches in the executive department—a bunch of masters of the universe in real estate, money management, finance, advertising, and hedge funds, in their own right.

I spent most of the rest of the day solidifying my questions for the annual meeting. I did, however, have a number of other media interviews.

A Growing Bundle of Nerves I must admit to having been a bit nervous as the day progressed, but not terribly so. I think I was just so darned excited for Saturday to come.

My son Noah finally arrived at the hotel. (He came in a separate group that left the New York area midday Friday.)

I gave him a big hug and kiss—I was so happy he was there to participate in the unique experience I was about to face.

In the early evening, Mario Gabelli invited me and Noah to a cocktail party and panel discussion for the benefit of Columbia Business School at the Hilton where I was staying. Among the speakers was my friend/ buddy/pal Lee Cooperman, who gave an excellent presentation for the students and alumni of Columbia, as well as Mario's other guests. The meeting was informative and well-attended—I saw Pershing Square's Bill Ackman and a lot of other hedge-hoggers in the audience.

MDC Partners' Miles Nadal, Noah and I then proceeded to the legendary Gorat's Steak House that Warren Buffett favors and always talks about. There we met Lee Cooperman, Mario Gabelli, an acquaintance from David Einhorn's Greenlight Capital organization, Vornado Realty Trust's Steve Roth, Cohen and Steers' Marty Cohen, my buddy/ pal/friend Mikey Salzhauer, and the *New York Times'* and *Squawk Box*'s Andrew Ross Sorkin.

The group was animated, and it was a very festive dinner. The conversation was great. Our discussions circled around Berkshire Hathaway—I told the group about a lot of little-known facts I had learned about Warren, and I entertained the group with some commonalities between the Oracle and myself.

Andrew reminisced about the previous meetings he had attended, and Steve Roth told some extraordinary stories about his experiences with Warren, who was on the board of directors of Vornado before Steve took control of the company in the late 1970s. Steve eventually bought out Warren's Vornado stock position. Others, like Lee, had equally interesting stories about Warren.

Later in the evening, Andrew—who was, for the fifth year, a panelist at the annual meeting—reminded me to have some alternative queries in the event that my questions were asked by others. Fortunately, I was already well prepared for that.

Our three-hour dinner finally ended, and we returned to the hotel, where I finished off the edits to my questions.

Noah and I awoke early Saturday, had some coffee and ran over to the convention center to reserve seats for my buddies. Though we arrived nearly one-and-a-half hour early, the entire convention center's seating was almost completely filled.

We managed to reserve eight seats in the nosebleed section, though there was still a reasonable view of the stage.

After putting T-shirts on the chairs (thanks, Mikey, for that thoughtful present of "Go Dougie Go—Omaha 2013" T-shirts for the group), Noah and I ventured down to the stage, where I was to present my questions.

From there, we went into the exhibition area next to the convention center, where many of Berkshire Hathaway's subsidiaries were selling merchandise—Fruit of the Loom, See's Candies, Benjamin Moore, Dairy Queen, and so on. Geico even had booths selling automobile insurance.

I spent nearly $250 on assorted merchandise to bring back to New York and Florida for my friends, and especially for two of my analysts—Kelley Hopkins and Nick Pollari—who helped me with my one-and-a-half month of researching for questions. Among the products I bought were Warren Buffett/Charlie Munger boxer shorts and Berkshire Hathaway hats and T-shirts. I even purchased five basketballs signed by "Handles," a member of the Harlem Globetrotters basketball team. (Naturally, "Sweet Georgia Brown," the Globetrotters theme song, was playing throughout the concession booths.)

The "Woodstock of Capitalism" Commences It was now time for the meeting to begin.

As I walked up to the stage, numerous members of the audience recognized me and mostly yelled out, "Good luck," though there were some Bronx cheers. I felt like a heavyweight fighter approaching the ring to the cheers and boos of the crowd. It was very exciting. In fact, this happened throughout the weekend as many of the Buffettphiles recognized me and either cheered or jeered me. It was all in good fun. (I think!)

Before getting up to the stage, Warren came up to me and wished me good luck—"Give it your best shot," he said. I introduced myself to Charlie Munger, who initially sat next to Buffett with the other members of Berkshire's board of directors.

I was then introduced to Berkshire board member and Microsoft Chairman Bill Gates, which for me was one of the highlights of the day.

Slowly, we all began to assemble on the stage.

On the left were the journalists—*Fortune*'s Carol Loomis, the *New York Times*' Andrew Ross Sorkin, and CNBC's Becky Quick. In the middle of the stage were Charlie Munger and Warren Buffett. On the right were Nomura's insurance analyst Cliff Gallant, Ruane Cunniff's Jonathan Brandt, and myself.

For the first time I grew nervous as I faced nearly 40,000 people in the Century Link Center crowd, and as the legendary Oracle sat only a few feet away from me. The entire board of directors, including Bill Gates, was in the first few rows in front of me.

As the meeting started, and throughout the first hour, I literally felt my heart thumping. I thought I was going to have a heart attack. Yup, that's how I felt.

But, in time, and after a hysterical 45-minute start—during which a "Dancing with the Stars" video was shown to the audience that included Charlie and Warren dancing to Psy's "Gangnam Style"—an almost eerie calm descended on me.

The best commercials for Coca-Cola, Geico, and other Berkshire subsidiary products were shown, and there was also a wonderful video parody of *Breaking Bad,* which saw Bryan Cranston and Aaron Paul reprising their roles as Walter White and Jesse Pinkman. Instead of cooking up meth, the drug-dealing duo opts to focus on peanut brittle, and Warren appears at their motor home in the desert and offers to buy out their peanut-brittle business. They have a stare-down—and Warren, of course, wins and buys their company. He calls Charlie Munger after the deal is agreed to and Charlie's response is priceless: "Brittle, bitches!"

Then there was video from Warren's congressional testimony in the early 1990s regarding the Salomon Brothers fiasco, as well as some clips from a Carol Loomis/Warren Buffett appearance on *The Daily Show with Jon Stewart.*

That was in addition to a very funny *Terminator* parody in which Warren wants to star in the movie with Arnold Schwarzenegger, only to be one-upped by Charlie.

Finally, a disco ball dropped in the convention center and the screen showed the Berkshire executives while the Village People song "YMCA" played.

Warren erupted from his chair and started enthusiastically dancing and doing the YMCA letters with his arms to the delight of the crowd. Everyone cheered and joined in.

I magically became collected, and I had regained my composure. I am not sure why, but perhaps it was the humor of the videos. I was calm and ready for the meeting to begin and excited to ask my questions.

The question-and-answer period commenced after Warren spent a few minutes on the first quarter's results.

Then he introduced the panelists. When he got to me, he said in his introduction that inviting a "credentialed bear" was an unprecedented move by a company and that he looked forward to the polemic.

Fortune's Carol Loomis asked the first question. Interestingly, the essence of her question—taken from an e-mail to her—embodied most of my first question that I intended to ask. Fortunately, I was prepared with some alternative ones!

My Conversation with the Oracle   I won't get into the questions now, but I will mention that I ad-libbed a bunch of times, starting with before I asked my fist question: "Warren and Charlie, thanks for the invitation today. I am honored. I am looking forward to the role of playing Daniel in the lion's den to both of you, and to the 45,000 of your closest friends and greatest admirers in the center today."

To my surprise, the crowd cheered for me.

At some risk, I started my first question off with a double entendre: "As it is said, Warren, size matters!"

My approach worked and didn't misfire. I think it even set up the tone well for the rest of my questions, putting everyone in a relaxed mood. My other attempts of humor worked, too. (Phew!)

Remember, I viewed my assignment as an opportunity to ask hard-hitting questions that were original, would elicit newsworthy responses, and allow investors and the crowd to get a different view (a skeptical one) about Berkshire Hathaway's prospects. At the same time, while asking pointed questions, I wanted to conduct myself with respect and to be courteous to the greatest investor of all time.

My six questions were diverse in context. They ranged from the issue of inevitable declining returns, which have been an outgrowth of Berkshire's remarkable success, to business strategy, investment process, a defense of short-selling, succession and so on.

I even issued a challenge to Warren in a question.

After he answered my first question, he lobbed me a "zinger" and a challenge: "Doug, you haven't convinced me to sell the stock, but keep trying!"

Warren answered most of my inquiries, though my last question—regarding his son Howard's eventual role as nonexecutive chairman of the board—was the one I felt he didn't answer fully. He may even have felt somewhat uncomfortable about it.

I also ad–libbed before that hard (and even uncomfortable) question when I framed it by saying, "Warren, you and I both have two sons that we love. You and I both have a son in the audience.

This question is not meant to be disrespectful, but I thought it was a question that must be asked."

That aside, there were a couple of spontaneous and amusing exchanges between Warren and myself, including the "Warren," "Doug," "Warren," "Doug" routine.

Another memorable moment: When I prefaced my questions in the afternoon by saying, "When you are gone, and we hope that's not for a long time," Warren quickly and cleverly quipped, "No one more than I."

I am also happy that I was successful in was bringing some levity into my serious questions, as I wanted to lighten things up. I even interjected a good quote from Mae West—another ad-lib—into one of my questions on investment process, as Warren has done over time in his Chairman's letters. The quote: "The score never interested me, only the game."

When the meeting broke up for an hour for lunch, I spent a lot more money buying souvenirs for my friends. Then I went to the special section reserved for board members and management for lunch and met a number of Berkshire's directors. For me, the highlight was when the husband of Warren's sister came up to me and introduced himself, telling me my first three questions were among the best ever asked at a Berkshire annual meeting.

At halftime, I also had a great interview with Susie Gharib on CNBC. I also did another interview with Lindsey Bell at *TheStreet*.

Overall, I couldn't be happier about my delivery and the substance of my questions. I believe they contributed to a value-added session by highlighting issues never previously discussed in this forum.

I hope Charlie and Warren agreed.

Interestingly, three members of the Berkshire Hathaway board of directors came over to introduce themselves to me after the meeting concluded—and they all said my questions were among the best in the last decade. Two of the directors said they were going to recommend to Warren that he have me back next year.

That would be some treat for me, as I would enthusiastically welcome the opportunity to challenge Charlie and Warren. I have a lot more questions to ask the Oracle.

My Berkshire Q&A Recap

5/7/2013

It's time to review the six questions that I presented to Charlie Munger and Warren Buffett at Berkshire Hathaway's annual shareholders meeting. I also have included their responses to my questions as well as six alternate questions that I was prepared to ask in the event that someone asked one of my primary questions ahead of me.

Going into the meeting, there were a number of subjects that I thought warranted discussion.

It was important for me to balance my hard-hitting and pointed questions with a courteous and respectful delivery, considering the extraordinary accomplishments of the men that I was addressing and the unique invitation to a short-seller who was negative on their company. Initially, each of my original six questions was far too lengthy (500–1,000 words). Given the setting and Warren's crafty ways of answering questions, my mission was to condense each into a tightly worded question.

That process took a surprisingly long time.

Let's start with the six questions I asked on Saturday. (I have marked with an asterisk the six primary questions that I had planned to ask. Three of my top six questions were previously asked so I used three of the alternate questions.)

1. Size matters: Berkshire's growth strategy—chasing elephants instead of gazelles?*
2. The Buffett factor: What happens when Warren has left us?

3. Does a Berkshire breakup make sense?*
4. Has Warren's investment process become less intense over time?
5. A short-selling challenge.*
6. Is Howard Buffett qualified to be nonexecutive chairman?

Question No. 1—Size Matters

Q: As it is said, Warren, "Size matters!"

In the past, Berkshire bought cheap or wholesale—for instance, Geico, MidAmerican Energy, the initial Coca-Cola purchase and Benjamin Moore. Arguably, your company has shifted to becoming a buyer of pricier and more mature businesses—for instance, IBM, Burlington Northern Santa Fe, Heinz and Lubrizol, which were done at price-to-sales, price-to-earnings and price-to-book-value multiples well above the prior acquisitions and after the stock prices rose.

Many of the recent buys might be great additions to Berkshire's portfolio of companies, however, the relatively high prices paid for these investments could potentially result in a lower return on invested capital. In the past you hunted gazelles, but now you are hunting elephants.

To me, the recent buys look like preparation for your legacy, creating a more mature, slower-growing enterprise. Is Berkshire morphing into a stock that has begun to resemble an index fund that is more appropriate for widows and orphans rather than past investors who sought out differentiated and superior compounded growth?

In the past, you have quoted Benjamin Graham, saying "Price is what you pay—value is what you get." Are your recent deals and large investments bringing Berkshire less value than the deals done previously?

A: Warren admitted that Berkshire won't grow as rapidly in the future as it has in the past but it will still generate a lot of incremental value. "We think we will do better than the giants of the past," he said. Charlie chimed in and said much of the same. Warren then exclaimed, "Doug, you haven't convinced me to sell the stock, but keep trying!"

Question No. 2—The Buffett Factor

"Warren," I said.

"Doug," he responded.

"Warren," I remarked again.

"Doug," he repeated.

And I felt that this exchange set the stage for a more relaxing repartee between us over the balance of the day.

Q: Much of Berkshire's returns over the past decade have been based on your reputation and your ability to extract remarkable deals from companies in duress as compared to the past when you conducted yourself more as a value investor, digging and conducting extensive analysis.

What gives you confidence that your successors' imprimatur will be as valuable to Berkshire as yours has been?

A: Warren responded by saying that when he is gone, Berkshire will remain the investor of last resort—the company will remain the refuge for distressed companies, as Berkshire will possess large amounts of capital and will be positioned to react quickly. "They will call Berkshire. And Berkshire's reputation will become only more solidified for providing capital in sound deals, when other people are frozen. When it happens when I'm not around, it will become more tied to the Berkshire brand." Charlie agreed.

Question No. 3—Does a Berkshire Breakup Make Sense? I started by saying, "When you are gone, and we hope that's not for a long time."

To which Warren quipped, "No one more than I!"

I then prefaced the question by saying that in response to a previous question, Buffett suggested that, in time, Berkshire might be more centralized in terms of management strategy.

Q: Warren, in the past, you have demonstrated a great respect for Dr. Henry Singleton, the founder and long-time CEO of the diversified conglomerate Teledyne.

You have written about Singleton:

"Henry is a manager that all investors, CEOs, would-be CEOs and MBA students should study. In the end, he was 100% rational, and there are very few CEOs about whom I can make that statement."

You have publicly stated that Singleton had the best operating and capital deployment record in American business.

Prior to his death, he broke up Teledyne into three companies. Dr. Singleton told our mutual friend Lee Cooperman that he did it for a couple of reasons.

There is one reason in particular I want to ask you about. According to Singleton, Teledyne was hard to manage for one CEO. What would you say about the Berkshire situation, given your company's greater complexity and the recent management issues over the past several years? And what is the advisability of restructuring Berkshire into separately traded companies organized along business lines?

A: Both Charlie and Warren spent some time responding to both the history of Teledyne, Singleton's role and Berkshire's structure. Buffett underscored his confidence in his current management team at the divisional levels. "Breaking Berkshire into several companies," he said, "I am convinced would produce poorer results."

Question No. 4—Has Your Investment Process Become Less Intense?

Q: Mae West once said, "The score never interested me, only the game."

Are you at that point now where the game interests you more than the score?

But before you answer, let me explain why I asked.

In the past, your research has been all-encompassing, whether measured in time devoted to selecting investments and acquisitions or in the intensity of analysis.

You were interested, in the old days, of knowing the slightest minutia about a company.

You once said in characterizing Ben Rosner, "Intensity is the price of excellence."

Your research style seems to have morphed over time from a sleuth-like analysis—American Express comes to mind, when you hired Henry Brandt (father of Ruane, Cunniff & Goldfarb's Jonathan on today's panel!); you and he conducted weeks of analysis, in site visits and channel checks.

Now, not so much in later investments. As an example, you famously thought of making the Bank of America investment in your bathtub.

There is an investment message of this transformation from being intense to less intense. Would you please explain the degree it has to do with the market, Berkshire's size or other factors?

A: Warren responded by saying that he finds running Berkshire to be the most interesting thing to do. "I have every bit of the intensity, though it's not manifested in the same way," he said. "I love thinking about Berkshire, about its investments, about its business. It's a part of me."

Charlie said, "It [research] is all cumulative."

In response to my Bank of America/bathtub reference, Warren quipped, "The bathtub wasn't the most important part!"

Question No. 5—A Short-Selling Challenge

Q: Warren, I am asking this next question because in the past you have been open to inviting your audience to apply for jobs. In 2002, you suggested that shareholders (who thought they were eligible) send in their qualifications if they were interested in seeking a seat on your board, and, again, in your 2006 letter, you advertised for a successor to Lou Simpson (former portfolio manager for Geico who retired in 2010). "Send me your resume," you said at the time.

In the past, you have discussed your views of short-selling. You have cited that stocks tend to rise over time, and you have expressed concerns regarding the asymmetry of reward vs. risk.

By contrast, the last 15 years has demonstrated that short-selling can be value-additive when done by professionals—for example, I believe Todd Combs had success as a short-seller before you hired him.

(Charlie then interrupted and said that Todd Combs "had so much success [in short-selling] that he stopped doing it," which drew laughter from the crowd.)

My question and challenge is would you ever reconsider committing capital to a short-selling strategy?

Would you or Berkshire consider being my "Homer Dodge," who invested in your partnership shortly after the original seven investors did?

Specifically, would either you or Berkshire Hathaway be willing to give my firm, Seabreeze Partners (specialists in short-selling), at least $100 million in a managed account (for no less than two years) that would be committed solely to a short-selling strategy?

If the Seabreeze account failed to outperform the change in Berkshire Hathaway's book value, all the earned fees (over the period) will be contributed to six charities in equal amounts: The Sherwood Foundation (the charity your daughter founded) and two other charities of your choice plus three charities of my choice, including Jewish Federation of Palm Beach County.

And even if Seabreeze did outperform Berkshire, 25% of the earned fees would be contributed to the charities.

I added that in a previous answer to a question, Buffett emphasized that he was technophobic and reluctant to invest in the technology sector. I emphasized that technology has been a disruptive force in a number of industries by virtue (or lack thereof) of its adverse impact on company business models. This provides a fertile ground for short-selling candidates.

A: Denied.

Charlie was emphatic. "No," he said.

Asked why, Warren uttered what I thought was the best line of the day, "We don't like trading agony for money."

Buffett then added, "But we wish you well."

Question No. 6—Is Howard Buffett Qualified to be Berkshire's Nonexecutive Chairman

Q: Warren, like you, I have two sons that I love.

Like you, I have a son in the audience.

This question is not meant to be disrespectful, but it is a question that I believe should be asked.

Someday your son will be Berkshire's nonexecutive chairman.

Berkshire is a complex business, growing more complex as the years pass.

Howard has never run a diversified business nor is he an expert in enterprise risk management.

Best as we know, he hasn't made material stock investments nor has he ever been engaged in taking over a large company.

Other than the accident of birth, how is he the most qualified person to take this role? Why should someone who has spent so little time with the company's managers suddenly become eligible for the position?

A: The response to this question, I felt, was the weakest of the six responses. Warren said that Howard would be the guardian of Berkshire's culture. "If a chief executive doesn't work out, having a chairman who cares deeply about the company's culture will make fixing the problem much easier."

Following is a list of the six unasked questions. (Again, I have marked with an asterisk the six primary questions that I had planned to ask. Three of my top six questions were previously asked, so I used three of the alternate questions.)

1. Is Berkshire too big to outperform?*
2. Are some of Berkshire's bank moats damaged or disappearing?*
3. Is the stock market overvalued by your metrics?*
4. Missed deals?
5. Regrets?
6. Is your optimism justified?

Unasked Question No. 1—Is Berkshire Too Big to Outperform? Historically, Berkshire's outperformance over the past 40-plus years has been spectacular. However, sustaining that growth is becoming more difficult to achieve.

You noted in your 2007 annual letter that, "Berkshire's past record can't be duplicated or even approached." And in almost every letter since that, you have uttered the same theme.

In the sole year of the last four (in 2011) that Berkshire succeeded in outperforming the share price of the S&P 500, it did so by a mere 2.5%. Even five years ago (in 2008), when performance was strong on a relative basis, Berkshire still recorded a negative return of −9.6% (while the S&P dropped by a staggering −37%).

Explain how Berkshire can persist in outperforming the markets while you continue to expand the size of your company.

Note: This question (one of my top six initially) was somewhat close to Carol Loomis's first question, so I canned it.

Unasked Question No. 2—Are Some of Berkshire's Bank Moats Damaged or Disappearing? A changing bank regulatory climate has put constraints on leverage and has produced less robust returns on assets and capital. As well, banking has become more homogenous and less differentiated, what Charlie and you describe as, "standing on tiptoe at a parade"—when one bank offers a new product, every bank has to offer or match it.

Given the fact that the banking industry has a lower profit growth rate potential going forward (think of it as damaged and shrinking moats of profitability), why is Berkshire continuing to acquire shares and becoming more exposed to banks, specifically Wells Fargo?

Note: This question, too, was one of my six original questions. But Charlie and Warren had already discussed the impact of Dodd–Frank legislation on reducing bank industry returns.

Unasked Question No. 3—Is the Stock Market Overvalued by Your Metrics? Warren, generally, you abide by Casey Stengel's old adage, "Never make predictions, especially about the future," and rarely make public comments about the market.

In 1999, however, you said, "One has to be wildly optimistic to believe that corporate profits as a percent of GDP can, for any sustained period, hold much above 6%." Today, that ratio has been stretched to over 10%, or 70% above 1999's level.

In the same year, you stated that interest rates "act to stock prices like gravity acts on matter." Today, interest rates are at generational lows and have little to go but up due to the "invisible pull of gravity."

Despite these concerns, you said recently on CNBC that you're buying stocks.

If interest rates are unlikely to fall much further and corporate profitability in relation to GDP must drop, then stocks, by your two key measures, are meaningfully overpriced today.

It's got to be one of two alternatives. Which is it, Warren? Are investors seriously overestimating future profit growth? Or is it different this time so that neither interest rates nor profit margins will mean-revert—that these factors have lost their relevance and investors are right?

Note: This question was among my first six, but it was asked by another questioner, though I forgot which one.

Unasked Question No. 4—Missed Deals? Over the past five years, you have mentioned that a number of deals that you worked on have never come to pass. I assume you signed confidentiality agreements in which you can't disclose the names of the companies. What industries did you pursue and why? What is it about the deals that attracted you and what business qualities/profiles were you looking for? If they don't have something in common, can you pick one, even the most important one that you missed and didn't get?

Unasked Question No. 5—Regrets?

Q: Mae West also said, "You only live once, but if you do it right, once is enough."

But everyone has regrets. What business regrets do you have?

Unasked Question No. 6—Is Your Optimism Justified?   Mark Twain said, "The man who is a pessimist before the age of 40 knows too much—if he is an optimist after it, he knows too little."

You seem to be growing more optimistic with age. In a new normal world, what do you see that makes you so optimistic?

Summary   Based on my previous company analysis, the recent quarterly results and after listening to the responses to my questions from Charlie and Warren on Saturday, I remain resolute in my view, and I plan to remain short on Berkshire's shares.

The Rabbi and the Oracle

6/4/2013

I spent two months researching for my questions that I asked at the Berkshire Hathaway annual shareholders meeting in early May.

> *"The nice thing about an agnostic is you don't think anybody is wrong."*
>
> —Warren Buffett

Part of my process was to interview a number of individuals who knew Warren Buffett but not on a business level. Some of those interviews were revealing and, in part, formed the basis of the questions I finally asked Warren and Charlie.

I want to pass on what I think is the one of the nicest tales I learned about, one that is not well known and has a beautiful ending.

It is the story of the relationship between Rabbi Myer Kripke and Warren Buffett. (Heartfelt thanks to Radine and several others who initially related the story to me.)

Kripke came from a middle-class family in Toledo, Ohio. He traveled to New York City 83 years ago to attend New York University and the Jewish Theological Seminary on 122nd Street.

At the Jewish Theological Seminary (the flagship institution of the Jewish Conservative movement), he met a Brooklyn girl, Dorothy Karp, and they married seven years later at the Seminary. The couple had little money, and the Seminary didn't charge the couple for the wedding.

Kripke, then a rabbi, worked at synagogues in Racine, Wisconsin; Long Island, New York; and New London, Connecticut. In the mid-1940s, he became the rabbi at Beth El Synagogue in Omaha, Nebraska. (Dorothy and Myer Kripke are the parents of three children, including the noted philosopher, Princeton University's Saul Kripke.)

In the early 1960s, while performing his rabbinical duties, Rabbi Kripke's wife authored several books on Jewish studies and beliefs. One of the books, *Let's Talk About God*, was read by Warren's wife Susie. (Susie Buffett's father was a minister in the Disciples of Christ Church, and Warren Buffett's parents were Presbyterians. Warren is religiously agnostic.) After learning that the Kripkes lived around the corner from the Buffetts, Susie telephoned Dorothy Kripke, and they soon became good friends.

At the time, Dorothy Kripke had developed a brain disorder and was usually bedridden. Once every week, Susie Buffett would take Dorothy to physical therapy. When she was well enough, the Buffetts and the Kripkes would play bridge together at their houses.

In time, the couples became closer, and the Buffetts began to host the Kripkes (with some other friends) at their house for Thanksgiving dinner. The Kripkes were kosher, and it became a tradition that Susie would serve the Kripkes tuna salad for the holiday and turkey for the other guests.

At the time, Warren had accumulated some wealth but nothing monumental. He was managing several partnerships for a small cadre of investors (mostly his family), and few had heard of him—he had not yet been crowned the Oracle of Omaha.

Rabbi Kripke never earned more than $35,000 in any year, but the Kripkes had been saving their money and, combined with an inheritance, had accumulated nearly $70,000. Myer Kripke's wife Dorothy implored him to "invest the money with your friend Warren." Three years later, he got the courage to ask Warren to invest his worldly savings, and Warren accepted the money into his partnership. When Warren closed his partnership, he suggested that the rabbi roll his investment into Berkshire Hathaway's shares, which he did.

In 1976 Rabbi Kripke retired from his Congregation in Omaha and began to teach at a Jesuit school, Creighton University. He also began to write for a Jewish newspaper.

Fast-forward 30 years after the time Rabbi Kripke invested in Warren's partnership and in Berkshire Hathaway—his original investment of about $70,000 was now worth almost $25 million.

The Kripkes, despite their enormous worth, were never big spenders. They never owned any real estate and lived in an apartment in Omaha that they rented for less than $1,000 a month.

> *"Dorothy once asked me, 'Wouldn't you like to buy a better car?' I said, 'There's nothing wrong with a Chevrolet.'"*
>
> —Rabbi Myer Kripke

By the mid-1990s, the rabbi's (now almost 85 years old) wife's health had deteriorated, and she was moved to a nursing home.

Rabbi Kripke felt he had a debt to the Jewish Theological Seminary, and, in 1996, he called Rabbi Carol Davidson, the Director of Planned Giving at the Seminary to make a gift of $100,000. At a meeting at Rabbi Kripke's house in Omaha, Rabbi Davidson suggested that Myer donate the money to help fix the Seminary's high tower—it housed the library where Myer studied decades ago—that was almost destroyed by a fire 30 years earlier (ironically, the same year that Myer gave his life savings to Warren).

Rabbi Kripke asked Rabbi Davidson how much would it cost to repair the entire tower, and she responded $7 million. "We'd like to do the entire amount," Myer said.

> *"Listen, I'm a rabbi, I believe it was destined. No such thing as coincidence here. . . . Most people would have considered putting everything into one investment stupid. . . . I guess it was stupid. It was chance, just chance."*
>
> —Rabbi Myer Kripke

In December 1996, the Kripkes donated $7 million (plus an additional $8 million was contributed in a deferred gift through family trusts), and the tower was fully repaired in 1997–1998.

And that, as Paul Harvey would say, is the rest of the (beautiful) story.

Lessons Never Learned

3/18/2014

"We learn from history that we do not learn from history."

—Georg Wilhelm Friedrich Hegel

Back 45 years ago, a successful investment manager wrote what follows in a letter to his limited partners:

> The investing environment . . . has generally become more negative and frustrating as time has passed: Maybe I am merely suffering from a lack of mental flexibility. (One observer commenting on security analysts over 40 stated: "They know too many things that are no longer true.")
>
> However, it seems to me that: (1) opportunities for investment that are open to the analyst who stresses quantitative factors have virtually disappeared, after rather steadily drying up over the past 20 years; (2) our $100 million of assets further eliminates a large portion of this seemingly barren investment world, since commitments of less than about $3 million cannot have a real impact on our overall performance, and this virtually rules out companies with less than about $100 million of common stock at market value; and (3) a swelling interest in investment performance has created an increasingly short-term-oriented and (in my opinion) more speculative market.

I feel very much like that 38-year-old investment manager, whose views arguably apply to the investment backdrop today.

That investment manager was Warren Buffett, and the paragraphs were extracted from the Buffett Partnership letter to limited partners in May 1969, in which Warren explained his decision to close his investment partnership. ("Therefore, before year-end, I intend to give all limited partners the required formal notice of my intention to retire.")

Warren went on in the letter:

> Quite frankly, in spite of any factors set forth on the earlier pages, I would continue to operate the Partnership in 1970, or even 1971, if I had some really first-class ideas. Not because I want to

but simply because I would so much rather end with a good year than a poor one. However, I just don't see anything available that gives any reasonable hope of delivering such a good year and I have no desire to grope around, hoping to "get lucky" with other people's money. I am not attuned to this market environment, and I don't want to spoil a decent record by trying to play a game I don't understand just so I can go out a hero.

I recently highlighted my concerns with emerging sectors of market froth/speculation, and I referenced a 1997 *Barron's* editorial I wrote, "Kids Today." I authored that Other Voices contribution to *Barron's* when I was approximately the same age that the Oracle of Omaha was when he wrote his 1969 letter in which he said, "If I am going to participate publicly, I can't help being competitive. I know I don't want to be totally occupied with outpacing an investment rabbit all my life. The only way to slow down is to stop."

Warren closed his 1969 letter with the following paragraph:

Some of you are going to ask, "What do you plan to do?" I don't have an answer to that question. I do know that when I am 60, I should be attempting to achieve different personal goals that those which had priority at age 20. Therefore, unless I now divorce myself from the activity that has consumed virtually all of my time and energies during the first 18 years of my adult life, I am unlikely to develop activities that will be appropriate to new circumstances in subsequent years.

As we all know, Warren Buffett, it turned out, was just starting his remarkable and unparalleled investment career in 1969. As it is said, "the best was yet to come" with his stewardship of Berkshire Hathaway in the decades ahead. (That, as news commentator Paul Harvey used to remind us on the radio, is the rest of the story.)

And to this day, Warren has not slowed down, though he will be 84 years young this August.

In closing, Warren's 1969 words and my 1997 editorial are two reminders to us all of how markets might not repeat themselves but they certainly rhyme.

Be forewarned.

Surprises

Introduction

Never make predictions, especially about the future.
—Casey Stengel

By means of background, in December 2002, I set out and prepared a list of possible surprises for the coming year, taking a page out of the estimable Byron Wien's playbook, who originally delivered his list while chief investment strategist at Morgan Stanley then Pequot Capital Management and now at Blackstone.

Lessons Learned over the Years

There are five core lessons I have learned over the course of my investing career that form the foundation of my annual surprise lists:

1. How wrong conventional wisdom can consistently be;
2. That uncertainty will persist;

"I'm astounded by people who want to 'know' the universe when it's hard enough to find your way around Chinatown."

—Woody Allen

"Let's face it: Bottom-up consensus earnings forecasts have a miserable track record. The traditional bias is well known. And even when analysts, as a group, rein in their enthusiasm, they are typically the last ones to anticipate swings in margins."

—UBS's top 10 surprises for 2012

3. To expect the unexpected;
4. That the occurrence of black swan events is growing in frequency; and
5. With rapidly changing conditions, investors can't change the direction of the wind, but we can adjust our sails (and our portfolios) in an attempt to reach our destination of good investment returns.

Consensus Is Often Wrong

It is important to note that my surprises are not intended to be predictions but rather events that have a reasonable chance of occurring despite being at odds with the consensus. I call these "possible improbable" events. In sports, betting my surprises would be called an *overlay*, a term commonly used when the odds on a proposition are in favor of the bettor rather than the house.

The real purpose of this endeavor is a practical one—that is, to consider positioning a portion of my portfolio in accordance with outlier events, with the potential for large payoffs on small wagers/investments.

Since the mid-1990s, Wall Street research has deteriorated in quantity and quality (due to competition for human capital at hedge funds, brokerage industry consolidation and former New York Attorney General Eliot Spitzer–initiated reforms) and remains, more than ever, maintenance-oriented, conventional, and groupthink (or groupstink, as I prefer to call it). Mainstream and consensus expectations are just that, and in most cases, they are deeply embedded into today's stock prices.

It has been said that if life were predictable, it would cease to be life, so if I succeed in making you think about (and possibly position for) outlier events, then my endeavor has been worthwhile.

Nothing is more obstinate than a fashionable consensus, and my annual exercise recognizes that over the course of time, conventional wisdom is often wrong.

As a society (and as investors), we are consistently bamboozled by appearance and consensus. Too often, we are played as suckers, as we just accept the trend, momentum and/or the superficial as certain truth without a shred of criticism. Just look at those who bought into the success of Enron, Saddam Hussein's weapons of mass destruction, the heroic home-run production of steroid-laced Major League Baseball players Barry Bonds and Mark McGwire, the financial supermarket concept at what was once the largest money center bank Citigroup, the uninterrupted profit growth at Fannie Mae and Freddie Mac, housing's new paradigm (in the mid-2000s) of noncyclical growth and ever-rising home prices, the uncompromising principles of former New York Governor Eliot Spitzer, the morality of other politicians (e.g., John Edwards, John Ensign, and Larry Craig), the consistency of Bernie Madoff's investment returns (and those of other hucksters) and the clean-cut image of Tiger Woods.

> *"Consensus is what many people say in chorus but do not believe as individuals."*
>
> —Abba Eban (Israeli foreign minister from 1966 to 1974)

In an excellent essay published two years ago, GMO's James Montier made note of the consistent weakness embodied in consensus forecasts. As he puts it, "economists can't forecast for toffee."

> They have missed every recession in the last four decades. And it isn't just growth that economists can't forecast; it's also inflation, bond yields, unemployment, stock market price targets and pretty much everything else. . . .
>
> If we add greater uncertainty, as reflected by the distribution of the new normal, to the mix, then the difficulty of investing based upon economic forecasts is likely to be squared!
>
> —*James Montier*

25 Surprises for 2003

12/12/2002

1. Retail spending drops precipitously in the first half of the year as a spent-up (not pent-up) consumer retrenches.
2. The Fed lowers interest rates and reduces margin requirements.
3. Home prices suffer their first annual decline in years, reflecting plunging consumer confidence, a rising unemployment rate and growing economic uncertainty.
4. The major market indices are flat on the year, but the year is volatile. The DJIA experiences a 750-point swing in one day.
5. Stilwell Financial, parent company of the Janus family of funds, is acquired by Fidelity Management. Fidelity goes public.
6. AOL Time Warner's AOL division experiences a net reduction in subscribers and Chairman Steve Case is forced out. Microsoft acquires the AOL division.
7. No further significant corporate frauds are discovered.
8. A previously well-regarded conglomerate is besieged by a liquidity crisis.
9. Ford experiences large losses. Chairman William Ford Jr. resigns.
10. Democratic presidential aspirant Al Gore bows out of the race, and a unified party rallies behind Massachusetts Sen. John Kerry, who is unopposed in the Democratic primaries. Vice President Dick Cheney leaves his post due to health problems and is replaced by Colin Powell. John McCain declares himself as a presidential candidate. Bill and Hillary Clinton divorce.
11. There are no major terrorist threats in the United States, but Israel is attacked.
12. No evidence of a weapon buildup is found in Iraq by U.N. inspectors. There is no U.S.-Iraq war.
13. The Japanese banking industry writes off nearly $1 trillion of loans. The Japanese yen plummets, and, as occurred in Brazil, the World Bank bails out Japan in the largest financing package in history.
14. The yield on the 10-year U.S. note drops to 3.25% as growing signs of deflation appear.
15. Germany's economic condition deteriorates dramatically amid that country's political overhaul.

16. Philip Morris cuts its dividend.
17. A major retailer files for bankruptcy.
18. A natural disaster devastates a major population area.
19. Tiger Management's Julian Robertson returns to the hedge fund business. George Soros officially retires.
20. General Electric again lowers its profit guidance.
21. Former New York City Mayor Rudy Giuliani announces his intention to run for senator of New York.
22. Merger and acquisitions activity hits a 25-year low.
23. Disney Chairman Michael Eisner is replaced.
24. Robert Rubin leaves Citigroup.
25. Tiger Woods wins three majors, the New York Yankees win the World Series, the University of Florida wins the NCAA basketball championship, the New York Islanders win the Stanley Cup, Toccet wins the Kentucky Derby, Army defeats Navy, the New York Jets win the Super Bowl, and the New Jersey Nets win the NBA championship.

Surprises in Store for 2004

11/26/2003

Some of my surprises were on target last year; to be precise, about one-third of the "possible improbables" came true. In particular, the following events had a familiar ring for readers of my "2003 surprises":

- We saw a 3.25% yield on the 10-year Treasury note.
- There was further deterioration in AOL's subscriber base, and Steve Case was ousted.
- The European economy was moribund during 2003's first half.
- The New Jersey Nets basketball team enjoyed surprising success.
- General Electric had lower earnings guidance.
- Democratic aspirant Al Gore bowed out of the presidential race.
- There were no major terrorist acts in the United States.
- UN inspectors found no evidence of a weapon buildup in Iraq.

Here is my list of possible surprises for 2004:

1. A revolution in Venezuela overcomes the existing regime in early 2004—four South American presidents have been toppled over the

past four years—cutting off oil production in that region and forcing crude oil to trade over $50 a barrel. The consumer is paralyzed, and retail sales nosedive. Rising energy prices and other cost-push pressures (such as health care and insurance) cause a mini panic in the world equities markets, and share prices plummet by more than 15% in a brief three-week period. At the same time, the U.S./China rift widens, and an all-out trade war ensues (albeit briefly), crippling the U.S. apparel business.

2. Interest rates plummet and the yield on the 10-year Treasury note makes a new low, briefly breaking below the 3% mark by midyear. We end 2004 at about the same levels that exist today.

3. Facing rising energy prices, the automobile industry's fortunes erode dramatically as the consumer is nonresponsive to further incentives. Ford loses more than $1 billion in the second quarter of the year. William Ford Jr. steps down.

4. With the cost of capital declining to unprecedented low levels, a relatively quick restoration of order in South America and the emergence of an overall calm in Iraq (as President Bush orders more troops in to stabilize that country), merger activity explodes and stock prices follow suit. The world equities markets end the year nearly 30% higher than the May lows and close at about 15% higher than year-end 2003 levels. Financial stocks and, briefly, oil stocks are the principal market leaders, but technology stocks languish throughout the entire year (portability proves to be a nonevent) and end the year slightly lower than at 2003's year-end.

Internet stocks prove to be one of the worst performing sectors of the market, after New York Attorney General Spitzer sues eBay and Amazon for nonpayment of state sales taxes.

Despite a widespread belief that housing activity will fall off the cliff, the rise in home prices (fueled by ever-lower mortgage rates) continues apace and begins to resemble the bubble in the Nasdaq of the late 1990s.

5. Beginning at midyear, Genworth Financial, the General Electric spinoff, embarks on a series of high-profile acquisitions (which include CNA Financial, Fidelity Financial and H&R Block), spurring an unprecedented round of industry consolidation in the financial sector.

6. After the mini panic in the markets in the first half, and in response to Genworth Financial's takeover announcements, the following acquisitions are announced and consummated:
   - Merck acquires Schering-Plough.
   - Fidelity acquires Janus.
   - News Corporation and MGM Mirage acquire a loss-ridden DreamWorks.
   - JPMorgan acquires Countrywide Credit.
   - Fifth Third Bank acquires National Commerce Financial.
   - Wachovia acquires First Tennessee.
   - GrupoTelevisa acquires Univision.
   - Wells Fargo acquires Capital One.
   - Tyco acquires Toll Brothers.
   - Citigroup acquires Alliance Capital.
   - Polo Ralph Lauren is acquired in a leveraged buyout.
   - Nike acquires Gap Stores.

7. The initial public offering (IPO) and secondary markets launch a meaningful comeback during the second half of the year. Indeed, the IPO market heats up and, similar to rising home prices, begins to resemble the bubble of 1999–early 2000 (something no one presumed likely).

8. Fidelity goes public in an IPO that doubles in the first day of trading.

9. A well-known and large hedge fund fraudulently misprices its portfolio of private investments and has a run on its assets. Calls for stricter regulation of hedge funds gain momentum as the Senate conducts public hearings.

10. Time Warner sells its AOL division to Kohlberg Kravis Roberts in a leveraged buyout during the third quarter after settling SEC charges in early January 2004 and as subscriber losses moderate.

11. Marsh & McLennan sells its Putnam subsidiary to Warren Buffett's Berkshire Hathaway. Marsh shares rise by more than 50% in the aftermath of the sale.

12. A low-cost airline carrier, which turned out to scrimp on maintenance and pilot training, crashes.

13. Tiger Management's Julian Robertson reemerges as a major force in the hedge fund community—after raising more than $5 billion for a new partnership.

14. Eliot Spitzer announces that he has no intention to run for public office and enters the private sector.

15. Robert Rubin leaves Citigroup and replaces an aging Hank Greenberg as AIG's chairman.

16. A unified Democratic Party rallies behind Massachusetts Sen. John Kerry after three state primaries. However, President George Bush wins the presidential election in one of the largest pluralities in history as Sen. Kerry wins only two states in the general election.

17. SunTrust distributes its 122 million shares of Coca-Cola in a secondary offering.

18. Freddie Mac's former executives are jailed, precipitating more restrictive rules governing derivative accounting at government-sponsored agencies and at other financial institutions. Rudy Giuliani is appointed Freddie Mac's chairman.

19. Bernie Ebbers, Dennis Kozlowski, and Scott Sullivan receive maximum-length jail sentences.

20. Disney's Michael Eisner is replaced by an executive at Procter & Gamble. Fed Chairman Alan Greenspan resigns owing to poor health.

21. The New York Stock Exchange (NYSE), in a stunning reversal, goes fully electronic by year end. John Reed remains as chairman and orchestrates the transformation. Goldman Sachs takes a $6.7 billion goodwill impairment charge off its 2000 acquisition of Spear Leeds, and LaBranche liquidates its assets.

22. Henry Blodget is hired as a research analyst by a second-tier Wall Street firm.

23. There are no major terrorist acts in the United States and limited disturbances outside our country during the year.

Some Surprises in Store for 2005

12/6/2004

Many of my surprises were on target last year; to be precise, almost one-half of the "possible improbables" came true, up from only one-third of my 2003 surprises coming to fruition.

In particular, the following actual events had a familiar ring for readers of my 2004 surprises.

- The No. 1 and most audacious forecast—that of a crude oil price of more than $50 a barrel—was realized.
- My interest forecast was spot-on (and equally audacious, at the time). I called for a bottoming-out in the 10-year yield at 3.20% when most were looking for an increase in interest rates (we were only a few basis points away) and a year-end yield close to the same levels of December 2003.
- The emergence of calm in Iraq, an absence of domestic terrorist incidents, still-low interest rates and an increase in merger and acquisitions activity contributed to a marked improvement in equities during the second half of the year. (It was an improvement, albeit far from our surprise of a 30% increase from the May lows and a 15% improvement year over year.)
- Merger activity accelerated, with, as expected, a plethora of bank stock deals leading the way.
- The automobile industry's fortunes declined dramatically.
- Despite widespread belief that housing activity would fall off the cliff, my expectation of a further rise in home prices, which began to resemble the bubble in the Nasdaq in the late 1990s, was realized.
- The IPO and secondary markets launched a meaningful comeback during the second half of the year.
- Calls for stricter hedge fund legislation made strong inroads.
- A unified Democratic Party rallied behind Sen. John Kerry, who won the party's presidential nomination.
- Questionable accounting practices at Freddie Mac led to more restrictive rules governing derivative accounting.
- The NYSE, in a stunning reversal, made plans to go fully electronic.
- There were no terrorist acts in the United States.

Possible Surprises in 2005

1. After a lackluster holiday retail season, the consumption binge of the last decade comes to an abrupt halt. Retail sales turn negative and home prices plummet (first on the East and West Coasts, then in the rest of the country) while (cost-push) inflation accelerates. The mini

panic of 2005 occurs—during a two-day period the stock market drops by 9%—as stagflation concerns surface.

2. U.S. equity prices drop by double-digit percentages in the first half of 2005 and, unlike 2004, show no recovery after the initial drop for the balance of the year.

3. The Japanese Nikkei is among the best-performing equity markets in the world; the London market is among the worst-performing equity markets.

4. In the face of a precipitous drop in the U.S. dollar (with the euro briefly trading at 1.55), the Fed drops its gradualist approach to monetary policy. Taking a tune from the Fed's moves in May and November 1994, the Fed tightens by 50 basis points and then by 75 basis points on two consecutive Fed meetings.

5. The year 2005 brings another large-scale, Long-Term Capital–like failure precipitated by an astonishingly large derivative loss that three major U.S. and overseas money center banks are partially on the hook for.

6. Europe sinks into a recession in the second quarter. The United States sinks into a recession in the fourth quarter.

7. After a brief move back above $50 a barrel, crude oil trades back to less than $30 a barrel as demand slackens in the face of a worldwide economic slump.

8. There are no major terrorist acts in the United States. England, however, becomes the target of a surprise contamination of that country's water supply by al Qaeda. Equity markets in England are closed for a 10-day period, and the price of agricultural commodities rises dramatically (reminiscent of 2004's rise in the price of crude oil).

9. The Bush administration imposes a national sales tax in an unsuccessful attempt to balance the budget. In the face of a world-wide downturn, the tax is repealed within six months.

10. Warren Buffett raises Berkshire Hathaway's stake in Coca-Cola to 13% by purchasing in a private transaction all 122 million shares owned by SunTrust. Berkshire Hathaway goes on a buying spree as equities tumble. Berkshire acquires Dow Jones at $58.50 a share and two troubled, publicly held reinsurers.

11. Citigroup's Bob Rubin takes over the reins at AIG from Hank Greenberg, who retires.

12. The junk bond market records its worst performance in more than a decade and underperforms almost every asset class in 2005.

13. The gold market records the best performance of any asset class in 2005, briefly touching $575 an ounce.

14. Housing stocks make nominal new highs as interest rates decline, but a series of order disappointments and guide-downs for 2006 make this sector among the worst-performing areas of the U.S. equity market as the inventory of unsold homes experiences a parabolic rise.

15. A subprime lender or subprime insurer fails.

16. A computer hacker generates a serious virus that infects a large portion of the Internet. This causes a problem for several weeks at Amazon, Google, eBay, Yahoo!, AOL, and many other sites.

17. Democratic aspirant Al Gore reemerges on the political scene. New York Sen. Hillary Clinton announces her intention not to enter the 2008 presidential race. Both former President Clinton and Chelsea Clinton announce their candidacies for political offices. Late in the year, Tom Ridge announces his intention to seek the Republican nomination for the 2008 presidential election.

18. Time Warner sells its AOL division to Marc Cuban in a leveraged buyout after the company settles Securities and Exchange Commission (SEC) and Justice Department charges and as subscriber defections moderate.

19. AOL founder Steve Case re-emerges on the corporate scene as the CEO of an Internet start-up that goes public and records the largest percentage rise in history of any initial public offering during its first day of trading.

20. Tyco embarks on a series of high-profile acquisitions.

21. The SEC's experiment in eliminating the downtick rule is abandoned coincidently with the double-digit decline in stock prices during the first half of 2005.

22. There is a major accounting irregularity (spring-loading earnings) uncovered in a highly regarded industrial conglomerate famous for its acquisitive appetite. Larry Summers leaves his post as president of Harvard University and becomes chairman of this troubled company.

23. Sumner Redstone gives Howard Stern permission to leave Infinity Radio earlier than his contractual responsibility and Sirius Satellite

Radio briefly trades at $10 a share. Subscription levels at Sirius fail to reach expectations, however, and the stock halves.

24. Health maintenance organizations (HMOs) become the new focus of New York Attorney General Eliot Spitzer.

25. The New York Jets win the Super Bowl, the University of Illinois wins the NCAA Basketball Tournament, and the New York Yankees capture the World Series. Pete Rose is elected to the Baseball Hall of Fame, and Barry Bonds is barred from baseball for steroid use.

Surprises for 2006

12/27/2005

About a fifth of last year's predicted surprises actually happened, which was down from the prior two years—nearly one-half of our prognostications proved prescient in 2004 and about one-third in 2003.

Two of our most accurate surprises related to markets and asset classes. We posited that the Nikkei would be among the best-performing markets in the world. Several emerging markets outperformed Japan, but Japan was probably the best performer among the more liquid international indices.

We suggested that the price of gold could briefly touch $575 an ounce (it hit $540) and would be the best asset class extant. Indeed, few markets rivaled gold in 2005.

Parts of Europe sank into a recession in the second quarter.

We said Hank Greenberg would unexpectedly retire from AIG; he did, though not voluntarily.

We thought the AOL division would be sold (to either Marc Cuban or Warren Buffett); recently a 5% position was sold to Google.

We envisioned a flattening in home prices in the late summer (and a buildup in inventory of unsold homes); this has transpired.

Let's move on to my list for 2006:

1. Anti-U.S. rhetoric in South and Central America becomes kinetic in 2006 and has broad market and economic implications. Presidential elections in nine Latin American countries put a plethora of

left-wingers in power, causing consternation in the Bush administration. Coupled with more aggressive nationalistic moves by Venezuela's Hugo Chavez, we see a turn to sweeping anti–U.S. policies.

This new wave of socialism and left-wing presidents contributes to a
series of moves to nationalize certain industries, and supply disruptions in
certain countries in South America are destabilizing, resulting in much
higher commodity prices during the year (including oil, natural gas,
copper, tin, and grain). The CRB Index approaches 375 (now at 326).

Fears of stagflation befall economies and markets dependent on
imports of goods from South America. Crude climbs to over $80 a
barrel, and the DJIA bottoms at 9,000–9,250 during the early
summer (and closes the year at the 10,000 level). Gold trades above
$675 an ounce sometime during the year.

2. Senate Judiciary Committee hearings on secret domestic wiretaps
authorized by President Bush—made without applying for a warrant
from the court that handles sensitive national security issues—find that
the surveillance operation was far broader than admitted by the
administration.

A special prosecutor begins an aggressive assault on the White
House that results in Vice President Richard Cheney taking the fall
for the administration and resigning by midyear. The president's
popularity plunges as memories of Watergate are resurrected and the
Democratic Party takes a large lead in preliminary presidential polls.
Condoleezza Rice is selected to replace Cheney as vice president.

3. The Fed, responding to the appearance of continued economic
strength in fourth-quarter 2005 and in January 2006, continues to
take the federal funds rate higher, just as the economy is about to
sour. Bernanke pushes for and proceeds with a 50-basis-point
increase in his first meeting as chairman of the Fed. (It turns out
to be the last rate change over the balance of 2006.)

As the Fed and ECB continue tightening and the Bank of Japan
ends its easing, bond yields initially rise early in 2006, but in the
second half of the year, the 10-year U.S. note's yield dips to 3.65% as
the market's focus moves toward potential rate cuts by the Fed and a
potential recession in late 2006 or early 2007.

4. By early in the second quarter of 2006, the consumption binge of the
last decade comes to an abrupt halt. Retail sales turn negative as the

American consumer (the straw that has stirred the drink of the world economies) folds like a cheap suit, and several former high-flying specialty retailers—such as Abercrombie & Fitch, Williams-Sonoma, Urban Outfitters, and so forth—exhibit surprisingly poor same-store sales.

Weakness in personal consumption is exacerbated by many external shocks, including rising commodity prices, lower home prices (leading to weakening job creation and the lost ability to extract equity), stretched affordability of the first-time and repeat homebuyer to purchase a new home, the absence of personal savings (and a safety net), rising debt-service requirements (proliferation and reset of floating-rate and interest-only loans), changes in credit-card payment requirements, and so forth.

5. A number of small-scale terrorist acts occur in the United States. A failed attempt to contaminate a major region of the U.S. water supply sends already high agricultural product prices (in large measure reflecting South America's instability) to record levels, creating another inflationary scare.

6. After the 50-basis-point increase in the fed funds rate and an uneventful January in the markets, stocks drop abruptly then quickly rally back. A conspicuous slowdown in retail sales hits equities again, however, and stocks only recover half of those losses.

The rise in commodity prices and the CRB Index (affected by political unrest in South and Central America and a rise in agricultural prices due to a terrorist act) bring the DJIA down to the 9,000–9,250 level in early summer, where it settles in for the balance of the year, though another sharp late-year rally brings the DJIA back to about 10,000 by year-end.

Volatility during this period rises dramatically—the S&P 500 routinely has 2% daily moves, acting more like a commodity than a stock index. Mutual fund inflows drop precipitously.

7. With confidence in the markets and economies deteriorating, merger-and-acquisition activity slows to a crawl. One large private-equity firm returns over $5 billion to its investors.

8. The best-performing equity strategy in 2006 is short-selling; the worst is aggressive growth (long-only). The junk-bond market records its worst performance in over a decade and underperforms

almost every asset class in 2006. The cable stocks, old media and high-yielding stocks (such as regional telecom companies) are among the best sectors. General Motors muddles through and ends the year with a gain of 25% (leading all other components of the DJIA) after Steve Miller (with financial assistance and the managerial support of Wilbur Ross) takes over the helm in a broad management shakeup.

Coca-Cola is a close second (buoyed by more stock purchases by Warren Buffett), and Verizon is the third-best performing member of that index. On the downside, the popularity of the exchanges (Chicago Mercantile, International Securities Exchange, Nasdaq, Chicago Board of Trade, etc.) wanes, and the stocks lead most sectors to the downside in 2006.

9. Corporate profits for 2006 are flat, decelerating sharply from the 7% increase recorded in first-quarter 2006.

10. The U.S. dollar's strong momentum and new paradigm bullishness in 2005 yields to weakness in 2006. As trade tensions mount with China (which in turn fails to ante up on its continued financing of U.S. consumption), inflation abruptly rises (within the context of supply disruptions) and the focus comes back to the U.S. current account deficit (reaching $900 billion, or 6.9% of GDP in 2006) and a stagnating economy as a consequence of reduced confidence in the president.

The current surge in tax revenue, which produced a reduction in the federal deficit, is reversed as tax-revenue growth normalizes back toward that of nominal GDP. Contributing to an expanding deficit are the Medicare prescription drug plan, spending on unmet infra-structure needs, the Homeland Investment Act (which encouraged repatriation of foreign profits to be taxed at low rates), hurricane rebuilding efforts, a pickup in bonuses (and other nonstandard income), and the normalization of individual nonwithheld and corporate taxes (both having previously benefited from a rising stock market and an increase in the value of homes, which served to increase capital gains).

11. There are three large-scale failures on the lines of Long-Term Capital Management—two in Asia and one in Europe—precipitated by an astonishingly large derivative loss for which two major U.S. and several overseas money center banks are partially on the hook.

12. A computer hacker launches a successful attack on a widely used open-source application of the Internet (which extends to closed, proprietary sites) causing chaos and turmoil over a month-long period at Amazon, Google, eBay, Yahoo!, AOL, and many other sites. The Internet HOLDRs Index drops by 20% in two weeks.

13. Google faces numerous legal and competitive challenges in 2006. Its leadership in search is threatened not by Microsoft or Yahoo! but by a cadre of high-profile engineers within the company itself who embark on their own search mission.

    The new competitive player is taken public by Goldman Sachs and has an instant valuation in excess of $25 billion after its IPO. Google's shares briefly touch $200 a share during the year as competition among the older and the new entities intensifies.

    Further hurting Google will be an attempt by the Federal Communications Commission to extend the definition of decency laws to the Internet, an adverse court ruling in the Google Book Search case, a patent issue that is brought up in the courts by content providers and a major privacy scandal involving the U.S. government.

    Most importantly, a suit claims Google has become a Web monopoly and is violating U.S. antitrust law. Microsoft's Vista is more successful than expected, and MSN search experiences a surprising gain of 10 points of search share after hiring two senior Google engineers who introduce massive changes such as eliminating clutter from its home page.

    A high-profile, content-rich media company will make available a free video product, hurting the launch of Google Video. Finally, Google will release far fewer services this year, disappointing investors, as the company realizes it must go through a consolidation phase in which it makes its existing services scale better.

14. Apple (and its iTunes) will not be immune from the problems facing Google as the music industry decides on new ways to control its distribution, just like in the good old days. In other Internet happenings: TiVo and Netflix will merge and the China Internet bubble will deflate.

15. Amid the market's gloom and doom, Warren Buffett goes on a buying spree (which emphasizes acquisitions in old media and the real estate industry). Berkshire Hathaway acquires Dow Jones & Company after

a proxy contest is instituted by some of the younger members of the Bancroft family. Buffett expands his involvement in the real estate sector after buying Countrywide Credit and a troubled, publicly held, substandard mortgage originator.

16. The bitter differences between New York Attorney General Eliot Spitzer and Ken Langone get more heated and Langone announces his candidacy for the Republican nomination for governor in opposition to Democrat Spitzer. With corporate contributions to his candidacy breaking all-time records and the backing of Hank Greenberg and former Goldman Sachs Chief John Whitehead, Langone narrowly defeats Spitzer in the general election. Langone resigns shortly into his governorship, saying he has made his point, and he directs Nassau County Executive Thomas Suozzi to replace him.

17. Carl Icahn means business this time with Time Warner. Enlisting Steve Case to run the company and Calpers (and two other large financial institutions provide the rest of the financing), he initiates a partial tender for a quarter of the company at $22 a share during the second quarter.

    Similar to the legendary cult movie *Putney Swope*, he swiftly gains control of the company's board of directors by the end of the third quarter. Toward year-end, Steve Case—in concert with Microsoft and Berkshire Hathaway—pays $18 billion for the AOL division of Time Warner.

18. Citigroup begins to undo some of the acquisitions that occurred during the Weil regime. Smith Barney is spun off to shareholders.

19. Vice President Condoleeza Rice (see Surprise No. 2), seen as a force of honesty and integrity, emerges as the leading contender for the Republican presidential nomination in 2008. Sen. Hillary Clinton decides to bow out as a candidate. She and the other Democratic presidential hopefuls uncharacteristically throw their early support behind Sen. Evan Bayh of Indiana.

20. There are no further meaningful natural disasters.

21. Osama bin Laden is found dead.

22. The hedge fund industry suffers outflows—in marked departure from the last decade—as the industry (similar to in the mid-1970s) fails to insulate investors from the bear market of 2006.

23. A large corruption scandal in Russia hits the emerging markets late in the year.

24. Japan's Nikkei—oblivious to the chaos in other world markets—continues to climb and briefly reaches the 20,000 level.

25. Economic growth continues apace in China and India, but a furious debate regarding the offshoring of information technology and service jobs continues, sparking a round of legislative protectionist initiatives. As a result, trade tensions mount among the United States, India, and China.

25 Surprises for 2007

12/11/2006

About one-third of last year's predicted surprises actually happened, up from 20% in 2005. Nearly one-half of our prognostications proved prescient in 2004 and about one-third in 2003.

Our most accurate sprang from a variant view of prices of a broad range of commodities—specifically the prices of the CRB Index, crude oil and gold. We expected the CRB Index to approach 375 (it stood at only 326 when the surprise list was published a year ago and peaked at 368 in early summer); we expected the price of crude to rise to $80 per barrel (exactly the price crude hit in July) and suggested that gold might rise to above $675 per ounce (gold reached $740 in May 2006). Our expectation of a sharp drop in the U.S. dollar was also realized.

- We accurately assessed the Fed's continued interest rate increases (despite the general view that the Fed would pause) earlier in the year. At the same time, our variant view that bond yields would rise in the first half of 2006 and then decline in the year's second half (in the face of a deceleration in the rate of domestic growth) was spot-on.

- We were also spot-on that the rate of growth in retail sales would slow in the second quarter of 2006 and that several high-flying specialty retailers such as Williams-Sonoma and Urban Outfitters would have disappointing same-store sales, although a large drop in crude oil and natural gas restored retail strength in the early fall.

- As we suggested, a Long-Term Capital–like hedge fund failure did occur, as Connecticut-based Amaranth's losses were on a par with the losses generated at LTC.
- As forecast, China and India's economic growth surprisingly continued in an uninterrupted fashion, but the outgrowth of weak median incomes for the average American worker stimulated more than 27 separate pieces of anti-China trade legislation in Congress.

25 Possible Surprises in 2007

1. Private-equity deals begin the year in a spectacular fashion, with two separate $50 billion acquisitions in January. A consortium of Silver Lake Partners, The Blackstone Group, Kohlberg Kravis Roberts, Texas Pacific, Bain Capital, and Goldman Sachs acquire Texas Instruments. Kohlberg Kravis Roberts leads a syndicate in the takeover of Caterpillar, the 55th largest company in the S&P 500.

   Later in the month, one of the largest buyouts in the history of the media and entertainment industry is made by Bain Capital and Thomas H. Lee Partners when they acquire CBS for $30 billion.

   In early February, Goldman Sachs (teaming up with Warren Buffett's Berkshire Hathaway) announces that it is considering a going-private transaction. The Goldman deal is abandoned three months later, as a fractured mortgage market leads to a standstill in deal making as the capital markets (and underwriting activity) seize up.

2. Robert E. Rubin returns to his brokerage roots and becomes the CEO and chairman of Salomon Brothers/Smith Barney after Citigroup decides to break up into three separate companies: a domestic money-center bank (Citibank), an investment banking/retail brokerage (Salomon Brothers/Smith Barney) and an international consumer finance company (Citiglobal).

3. Based on misleading government statistics, the housing market appears to stabilize in the first quarter of 2007. For a few months, those forecasting a bottom in residential real estate appear vindicated. Evidence of cracks in subprime credit is ignored, with housing-related equities soaring to new 52-week highs by March 1.

4. Continued heavy cancellations of home contracts, however, which are included in the government releases on homes sold and cause an erroneous inventory of unsold units for sale, lead to:
   - A dumping of homes on the market in the spring;
   - A quantum increase in the months of unsold housing inventory; and
   - A dramatic drop in the average home selling price.

   Sales of existing and new homes take another sharp leg lower as we enter what I've dubbed "The Great Housing Depression of 2007."

   Importantly, the financial intermediaries that source mortgage financing/origination begin to feel the financial brunt of "The Great Mortgage Bubble of 2000–2006" after years of creative but nonsensical, low-documented or nondocumented lending behavior.

5. Foreclosures steadily rise over the course of the year to nearly 3 million homes in 2007 vs. about 1.2 million in 2006. Deep cracks in the subprime market spread to other credits in the asset-backed securities market as a lumpy and uneven period of domestic economic growth takes its toll. In a similarly abrupt and dramatic manner, credit spreads fly open and revert back to mean valuations, as previously nonchalant investors are awakened to the reality of credit risk.

6. The magnitude of the credit problems in mortgages takes its toll on the hedge fund industry, which is much more exposed to real estate than generally recognized. A handful of multibillion-dollar, derivative-playing hedge funds bite the dust in the aftermath of the housing debacle. Several California-based industrial banks fail (the West Coast is always at the leading edge of financial creativity and leverage), and a large brokerage firm, heavily involved in fixed-income market-making and trading, faces material losses, and its debt ratings are downgraded. As the financial contagion spreads, rumors of a $10 billion-plus derivative loss at JPMorgan Chase (which ultimately prove to be false) spark the largest one-day percentage drop in its shares in the past 15 years.

7. In a panic, Congress announces a series of hearings on the derivative industry, and the Fed reduces the fed funds rate by 50 basis points in each of three consecutive meetings. Those efforts are too late to

affect the already weakening economy as the long tail of housing begins to affect not only consumer confidence and spending but also other peripheral areas of the economy.

8. Commodity prices begin to collapse even before the mortgage market fiasco, but the onset of the decline is initially ignored by stock market investors. The CRB Index moves below 300. Notably, crude oil falls under $50 in a deflationary scare as interest rate cuts fail to revive the economy. The yield on the 10-year U.S. note falls to below 4% and stays there over the balance of the year.

9. Corporate profits for 2007 end up virtually flat year over year, but the pattern is inconsistent. After rising 8% in first quarter 2007, corporate profits are down 5% in second quarter 2007, up by 2% in third quarter 2007 and back down by 4% in fourth quarter 2007.

10. Equity-market volatility, similar to credit spreads, rises exponentially. The S&P 500 routinely has 2% daily moves, acting more like a commodity than a stock index. Mutual fund and hedge fund redemptions rise dramatically.

11. Stocks begin 2007 the way they ended 2006—very strong—and the S&P 500 temporarily breaches 1,450 in February. But by the end of the second quarter, under the brunt of the mortgage implosion, stocks drop nearly 15% and remain relatively range-bound for the rest of the year. The S&P 500 ends the year at around 1,250, dropping by about 11% in 2007.

Reflecting the deflationary threats, one of the best-performing groups of 2006, industrial materials, morphs into the worst-performing group in 2007. With credit spreads flying open, the junk-bond market records its worst performance in over two decades and substantially underperforms almost every asset class in 2007. Technology, pinched by an abrupt demand plunge in consumer electronics, a listless response to Microsoft's Vista and a drop in business spending, ends the year with a 20% decline in value.

12. Fidelity Management announces the introduction of its first dedicated short equity product. Alliance Capital follows with a similar product shortly thereafter.

13. With confidence in the markets and economies ebbing, merger-and-acquisition activity slows to a crawl by May. Several leading universities and endowments, which previously underwrote large

private-equity commitments, announce that they are dramatically reducing their exposure to that asset class.

As the capital markets falter, institutional funds committed to real estate are also reined in, initially leading to a marked slowdown in the recent appreciation in office building values. While broadening economic weakness leads to only a slight rise in office vacancy rates, as the year progresses, vacancy rates deteriorate more noticeably. Real estate investment trust (REIT) shares get hit hard (and fall below net asset values), as the historic relationship between REIT dividend yields and the yield on the 10-year U.S. note mean regresses.

14. A well-known corporate raider finds himself with a concentrated portfolio of illiquid investments and suffers large losses. ESL's Ed Lampert cagily watches the early-year private-equity euphoria and does nothing, opting to shore up his liquidity. But as equity prices drop in the second half, he is joined by several previous corporate partners in making a large acquisition in the entertainment/media field by year-end.

15. America's growing dependency on convergence and connectivity (computers control power delivery, communications, aviation and financial services) becomes a battleground and launching pad for a series of cyberterrorism acts by a terrorist group in early 2007.

The first few virtual attacks are ignored and have no effect on the market or on the Internet. During a chaotic weeklong period after the July Fourth holiday, however, an attack renders the Internet partially ineffective, threatening to eradicate crucial information storage bases and to stop commerce and communication.

16. There are several political surprises in 2007. Most significant is that New York Sen. Hillary Clinton, citing personal issues, announces that she will not run for the Democratic presidential nomination in 2008 and that she will throw her support to former Vice President Al Gore's candidacy. Democratic hopefuls Barack Obama, John Kerry, Evan Bayh, and Joe Biden do not pursue the nomination, leaving Senator John Edwards as Gore's only viable competition.

On the other side of the ledger, Newt Gingrich is an early aspirant to the Republican nomination and, surprisingly, is in a dead heat in early polls against the favorite, Sen. John McCain, with Mitt Romney and Condoleezza Rice far behind. Rudy Giuliani does not enter the race after a *New York Times* investigative report uncovers some questionable business dealings.

17. After New York Yankee baseball team owner George Steinbrenner falls seriously ill, SAC Capital Partners' legendary Steve Cohen acquires a majority control of the New York Yankees and, at year-end, retires from active management at his hedge fund.

18. Wal-Mart fails to come out of its funk and reports five consecutive months of negative same-store sales. Overall retail spending follows the housing decline and briefly falls to levels that haven't been seen since the last recession as consumer confidence drops to lows not seen in more than 15 years. Purchases of discretionary items such as motorcycles, high-end kitchen appliances and jewelry suffer.

19. Google marches on, proving its skeptics wrong, and dramatically exceeds sales, profit and cash-flow expectations. Its shares approach the $650 level by early spring, after rising by more than $100 the day after first-quarter earnings are announced. Though results continue to beat expectations in the second and third quarters, the shares take a large hit after its domination and monopolistic position in search is questioned by legislators in a series of congressional hearings later in the year.

20. Saddam Hussein is assassinated in jail even before his appeal is concluded. Osama bin Laden is found dead, and initial reports indicate he has been dead for more than 12 months.

21. A series of corruption scandals in Russia hits the emerging markets in 2007, which further exacerbates the impact of uneven worldwide economic conditions and difficulties in the mortgage markets.

22. A large hedge fund lowers its investment management fees (to 0.5%) and incentive fees (to 10%). This effort, combined with the overall market weakness in 2007, leads to a 50% reduction in the number of hedge funds over the next 12 months.

23. With the hedge fund ranks diminished, commodities dropping in value and the appeal for alternative investments (private equity, real estate, etc.) moderating, the bullish chorus for a global liquidity case for equities becomes a faint whisper.

24. Maria Bartiromo leaves CNBC to join Joy Behar, Rosie O'Donnell, and Barbara Walters on ABC's *The View*. (At the same time, Elisabeth Hasselbeck gets booted off the show!) Another well-known CNBC anchor leaves to join a large hedge fund.

25. Amid the early 2007 stock market euphoria, Jim Cramer's *Mad Money* show goes prime time on CBS. But it is canceled during the midyear market meltdown and returns to CNBC by the fall. CNBC extends the show to two hours by year-end after *Cramer: The Movie* reaps $38 million in its first weekend.

20 Surprises for 2008

12/31/2007

Almost half of last year's predicted surprises actually transpired, up from one-third in 2006 and from 20% in 2005. Nearly one-half of the prognostications proved prescient in 2004 and about one-third in the first year of surprises in 2003.

But it wasn't the quantity of the correctly predicted surprises that made 2007's list a remarkable success, it was the quality, as I hit on nearly every major variant theme: the severity of the housing depression, the turmoil and write-downs in the credit markets, the curtailing of private-equity deals and the reawakening of equity market volatility.

Consider just a couple of these quotes from our surprise list for 2007:

- "A fractured mortgage market leads to a standstill in deal-making as the capital markets (and underwriting activity) seize up."
- In early 2007, "evidence of cracks in subprime credit is ignored, with housing-related equities soaring to new 52-week highs by March 1. . . . A dumping of homes on the market in the spring; a quantum increase in the months of unsold housing inventory; and a dramatic drop in the average home price. . . . Sales of existing and new homes take another sharp leg lower as we enter what I've dubbed 'The Great Housing Depression of 2007.' Importantly, the financial interme-diaries that source mortgage financing/origination begin to feel the financial brunt of 'The Great Mortgage Bubble of 2000–2006' after years of creative but nonsensical lending behavior."

It will be hard to do it again and beat last year's surprises, but without further ado, here is my surprise list for 2008.

1. The housing depression of 2007 morphs into the retail spending depression of 2008. Stubbornly high inflation coupled with a deceleration in the rate of job growth, which turns into job losses by midyear, and an absence of innovation (a creativity void in consumer electronic products and apparel) lead to an unprecedented and abrupt drop in personal consumption expenditures.

The Retail HOLDRs (RTH) exchange-traded fund declines from $94 to $80. Despite their apparent "value" today, retail stocks, especially women's apparel, are among the worst-performing stocks in the first half of 2008.

2. Under pressure from slowing consumer spending, disappointing capital spending and higher commodities, corporate profits drop 10% in 2008. Importantly, the pattern of economic activity grows increasingly inconsistent and lumpy, providing a difficult backdrop for corporate managers and investment managers to navigate.

3. The S&P 500 falls by 5% to 10% in 2008, and 2007's laggards and leaders continue to be the same laggards and leaders in the coming year.

4. With a continuation of the credit and liquidity crises and an increased recognition that financial retrenchment will take years (not months), volatility pushes even higher. Daily moves of 1% to 2% become more commonplace, serving to further alienate the individual investor.

5. The Fed embarks upon a series of moves to ease monetary policy in 2008. Nearly every meeting is accompanied by a 25-basis-point decrease in the federal funds rate even despite continued inflationary pressures.

Nevertheless the economy fails to revive as the Fed pushes on a string.

6. Growth in the Western European economies deteriorates throughout the year, and the markets in England and France drop at twice the rate of the U.S. market.

7. The Chinese juggernaut continues apace and, despite continued protestations of a market bubble, the Chinese market doubles again in 2008.

8. The Japanese market puts on a surprising resurgence as the world's investors respond to compressed valuations (vis-à-vis peer regions), reasonable multiples (absolutely and against Japanese bond yields), accelerated M&A activity, share buybacks and relatively strong corporate profit growth.

9. The administration's proposal to revive the housing market falls on
    its face (as the housing bust accelerates), and President Bush enlists a
    well-placed Democrat and former cabinet member to become the
    U.S. housing czar, who has the primary charge to propose and
    administer a massive Marshall Plan for housing.

    Several high-profile housing-related bankruptcies occur in 2008,
    including Countrywide Financial, Beazer Homes, Hovnanian, Stan-
    dard Pacific, WCI Communities, and Radian Group.

10. Financial stocks fail to recover. No financial company is immune to
    the eroding market conditions, the spike in market volatility, the
    uneven direction in commodities and currency prices. Even the leader
    of the pack, Goldman Sachs, makes several bad bets in the derivative,
    currency and commodity markets, and its shares begin to underper-
    form its peers as profit forecasts move lower.

    Citigroup halves its dividend, and the shares briefly trade in the
    mid-$20s. Asset sales and write-downs leave the bank crippled, and in
    late 2008 (after another capital infusion by Abu Dhabi), Citi is merged
    with Bank of America. Its new name is its old name: CitiBank.

    Bear Stearns is acquired by HSBC in a take-under (well below
    today's price), as investor Joe Lewis loses nearly $350 million on his
    near-10% position in the brokerage firm.

    Mutual fund outflows and uncertainty regarding the integrity of
    money market funds result in the asset-management stocks being
    among the worst-performing sectors in 2008. With private-equity
    deals at a standstill, Blackstone shares trade down close to $10 a share.
    Late in the year, CEO Stephen Schwarzman and his management
    group take the company private.

11. With the economy weakening and corporate profits tumbling,
    investors pay up—real up—for growth. The three horsemen—
    Research In Motion, Apple Computer, and Google—move into
    bubble status, and short interest triples as the naysayers increase their
    bets. Their shares double in 2008 even as most equities decline.

    Technology disappoints, as it becomes clear by the beginning of
    the second quarter that "double ordering" inflated recent revenue
    gains as the weakening consumers' appetite for electronics founders.
    Rapidly growing biotech names are embraced as their price-to-
    earnings ratios (P/Es) grow high into the sky and they become the

new big thing and market leaders. Housing-centric equities continue to deflate and mop up the rear.

12. Although private-equity M&A activity remains moribund, 2008 is highlighted by numerous mergers of equals as a weak U.S. economy necessitates the need for a strategy that produces synergies and cuts costs. Yahoo! and eBay merge. So do Amazon and Overstock.com.

13. A weakening economy will also hasten a number of divestitures. General Electric will sell NBC Universal to Time Warner, which will not sell or spin off AOL.

14. Reversing its recent strength, the U.S. dollar's value falls by over 10% in 2008 (and gold rises to over $1,000 an ounce). Despite the weak domestic economy, foreign reserve diversification efforts and the demand for higher interest rates cause the yield on the 10-year U.S. note to move higher throughout the year.

15. The price of crude oil, insensitive to a weakening world economy, eclipses $135 per barrel after an exogenous event of terrorism, supply disruptions or political upheaval. The $100 level becomes the new $70. Surprisingly, energy stocks react in a muted fashion to the rip in price, as, by midyear, the Democratic Party's populist view of a windfall tax on energy companies gains increased acceptance.

16. The Internet becomes the tactical nuke of the digital age. The Web is invaded on many levels as governments, consumers and investors freak out. First, an act of cyberterrorism occurs that compromises the security of a major government (similar to the attacks this year emanating from the Chinese military aimed at the German Chancellery) or uses a denial-of-service attack against media and e-commerce sites.

    Second, a major data center will fail and will be far worse than the 1988 Cornell student incident that infected about 5% of the Unix boxes on the early Internet.

    Third, cybercrime explodes exponentially in 2008. Financial markets will be exposed to hackers using elaborate fraud schemes (like liquidating and sweeping online brokerage accounts and shorting stocks, then employing a denial-of-service attack against the company). Fourth, Storm Trojan reappears.

17. The hedge fund community (especially of a quant kind) is disintermediated in 2008. Outflows accelerate, abetting an already

conspicuous trend of rising volatility in a market that behaves more like a commodity than ever.

18. There are several major Enron-like accounting scandals in 2008, causing investor confidence to plummet. These will come in some large financial and industrial (roll-up) companies in Europe and the United States.

19. Democrats Clinton/Kerrey and Republicans McCain/Crist represent their parties in the presidential/vice presidential contest in November. Ron Paul becomes the Libertarian candidate.

   In a remarkably close election (reminiscent of the Bush/Gore battle of 2000), the Democrats grab the White House.

20. The politics of trade become more fractious (even in the Republican Party), as angst about globalization escalates in the United States, reflecting inequalities and a cyclical contraction in our domestic economy. Doha dies. And the new big things (and the source of liquidity for the capital markets)—namely, sovereign wealth funds—become targets of American politicians (and suppress U.S. equities further).

20 Surprises for 2009

12/29/2008

Our surprise list for 2008 proved to be our most successful ever, with 60% of last year's "possible improbables" proving to be materially on target. Almost half of the prior year's predicted surprises actually came to pass, up from one-third in 2006 and from 20% in 2005.

Nearly of one-half 2004's prognostications proved prescient and about one-third in the first year of our surprises for 2003.

Investing based on some of my outlier events over the past 12 months would have yielded good absolute and relative returns and would have protected investors somewhat from the market's downdraft.

My surprise list for 2008 hit on a number of themes that dominated the investment landscape this year: the extent of the weakness in worldwide economic activity, the severity of the housing downturn, the collapse of retail spending, the obliteration of the hedge fund industry, the reawakening of market volatility, the spike in oil, the cessation of private equity deals and the steady drop in large bank shares.

- "The housing depression of 2007 morphs into the retailing depression of 2008."
- "With a continuation of the credit and liquidity crises and an increased recognition that financial retrenchment will take years (not months), volatility pushes even higher. Daily moves of 1% to 2% become more commonplace, serving to further alienate the individual investor."
- "The hedge fund community is disintermediated in 2008. Outflows accelerate, abetting an already conspicuous trend of rising volatility in a market that behaves more like a commodity than ever."
- "Job losses begin in mid-2008."
- "An unprecedented and abrupt drop in personal consumption expenditures occurs."
- "Retail stocks, especially women's apparel, are among the worst-performing stocks in 2008."
- "The Fed embarks upon a series of moves to ease monetary policy in 2008. Nearly every meeting is accompanied by a 25-basis-point decrease in the federal funds rate, even despite continued inflationary pressures. Nevertheless, the economy fails to revive as the Fed pushes on a string."
- "Growth in the Western European economies deteriorates throughout the year."
- "Financial stocks fail to recover. No financial company is immune to the eroding market conditions, spike in market volatility, the uneven direction in commodities and currency prices. Even the leader of the pack, Goldman Sachs, makes several bad bets in the derivative, currency and commodity markets, and its shares begin to underperform its peers as profit forecasts move lower. Citigroup halves its dividend. . . . Asset sales and write-downs leave the bank crippled."
- "Bear Stearns investor Joe Lewis loses nearly $350 million on his near-10% position in the brokerage firm."
- "Mutual fund outflows and uncertainty regarding the integrity of money market funds result in the asset-management stocks being among the worst-performing sectors in 2008."

- "With private-equity deals at a standstill, Blackstone shares trade down close to $10 a share."
- "Reversing its recent strength, the U.S. dollar's value falls by over 10% in 2008, and gold rises to over $1,000 an ounce."
- "The price of crude oil eclipses $135 a barrel."
- "There are several major Enron-like accounting scandals in 2008, causing investor confidence to plummet; these will come in some large financial companies in Europe."

Without further ado, here is my list of 20 surprises for 2009. In doing so, we start the new year with the surprising story that ended the old year, the alleged Madoff Ponzi scheme.

1. **The Russian mafia and Russian oligarchs are found to be large investors with Madoff.**

   During the next few weeks, a well-known CNBC investigative reporter documents that the Russian oligarchs, certain members of the Russian mafia and several Colombian drug cartel families have invested and laundered more than $2 billion in Madoff's strategy through offshore master feeders and through several fund of funds. There are several unsuccessful attempts made on Madoff's and/or his family's lives. With the large Russian investments in Madoff having gone sour and in light of the subsequent acts of violence against his family, U.S./Russian relations, which already were at a low point, are threatened. Madoff's lawyers disclose that he has cancer, and his trial is delayed indefinitely as he undergoes chemotherapy.

2. **Housing stabilizes sooner than expected.**

   President Obama, under the aegis of Larry Summers, initiates a massive and unprecedented Marshall Plan to turn the housing market around. His plan includes several unconventional measures: Among other items is a $25,000 tax credit on all home purchases as well as a large tax credit and other subsidies to the financial intermediaries that provide the mortgage loans and commitments. This, combined with a lowering in mortgage rates (and a boom in refinancing), the bankruptcy/financial restructuring of three public homebuilders (which serves to lessen new home supply) and a flip-flop in the benefits of ownership vs. the merits of renting, trigger a second-quarter 2009 improvement in national housing activity, but the rebound is uneven.

While the middle market rebounds, the high-end coastal housing markets remain moribund, as they are impacted adversely by the Wall Street layoffs and the carnage in the hedge fund industry.

3. The nation's commercial real estate markets experience only a shallow pricing downturn in the first half of 2009.

President Obama's broad-ranging housing legislation incorporates tax credits and other unconventional remedies directed toward nonresidential lending and borrowing. Banks become more active in office lending (as they do in residential real estate lending), and the commercial mortgage-backed securities market never experiences anything like the weakness exhibited in the 2007 to 2008 market. Office REIT shares, similar to housing-related equities, rebound dramatically, with several doubling in the new year's first six months.

4. The U.S. economy stabilizes sooner than expected.

After a decidedly weak January-to-February period (and a negative first-quarter 2009 GDP reading, which is similar to fourth-quarter 2008's black hole), the massive and creative stimulus instituted by the newly elected president begins to work. Banks begin to lend more aggressively, and lower interest rates coupled with aggressive policy serve to contribute to an unexpected refinancing boom. By March, personal consumption expenditures begin to rebound slowly from an abysmal holiday and post-holiday season as energy prices remain subdued, and a shallow recovery occurs far sooner than many expect. Second-quarter corporate profits growth comfortably beats the downbeat and consensus forecasts as inflation remains tame, commodity prices are subdued, productivity rebounds, and labor costs are well under control.

5. The U.S. stock market rises by close to 20% in the year's first half.

Housing-related stocks (title insurance, home remodeling, mortgage servicers, and REITs) exhibit outsized and market-leading gains during the January-to-June interval. Heavily shorted retail and financial stocks also advance smartly. The year's first-half market rise of about 20% is surprisingly orderly throughout the six-month period, as volatility moves back down to pre-2008 levels, but rising domestic interest rates, still-weak European economies and a halt to China's economic growth limit the stock market's progress in the back half of the year.

6. A second-quarter "growth scare" bursts the bubble in the government bond market.

The yield on the 10-year U.S. Treasury note moves steadily higher from 2.10% at year-end to over 3.50% by early fall, putting a ceiling on the first-half recovery in the U.S. stock market, which is range-bound for the remainder of the year, settling up by approximately 20% for the 12-month period ending December 31, 2009. Foreign central banks, faced with worsening domestic economies, begin to shy away from U.S. Treasury auctions and continue to diversify their reserve assets. By year-end, the U.S. dollar represents less than 60% of worldwide reserve assets, down from 2008's year-end at 62% and down from 70% only five years ago. China's 2008 economic growth proves to be greatly exaggerated as unemployment surprisingly rises in early 2009 and the rate of growth in China's real gross domestic product (GDP) moves toward zero by the second quarter. Unlike more developed countries, the absence of a social safety net turns China's fiscal economic policy inward and aggressively so. Importantly, China not only is no longer a natural buyer of U.S. Treasuries but it is forced to dip into its piggy bank of foreign reserves, adding significant upside pressure to U.S. note and bond yields.

7. Commodities markets remain subdued.

Despite an improving domestic economy, a further erosion in the Western European and Chinese economies weighs on the world's commodities markets. Gold never reaches $1,000 an ounce and trades at $500 an ounce at some point during the year. (Gold-related shares are among 2009's worst stock market performers.) The price of crude oil briefly rallies early in the year after a step up in the violence in the Middle East but trades in a broad $25 to $65 range for all of 2009 as President Obama successfully introduces aggressive and meaningful legislation aimed at reducing our reliance on imported oil. The price of gasoline briefly breaches $1.00 a gallon sometime in the year. The U.S. dollar outperforms most of the world's currencies, as the U.S. regains its place as an economic and political powerhouse.

8. Capital spending disappoints further.

Despite an improving economy, large-scale capital spending projects continue to be delayed in favor of maintenance spending.

Technology shares continue to lag badly, and Advanced Micro Devices files bankruptcy.

9. The hedge fund and fund-of-funds industries do not recover in 2009.

The Madoff fraud, poor hedge fund performance, and renewed controversy regarding private-equity marks (particularly among a number of high-profile colleges such as Harvard and Yale) prove to be a short-term death knell to the alternative investments industry. As well, the gating of redemption requests disaffects high net worth, pension plan, endowment and university investors to both traditional hedge funds and to private equity (which suffers from a series of questionable and subjective marking of private-equity deal pricings at several leading funds). Three of the 10 largest hedge funds close their doors as numerous hedge funds reduce their fee structures in order to retain investors. Faced with an increasingly uncertain investor base, several big hedge funds merge with like-sized competitors in a quickening hedge fund industry consolidation. By year-end, the number of hedge funds is down by well over 50%.

10. Mutual fund redemptions from 2008 reverse into inflows in 2009.

The mutual fund industry does not suffer the same fate as the hedge fund industry. In fact, a renaissance of interest in mutual funds (especially of a passive/indexed kind) develops. Fidelity is the largest employer of the graduating classes (May 2009) at the Wharton and Harvard Business Schools; it goes public in late 2009 in the year's largest IPO. Shares of T. Rowe Price and AllianceBernstein enjoy sharp price gains in the new year. Bill Miller retires from active fund management at Legg Mason.

11. State and municipal imbalances and deficits mushroom.

The municipal bond market seizes up in the face of poor fiscal management, revenue shortfalls and rising budgets at state and local levels. Municipal bond yields spike higher. A new municipal TARP totaling $2 trillion is introduced in the year's second half.

12. The automakers and the UAW come to an agreement over wages.

Under the pressure of late first-quarter bankruptcies, the UAW agrees to bring compensation in line with non-U.S. competitors and exchanges a reduction in retiree health care benefits for equity in the major automobile manufacturers.

13. The new administration replaces SEC Commissioner Cox.

Upon his inauguration, President Obama immediately replaces SEC Commissioner Christopher Cox with Yale professor Dr. Jeffrey Sonnenfeld. The new SEC commissioner recommends that the uptick rule be reinstated and undertakes a yearlong investigation/analysis into the impact of ultra-bear ETFs on the market. Later in the year, the administration recommends that the SEC be abolished and folded into the Treasury Department. Dr. Sonnenfeld returns to Yale University.

14. Large merger of equals deals multiply.

Economies of scale and mergers of equals become the M&A mantras in 2009, and niche investment banking boutiques such as Evercore, Lazard and Greenhill flourish. Goldman Sachs and Citigroup announce a merger of equals, but Goldman maintains management control of the combined entity. Morgan Stanley acquires Blackstone. Disney purchases Carnival. Microsoft acquires Yahoo! at $5 a share.

15. Focus shifts for several media darlings.

Though continuing on CNBC, Jim Cramer announces his own reality show that will air on NBC in the fall. At the time his reality show premieres, he also writes a new book, *Stay Mad for Life: How to Prosper From a Buy/Hold Investment Strategy.* Dr. Nouriel Roubini continues to talk depression, but the prices of his speaking engagements are cut in half. He writes a new book, *The New Depression: How Leverage's Long Tail Will Result in Bread Lines. Kudlow & Company's* Larry Kudlow proclaims that it's time to harvest the "mustard seeds" of growth and, in an admission of the Democrats' growing economic successes, officially leaves the ranks of the Republican Party and returns to his Democratic roots. Yale's Dr. Robert Shiller adopts a variant and positive view on housing and the economy, joining the bullish ranks, and writes a new book, *The New Financial Order: Economic Opportunity in the 21st Century.*

16. The Internet becomes the tactical nuke of the digital age.

The Web is invaded on many levels as governments, consumers and investors freak out. First, an act of cyberterrorism occurs that compromises the security of a major government or uses a denial-of-service attack against media and e-commerce sites. Second, a major data center will fail and will be far worse than the 1988 Cornell student incident that infected about 5% of the Unix boxes on the early Internet. Third, cybercrime explodes exponentially in 2009. Financial markets will be exposed to hackers using elaborate fraud schemes (such as liquidating and sweeping online brokerage accounts and shorting stocks, then employing a denial-of-service attack against the company). Fourth, Storm Trojan reappears. (Same as last year.)

17. A handful of sports franchises file bankruptcy.

Three Major League Baseball teams fail in the middle of the season and seek government bailouts in order to complete the season. The Wilpon family, victimized by Madoff, sells the New York Mets to SAC's Steve Cohen. The New York Yankees are undefeated in the 2009 season, and Madonna and A-Rod have a child together (out of wedlock).

18. The Fox Business Network closes.

Racked by large losses, Rupert Murdoch abandons the Fox Business Network. CNBC rehires several prior employees and expands its programming into complete weekend coverage. Two popular CNBC commentators "go mainstream" and become regulars on NBC news programs.

19. Old, leveraged media implode.

The worlds of leverage and old media collide in a massive flameout of previous leveraged deals. Univision and Clear Channel go bankrupt. The *New York Times* teeters financially.

20. The Middle East's infrastructure build-out is abruptly halted owing to market conditions.

Lower oil prices, weakening European economies and a broad overexpansion wreak havoc with the Middle East's markets and economies.

20 Surprises for 2010

12/21/2009

Once again, 2009 proved how wrong "groupstink" and conventional wisdom can be.

While I failed to surpass our most successful year of surprises in 2008, during which 60% of the year's "possible improbables" were on target, I still had a very successful surprise list in 2009, with approximately half of our predicted surprises actually coming to pass. In fact, over the past three years (since and including 2007), at least 50% of our surprises proved accurate, which is up from one-third in 2006 and from 20% in 2005. Nearly one-half of 2004's prognostications proved prescient, and about one-third came to pass in the first year of our surprises for 2003.

Investing based on some of my outlier events over the past 12 months would have yielded good absolute and relative returns, would have protected investors somewhat from the market's downdraft into early March, and would have helped investors navigate the market's historic recovery over the past eight months.

My surprise list for 2009 hit on a number of important themes that dominated the investment and economic landscape this year. Most important, despite the economic and credit despair that existed 12 months ago, I accurately predicted the surprise that the economy and the housing market would recover well ahead of expectations. On the negative side, I was correct in predicting cascading financial conditions for U.S. municipalities and in the forecast for an abrupt halt in the Middle East infrastructure build.

Below is a list of the accurate surprises from last year's list:

- The Russian mafia and Russian oligarchs are found to be large investors with Madoff.
- Housing stabilizes sooner than expected.
- The nation's commercial real estate markets experience only a shallow pricing downturn in the first half of 2009.
- The U.S. economy stabilizes sooner than expected.
- Capital spending disappoints further.
- Mutual fund redemptions from 2008 reverse into inflows in 2009.
- State and municipal imbalances and deficits mushroom.
- The Internet becomes the tactical nuke of the digital age.
- A handful of sports franchises file bankruptcy.
- Old, leveraged media implode.
- The Middle East's infrastructure build-out is abruptly halted owing to market conditions.

So, without further ado, here is my list of 20 surprises for 2010:

1. There is a glaring upside to first-quarter 2010 corporate profits (up 100% year over year) and first-quarter 2010 GDP (up 4.5%).

It grows clear that, owing to continued draconian cost cuts, coupled with a series of positive economic releases and a long list of company profit guidance increases in mid to late January and early February, there is a very large upside to first-quarter GDP (up 4.5%) and, even more important, to S&P profit growth (which doubles). The upside on both counts is in sharp contrast to more muted growth expectations. While corporate managers, economists and strategists raise earnings per share, full-year growth and S&P target estimates, surprisingly, the U.S. equity market fails to respond positively to the much better growth dynamic, and the S&P 500 remains tightly range-bound (between 1,050 and 1,150) into spring 2010.

2. Housing and jobs fail to revive.

An outsized first-quarter 2010 GDP (up 4.5.%) print is achieved despite a still-moribund housing market and without any meaningful improvement in the labor market (excluding the increase in census workers), as corporations continue to cut costs and show little commitment to adding permanent employees.

3. The U.S. dollar explodes higher.

After dropping by over 40% from 2001 to 2008, the U.S. dollar continued to spiral lower in the last nine months of 2009. Our currency's recent strength will persist, however, surprising most market participants by continuing to rally into first quarter 2010. In fact, the U.S. dollar will be the strongest major world currency during the first three or four months of the new year.

4. The price of gold topples.

Gold's price plummets to $900 an ounce by the beginning of second quarter 2010. Unhedged, publicly held gold companies report large losses, and the gold sector lies at the bottom of all major sector performers. Hedge fund manager John Paulson abandons his plan to bring a new dedicated gold hedge fund to market.

5. Central banks tighten earlier than expected.

China, facing reported inflation approaching 5%, tightens monetary and fiscal policy in March, a month ahead of a Fed tightening of 50 basis points, which, with the benefit of hindsight, is a policy mistake.

6. A Middle East peace is upended due to an attack by Israel on Iran.

Israel attacks Iran's nuclear facilities before midyear. An already comatose U.S. consumer falls back on its heels, retail spending plummets, and the personal savings rate approaches 10%. The first-quarter spike in domestic growth is short-lived as GDP abruptly stalls.

7. Stocks drop by 10% in the first half of next year.

In the face of renewed geopolitical tensions and reduced world-wide growth expectations, stocks drop as the threat of an economic double-dip grows. Surprisingly, though, the drop in the major indices is contained, and the U.S. stock market retreats by less than 10% from year-end 2009 levels.

8. Goldman Sachs goes private.

Goldman Sachs stock drops back to $125 to $130 a share, within $15 of the warrant exercise price that Warren Buffett received in Berkshire Hathaway's late-2008 investment in Goldman Sachs. Sick of the unrelenting compensation outcry, government jawboning, and associated populist pressures, Warren Buffett teams up with Goldman Sachs to take the investment firm private. The deal is completed by year-end.

9. Second-half 2010 GDP growth turns flat.

The Goldman Sachs transaction stabilizes the markets, which are stunned by an extended Middle East conflict that continues through-out the summer and into the early fall. While a diplomatic initiative led by the United States serves to calm Mideast tensions, flat second-half U.S. GDP growth and a still high 9.5% to 10.0% unemployment rate caps the U.S. stock market's upside and leads to a very dull second half, during which share prices virtually flatline (with surprisingly limited rallies and corrections throughout the entire six-month period). For the full year, the S&P 500 exhibits a 10% decline vs. the general consensus of leading strategists for about a 10% rise in the major indices.

10. Rate-sensitive stocks outperform; metals underperform.

Utilities are the best performing sector in the U.S. stock market in 2010; gold stocks are the worst performing group, with consumer discretionary coming in as a close second.

11. Treasury yields fall.

The yield of the 10-year U.S. note drops from 4% at the end of the first quarter to under 3% by the summer and ends the year at approximately the same level (3%). Despite the current consensus that higher inflation and interest rates will weigh on the fixed-income markets, bonds surprisingly outperform stocks in 2010.

A plethora of specialized domestic and non–U.S. fixed-income exchange-traded funds are introduced throughout the year, setting the stage for a vast speculative top in bond prices, but that is a late-2011 issue.

12. Warren Buffett steps down.

Warren Buffett announces that he is handing over the investment reins to a Berkshire outsider and that he plans to also announce his in-house successor as chief operating officer by Berkshire Hathaway's annual shareholders meeting in 2011.

13. Insider trading charges expand.

The SEC alleges, in a broad-ranging sting, the existence of extensive exchange of information that goes well beyond Galleon's Silicon Valley executive connections. Several well-known, long-only mutual funds are implicated in the sting, which reveals that they have consistently received privileged information from some of the largest public companies over the past decade.

14. The SEC launches an assault on mutual fund expenses.

The SEC restricts 12b-1 mutual fund fees. In response to the proposal, asset management stocks crater.

15. The SEC restricts short-selling.

The SEC announces major short-selling bans after stocks sag in the second quarter.

16. More hedge fund tumult emerges.

Two of the most successful hedge fund managers extant announce their retirement and fund closures. One exits based on performance problems, the other based on legal problems.

17. Pandit is out and Cohen is in at Citigroup.

Citigroup's Vikram Pandit is replaced by former Shearson Lehman Brothers Chairman Peter Cohen. Cohen replaces a number of senior Citigroup executives with Ramius Partners colleagues. Sandy Weill rejoins Citigroup as a senior consultant.

18. A weakened Republican Party is in disarray.

Sarah Palin announces that she has separated from her husband, leaving the Republican Party firmly in the hands of former Massachusetts Governor Mitt Romney. An improving economy in early 2010 elevates President Obama's popularity back to pre-inauguration levels, and, despite the market's second-quarter decline, the country

comes together after the Middle East conflict, producing a tidal
wave of populism that moves ever more dramatically in legislation
and spirit. With the Democratic tsunami revived, the party wins
November midterm elections by a landslide.

19. Tiger Woods makes a comeback.

Tiger Woods and his wife reconcile in early 2010, and he returns
earlier than expected to the PGA tour. After announcing that his wife
is pregnant with their third child, both the PGA tour's and Tiger
Woods' popularity rise to record levels, and the golfer signs a series of
new commercial contracts that insure him a record $150 million of
endorsement income in 2011.

20. The New York Yankees are sold to a Jack Welch–led investor
group.

The Steinbrenner family decides, for estate purposes, to sell the
New York Yankees to a group headed by former General Electric
Chairman Jack Welch.

15 Surprises for 2011

12/27/2010

Last year's surprise list had relatively poor results. Only about 40% of my
surprises were achieved in 2010, well under the success ratio in previous
years. By means of background, about 50% of my 2009 surprises were
realized, 60% in 2008, 50% in 2007, one-third in 2006, one-fifth in
2005, 45% in 2004, and one-third came to pass in the first year of our
surprises in 2003.

While my surprise list for 2010 hit on some of the important themes
that dominated the investment and economic landscape this year, I failed
to expect the announcement of further quantitative easing and did not
accurately gauge investors' animal spirits that followed the proclamation
of QE2.

Below are some of my meticulous surprises from last year's list:

- *Economy*. Real GDP and corporate profit growth was, as I suggested,
  far better than expected during the first half of 2010, and my surprise
  that U.S. equities would weaken (and that P/E ratios would contract)

despite that strength was accurate (in that stocks exhibited a negative return during that period).

- *Housing and jobs.* Despite the overall economic strength, both housing and employment failed to recover.
- *Interest rates.* My surprise that the yield on the 10-year U.S. note would fall under 3% by midyear and end 2010 at about 3% was prescient.
- *SEC investigations.* The broadening of the SEC's assault on insider trading was a featured story in 2010.
- *The Oracle of Omaha.* Though Warren Buffett is still at the helm, our surprise that he would announce a possible successor was accurate.
- *Hedge funds.* Brilliant and legendary hedge-hogger Stanley Druckenmiller announced that he was leaving the investment business—in line with our surprise that a leading hedge-hogger would announce his retirement.

What follows is my list of 15 Surprises for 2011—reduced from 20 surprises in previous year in order to be more on point. I have listed my surprises in four categories—economic (surprise Nos. 1–3), stock market (surprise Nos. 4–6), political (surprise Nos. 7–9) and general (surprise Nos. 10–15).

1. In line with consensus, the domestic economy experiences a strong first half, but several factors conspire to produce a weakening second half, which jeopardizes corporate profit growth forecasts.
   - The improving momentum of domestic growth at the end of 2010 continues into the first half of 2011 but proves ephemeral by the summer.
   - That improving momentum turns out to be nothing more than a brief respite and "recession fatigue," as reality and a new normal sets in.
   - Americans remain in a foul mood, as the jobs market fails to improve despite the recent downtick in claims.
   - Over there, multiple country austerity programs move Europe back into recession by year-end 2011. (Share prices of many large multinational industrials falter in the year's second half.)

- China continues to tighten, but inflation remains persistent, economic growth disappoints (see surprise No. 15), and its stock market weakens further.
- Political gridlock and inertia in tackling the deficit incite the bond vigilantes. The yield on the 10-year U.S. note rises above 4.50% by the spring (see surprise No. 2).
- Trust continues to be lost, as the uncertainty brought by changes in the administration (see surprise No. 7) and the emergence of a third political party (see surprise No. 8) adversely impact consumer and corporate confidence.
- Housing fades under the pressure of higher mortgage rates and the supply of shadow inventory coming onto the market in an avalanche of foreclosures. (A housing czar is named to implement a Marshall Plan for housing.)
- An across-the-board spike in commodities pressures corporate profit margins and real disposable incomes (see surprise No. 3).
- Price controls are briefly considered (and then rejected) by the Obama administration as oil soars to over $125 a barrel.

"The first thing we do, let's kill all the lawyers."

—William Shakespeare, *Henry VI, Part 2*

"The day the Fed came into being in 1913 may have been the beginning of the end, but the powers it obtained and the mischief it caused took a long time to become a serious issue and a concern for average Americans."

—Ron Paul, *End the Fed*

2. Partisan politics cuts into business and consumer confidence and economic growth in the last half of 2011.

Increased hostilities between the Republicans and Democrats become a challenge to the market and to the economic recovery next year. As the 2012 election moves closer, President Obama reverses his seemingly newly minted centrist views, as newly appointed Vice President Hillary Clinton becomes the administration's pit bull against the Republican opposition.

On the other side of the pew, as chairman of the Subcommittee on

Domestic Monetary Policy, Congressman Ron Paul's fervent criticism of monetary policy and the lack of transparency of the Fed leads to further friction between the parties.

Sarah Palin, who can see the 2012 presidential election from her home in Alaska, continues her barbs against the opposition party and holds a large lead to be her party's presidential candidate in early 2011, but continued verbal and nonverbal blunders and policy errors coupled with an announcement that she has separated from her husband cause Palin to announce that she will not run on the Republican ticket.

> *"'Refudiate,' 'misunderestimate,' 'wee-wee'd up.' English is a living language. Shakespeare liked to coin new words, too. Got to celebrate it!'"*
>
> —Sarah Palin

Massachusetts's Mitt Romney, Wisconsin's Paul Ryan, and South Dakota's John Thune emerge as the leading Republican presidential candidates by year-end 2011.

The resulting bickering yields little progress on deficit reduction. Nor does the rancor allow for an advancement of much-needed and focused legislation geared toward reversing the continued weak jobs market.

The yield on the 10-year U.S. note, despite a sputtering economic recovery visible by third quarter 2011, rises to over 4.25%, as the bond vigilantes take control of the markets. The rate rise serves to put a further dent in the U.S. housing market, which continues to be plagued by an avalanche of unsold home inventory into the market as the mortgage put-back issue is slowly resolved.

During the second half of the year, housing stocks crater, and the financial sector's shares erase the (sector-leading) gains made in late 2010 and early 2011.

3. Rising commodities prices become the single greatest concern for U.S. stock market and economy.

Scarcity of water boosts agricultural prices and causes a military confrontation between China and India. The continued effect of global warming, the resumption of swifter worldwide economic growth in 2011, normal population increases and an accelerated industrialization in emerging markets (and the associated water contamination and pollution that follows) contribute importantly to more droughts and the growing scarcity of water, forcing a continued and almost geometric rise in the price of agricultural commodities (which becomes one of the most important economic and stock market themes in 2011). Increased scarcity of water and higher agricultural commodity prices (corn, wheat, beans, etc.) not only have broad economic consequences, but they become a destabilizing factor and serve as the basis for a developing powder keg in the relations between China and India.

China has about 23% of the world's population but only approximately 7% of the world's fresh water supply. Moreover, China's water resources are not distributed proportionately; the 550 million residents in the more industrialized northern area of the country are supported by only one-fifth of the fresh water and the 700 million in the southern region of China have the other 80% of the country's fresh water supply. The shared resources of water supply have been a focal point of conflict between China and India since the 1962 Indo-China War.

My big surprise is that in early 2011, tension intensifies based on a decision by the Chinese government to materially expand the plans for the diversion of the 1,800-mile long Brahmaputra River, which hugs the Chinese border before dipping into India, from the south back up to the water-deprived northern China area in an expansion of the Zangmu Dam project, original construction plans of which were announced earlier this year.

At first, trade sanctions are imposed by India against China. Later in the year, the impoverished northeastern India region is the setting for massive protests aimed at China; ultimately, groups of Indian rebels, fearful of reduced availability of fresh water and the likelihood of flooding, actually invade southern China in retaliation.

4. The market moves sideways during 2011.

While the general consensus forecast is for a rise of about 10% to 15% for the S&P 500 in 2011, the index ends up exactly where it closes the year in 2010. A flat year is a fairly rare occurrence. Since 1900, there have been only six times when the averages recorded a year-over-year price change of less than 3% (plus or minus); 2011 will mark the seventh time.

With a return profile reminiscent of the sideways markets of 1953 (–0.80%), 1960 (–0.74%) and 1994 (+1.19%), the senior averages also exhibit one of the least volatile and narrowest price ranges ever. The S&P 500 never falls below 1,150 and never rises above 1,300, as the tension between the cyclical tailwind of monetary ease and the cyclical economic recovery it brings are offset by numerous nontraditional secular challenges

> *Neither a borrower nor a lender be;*
>
> *For loan oft loses both itself and friend,*
>
> *And borrowing dulls the edge of husbandry.*
>
> —William Shakespeare, Hamlet

(e.g, fiscal imbalances in the United States and Europe; a persistently high unemployment rate that fails to decline much, as structural domestic unemployment issues plague the jobs market and the continued low level of business confidence reinforced by increased animosity between the Republicans and Democrats exacerbates an already weak jobs market and retards capital-spending plans, etc.).

Despite the current unambiguous signs of an improving domestic economy, as the year progresses, the growing expectation of consistently improving economic growth and a self-sustaining recovery is adversely influenced by continued blows to confidence from Washington, D.C., serving to contribute to a more uneven path of economic growth than the bulls envision.

With traditional economic analysis again failing to accurately predict the path of economic growth (as it did in 2008–2009), behavioral economic analysis, linking psychology to the business cycle, gains popularity. Yale's Dr. Robert Shiller and former Fed Chairman Dr. Alan Greenspan write books on behavioral economics that become the No. 1 and No. 2 books on the *New York Times'* nonfiction bestseller list.

The sideways market of 2011 will prove to be a good year for opportunistic traders but a poor one for the buy-and-hold crowd as neither the bulls nor the bears will be rejoicing next Christmas.

5. Food and restaurant companies are among the worst performers in the S&P 500.

(This surprise is an extension of surprise No. 3.) Several well-known multinational food companies and a host of domestic restaurant chains face margin and earnings pressures, as they are unable to pass the violent rise in agricultural costs on to the consumer. Profit guidance for 2011 is taken down by Kellogg, Kraft, General Mills, and many other exposed food companies.

Publicly traded restaurant chains such as Darden Restaurants, McDonald's, Yum! Brands, Brinker International, and Ruby Tuesday all take a hit owing to the abrupt contraction in profit margins as product demand swoons in the face of higher prices. As a consequence, food companies and restaurant chains are among the worst performers in the S&P next year.

6. The shares of asset managers suffer.

I expect a series of populist initiatives by the current administration beginning with a frontal assault on mutual fund 12b-1 fees. The asset managers—Franklin Resources, T. Rowe Price and Waddell & Reed—are exposed.

7. Vice President Joe Biden and Secretary of State Hillary Clinton switch jobs by midyear 2011, 18 months before the 2012 presidential election.

It is generally recognized that President Obama has been seriously weakened politically, but the situation gets worse early next year. A sustained and high level of unemployment and a quiescent housing market fail to revive, forcing the administration to consider some radical changes in order to survive in the presidential election of 2012. (While such a switch is unconventional, this move can be accomplished as the 25th Amendment sets out that the majorities in both houses of Congress would have to confirm Vice President Clinton; Secretary of State Biden would only have to be confirmed by the Senate.)

The other benefits to the switcheroo:

- Hillary Clinton would have almost a year and a half of experience and credibility in the vice president's office.
- She would be well prepared to campaign for a Democratic ticket.
- An Obama/Clinton ticket would be viewed by many as unbeatable. Clinton is a relentless campaigner, and she would be a far more effective drawer of votes than Biden. (Consider how many votes Obama and Clinton combined received in the 2008 presidential primary campaign.)

- Clinton will be seen as very capable of deflecting the women's vote from Sarah Palin in 2012.
- Clinton still likely harbors dreams of the White House. She would immediately become the overwhelming favorite to garner the Democratic Party's presidential nomination in 2016. She would be 69 years old at that time.
- On experience alone, Clinton would be considered far more qualified than most of the other Republicans now being considered (e.g., Bobby Jindal, Mitt Romney and Tim Pawlenty).
- Fears of former-president interference in the White House have dissipated. Bill Clinton has stayed out of the limelight and has been discreet with regard to his private life.

8. Speaker of the House John Boehner is replaced by Congressman Paul Ryan during the summer.

   A tearful Boehner proves too dogmatic. Within the context of a gridlock-impacted interest rate rise and slowing economy coupled with the emergence of a threat from an increasingly powerful third party (see surprise No. 9), Wisconsin's Paul Ryan replaces Boehner.

9. A new political party emerges.

   Screwflation becomes a theme that has broadening economic social and political implications. Similar to its first cousin stagflation, screwflation is an expression of a period of slow and uneven economic growth, but, in addition, it holds the existence of inflationary consequences that have an outsized impact on a specific group. The emergence of screwflation hurts just the group that authorities want to protect—namely, the middle class, a segment of the population that has already spent a decade experiencing an erosion in disposable income and a painful period (at least over the past several years) of lower stock and home prices.

   Importantly, quantitative easing is designed to lower real interest rates and, at the same time, raise inflation. A lower interest rate policy hurts the savings classes—both the middle class and the elderly. And inflation in the costs of food, energy and everything else consumed (without a concomitant increase in salaries) will screw the average American who doesn't benefit from QE2.

   Stagnating wages and ever-higher food and other costs energize Middle America, the chief victim of screwflation, and a new party, the American Party, emerges chiefly through a viral campaign begun on Facebook. This centrist initiative initially is endorsed by several independent Republican and Democratic congressmen, but a ratification by Senator Joe Lieberman (Connecticut) leads to several senatorial endorsements as it becomes clear that the American Party's ranks are growing rapidly. (Both the Tea Party and Sarah Palin abruptly disappear from the public dialogue.)

By the end of 2011, between 5% and 10% of all U.S. voters are believed to be members of the American Party. With its newfound popularity, the American Party asks New York City Mayor Bloomberg to become its leader. By year-end 2011, he has not yet made a decision.

10. The price of gold plummets by more than $250 an ounce in a four-week period in 2011 and is among the worst asset classes of the new year.

The commodity experiences wild volatility in price (on five to 10 occasions, the price has a daily price change of at least $75), briefly trading under $1,050 an ounce during the year and ending the year between $1,100 and $1,200 an ounce.

By means of background, the price of gold has risen from about $250 an ounce 11 years ago to about $1,370 an ounce today—compounding at more than a 16% rate annually. As a result, investing in gold has become de rigeur for hedge-hoggers and other institutional investors—and in due course gold has become a favored investment among individual investors.

My surprise is that next year the price of gold has the potential to become the modern-day equivalent of Hans Christian Andersen's "The Emperor's New Clothes," a short tale about two weavers who promise an emperor a new suit of clothes that are invisible to those unfit for their positions, stupid or incompetent. When the emperor parades before his subjects in his new clothes, a child cries out, "But he isn't wearing anything at all!"

With a finite supply, gold has historically been viewed as a tangible asset that increases in value during uncertain (and inflationary) times. No wonder it has become such a desirable asset class following the Great Decession and credit crisis of 2008–2009. Gold bugs remind the nonbelievers that for thousands of years, gold has been a store of value and, given the current state of the world's financial system, gold is the best house in a bad neighborhood of asset classes.

But gold, which may be the most crowded trade around, is viewed now as a commodity for all seasons—during inflation, deflation, low or high economic growth.

There is a body of thought that maintains gold holds little value, that it is only a shiny metal with limited industrial value that throws off no income or cash flow (and, as such, its value cannot be determined or analyzed with any precision based on interest rates or any other measure). Those nonbelievers compare the dizzying price of gold to the unsustainable rise in comic book prices (and other collectibles) in the early 1990s, Internet stock prices in early 2000 or home prices in 2006–2007.

Here is how Oaktree Management's Howard Marks draws a colorful parallel between gold and religion:

> My view is simple and starts with the observation that gold is a lot like religion. No one can prove that God exists . . . or that God doesn't exist. The believer can't convince the atheist, and the atheist can't convince the believer. It's incredibly simple: Either you believe in God or you don't. Well, that's exactly the way I think it is with gold. Either you're a believer or you're not.

What we do know is that gold is valued in an auction market based on the price where buyers ("the believers") and sellers ("the atheists") meet.

With an inability to gauge gold's intrinsic value, wide price swings remain possible. And wide price swings are what I expect in 2011.

There are numerous catalysts that can contribute to a surprising weakness in the price of gold in the upcoming year. But most likely, a large drop in the price of gold might simply be the result in a swing in sentiment that can be induced by a number of factors—or maybe even sentiment that the emperor (and gold investors/traders) isn't wearing anything at all:

• Investors might grow increasingly comfortable in a self-sustaining, inflation-free worldwide economic recovery.

- Interest rates could ratchet higher, providing competition for non-income-producing assets (such as gold).
- The world stock markets could surprise to the upside, reducing investors' interest in real assets (such as gold).
- The U.S. government might (astonishingly) address the deficit.

In addition, there are numerous cautionary and anecdotal signs that are reminiscent of prior unsustainable asset class cycles or bubbles:

1. Macro funds, such as those managed by John Paulson, have outsized weightings in gold or even have established dedicated gold hedge funds.
2. On Okeechobee Boulevard in West Palm Beach, Florida, hand-held placards that used to advertise condominiums and single-family homes for sale (during the housing bubble) have been replaced by handheld signs advertising "We Buy Gold." On this well-populated street, gold-exchange stores have replaced the omnipresent real estate and cell-phone stores of the last specula-tive cycle. ("We Buy Gold," "Sell Your Unwanted Gold," "Get Cash Now For Your Gold" are names of a few of the retail outlets).
3. Gold is even being dispensed in an ATM in the Town Center Mall in Boca Raton, Florida and at a hotel in Abu Dhabi.
4. The company that dispenses the gold is PMX Communities, a Boca Raton-based concern listed on the Pink Sheets. According to a recent release, the ATM gold-dispensing machines now operate in 12 locations around the world.
5. My spam e-mails normally consist of Viagra and "male enlarge-ment" solicitations, but offers to buy gold have been on the rise over the last few months.

11. Among the most notable takeover deals in 2011, Microsoft launches a tender offer for Yahoo! at $21.50 a share.

   With the company in play, News Corporation follows with a competing and higher bid. The private-equity community joins the fray. Microsoft ultimately prevails and pays $24 a share for Yahoo!.

   Currently, Yahoo! is universally viewed as a dysfunctional company, and few expect that Microsoft has an interest in the company. But a deal could be profitable and advantageous (more critical mass and immediate exposure to the rapidly growing Chinese market) to Microsoft:

- Microsoft is hemorrhaging cash in its Internet operations (estimated $2.5 billion of losses in the past 12 months). Yahoo! will immediately contribute $1.25 billion-plus of cash flow. (Applying a normal multiple, 6× to 9× creates $8.5 billion of value to Microsoft from Yahoo!'s current earnings before interest, taxes, depreciation, and amortization).
- Yahoo! boasts net cash of $3.4 billion.
- Yahoo!'s public holdings total $9.5 billion of value (Alibaba and Yahoo! Japan).
- Yahoo!'s private holdings total $6 billion.
- Yahoo! owns 40% of private Alibaba through two assets:
  1. A call option on Chinese search via Microsoft joint venture. Based on the value of Baidu, if Yahoo! gets a 10% share of the $50 billion Chinese search market, the value is $5 billion—the value to Yahoo! is about $1 billion for each 10% of search share (40% of 50%).
  2. 40% of AliPay. This is the elephant in the room. Current AliPay payments are about two thirds of PayPal, but the company is growing much faster than PayPal, and its market potential is far greater. PayPal is currently worth $18 billion—making AliPay valued at $12 billion. Yahoo!'s 40% is worth $5 billion now but will easily be $10 billion in three years.

By means of background, on February 1, 2008, Microsoft offered $31 a share, or $45 billion, to acquire Yahoo! in an unsolicited bid that included a combination of stock and cash. At that time, Yahoo!'s shares stood at $19 a share, and Microsoft was trading at $32 a share. (Today Microsoft trades at $27 a share, and Yahoo! trades at $16 a share.)

Yahoo! rejected the bid, claiming that it "substantially undervalued" the company and was not in the interest of its shareholders. In January 2009, Carol Bartz replaced Yahoo! cofounder Jerry Yang, and six months later Microsoft and Yahoo! entered into a search joint venture.

12. The Internet becomes the tactical nuke of the digital age.

Cybercrime likely explodes exponentially as the Web is invaded by hackers. A specific target next year will be the NYSE, and I predict an attack that causes a weeklong hiatus in trading and an abrupt slowdown in domestic business activity.

13. The SEC's insider trading case expands dramatically, reaching much further into the canyons of some of the largest hedge funds and mutual funds and to several West Coast–based technology companies.

This surprise is an extension of surprise No. 13 from last year's 20 Surprises for 2010:

Insider trading charges expand. The SEC alleges, in a broad-ranging sting, the existence of an extensive exchange of information that goes well beyond Galleon's Silicon Valley executive connections. Several well-known, long-only mutual funds are implicated in the sting, which reveals that they have consistently received privileged information from some of the largest public companies over the past decade.

The next SEC target is directed at some of the world's largest tech companies, including one of the leading manufacturers of flash memory cards, one of the largest contract manufacturers and a big producer of integrated circuits. A high-profile, very senior executive in one of these companies is implicated and is forced out of his position.

With the depth of the investigations moving toward the center of some of the largest hedge and mutual funds, many of the more active traders are temporarily in "lockdown" mode as the hedge fund community's trading activity freezes up.

- NYSE volume and price volatility dry up (see surprise No. 4 on the sideways market).
- Fox Business Network closes because of lack of interest.
- CNBC reduces its live broadcasting schedule and resorts to paid programming before 6 A.M. and after 8 P.M.
- Particularly hard-hit is Greenwich, Connecticut—the home of many of the biggest hedge-hoggers who are alleged to have committed insider trading violations. The residential real estate market in Greenwich collapses.

14. There is a peaceful regime change in Iran.

15. China overplays its economic hand by implementing multiple tightening and by its unwillingness to allow its currency to appreciate.

The region's GDP climbs by only 5% in 2011.

15 Surprises for 2012

12/27/2011

While I had a reasonably successful surprise list for 2011, with about half my surprises coming to fruition, the real story was that I achieved something that is almost impossible to accomplish.

My most important surprise (No. 4) was that the S&P 500 would end the year at exactly the same price that it started the year (1,257) and that the range over the course of the year would be narrow (between 1,150 and 1,300).

As explained below, both predictions were remarkably close to what actually occurred.

My Biggest Surprise for 2011 Was Eerily Prescient   As we entered 2011, most strategists expressed a sanguine economic view of a self-sustaining domestic recovery and shared the view that the S&P 500 would rise by about 17% and would end the year between 1,450 and 1,500 vs. a year-end 2010 close of 1,257.

By contrast, I called for a sideways market, stating that the S&P would be exactly flat year over year. To date, that surprise has almost come true to the exact S&P point. Remarkably, at around midday last Friday, December 23, the S&P 500 was trading at 1,257—Friday's closing price was 1,265—precisely the ending price on December 31, 2010. (There are still four trading days left in the year, so technically the exercise is not yet over.)

A flat year is a much rarer occurrence than many would think. According to The Chart Store's Ron Griess, in the 82 years since 1928, when S&P data was first accumulated, the index was unchanged in only one year (1947). And in only three of the 82 years was the annual change in the S&P 500 under 1%—1947 (0.00%), 1948 (−0.65%) and 1970 (+0.10%).

In addition to the amazing accuracy of my variant S&P forecast, my forecast for the index's full-year trading range was almost as precise—in both content and from the standpoint of causality.

As I wrote, a year ago, the S&P 500 would exhibit "one of the narrowest price ranges ever."

The surprise expected was that the S&P would never fall below 1,150 (it briefly sold at 1,090) and never rise above 1,300 (it briefly traded at

1,360), "as the tension between the cyclical tailwind of monetary ease and the cyclical economic recovery it brings are offset by numerous nontraditional secular challenges (e.g., fiscal imbalances in the United States and Europe; a persistently high unemployment rate that fails to decline much, as structural domestic unemployment issues plague the jobs market and the continued low level of business confidence reinforced by increased animosity between the Republicans and Democrats exacerbates an already weak jobs market and retards capital-spending plans, etc.)." I went on to write, "Despite the current unambiguous signs of an improving domestic economy, as the year progresses, the growing expectation of consistently improving economic growth and a self-sustaining recovery is adversely influenced by continued blows to confidence from Washington, D.C., serving to contribute to a more uneven path of economic growth than the bulls envision."

How Did My Other Surprises for 2011 Fare?   Last year's surprise list achieved about a 50% success ratio. Forty percent of my 2010 surprises were achieved, while I had a 50% success rate in 2009, 60% in 2008, 50% in 2007, one-third in 2006, 20% in 2005, 45% in 2004, and one-third came to pass in the first year of my surprises in 2003.

My surprise list for 2011 hit on some of the important themes that dominated the investment and economic landscape this year. Below is a list of some of my accurate surprises from last year's list.

- *Markets:* As discussed previously, the market was practically unchanged in 2011, and the year's range almost perfectly coincided with my No. 4 surprise. Also, group performance surprises were fulfilled—for instance, "During the second half of the year, housing stocks crater, and the financial sector's shares erase the (sector-leading) gains made in late 2010 and early 2011." I also was correct in expecting asset managers' shares to fall lower and underperform.
- *The U.S. economy:* Real GDP in the United States, as I expected, was disappointing at about half consensus growth expectations. Screw-flation of the middle class was a dominant theme, and I incorporated screwflation in my surprise list. Americans, I thought, would remain in a foul mood, as the jobs and housing markets failed to improve to the degree expected by most. My surprise of social unrest was also

realized around the world—over there in the Arab Spring and over here in the Occupy Wall Street movement.

- *The European economy:* Over there, as I suggested a year ago, "multiple country austerity programs moved Europe back into recession by year-end 2011."
- *China's economy:* I wrote that "China continues to tighten, but inflation remains persistent, economic growth disappoints and its stock market weakens further." All happened.
- *U.S. politics:* I wrote "increased hostilities between the Republicans and Democrats become a challenge to the market and to the economic recovery next year. As the 2012 election moves closer, President Obama reverses his seemingly newly minted centrist views. . . . The resulting bickering yields little progress on deficit reduction. Nor does the rancor allow for an advancement of much-needed and focused legislation geared toward reversing the continued weak jobs market." Trust in our leaders was indeed lost throughout 2011—approval ratings hit an all-time low during 2011 for Congress and for the president—and political gridlock and inertia adversely impacted sentiment as confidence figures plummeted by late summer.
- *Republican presidential candidate:* Mitt Romney, as expected, is the Republican Party's presidential frontrunner (but Ryan and Thune never were in the fray).
- *Commodity prices:* Throughout the year, "the rise in the price of commodities was one of the primary market themes and concerns."
- *Gold:* I was correct in expecting volatility in the price of gold but very wrong in the direction of the price of gold when I wrote, "The price of gold plummets by more than $250 an ounce in a four-week period in 2011 and is among the worst asset classes of the new year. The commodity experiences wild volatility in price (on five to 10 occasions, the price has a daily price change of at least $75), briefly trading under $1,050 an ounce during the year and ending the year between $1,100 and $1,200 an ounce."
- *Takeovers:* Though Microsoft has not yet made a bid, my Yahoo! deal surprise turned out to be materially correct. "Among the most notable takeover deals in 2011, Microsoft launches a tender offer for Yahoo!. . . . The private equity community joins the fray."

- *Internet as the tactical nuke of the digital age:* "Cybercrime likely explodes exponentially as the Web is invaded by hackers." Dead on, as serious hacking incidents are occurring with increased frequency.
- *Expanding insider trading charges:* It was a record year of insider trading indictments and convictions, from Raj to many other ne'er-do-wells (including research network consultants, hedge funds, corporations and even a member of the board of directors of Goldman Sachs). "The SEC's insider trading case expands dramatically, reaching much further into the canyons of some of the largest hedge funds and mutual funds and to several West Coast-based technology companies." (Some of us even learned this year for the first time that Congress is legally permitted to be in the insider trading game.)

Where did my surprises for 2011 go wrong?

- Though the price of gold was volatile (and did sustain quick $200-per-ounce drops), it did not fall and was among the best asset classes in 2011.
- There was no military confrontation between China and India over water rights.
- The price of oil didn't soar to over $125 a barrel.
- The yield on the 10-year U.S. note did not spike to 4.25%.
- Food and restaurant stocks were not among the worst-performing market sectors.
- Hillary Clinton and Joe Biden did not switch jobs, though Clinton is resigning her post as secretary of state.
- While Speaker of the House John Boehner's tenure has been uneven, he was not replaced by Paul Ryan.
- A third political party did not appear (though it is never too late).
- There was no peaceful regime change in Iran.

My 15 Surprises for 2012   My new surprises for 2012 represent a fundamental turn toward optimism and a marked departure from the pessimism expressed in my recent surprise list history.

For the last few years, since the financial and economic crisis of 2008–2009, caution, restraint and the word "no" have characterized and dominated the economic, social and political backdrop. In 2012, however, our surprise list moves toward an inflection point in which bolder steps, expansiveness and the word "yes" begin to dominate the political, economic and stock market stages.

This new, brighter and more positive narrative is the essence and the common thread contained in my surprise list for 2012. (And this year, following each surprise, I am introducing a specific strategy that might be employed in order for an investor to profit from the occurrence of these possible improbables.)

Surprise No. 1: The U.S. stock market approaches its all-time high in 2012   The beginning of the New Year brings a stable and range-bound market. A confluence of events, however, allows for the S&P 500 to eclipse the 2000 high of 1,527.46 during the second half of the year. The rally occurs as a powerful reallocation trade out of bonds and into stocks provides the fuel for the upside breakout. The market rip occurs in a relatively narrow time frame as the S&P 500 records two consecutive months of double-digit returns in summer/early-fall 2012.

Strategy: Buy out-of-the-money SPDR S&P 500 ETF (SPY) calls.

Surprise No. 2: The growth in the U.S. economy accelerates as the year progresses   The U.S. economy muddles through in early 2012, but, with business, investor and consumer confidence surging in the fall, real GDP accelerates to over 3% in the second half. Unemployment falls slightly more than consensus, but the slack in the labor market continues to constrain wage growth. Domestic automobile industry sales soar well above expectations, benefiting from pent-up demand and an aging U.S. fleet. Inflation is contained but begins to be worrisome (and serves as a market headwind) in late 2012. Corporations' top-line growth is better than expected, and wage increases are contained. Operating margins rise modestly as sales growth lifts productivity and capacity utilization rates. Operating leverage surprises to the upside, as 2012 S&P profits exceed $105 a share.

A noteworthy surprise is that the residential real estate market shows surprising strength. The U.S. housing market becomes much bifurcated (in a market of regional haves and have-nots), as areas of the country not impacted adversely by the large shadow inventory of unsold homes enjoy a strong recovery in activity and in pricing. The Washington, D.C., to Boston, Massachusetts, corridor experiences the most vibrant regional growth, while Phoenix, Las Vegas, and areas of California remain weak. The New York City market begins to develop a bubbly speculative tone. Florida is the only area of the country that has had large supply imbalances since 2007 that experiences a meaningful recovery, which is led by an unusually strong Miami market.

Strategy: Buy Home Depot, Lowe's, building materials and home-builders, and buy auto stocks such as Ford and General Motors.

Surprise No. 3: Former Presidents Bill Clinton and George Bush form a bipartisan coalition that persuades both parties to unite in addressing our fiscal imbalances The Clinton-Bush initiative, also known as "Simpson-Bowles on steroids," gains overwhelming popular support, and despite strenuous initial opposition, it forces the Democrats and Republicans (months before the November elections) to move toward a grand compromise on fiscal discipline and pro-growth fiscal policy. Interest rates remain subdued, growth prospects become elevated and a feel-good atmosphere begins to permeate our economy in a return of confidence and in our capital markets engendered by the Clinton-Bush initiative.

The Clinton-Bush initiative includes seven basic core policies that are accepted by both political parties.

1. A broad infrastructure program focused on a massive build-out and improvement of the U.S. infrastructure base—the restoration of our country's highways, bridges and buildings and an extensive Internet bandwidth expansion are embarked upon.
2. The annual increase in government spending is limited to the change in the CPI.
3. A comprehensive jobs plan includes new training programs—all veterans are made eligible to tuition subsidies to vocational schools and colleges.
4. A Marshall Plan for housing is introduced, highlighted by a nation-wide refinancing proposal adopted for all mortgagees (regardless of loan-to-values).
5. A series of new tax increases—including a plan to raise taxes on the families with an income in excess of $500,000 a year (a two-year income tax surcharge of 5%-10%) and some other more imaginative,

outside-the-box proposals (e.g., a tax on sugar products)—are introduced.

6. Mean test entitlements, freeze entitlement payouts, and gradually increase the Social Security retirement age to 70 years old.

7. A comprehensive plan is designed to rapidly develop all our energy resources.

Strategy: See No. 1 surprise strategy. Sell volatility.

Surprise No. 4: Despite the grand compromise, the Republican presidential ticket gains steam as year progresses, and Romney is elected as the forty-fifth President of the United States The U.S. moved to the left politically in the Democratic tsunami in 2008 and to the right politically as the Republican Party gained control of Congress in 2010; the 2012 election is the tiebreaker. The result of the tiebreaker is that Mitt Romney and Marco Rubio squeak by Barack Obama and Joseph Biden in the November 2012 election. All the five swing battleground states (Florida, Indiana, Missouri, North Carolina, and Ohio) go Republican. The Romney-Rubio ticket also wins the states of New Hampshire and Virginia, previously won by Obama in 2008, and the Republicans prevail (270 electoral votes to 268 votes) in one of the closest elections of all time.

Strategy: See No. 3 surprise strategy.

Surprise No. 5: A sloppy start in arresting the European debt crisis leads to far more forceful and successful policy The EU remains intact after a brief scare in early 2012 caused by Greece's dissatisfaction (and countrywide riots) with imposed austerity measures. The eurozone experiences only a mild recession, as the ECB introduces large-scale quantitative-easing measures that exceed those introduced by the Fed during our financial crisis in 2008–2009.

Strategy: Buy European shares. Buy iShares MSCI Germany Index Fund (EWG) and iShares MSCI France Index Fund (EWQ).

Surprise No. 6: The Fed ties monetary policy to the labor market In order to encourage corporations to invest and to build up consumer and business confidence, the Fed changes its mandate and promises not to tighten monetary policy until the unemployment rate moves below 6.5%, slightly above the level at which wage pressures might emerge (the nonaccelerating inflation rate of unemployment).

Strategy: Buy high-quality municipal bonds or the iShares S&P National AMT–Free Municipal Bond Fund (MUB).

Surprise No. 7: Sears Holdings declares bankruptcy In a spectacular fall, Sears Holdings shares are halted at $18 a share during the early spring, as vendors turn away from the retailer, owing to a continued and more pronounced deterioration in cash flow (already down $800 million 2011 over 2010), earnings and sales. With funding and vendor support evaporating, as paper-thin earnings before interest and taxes margins turn negative and cash flow is insufficient to fund inventory growth. The shares reopen at $0.70 after the company declares bankruptcy and its intention to restructure, as we learn, once again, that being No. 3 in an industry has little value—especially after store improvements were deferred over the past several years. A major hedge fund and a large REIT join forces in taking over the company. Ten percent to 15% of Sears' 4,000 Kmart and specialty stores are closed. More than 35,000 of the company's 317,000 full-time workers are laid off. As a major anchor tenant in many of the nation's shopping centers and with no logical store replacement, the REIT industry's shares suffer through the balance of the year, and the major market indices suffer their only meaningful correction of the year. Target and Wal-Mart's shares eventually soar in the second half of 2012.

Strategy: Buy out-of-the-money Sears Holdings puts, go long Target and Wal-Mart, and short the iShares Dow Jones U.S. Real Estate Index Fund (IYR).

Surprise No. 8: Cyberwarfare intensifies Our country's State Department's defenses are hacked into and compromised by unknown assailants based outside of the United States. Our armed forces are placed on Defcon Three alert.

Strategy: None.

Surprise No. 9: Financial stocks are a leading market sector After five years of underperformance, the financial stocks rebound dramatically and outperform the markets, as loan demand recovers, multiple takeovers permeate the financial intermediary scene and domestic institutions enjoy market share gains at the expense of flailing European institutions. With profit expectations low, three years of cost cutting and some revenue upside surprises (from an improving capital markets, a pronounced rise in M&A activity and better loan demand) contribute to better-than-expected industry profits.

Strategy: Buy JPMorgan Chase, Citigroup, and the Financial Select Sector SPDR (XLF).

Surprise No. 10: Despite the advance in the U.S. stock market, high-beta stocks underperform Though counterintuitive within the framework of a new bull-market leg, the market's low fliers (low multiple, slower growth) become market high fliers, as their P/E ratios expand.

With the exception of Apple, the high fliers—Priceline, Baidu, Google, Amazon and the like—disappoint. Apple's share price rises above $550, however, based on continued above-consensus volume growth in the iPhone and iPad. Profit forecasts for 2012 rise to $45 a share (up 60%). In the second quarter, Apple pays a $20-a-share special cash dividend, introduces a regular $1.25-a-share quarterly dividend and splits its shares 10–1. Apple becomes the AT&T of a previous investing generation, a stock now owned by this generation's widows and orphans.

Strategy: Long Apple (common and calls).

Surprise No. 11: Mutual fund inflows return in force With confidence renewed, domestic equity inflows begin to pour into equity mutual funds by midyear and approach a $100 billion seasonally adjusted annual rate by fourth quarter 2012. The share prices of T. Rowe Price and Franklin Resources double.

Strategy: Long Legg Mason, T. Rowe Price and Franklin Resources.

Surprise No. 12: We'll see merger mania Cheap money, low valuations and rising confidence are the troika of factors that contribute to 2012 becoming one of the biggest years ever for mergers and take-overs. Canadian companies are particularly active in acquiring U.S. assets. Canada's Manulife acquires life insurer Lincoln National, two large banks join a bidding war for E*Trade, and International Flavors & Fragrances and Kellogg are both acquired by non-U.S. entities. Finally, a Canadian bank acquires SunTrust.

Strategy: Long E*Trade, Lincoln National, International Flavors & Fragrances, Kellogg and SunTrust.

Surprise No. 13: The ETF bubble explodes   There are currently about 1,400 ETFs. During 2012, numerous ETFs fail to track and one-third of the current ETFs are forced to close. There are several flash crashes of ETFs listed on the exchanges. The ETF landscape is littered by investor litigation as investor losses mount. New stringent maintenance rules and new offering restrictions are imposed upon the ETF business. The formation of leveraged ETFs is materially restricted by the SEC.

Strategy: Avoid all but the largest ETFs.

Surprise No. 14: China has a soft landing (despite indigestion in the property market), and India has a hard landing   India becomes the emerging-market concern. With India's trade not a driver to GDP growth, its currency in free-fall, pressure to keep interest rates high by its central bank and signs of a contraction in October industrial output, India's GDP falls to mid-single-digit levels.

Strategy: Long iShares FTSE/Xinhua China 25 Index Fund (FXI); short WisdomTree India Earnings Fund ETF (EPI) and iPath MSCI India Index ETN (INP).

Surprise No. 15: Israel attacks Iran   The greatest headwind to the world's equity markets is geopolitical not economic. Israel attacks Iran in the spring, but, at the outset, the United States stays out of the conflict. Iran closes the Strait of Hormuz, and oil prices spike to $125 a barrel.

Strategy: Buy Schlumberger, ExxonMobil and other oil production and exploration stocks.

Five More Surprises for 2012

12/30/2011

Some of the possible improbables that I came up with while compiling my "15 Surprises for 2012" were not quite ready for prime time, but they can certainly serve as an addendum to that list.

Surprise No. 16: After it is disclosed that Bank of America is being forced to raise an additional $20 billion to $25 billion of capital, Brian Moynihan resigns as president and CEO of Bank of America.

Surprise No. 17: Reflecting upward-trending stock markets around the world, continued improvement in domestic high-frequency economic statistics and a contained European debt crisis, the CBOE Volatility Index falls to the 10–15 level during the second half of 2012.

Surprise No. 18: Facebook's IPO fizzles. The new offering is priced at a $70 billion equity capitalization but opens flat and breaks issue price in the first day of trading.

Surprise No. 19: A second-half growth scare briefly lifts the yield on the 10-year U.S. note to over 3%.

Surprise No. 20: Similar to Hewlett-Packard's former CEO Mark Hurd, three very high-profile executives of Fortune 500 companies are forced to resign after sexual harassment allegations.

15 Surprises for 2013

1/7/2013

It was a tough task repeating the success of my surprise list for 2011 over the past year.

This is particularly true since my most important surprise (No. 4) in 2011—namely, that the S&P 500 would end the year at exactly the same price that it started the year (1,257)—was eerily prescient. As well, in 2011, I basically nailed that the trading range over the course of that year would be narrow (between 1,150 and 1,300).

As we entered 2012, most strategists expressed a relatively sanguine economic view of a self-sustaining domestic recovery and an upbeat corporate profits picture but shared the view that the S&P 500 would rise but only modestly.

By contrast, I called for a much better equity market—one capable, in the second half of the year, of piercing the 2000 high of 1,527. As it turns out, the S&P 500 breached 1,480 to the upside in the fall—or about only 3% less than the 2000 peak.

How Did My Surprise List for 2012 Do?   Last year's surprise list achieved about a 50% hit ratio, similar to my experience in 2011. Forty percent of my 2010 surprises were achieved, while I had a 50% success rate in 2009, 60% in 2008, 50% in 2007, one-third in 2006, 20% in 2005, 45% in 2004, and one-third came to pass in the first year of my surprises in 2003.

Following is a report card of my 20 surprises for 2012 (I hit on 50% of the surprises).

Surprise No. 1: The U.S. stock market breaches the 2000 high of 1,527. Right.

I call this correct as:

1. This was a hugely out-of-consensus and bullish view;
2. The S&P came within 3% of 1,527; and
3. In September I reduced my year-end price close for the S&P 500 to 1,415. (It closed at 1,425.)

Surprise No. 2: The growth in the U.S. economy accelerates as the year progresses. Wrong.

Surprise No. 3: Former Presidents Bill Clinton and George Bush form a bipartisan coalition that persuades both parties to unite in addressing our fiscal imbalances. Wrong.

Surprise No. 4: Despite the grand compromise, the Republican presidential ticket gains steam as year progresses, and Romney is elected as the forty-fifth President of the United States. Wrong.

Surprise No. 5: A sloppy start in arresting the European debt crisis leads to far more forceful and successful policy. Right.

Surprise No. 6: The Fed ties monetary policy to the labor market. Right.

Surprise No. 7: Sears Holdings declares bankruptcy. Wrong.

Surprise No. 8: Cyberwarfare intensifies. Right.

Surprise No. 9: Financial stocks are a leading market sector. Right.

Surprise No. 10: Despite the advance in the U.S. stock market, high-beta stocks underperform, but Apple is a standout to the upside. Right.

Surprise No. 11: Mutual fund inflows return in force. Wrong.

Surprise No. 12: We'll see merger mania. Wrong.

Surprise No. 13: The ETF bubble explodes. Wrong.

Surprise No. 14: China has a soft landing (despite indigestion in the property market), and India has a hard landing. Right.

Surprise No. 15: Israel Attacks Iran. Wrong.

Surprise No. 16: Bank of America is forced to raise an additional $20 billion to $25 billion, and Brian Moynihan resigns as president. Wrong.

Surprise No. 17: The CBOE Volatility Index (VIX) falls to the 10 to 15 level during the second half of 2012. Right.

Surprise No. 18: Facebook's IPO fizzles and breaks issue price in the first day of trading. Right.

Surprise No. 19: A second-half growth scare briefly lifts the yield on the 10-year U.S. note to over 3%. Wrong.

Surprise No. 20: Three very high-profile executives of Fortune 500 companies are forced to resign after sexual harassment allegations. Right.

The Rationale behind My Downbeat Surprises for 2013   Last year my surprise list had an out-of-consensus positive tone to it, but this year it is noticeably downbeat relative to generally upbeat expectations.

As contrasted to 2012, when most were dour in market view (and wrong), the 2013 consensus is an optimistic one and now holds to the view that European economic growth is stabilizing while growth in China and in the United States is reaccelerating. The popular view goes on to believe that even our dysfunctional leaders in Washington will not upset the growing consensus that it is clear sailing for equities and trouble ahead for bonds.

Once again, the bullish consensus is tightly grouped with the expectation that the S&P 500 will close the year at 1,550 to 1,615 (up from 1,425 at the close of 2012) and that the 10-year U.S. note yield will trade at 2.50% or higher (up from 1.80% at the close of 2012).

These consensus views might prove too optimistic on stock prices and too pessimistic on bond prices. I believe that the U.S. stock market will make its 2013 high in the first two weeks of January, be in a yearlong range of 1,275 to 1,480 and close the year at 1,425 and that the 10-year U.S. note will be below 2% in the first six months of 2013.

Many of my more downbeat surprises for 2013 are an outgrowth of an aging economic recovery (now four years old), a maturing stock market (of a similar age) coupled with the recognition that running trillions of dollars in deficits while maintaining zero interest rates are unsustainable policy strategies.

I am also concerned that the multiplier being applied to the tax increases agreed to last week will be greater than many expect, serving to weigh on domestic economic growth.

As well, it is also my view that the trajectory of economic growth in 2013 (and corporate profits) will also be adversely impacted by the manner in which businesses and consumers react to the tax hikes and the growing animosity and contentiousness in Washington, D.C., in the months ahead.

Indeed, I fully expect the upcoming deliberations between the revenge-lusting Republicans in the House and the equally dogmatic and partisan incumbent president and Democratic Senate to not result in any meaningful cut in spending or entitlements reform. I do, however, expect these negotiations to have a direct and distinct adverse impact on economic growth, confidence and profits.

The dependency on our economy and on business and consumer confidence to Washington's ability to compromise and deliver intelligent policy will prove, at the very least, unsettling to the markets in the year ahead. At worst, it will undermine the economic expansion.

In addition, policy alternatives are diminishing.

U.S. monetary policy is now effectively shooting blanks, and fiscal policy will now turn out to be a drag on growth. Moreover, the likely reluctance and inertia by our leaders in addressing our budget will continue to turn off the individual investor class to stocks this year.

Finally, my ursine tone is also a reflection that, by most measures, the U.S. stock market is not meaningfully undervalued and that given the dynamic of the headwinds of slowing economic growth, a poor profit outlook and the developing weakness of policy are unlikely to be revalued upward in 2013 (as many strategists suggest).

Without Further Ado . . .   Following are my 15 surprises for 2013. This year I have reduced the surprise list from 20 to 15. As I did last year, following each surprise, I have included a specific strategy that might be utilized in order for an investor to profit from the occurrence of these possible improbables.

Surprise No. 1: The U.S. economy disappoints relative to consensus expectations Amid contentious and hyperpartisanship of political debate, consumer and business confidence sours, adversely impacting personal spending, job growth and capital spending plans:

- U.S. real GDP growth expands by only 1.5% (or less) in 2013.
- There is no grand bargain, as the debt ceiling and budget issues are kicked down the road.
- The only real development in the budget debate is that a financial transaction tax is adopted in exchange for a one-year increase in Medicare eligibility.

By midyear either Janet Yellen or Alan Blinder will replace Ben Bernanke as Fed Chairman, and the administration's entire economic advisory team will be turned over.

Question: How many politicians does it take to screw up our economy?

Answer: 537 (436 members of the House, 100 members of the Senate and one president).

The consensus view is that while the upcoming budget debate will likely get ugly and go down to the wire, a 10-year, $2 trillion agreement will be negotiated.

Unfortunately, the last meaningful agreement between the Republican and Democratic parties was the twenty-fourth-hour fiscal cliff compromise on January 1, 2013.

The squabbling and enmity of the recent fiscal cliff debate poisons all future budget talks. The Obama administration is unwilling to make spending concessions anywhere that is needed to make substantive progress on our fiscal deficit. The Republicans are equally entrenched in policy view.

"This subcommittee has demonstrated in hearings and comprehensive reports how various schemes have helped shift income to offshore tax havens and avoid U.S. taxes. . . . The resulting loss of revenue is one significant cause of the budget deficit and adds to the tax burden that ordinary Americans bear."

—Sen. Carl Levin (D–Mich.), Senate Permanent Subcommittee on Investigations

The debate grows increasingly contentious and vitriolic. Congressional Democrats, prodded by the president, introduce the idea of a wealth tax.

A Levin-led subcommittee investigation determines and highlights that Apple (which deferred taxes on over $35 billion in offshore income between 2009 and 2011) and many other companies—including Hewlett-Packard, Google, and Microsoft—have adversely impacted the budget deficit by unfairly allocating revenue and intellectual property offshore to lower the taxes they pay in the United States (and have even avoided taxes in the United States by moving subsidiaries to Nevada). The investigation reveals that Apple was a pioneer (as early as in the mid-1980s) of an accounting technique known as the "double Irish with a Dutch sandwich," which reduces taxes by routing profits through Irish subsidiaries and the Netherlands and then on to the Caribbean. The Levin subcommittee finds that this tax avoidance technique employed by Apple has been imitated by hundreds of other international companies.

The Democrats in Congress propose a closing of such corporate tax loopholes and more strict rules regarding non-U.S. tax havens. This creates a complete impasse when Republicans react violently to it. Congressional Republicans, on the other hand, offer sizable entitlement benefit cuts, which turn off the Democrats.

During the debate it becomes clear that the risks of destabilizing outcomes are rising (e.g., a technical default on U.S. debt and a downgrade by all of the major ratings agencies), and investors panic. The S&P 500 hits a low of 1,275.

The surprise is that there is no grand bargain in 2013 that brings our country closer to fiscal sustainability—indeed, there is virtually no bargain (on tax and entitlement reforms nor in discretionary spending cuts) in the new year at all.

The debt ceiling is finally raised, though only minor spending cuts are instituted. At the last moment, the Democrats agree to a one-year increase in Medicare eligibility in exchange for an Elizabeth Warren–inspired campaign (in conjunction with Congressional Democrats) to introduce a financial transaction tax to be imposed on securities trades by year-end. (See surprise No. 4.)

After the debate comes to a close it is apparent that the ability of the administration to enact previously sought gun control laws, immigration reform and other projects is in serious jeopardy.

Foreign leaders openly discuss the waning role of our country's leadership in the world. The U.S. dollar suffers as our standing in the global economy erodes.

Meanwhile, though the fiscal drag from last week's fiscal cliff agreement appears to many to be a manageable $250 billion–$280 billion (or less than 1.0% taken off U.S. GDP), the actual multiplier of this drag is greater than most are projecting (over 1.5%). The growing tortured debate, animosity, and fiscal uncertainty between both parties during the January–March period chill the economy further and adversely impact business and consumer confidence. Corporate fixed investment, hirings, and industrial production suffer, and it becomes clear that there is little economic momentum in the United States and that, among other issues, corporate pricing power is harmed by increased competition from non-U.S.-based companies.

Most market participants begin to accept the notion that the Fed is essentially out of bullets and can no longer impact our economy at the margin and that it doesn't possess the sort of durable and effective fiscal remedies that are needed to materially address the complexity of the secular challenges facing the country (education, the jobs market, etc.).

By midyear President Obama seeks scapegoats for economic policy failure. He replaces most of his team at the Council of Economic Advisers as well as Fed Chairman Bernanke (with Alan Blinder or Janet Yellen) a full six months before Bernanke's term is officially over in January 2014.

Despite recent concerns that the Fed will end quantitative easing, more easing lies ahead during 2013, and, in all likelihood, the amount of bond buying will be raised not ended or reduced (as suggested in the recent Fed minutes release).

A weaker-than-expected domestic economy in the first half of the year underscores the fragility of the consumer (in particular).

First-quarter 2013 real GDP is 0.5% to 1.0%, worse than consensus expectations. Second-quarter 2013 real GDP shows little improvement (but only to 1.0% to 1.5%) from the first quarter.

Overall full-year U.S. GDP disappoints relative to the consensus (and particularly relative to the Fed's forecast of 3% growth) and approximates 1.5% (or less) for all of 2013.

Strategy: Buy index puts in the first half of 2013.

Surprise No. 2: The 2013–2014 earnings cliff sinks the markets in 2013's first half The 2012 improvement seen in the residential real estate markets moderates, as sales activity/turnover and home price appreciation flattens.

Already refinancing applications (down 23%) and new mortgage applications (down 15%) have taken a bad fall in the last half of December 2012. Low interest rates from 2009 to 2012 have done their job in reviving the U.S. housing market, and that stimulus should be seen as bringing forward home sales—now it is up to the domestic economy to resuscitate demand.

On the latter point I am less optimistic about the foundation of growth for the U.S. economy and the financial fate of the consumer who is now just absorbing a new tax hike (see surprise No. 1). Finally, let's not lose sight that the Obamacare surcharge of 3.8% will be applied to home sales in 2013.

Retail sales suffer, as spent-up not pent-up consumers are stunned by having less money in their wallets.

In 2013 we discover that there is a limit to the consumer in the face of our dysfunctional leaders' inability to deliver a grand bargain. A payroll tax increase, higher top income tax rates and the Obamacare surcharge, coupled with disappointing capital spending and weak hirings, represent the brunt of the domestic growth shortfall relative to consensus expectations.

Surprisingly, automobile sales, benefiting from pent-up demand (much like housing last year) continue to improve slowly, to a surprisingly strong 16 million–17 million SAAR rate by year-end, and represent a standout feature of the domestic economy throughout the new year.

Wage growth is muted, interest rates remain low, and inflationary pressures are nonexistent, helping to keep profit margins from slipping too far. Nonetheless, slowing domestic economic growth and reduced final demand—personal consumption expenditures are further hurt by the droughts and rising food prices—weigh significantly on corporate profits.

Full-year 2012 S&P 500 earnings come in at $102 a share, while 2013 S&P profits disappoint at $95–$97 a share, well below consensus of about $106–$108 a share, top-down estimates of $107–$109 a share and bottom-up forecasts of $112–$113 a share.

Though starting out strong, the stock market in 2013 is a tale of two cities, with a weak first half and a stronger second half. The 2013 S&P 500 range is 1,275 to 1,480. The S&P 500 ends the year flat.

Beginning-of-the-year equity fund inflows, breathless optimism (of a technically inspired kind) and the initial excitement over the fiscal cliff resolution lift the S&P 500 to its yearly high in the first two weeks of January 2013. Unfortunately, the lack of intelligent, thoughtful leadership becomes ever more apparent in February–March, and ultimately the S&P 500 bottoms at about 1,275 (or at 13.5× my projected S&P profit surprise) during the spring.

The VIX exceeds 25, and risk premiums remain elevated amid the increased political rancor.

While dividend payout rates are low and corporate balance sheets in strong shape—there is less than meets the eye here, as it should be noted that much of the cash hoards are positioned in non-U.S.-taxed overseas accounts—a smaller amount of money is returned to shareholders, as dividend growth and share buybacks slow down while business confidence ebbs and the economy decelerates.

Though most believe that a spending deal will be forced by the pressures of a weakening stock market and economy, there is no agreement or real addressing of the deficit forthcoming despite a slide in equities and the backdrop of falling corporate profits and weaker economic growth taking center stage.

In the second half of 2013, coincident with a slow improvement in domestic growth, the market stages a persistent recovery back toward year-end 2012 levels of 1,425 (as investors get inured to the political dysfunction and grow increasingly accepting of a period of slowing secular economic growth), exactly duplicating the flat market experience of 2011.

The VIX falls back under 15 by the second half of the year.

I would emphasize that a flat year in the U.S. stock market is a much rarer occurrence than many would think. According to The Chart Store's Ron Griess, in the 84 years since 1928, when S&P data was first accumulated, the index was unchanged in only two years (1947 and 2011). In only four of the 83 years was the annual change in the S&P 500 under 1%: 1947 (0.00%), 1948 (−0.65%), 1970 (+0.10%), and 2011 (+0.0%).

Strategy: Buy index puts in the first half of 2013; short Market Vectors Retail ETF (RTH).

Surprise No. 3: A dysfunctional Washington, D.C., has profound political implications, and an influential third party (the People's Party) is formed

Despite widespread expectations of a 1992 repeat of a Bush vs. Clinton presidential contest in 2016, the consensus is proven wrong.

Shortly after a successful recovery from a concussion and blood clot, Bill and Hillary Clinton announce that they will divorce. Soon thereafter, Hillary Clinton declares that she has no intention to run as the Democratic presidential nominee for 2016, setting the Democratic leadership in turmoil.

Alienated, saddened and disappointed by the current political alternatives and a dysfunctional Washington, D.C., a meaningful movement of Democratic and Republican moderates toward the creation of a new and independent third party, known as the People's Party, gains steam.

Although it is early in the process and despite being initially reluctant, New York Mayor Michael Bloomberg becomes the standard-bearer of the People's Party, and he announces his intention to run for president.

The People's Party is named after the short-lived political party with the same name that was established in the late 1890s during the populist movement in the United States. Originally based among poor, white cotton farmers in the South and hard-pressed wheat farmers in the plains, it represented a radical crusading form of agrarianism that possessed a hostility toward banks, railroads and elites generally. Often it formed coalitions and was aligned with labor unions and generally was seen as anti-elitist and in opposition to established interests (in banking and railroads) and mainstream parties.

Several of the wealthiest Americans—including Bill Gates, Warren Buffett, and several well-known billionaire hedge fund managers—commit huge amount of financial and intellectual support to Bloomberg and the People's Party.

Surprisingly, Senator Elizabeth Warren (not Joe Biden or Andrew Cuomo) is viewed as the leading Democratic presidential candidate by year-end 2013, and Wisconsin Governor Scott Walker (not Marco Rubio or Jeb Bush) becomes the frontrunner for the Republican Party's presidential nomination.

Strategy: None.

Surprise No. 4: A tax on securities transactions is instituted in exchange for an increase in Medicare eligibility—its implementation has broadly negative ramifications for financial stocks and hedge funds In conjunction with Congressional Democrats (and in exchange for an increase in Medicare age eligibility), Senator Elizabeth Warren spearheads a successful campaign to force the House to introduce a financial transaction tax attached to all securities trades. The legislation is sold to Americans (and to the Republicans) as a way to:

1. Curb market volatility;
2. Reduce the disruptive role of high-frequency trading on the markets; and
3. Increase tax revenue.

The ramifications of this tax are broad—financial stocks suffer, and the hedge fund industry retrenches, consolidates and lowers fees.

> *"Speculators may do no harm as bubbles on a steady stream of enterprise. But the situation is serious when enterprise becomes the bubble on a whirlpool of speculation."*
>
> —John Maynard Keynes (when he first proposed a securities transaction tax in 1936)

The implementation of a financial transaction tax, weak capital markets, reduced merger and acquisition activity, continued pressure on net interest margins and poor loan demand lead to well-below-consensus bank and brokerage industry profits and underperforming stocks.

In 2013's macro-driven market, correlations remain at historically high levels, rendering excess return generation hard to deliver by the hedge fund community. Moreover, the implementation of a financial transaction tax pressures trading-based and high-frequency-trading hedge fund strategies to close, and nearly one third of the existing hedge funds close shop in 2013.

As pressure on returns intensifies, a large institutional manager introduces a menu of low-fee hedge funds that further accelerate hedge fund closures. Hedge fund management fees move toward 1% (or lower), and performance fees move toward 10%, as the industry begins to resemble the traditional money management industry.

Several large hedge funds lower fees and structure fees to more resemble Warren Buffett's hedge fund in the 1960s, which charged no management fee but took in 25% on performance above a 6% threshold return.

Strategy: Short Financial Select Sector SPDR (XLF) and Goldman Sachs.

Surprise No. 5: Under political, economic and stock market pressure, Obama begins to move back toward the center, but it is too late By midyear (after failed budget deficit debate) it will be clear to the president that his legacy is in serious jeopardy.

In response, Obama takes a surprising move to the center. His administration's team is turned upside down, and the president, in search of economic growth and a more vibrant jobs market, will approve legislation to allow fracking on federal lands. In addition, he completely turns around on his previous Keystone Pipeline stance and green lights the project.

Several previously somnolent regional bank stock prices positioned in areas of potential fracking activity revel in the administration's move. For example, Northwest Bancshares, a bank holding company right smack in the middle of Pennsylvania's fracking sites, rises by 25%.

The move fractures the Democratic Party and emboldens the Republicans. For both the president and the Republicans, it is too little and too late, as the approval ratings of both plummet to all-time lows and the aforementioned third party (led by Bloomberg) gains popularity (see surprise No. 3).

By year-end the People's Party is estimated to have as much as 20% of the national vote.

Strategy: Buy Northwest Bancshares.

Surprise No. 6: Despite a growing concern that interest rates will rise, the yield on the 10-year U.S. note remains range-bound The big up move in yields that I have long expected and that has now become consensus is delayed by at least another six months.

The yield on the 10-year U.S. note stays in a relatively tight range of between 1.5% and 2% in 2013, as slowing global growth remains the bond market's dominant influence.

Strategy: Buy bonds on weakness via iShares Barclays 20+ Year Treasury Bond Fund (TLT); short bonds on strength via ProShares UltraShort 20+ Year Treasury (TBT).

Surprise No. 7: There will be four market-influencing black swan events in 2013 As I have observed, there is a growing frequency of black swans around the world, and 2013 will be no exception—climate change and technological disruptions play a significant role on the financial markets this year:

1. *Another major drought lies ahead.* Droughts in the United States, Brazil and Russia have a knock-off impact on much higher commodity and food prices, experiencing a greater-than-5% rise in 2013. A 5%-plus rise in food prices further adversely impacts the consumer's purchasing power.
2. *A coronal mass ejection.* The sun emits solar flares (or coronal mass ejections) that penetrate the Earth's atmosphere and initially wipe out most GPS systems and disrupt numerous communications systems, electronic devices and power grids all over the world. Electricity is lost in several regions of the world for weeks. A mini panic ensues, as concerns about broader damage emerge.
3. *More flash crashes.* A series of mini flash crashes occur in the first six months of the year. One such flash causes a major bank to lose close to $2 billion. In part to raise revenue and in part to curb market volatility and to halt the proliferation of high-frequency trading, a securities transaction tax is instituted by year-end.
4. *A cyberattack.* The United States experiences a major cyberattack on the power grid or other key infrastructure target. The source of the attack is not detected. Cybersecurity stocks soar, while the overall market experiences a 3% to 4% drop.

Strategy: Buy Sourcefire and Palo Alto Networks.

Surprise No. 8: Apple's share price and earnings continue to disappoint in the first half of 2013 Last year, I wrote that Apple would be a positive surprise in 2012, though I turned negative on the company's fundamentals and share price in late September.

This year I have a negative surprise in store for Apple—at least for the first half of the year.

The aforementioned Senator Levin subcommittee investigations on offshore tax havens (see surprise No. 1) highlight Apple's tax-avoidance strategies. The share price drops below $500 a share in first quarter 2013, as investors begin to recognize that it is likely that Apple's future earnings will be taxed at a much higher rate than in the past.

Meanwhile, Apple's core operating profits disappoint due to a more competitive landscape, lessening demand for iPads and iPhones and emerging margin pressures. Apple's earnings estimates (and price targets) are cut, and full-year 2013 results fall short of $40 a share.

Microsoft's Surface sales start off poorly but gain traction by the end of 2013. Google Nexus, Amazon Kindle, Surface, and Samsung all sell at lower price points throughout the year, as price competition emerges in the tablet market.

Apple's consensus 2014 profit estimates move toward an expected year-over-year decline. The stock spends most of 2013 below $550 a share, but, in the last half of the year, two revolutionary product additions lift the share price to over $600 by year-end. (Samsung's stock performance continues to outpace that of Apple in all of 2013.)

In the third quarter Apple announces three new products in 2013: iTV, iMed, and iHomes.

iTV is a yawner, but the latter two are revolutionary product additions.

With iMed, Apple enters the medical information market, providing a platform for the medical field to keep, store and transfer records in real time. This expands the use of iPads exponentially.

Also introduced is the iHomes program, an iTunes-like software to control all electrical (and some non-electrical, like plumbing) elements in a home remotely. The software receives rave reviews from the *Wall Street Journal's* Walt Mossberg, after which Apple announces it will not license the software for use on Android devices. (Google shares drop 60 points on the announcement.)

Strategy: Avoid Apple in the first half of year; buy Apple and short Google in the second half of the year.

Surprise No. 9: The big market winners and losers of 2013   Over the past few years (2010–2012), Altisource Portfolio Solutions was my stock of the year. The shares of Altisource Portfolio Solutions, which traded at around $15 a share in late 2009, rose to nearly $130 a share several months ago.

So, what is the next Altisource Portfolio Solutions, and what will be the stock of the year for 2013?

My answer is that we don't have to go far from Altisource Portfolio Solutions. The stock of the year will be the recent spinoff of Altisource Portfolio Solutions, Altisource Asset Management. With a sharp trajectory of earnings growth (resembling that of Altisource Portfolio Solutions in 2010–2012), I expect Altisource Asset Management will trade over $150 a share sometime this year.

Last year's surprise large-cap stock was Bank of America, which, after dropping by over 50% in 2011, climbed by over 100% in 2012.

My surprise large-cap pick for 2013 is Ford.

Trading at $13.50 a share, I expect Ford's share price to rise to above $17.50 a share in 2013 based on a combination of surprisingly strong domestic automobile industry sales (in excess of 16 million SAAR) and a revaluation (upward) in the company's P/E ratio.

After an initial burst to the upside, overowned financial stocks (XLF, Morgan Stanley, Citigroup, Goldman Sachs, JPMorgan Chase and asset managers) are the big losers in 2013, as the financial transaction tax, weak capital markets, still-low interest rates and tepid merger and acquisition activity weigh on the sector.

Strategy: Long Altisource Asset Management and Ford.

Surprise No. 10: Takeover activity slows to a standstill   Though interest rates are low and there is an abundance of excess cash on corporations' balance sheets, economic uncertainty meaningfully curtails merger and acquisition activity in 2013.

There is one large exception: Oracle takes over Hewlett-Packard (at only a modest premium). Mark Hurd returns to become Hewlett-Packard's CEO. Hewlett-Packard's current CEO Meg Whitman rejoins Kleiner Perkins.

Strategy: Avoid investment and brokerage stocks.

Surprise No. 11: A comprehensive *New York Times* exposé reveals that all Chinese economic data has been fabricated   Strategy: Short iShares FTSE/Xinhua China 25 Index Fund (FXI).

Surprise No. 12: There is no reallocation out of bonds and into stocks in 2013   Despite a growing consensus that the reallocation trade is imminent and will reverse the trends of money moving out of stocks and into bonds (in place since 2007), outflows from domestic equity funds and inflows into bond funds continue throughout the year. In support, I would note that, according to AMG, bond/equity fund flows started 2013 just the way they ended last year, with large outflows totaling −$3.5 billion coming out of domestic equity funds and with inflows into fixed income.

Strategy: Short T. Rowe Price and Franklin Resources.

Surprise No. 13: Signs of life are found on Mars   There are signs of life on Mars but not in Washington, D.C.

The *Curiosity* rover conducts a chemical test in early 2013 that uncovers complex carbon-based compounds in Martian soil.

Strategy: None.

Surprise No. 14: Procter & Gamble splits apart into three separate companies, and Avon Products is courted   Another activist hedge fund investor joins Bill Ackman's Pershing Square and acquires a large position in Procter & Gamble. Under pressure from an expanding shareholder group, Procter & Gamble decides to split into three separate entities. The shares rise by $7 to $10 a share on the announcement.

As was the case of Procter & Gamble, several activist investors pressure Avon Products to consider being acquired.

Strategy: Long Procter & Gamble and Avon Products and out-of-the-money calls.

Surprise No. 15: There are numerous surprises in entertainment and in sports

- Move over Taylor Swift, as *The Voice*'s Cassadee Pope wins more Grammys than any new entertainer in history.
- The New York Yankees, seen as too old and too slow, shock the world and win the 2013 World Series.

- The Oklahoma Thunder win the NBA Championship.
- The Seattle Seahawks win the 2013 Super Bowl.
- Alabama trounces Notre Dame by 28 points in tonight's BCS Championship game, but Notre Dame's men's basketball team reaches the Final Four.
- Tiger Woods wins a major and comes close to a second win. He marries a famous entertainer.
- Three-year-old thoroughbred Violence wins the Kentucky Derby.
- I finish in first place at the World Series of Poker in November and win $8.2 million.

Strategy: None.

15 Surprises for 2014

1/6/2014

It takes me about three weeks of thinking and writing to compile and construct my annual surprise list column. I typically start with about 40 surprises, which are accumulated during the months leading up to my column. In the days leading up to this publication, I cull the list to come up with my final 15 surprises. (This year I include five also-ran surprises).

I often speak to the wise men and women in the investment and media businesses who give me some ideas. (This year I wanted to specifically thank Steve Einhorn and Lee Cooperman at Omega Advisors and The Lindsey Group's Peter Boockvar for their input.)

I have always associated the moment of writing the final draft (in the weekend before publication) of my annual surprise list with a moment of lift, of joy and hopefully with the thought of unexpected investment rewards in the New Year (e.g., Altisource Asset Management, my stock of the decade for 2013, spiked up by 1,200% during the year). This year is no different.

Above all, the publication of my annual surprise list is recognition that economic and stock market histories have proven that (more often than not) consensus expectations are off base.

My Surprises for 2013 Generally Proved to Be Wrong-Footed

While over recent years many of my surprise lists have been eerily prescient (e.g., my 2011 surprise that the S&P 500 would end exactly flat was exactly correct), my "15 Surprises for 2013" failed to achieve the successes of the past few years.

"How'm I doin'?"

—Ed Koch, former New York City mayor

In fact, my surprises were way off the mark last year. I needed a lifeline, a call to a friend or a do over.

As we entered 2013, most strategists expressed a cautious but constructive economic view of a self-sustaining domestic recovery, held to an upbeat (though not wide-eyed) corporate profits picture and generally shared the view that the S&P 500 would rise by between 8% and 10%. (A year ago the median S&P forecast for year-end 2013 was only 1,550, according to *Bloomberg*; the closing price in 2013 was 1,848.)

Those strategists proved to be correct on profit growth (but only because of several nonoperating factors), were too optimistic regarding domestic and global economic growth and, most importantly (as I did), grossly underestimated the animal spirits that resulted in a well-above-historic increase in P/E ratios that buoyed stock prices to their largest annual gain since the mid-1990s.

Many readers of this annual column assume that my surprise list will have a bearish bent. But I have not always expressed a negative outlook in my surprise list. For example, two years ago, my 2012 surprise list had an out-of-consensus positive tone to it, but 2013's list was noticeably downbeat relative to the general expectations. I specifically called for a stock market top in early 2013, which couldn't have been further from last year's reality, as January proved to be the market's nadir. The S&P closed at its high on the last day of the year and exhibited its largest yearly advance since 1997. (I steadily increased my fair market value calculation throughout the year, and, at last count, I concluded that the S&P 500's fair market value was approximately 1,645.)

How Did My Surprise List for 2013 Do?   My 15 surprises for 2013 had the poorest success rate since 2005's list (20%).

By comparison, my 2012 surprise list achieved about a 50% hit ratio, similar to my experience in 2011. Forty percent of my 2010 surprises were achieved, while I had a 50% success rate in 2009, 60% in 2008, 50% in 2007, one-third in 2006, 20% in 2005, 45% in 2004, and one-third came to pass in the first year of my surprises in 2003.

Below is a report card of my 15 surprises for 2013 (I hit on only about 20% of the surprises):

Surprise No. 1: The U.S. economy disappoints relative to consensus expectations. Right. (Though third-quarter GDP beat consensus by a hefty amount, the full year was close to my view and lower than consensus.)

Surprise No. 2: The 2013–2014 earnings cliff sinks the markets in 2013's first half. Wrong.

Surprise No. 3: A dysfunctional Washington D.C., has profound political implications and an influential third party (the People's Party) is formed. Wrong.

Surprise No. 4: A tax on securities transactions is instituted in exchange for an increase in Medicare eligibility—its implementation has broadly negative ramifications for financial stocks and hedge funds. Wrong.

Surprise No. 5: Under political, economic and stock market pressure, Obama begins to move back toward the center, but it is too late. Wrong.

Surprise No. 6: Despite a growing concern that interest rates will rise, the yield on the 10-year U.S. note remains range-bound. Wrong.

Surprise No. 7: There will be four market-influencing black swan events in 2013. Wrong. (Though numerous cyberattacks did occur throughout the year, and Sourcefire was acquired by Cisco.)

Surprise No. 8: Apple's share price and earnings continue to disappoint in the first half of 2013, but the shares rebound sharply in the second half. Right.

Surprise No. 9: The big market winner will be Altisource Asset Management. Right. (Indeed, I hit it out of the park on this one, as Altisource Asset Management, my "stock of the decade" climbed by 1,120%, to $940 a share.)

Surprise No. 10: Takeover activity slows to a standstill. Wrong. (Though M&A activity was muted relative to optimistic expectations.)

Surprise No. 11: A comprehensive *New York Times* exposé reveals that all Chinese economic data have been fabricated. Wrong.

Surprise No. 12: There is no reallocation out of bonds and into stocks in 2013. Wrong.

Surprise No. 13: Signs of life are found on Mars. Right.

Surprise No. 14: Procter & Gamble splits apart into three separate companies, and Avon Products is courted. Wrong.

Surprise No. 15: There are numerous surprises in entertainment and in sports (Cassadee Pope, New York Yankees, Oklahoma Thunder, Seattle Seahawks, Alabama, Tiger Words, Kentucky Derby, World Series of Poker). Wrong. (Though I did forecast the exact Alabama–Notre Dame point differential in the Bowl Championship Series National Championship Game.)

The Rationale behind My Downbeat Surprises for 2014   There are numerous reasons for my downbeat theme this year. Below are a few (in no order of importance):

- Corporate profit margins (70% above historical averages) are stretched to 70-year highs, so earnings are exposed.
- Second-half 2013 strength in domestic economic growth has been boosted by nonrecurring inventory accumulation. Some more recent signs (e.g., automobile sales, retail spending and housing data) suggest a deceleration in growth may lie ahead.
- The baton exchange from Helicopter Ben to Whirlybird Janet could be unkind to the markets. On average, a change in the Fed chair has resulted in about a 7% drop in the major stock indices.
- Quantitative easing may not be a continued tailwind for stocks. As Peter Boockvar wrote, "QE doesn't create a safer world, it is just a temporary high and the danger always comes on the flip side as previously seen. . . . QE puts beer goggles on investors by creating a line of sight where everything looks good, but the Fed's current plan is to end it by year-end."
- Sentiment measures are elevated to historically bullish levels. This is seen not only in the disparity between bulls and bears (in the popular surveys) but also manifested in the third-highest margin debt to GDP in history.
- Valuations (P/E ratios) rose by nearly 25% in 2013 vs. only 2% annually since the late-1980s.
- The Shiller P/E ratio is at or near historic highs (excluding the bubble of the late-1990s).

- According to JPMorgan, the S&P 500 is now more expensive on a forward P/E basis than it was at its previous peak in October 2007.
- Interest rates might pose more of a threat than is generally viewed. The rose-colored glasses being worn by investors might be cleared in the year ahead, as the withdrawal from QE and low rates might be harsher.
- A year ago, market enthusiasm was muted. Today there are no cautionary forecasts for the S&P for the next 12 months.

My 15 Surprises for 2014   As I did last year, following each surprise, I have included a specific strategy that might be employed in order for an investor to profit from the occurrence of these "possible improbables."

Following are my 15 surprises for 2014 (and five also-rans that didn't make the list).

Surprise No. 1: Slowing global economic growth and fears of stagflation emerge   At the core of this year's surprise list is that the U.S. economy disappoints (with domestic real GDP growing at 1.75% or less, half the expected rate offered by the consensus) relative to consensus expectations. Many (e.g., Harvard's Martin Feldstein) are worried about the economy overheating, but global growth also fails to meet forecasts (and is only 2.5% against consensus forecasts of 3.6%-plus).

The case for slowing growth is not necessarily quartered and dependent on rising interest rates. Rather, central to my surprise is a spent-up not pent-up consumer whose fragility may be exposed and an uptick in economic inequality, as trickle-down policy grows increasingly ineffective.

The recent rise in unemployment claims, higher gas prices, slowing population growth, the higher costs of health care, slowing retail sales and a pause in domestic automobile and housing activity likely presage that slowing growth is in store for 2014.

U.S. real GDP growth is under 2%, and worldwide growth is under 3%, making the difference between anemic growth and recession increasingly one of semantics. (*Note:* The U.S. stock market has a forward P/E ratio of nearly 17× with a 2% real GDP growth rate, while China has a forward P/E ratio of about 7.5× with a 7% real GDP growth rate.)

The Fed's tapering will be put on hold in response to slowing growth, and some within the Fed, including Whirlybird Janet Yellen, argue for increased levels of quantitative easing. Half the Fed members are reluctant to add "more cowbell," however, so there is no additional QE and the new Fed Chair's more aggressive monetary policy views are repudiated.

Pressure is placed on both parties in Washington, D.C., to introduce more radical and aggressive fiscal policies in order to stimulate domestic economic growth by year-end.

Major droughts in the United States, Brazil, and Russia have a knock-off impact on much higher commodity and food prices, experiencing a greater-than-5% rise in 2014 (negatively impacting the consumer's purchasing power).

The drought brings on stagflation concerns. Other supply disruptions fuel some cost-push commodity price inflation even though economic growth is weak relative to expectations.

The risk of an exogenous shock expands, and further downgrades of global growth could put the United States and Europe in a deflationary headlock, finding both regions in a light liquidity trap.

Even though interest rates grind a bit higher in early 2014, the rise is mild, and the yield on the 10-year U.S. note spends most of the year between 2.5% and 3%.

Surprisingly (with a stable rate picture), the housing market is further disrupted. Mortgage rate and home price sensitivity are underestimated, as double-digit home price increases in 2013 dwarf modest rises in incomes. As a result, affordability suffers, and real buyers are priced out of the market. Traffic and orders drop off as the year proceeds. The accumulation of homes to rent by new-era buyers (hedge funds, private equity, etc.) precipitates further weakness in the U.S. housing market— indigestion in the rental markets develops, as there is an inability to absorb the units. By the second half of 2014, year-over-year home prices turn mildly negative.

A new homebuyer tax credit is considered in late 2014 in order to stimulate residential real estate markets.

Refinancings evaporate, serving to put pressure on household cash flow and personal consumption expenditures. The unemployment rate remains sticky (hanging around 7%), and consumer confidence falls.

The expected recovery in capital spending fails to materialize in 2014.

Companies slow down their share repurchase programs (which buoyed EPS last year), balking at higher stock prices and recognizing that the economics of debt offerings to fund repurchases are less compelling from a return-on-investment standpoint than they were in 2013.

Strategy: Buy index puts, sell index calls, or purchase inverse ETFs.

Surprise No. 2: Corporate profits disappoint Slower global economic growth impedes corporate profit growth. (See previous section, "The Rationale behind My Downbeat 2014 Expectations," for more reasons.)

As we approach earnings season, I estimate that 2013 S&P earnings approximate $108.50 a share.

For 2014, the consensus estimates that the S&P 500 will achieve profits of about $116 to $120 a share. (Recently, those projections have been skewing higher and seem to be moving to closer to $120 a share.) My base case estimate is for $112 a share, a gain of under 5% (year over year), which is, again, below consensus.

Slowing sales, a contraction in margins, the reduced influence/benefit from aggressive monetary policy and political uncertainties are some of the reasons why my baseline earnings expectation is for below-consensus 2014 S&P 500 profits.

Strategy: Buy index puts, sell index calls, or purchase inverse ETFs.

Surprise No. 3: Stock prices and P/E multiples decline While the S&P 500 closed 2013 at its yearly high, equities will close 2014 at their yearly low.

Stocks trade in a relatively narrow range over the next six months but fall in the second half, ending the year at their low, with a decline of between 5% and 15%.

Valuations decline in 2014. Last year's animal spirits subside as P/E multiples, which increased by nearly 25% in 2013, fall by about 15% in 2014.

Strategy: Buy index puts, sell index calls, or purchase inverse ETFs.

Surprise No. 4: Bonds outperform stocks Bonds outperform stocks in 2014.

Against the backdrop of a decline of between 5% and 15% in the U.S. stock market, the return on long-dated, taxable U.S. bonds is close to 10%.

Interest rates decline from 2013's year-end levels. The yield on the 10-year U.S. note ends the year between 2.5% and 3%.

Closed-end municipal bond funds are among the best asset classes during the year, achieving a total return of about 15% in 2014.

Strategy: Buy iShares 20+ Year Treasury Bond ETF (TLT), Power-Shares Build America Bond Portfolio (BAB), BlackRock Municipal Target Term Trust (BTT), Eaton Vance Municipal Income Term Trust (ETX), BlackRock Investment Quality Municipal Trust (BKN), Nuveen Select Quality Municipal Fund (NQS), Nuveen Premium Income Municipal Fund II (NPM), Nuveen Dividend Advantage Municipal Fund (NAD), Nuveen Municipal Market Opportunity Fund (NMO), Nuveen Municipal Advantage Fund (NMA), Invesco Pennsylvania Value Municipal Income Trust (VPV), Invesco California Value Municipal Income Trust (VCV), Nuveen Quality Income Municipal Fund (NQU), Nuveen Premium Income Municipal Fund (NPI) and Nuveen New York AMT-Free Municipal Income Fund (NRK).

Surprise No. 5: A number of major surprises affect individual stocks and sectors

- Citigroup outperforms Bank of America.
- Starbucks shares fall by 25% as consumers finally balk at the company's expensive product offerings.
- 3-D printing stocks halve in price.
- Apple's shares drop back under $500 a share, never breaching $600 to the upside and spending most of the year under $525 a share as profit estimates are again shaved. (Icahn dumps the shares; see more on Icahn in also-ran surprises.)
- Amazon reports a huge earnings beat in the first half of 2014—the shares trade over $550 a share and are a standout in the moribund high-beta, speculative sector.
- Goldman Sachs goes private (a previous-year surprise).
- My "stock of the decade," Altisource Asset Management, doubles in price to $2,000 a share after rising by 1,200% in 2013.
- My 2014 "stock of the year," Monitise, triples in price (after doubling last year).

- The latest hedge fund hotel, General Motors, drops by 20% in 2014 as automobile sales stall.
- Consumer staples and master limited partnerships are among the top performing sectors.
- Retailers, transportation and housing shares are among the bottom performing sectors.

Strategy: Buy Citigroup/short Bank of America pair trade, short Starbucks, short 3D Systems, short Apple calls, buy Amazon common and calls, buy Goldman Sachs, buy Altisource Asset Management, buy Monitise, short GM, buy Consumer Staples Select Sector SPDR (XLP), short Consumer Discretionary Select Sector SPDR (XLY) and Market Vectors Retail ETF (RTH), and short Power-Shares QQQ (QQQ).

Surprise No. 6: Volkswagen AG acquires Tesla Motors Strategy: Buy Tesla Motors common and calls.

Surprise No. 7: Twitter's shares fall by 70% as a disruptive competitor appears Strategy: Short Twitter common and buy TWTR puts.

Surprise No. 8: Buffett names successor Against all of his previous protestations, Berkshire Hathaway's Warren Buffett announces the name of his successor.

Strategy: None.

Surprise No. 9: Bitcoin becomes a roller coaster Bitcoin scores acceptance as a virtual currency from Amazon and eBay in early 2014 and climbs to over $7,500 in value by midyear.

The Winklevoss twins make nearly $350 million on paper from their investment in bitcoin.

Just at the time that bitcoin begins gaining legitimacy as a currency, improprieties in the calculation of the supply of bitcoins are found. A fraudulent double-spend attack wreaks havoc and significantly disrupts the bitcoin market. At the same time, a selfish miner (who does not release solutions to solved cryptopuzzles and minds a branch in secret) successfully attacks the bitcoin system and gains control of over 55% of the total network hashing power.

The value of bitcoin falls by nearly 70% in a two-week period and closes back under $1,000 by year-end.

Several momentum-based hedge funds that got long fail spectacularly.

Strategy: Buy and then short bitcoins.

Surprise No. 10: The Republican Party gains control of the Senate and maintains control of the House
As a result, President Obama becomes a lame duck president who is unable to launch any new policy initiatives.

The S&P 500 soars to over 2,100.

Strategy: Buy everything.

Surprise No. 11: Hillary Clinton bows out as a presidential candidate
Revelations made by a *New York Times* investigative reporter precede an announcement that Bill and Hillary Clinton plan to divorce. Shortly thereafter Hillary Clinton officially bows out of the 2016 presidential contest. Elizabeth Warren emerges as a Democratic presidential frontrunner (a 2013 surprise).

Strategy: None.

Surprise No. 12: Social unrest and riots appear in the United States
Riots break out in select major cities as inequality and the screwflation of the middle class gain center stage.

Middle-class income, purchasing power and discretionary incomes continue to stagnate. Zero interest rates, quantitative easing, trickle-down economics and a higher stock market fail to solve the structural decline in labor's share of the economy.

Local municipalities raise costs and reduce their levels of services. With property values topping out, pension/health care costs rising and economic growth slowing, the decline in government services accelerates—and so does taxation. As an example, the U.S. Postal Service reduces home delivery (in favor of more post office boxes and less frequent daily service). Local "junk fees" on parking tickets, permits, recreational entrance, etc. are instituted. As well, fees for trash pickup are raised dramatically and, in certain cases, trash pickup is eliminated.

Pressured politicians introduce a national wealth tax (also a 2013 surprise) that is authorized by Congress late in the year.

Strategy: None.

Surprise No. 13: Africa becomes a new hotbed of turmoil, and South Africa precipitates an emerging debt crisis Politics and economics form a potentially toxic cocktail.

Africa triggers an emerging-market crisis and becomes a flashpoint of geopolitical risk and political turmoil as the region's untapped oil wealth is recognized.

Not long ago, South Africa was meant to be the "S" in the BRICS, alongside fast-growing Brazil, Russia, India and China. The rand, however, is in steep decline, and the nation has growing budget and trade deficits and slowing growth, so it can hardly claim membership in that club right now.

At some point in 2014, the ratings agencies will downgrade South Africa, foreign money will flee, and the country will be in a full-blown financial crisis that will trigger a wider selloff in the emerging markets and could highlight problems at emerging-market central banks (which are already suffering from slowing economic growth, an acceleration in inflation, etc.).

Potentially changing regimes due to national elections in Brazil, India, Indonesia and Turkey cause those countries to join South Africa in the emerging markets' bumpy ride, which is further impacted by U.S. dollar strength caused by the Fed's tapering.

If the crisis intensifies and expands beyond South Africa, a contagion into the developed banks could raise additional concerns and pull down money center bank shares.

Strategy: Short iShares MSCI South Africa ETF (EZA), iShares MSCI Emerging Markets ETF (EEM) and Financial Select Sector SPDR (XLF).

Surprise No. 14: The next big thing? A marijuana IPO rises by more than 400% on its first day of trading Marijuana is legalized in many more states, and the largest (to date) marijuana grower/retailer goes public in a Goldman Sachs-led IPO that soars by 400% in the first day of trading.

Numerous copycat marijuana related IPOs follow.
Strategy: None.

Surprise No. 15: An escalation of friction between China and Japan hints at war-like behavior between the two countries Global trade and stocks suffer.

Strategy: Short iShares China Large-Cap ETF (FXI) and SPDR S&P 500 ETF Trust (SPY).

Five Also-Ran Surprises

1. *Also-Ran Surprise No. 1:* Changes seen at CNBC, NBC, CNN, and Fox Business.
   - Michelle Caruso-Cabrera joins Fox Business as the morning anchor.
   - Erin Burnett leaves CNN and rejoins CNBC.
   - Carl Quintanilla leaves CNBC and permanently joins NBC's *The Today Show.*
     Strategy: None.
2. *Also-Ran Surprise No. 2:* Crude oil trades at $75 a barrel.
     A quiescent period of Middle East peace, more U.S. energy discoveries (and an increased pace of energy independence) and slowing global economic growth adversely impact energy prices.
     Strategy: Short crude oil and energy stocks.
3. *Also-Ran Surprise No. 3:* Despite lower stock prices the VIX trades under 10.
     Strategy: Short VIX.
4. *Also-Ran Surprise No. 4:* Gold trades under $1,000 an ounce.
     Strategy: Short SPDR Gold Trust (GLD) and gold miner shares.
5. *Also-Ran Surprise No. 5:* Carl Icahn's fund loses 15% to 20%.
     He is only human.
     Strategy: None.

Epilogue

This book is intended to serve as a kaleidoscope of my experiences in the markets.

Over the past 15 years, the purpose of my writings on *TheStreet* has been to identify and highlight the dominant investing trends and to deliver potentially profitable investment ideas.

My approach as a contrarian is to provide differentiated and (hopefully) hard-hitting analysis incorporated in an (again, hopefully) enjoyable writing style. As the crowd usually outsmarts the remnants, I have, as an outside-of-consensus thinker and investor, taken my lumps, lost some friends and even made some enemies (of the managements of companies I have shorted).

Though a contrarian, I fully recognize that stocks have, over history, been undeniably higher and the gravitational pull that accompanies that fact.

Berkshire Hathaway's Warren Buffett wrote: "In the 20th century, the United States endured two world wars and other traumatic and expensive military conflicts; the Depression; a dozen or so recessions and financial panics; oil shocks; a flu epidemic; and the resignation of a disgraced president. Yet the Dow rose from 66 to 11,497."

Since I began to write for Jim Cramer's *TheStreet* in 1998, our country has endured a speculative blow off (and collapse) of 75% in the Nasdaq market, several (terrible and tragic) terrorist attacks on our soil (September 11, 2001), corporate scandals (at Tyco, Enron, and others), the deepest recession since the Great Depression and an extended European credit/economic crisis. Yet the Dow rose from about 8,000 to nearly 17,000.

That said, markets have been and are likely to continue to be cyclical and volatile. Unless you have a forever investing time frame (similar to Warren Buffett), we must be vigilant and aware of influences that can derail the capital markets from time to time.

In his 2014 commencement speech at Harvard University, Michael Bloomberg remarked, "There is no easy time to say hard things." My credo over the past 15 years has been to write exactly what I am thinking regardless of how unpopular my investment positions and views have been.

Wherever it leads, on every economic and investment issue, I have followed the body of evidence, attended to my analysis, and I have listened to wise and accomplished investment professionals whom I have befriended. On the latter point, it has been my experience that the more we accept diversity of opinion, the stronger our investment decisions will be.

My millions of words over a decade and a half have been written to focus traders and investors on profitable strategies.

It is important, however, to recognize that the psychology and sentiment of the investor class is that fear almost always dissolves with a rise in stock prices (and for investors to be fearful when stock prices fall).

Things are not always as they seem, as fantasy is often confused with progress. In its extreme, as we learned in 2007–2008, markets convulse as stability and complacency morph into instability and fear.

As we enter 2015 and after a near trebling in the S&P 500 since the generational bottom in 2009, we must recognize that much fear has been driven from Wall Street.

This is somewhat surprising, as, at the present time, the trajectory of global economic growth remains subpar and, importantly, dependent on the continued aggressive monetary policies of the world's central bankers.

To some degree, central bankers' efforts have prevented natural price discovery in many asset classes, and their actions have caused investors to lower their guards, adopting something of a false sense of security that there is limited market downside.

Fueled by new market highs and easy money, market observers are now growing more optimistic. Sentiment measures are at or are approaching five-year highs.

But consensus views and investor sentiment are often notoriously wrong-footed. As an example, find me the forecaster who called for a 2.50% yield on the 10-year U.S. note and 1950 on the S&P 500 this year, and you would have found a liar.

Over history, a Minsky moment—that is, market turmoil following an extended period of speculation and/or unsustainable growth—sometimes occurs when complacency sets in, as stability is often the prelude to instability.

Particularly worrisome is that we might have entered one of the great bull markets in complacency, with enthusiasm rapidly building (as it typically does in a maturing and eventually vulnerable stock market cycle). Bulls have rarely been more self-confident in view, but there are numerous dangers to the bull market in stocks that are being ignored by many, including tepid and uneven economic growth, which is still (five years after the Great Decession) dependent on exaggerated and extreme implementation of monetary policy; a growing schism between haves and have-nots (after the failure of QE); weak top-line growth; vulnerability to corporate profits (and profit margins); a consumer sector that is spent-up, not pent-up; and so on.

It is often the case that the more stable things appear, the more dangerous the ultimate outcome will be, because people start to assume everything will be all right and end up doing stupid things.

Fundamentally, things appear fine, but there is less than meets the eye.

The two-year cumulative 2013–2014 gain in S&P profits is estimated to be under 10%, but the price of the S&P 500 has already risen by close to 40% since year-end 2012. The difference has been a rise in both animal spirits and in P/E ratios.

Arguably, valuations are stretched. While corporate profits are at all-time records, profit margins are near-60-year highs and nearly 70% above the average level of the past six decades. Equally important, the factors that have contributed to the expansion in margins (low interest rates, productivity gains, and banking industry reversals of loan-loss provisions) are likely to deteriorate in the years ahead. Looking at nominal or stated profits (projected at \$117 to \$120 a share for the S&P 500) rather than normalized earnings (to account for degradation in profit margins) could prove to be a fool's errand, just like the mistake that was made back at the generational bottom, when trailing earnings of only \$45 a share understated normalized corporate profitability. At that time in 2009, investors were as reluctant to buy as they are emboldened to buy in 2014.

Above all, there is most definitely a bubble in the belief that central bankers can guide the economy higher and into a self-sustaining trajectory of growth despite the absence of tax and regulatory reforms and without a well-thought-out fiscal mission. It's been five years and we are not yet there. Importantly, bubbles are not the mandatory starting point to corrections, as stocks often fall from excessive valuation rather than bubbles.

While equities are less frothy than fixed income, I don't feel as though stocks are inexpensive or compelling buys at the margin. Nor do I buy the either/or argument, as cash is an asset class—during numerous times in history, not losing money (and being in cash) has been a reasonable alternative to being in risk assets.

Relative to actual economic growth, since 2009 the U.S. stock market has been forgiving—perhaps too much so. Each year since the Great Decession, the consensus has delivered the promise of self-sustaining U.S. economic growth, and each year that has led to a series of rationalizations. In 2014's first quarter, the excuse was bad weather; in previous years, it has been other factors. The run rate for the domestic economy has only been about 2% growth per year and has failed to reaccelerate to escape velocity.

Going forward, the current mix of fiscal and monetary policy likely insures continued subpar growth. Though it has maintained its second-half optimism recently, I expect that the Fed will, once again, end up lowering its official economic forecast for 2014–2015.

Most economists have predicted escape velocity for the U.S. economy since 2011. They have been wrong-footed and might continue to be, reminding me of John Kenneth Galbraith's comment that "the only function of economic forecasting is to make astrology look respectable."

The recovery and wealth effect has not been broad based; it has been lopsided, favoring the wealthy and invested class while disfavoring the savings class, who are penalized by zero-interest-rate policy. Meanwhile policy has not trickled down to the average Joe, who continues to suffer from stagnating wages and higher costs of the necessities of life.

In summary:

- Fear has been driven from Wall Street, and there is no concern for downside risk.
- Global economic growth is falling short of earlier forecasts, while a number of regions are flirting with deflation.
- While economic growth has relied on central bank policy, in the absence of regulatory and fiscal reform, QE's impact is now materially moderating.
- S&P 500 profits are estimated to have risen by only about 10% in 2013–2014, against a near 40% rise in the index.
- Though fundamentals remain soft (with sales and profit growth muted), bulls are self-confident in view as share prices propel ever higher.
- Bullish sentiment is at an historical extreme.
- Shorts are an out-of-favor, endangered and ridiculed species.
- There is less to valuation than meets the eye.

Benjamin Disraeli once suggested, "What we have learned from history is that we haven't learned from history."

Today most strategists see a consistent period of economic and earnings growth ahead. But business cycles have not been repealed, and I am increasingly skeptical that the path to growth will be even.

As has been the case since 1998, we should expect the unexpected over the next 15 years. Indeed, the only certainty I see is the lack of certainty, as our financial future may be visualized but it may never be absolutely known.

My advice for the next 15 years? Get ready to prepare for the next mini Minsky moment—it could be on our investment doorstep sooner than many currently expect.

For as Warren Buffett also said, "A bull market is like sex. It feels the best right before it ends."